Education of a
Guardian Angel:
Training a Spirit Guide

By:
Annie Stillwater Gray

OZARK
MOUNTAIN
PUBLISHING

For permission, serialization, condensation, adaptions, or for our catalog of other publications, write to Ozark Mountain Publishing, Inc., P.O. box 754, Huntsville, AR 72740, ATTN: Permissions Department.

Library of Congress Cataloging-in-Publication Data

Gray, Annie Stillwater -1946

Education of a Guardian Angel: Training a Spirit Guide by Annie Stillwater Gray

Understanding how a guardian angel or spirit guide is educated and trained.

1. Angels   2. Spirit Guides   3. Training of a Spirit Guide 4. Metaphysics

1. Gray, Annie Stillwater, 1946 II. Guardian Angels III. Title

Library of Congress Catalog Card Number: 2014933818

ISBN: 9781886940475

Cover Design: enki3d.com

Book set in: Times New Roman, Book Antiqua

Book Design: Tab Pillar

Published by:

PO Box 754

Huntsville, AR 72740

800-935-0045 or 479-738-2348 fax: 479-738-2448

WWW.OZARKMT.COM

Printed in the United States of America

Dedication

To all alive on Earth now
And those who are to come.

---Darcimon Stillwater---

Acknowledgements

To my teachers and all who helped me
Along the path to become a Spirit Guide,
And to my dear partner,
Angel, Annie Stillwater Gray,
Who patiently listened to me tell this story
And then wrote every word.
Also, her efforts to make sure this book is published
Are to be commended.

Thanks to Dolores Cannon
and Ozark Mountain Publishing
for having the foresight to recognize the value
in this story and the information it imparts.

---Darcimon Stillwater---

Table of Contents

Introduction

When the Spirit Guides asked me to write a true life account of my experiences, I had doubts and a great many questions. I knew that Spirit Guides are non-judgmental and have an abundance of compassion—how else could they deal with human beings on a regular basis? But writing my true life account? I was a bit uncomfortable with the idea.

"This is very personal," I said to my Spirit Guide. "I don't know if I can write about some of these things."

Darcimon Stillwater is my Life Guide, the Spirit Guide who has chosen to watch over me for the duration of my life on Earth and beyond. Every human has a Life Guide, sometimes called "a guardian angel." The term "guardian angel" is used only by humans as referring to Spirit Guides. Such references are found in the Bible.

When I voiced my misgivings about this project, my Life Guide, Darci, patiently explained that my human identity did not really matter.

"Use another name if you wish," he told me. "What is important is that our story be told."

Darci then told me the Master Guides said, "It is time for humans and their Spirit Guides to work together for the benefit of planet Earth and all upon her. Indeed, it is time for humans to know they can have a close relationship with their Guides, for the relationship between a human and a Spirit Guide is and has always been sacred. In fact, now a combination of factors is making conscious contact and communication between Guides and humans a reality."

"When people know our story," Darci continued, "they will see that they, too, can have an intimate association with their Spirit Guides. Humans need this now. Our story is essential to the evolution of humanity. It must be told."

1

After hearing this, I could not refuse the task. As I relate this tale from Darci's viewpoint, keep in mind that every word is true and has been written just as he said it to me.

Remember also that you as the reader have the opportunity to live your own story with your Spirit Guides, your own guardian angels. The time is right for you to not only know your Guides but also to develop a deep relationship with them to improve your life and life on Earth.

It is a challenging and joyful undertaking. Darci and I encourage you to begin. We hope our story will help.

Chapter One:
My Death, My Opportunity

My name is Darcimon Stillwater though I have had many names. I am a Spirit Guide, and this is my story. The last time I walked the Earth was in Jane Austen's time. Since my death in 1836, I have been very busy. That last human lifetime was one of leisure compared to what next occurred for me.

As soon as I died and my Spirit left my physical body, I was approached by a group of very tall, resplendent Beings. I learned later that these were Angel Initiates. They had been in training and were about to graduate, as it were, to the level where they could begin their work and play as Angels. The tallest and most magnificent of these Beings glided towards me. I had been very ill and had died of fever and infection, so my Spirit was dull and weak.

The first motion this Angel Initiate made was to encircle me with her arms and lift me up. The sensation was incredible and exhilarating. I was flooded with love, energized with light, and felt myself becoming taller and vibrating faster. What was left of my illness from my life in an Earth body was gone. My Spirit was rejuvenated, and I began my long journey to becoming a Spirit Guide, or guardian angel, if you will.

I had, you see, earned the opportunity to move on to the Spirit Guide plane. I learned this next as the group of Angel Initiates gently floated my regenerated Soul into a circular hall. This place was very busy with much activity happening around the outer rim. However, I was brought to the center where a great luminous Being sat in an oval chair. The Angel Initiates indicated that I should stand before this Being as they grouped in a semi-circle behind me.

Still disoriented from my passage out of the Earth realm, I found it difficult to focus. The great Being took my face in his hands and lifted it toward his. When his hands touched my head, my perception became extremely clear, and I began to understand the language that was being spoken around me.

The Being used this multi-dimensional language to say to me, "You have done well. You walked your life on Earth with integrity and showed much love and compassion. An opportunity is now yours. You are welcome to study to become a Spirit Guide."

In my last Earth life, I had attended church and had read the Bible, so I knew about Angels, even guardian angels, yet had never entertained the idea that every human has a personal Spirit Guide. In my innocence as someone newly arrived, I asked, "What is a Spirit Guide?"

The Great Being, who appeared to me as a phosphorescent Buddha, smiled and scooped me towards him with one hand and gathered another Spirit with his other one. He nodded at us both. A flash of magenta light transported the other Spirit and me to a private compartment, small and circular with an open top. Light radiated from the walls.

The Spirit before me was a gentleman in a purple robe. His face seemed somehow familiar.

"You recognize me," he smiled.

"I think so," I nodded.

"And well you should. I am your Spirit Guide. I have watched over you for your last two Earth lifetimes, and we also walked the Earth plane together many hundreds of years ago."

Speechless, all I could manage was a feeble nod indicating that he go on.

"I am Aleron. It has been my joyful duty to guide and look after you as you made your way through your life in England from 1785 to 1836. I can answer all your questions about becoming a Spirit Guide, for, you see, I am one."

Looking at me, he recognized my astonishment and resulting muteness, so he continued, "Becoming a Spirit Guide is hard but joyful work. You will study for a long time before you are assigned a human to help. You have been selected as a possible candidate for this training because you showed yourself worthy during your last few Earth lifetimes and also through some of your growth experiences on other planes."

He went on, "What is important here is that you understand that this is a major transition and a great opportunity for you. If you choose to do this, you will never have to walk the Earth again. You have graduated from the lessons that come through being human. You can move on."

"The Earth is beautiful," I managed to say.

Aleron put his hands on my shoulders. I felt so loved.

"Of course. Your love for the beautiful Earth plane is one of the reasons you would make an excellent Spirit Guide. You see, the Spirit Guide Realm is interconnected with the Earth plane. You would be serving the great Earth Mother by helping humans, one in particular, as I have helped and guided you."

Aleron continued, "Do you remember when you were ten years old, and a school chum goaded you into stealing some of your father's precious coins?"

"Mattie!" I said as the memory flashed into my mind. "He had a set of marbles. I wanted them so much. Mattie—what a character!"

"What else do you remember?" Aleron drew closer.

"I recall sneaking into my father's study, his library. He had shown me his collection of coins so I knew where they were."

"Go on." Aleron's eyes were luminescent.

"I was just about to open his drawer when I got a splinter from the wood. Ow! It stung! I remember being puzzled because the desk was smoothly finished."

"The splinter was my doing."

"You gave me that splinter?"

"In a manner of speaking. We Spirit Guides can help manifest circumstances on Earth—indirectly."

"Indirectly?"

"Through humans. What happened next?"

"I forgot about stealing the coins and tended to my splinter."

"This is just one example of the way I have worked on your behalf. There is much to show you. Follow me."

With that he turned, and as I took a step, we changed locations. Now we were under a dome with lighted walls. A group of beings was sitting in a circle with a tall, very lustrous teacher in the center.

"Where are we, Aleron?"

"It's a classroom of sorts. This group of Spirit Guides-in-training is going over the Spirit Guide Creed, and I thought you would like to witness this."

As the center figure turned, she radiated sparkles of light.

"She must be a very high Being," I remember thinking to myself as the voices of those in the circle joined in saying the words I would come to know so well.

"As Spirit Guides, we walk in light.
We come to the Earth plane to guide humans.
We work always from uncompromising, unconditional LOVE.
We are non-judgmental.
We do not frighten or scare anyone.
We stay close to the humans we watch over, stepping back when they request privacy.
We use all our resources as Spirit Guides to help and to heal."

Once the Spirit Guide Creed was spoken, orbs of light pulsed from the teacher, and every being in that circle became brighter. Even I felt the waves and was exhilarated by them.

"Aleron, this is something I think I can do—I believe I want to do."

"Patience, Darci. There is much for you to learn. The work of a Spirit Guide is not easy. I consider myself fortunate for having you as my assigned human. Other Guides have much tougher jobs. You will see."

Again Aleron took one step, and the minute I did, the scene changed. It seemed we were back on Earth, yet Aleron and I were perched near the ceiling of a hovel. The floor was dirt, and there was only one tiny stream of light filtering through a small hole that served as a window. Below us was a man in despair.

Standing behind him was an illuminated Being, a woman. She looked as if she could be his grandmother, but she was glowing. She had her hands on his shoulders and was radiating light to and around him. Snarling and flailing his arms, the poor man leapt up and away from the Spirit Guide.

"Not all are receptive to help," said my Guide.

Aleron then turned to me, his eyes filled with compassion. "You may have a difficult road as a Spirit Guide. Humans have free will, and the human to whom you are assigned may be like this fellow or worse."

"What does it matter?" I asked. "It is the human's choice not to accept help. How does this affect the Guide?"

Aleron motioned to the scene below us. The man was angry now. He shook his fist and cursed. The gentle grandmother Guide again came towards the troubled human, reaching out to comfort him, but the man, who obviously could not see the golden-lighted Guide, stormed right through her and slammed his hands and head on the wall. Then I noticed a change in the Guide. Her beautiful golden radiance dimmed, and she seemed smaller.

"What is happening to the Spirit Guide?" I asked in alarm.

Aleron put his arm around me. I felt flooded with warmth and love.

"The relationship between a Spirit Guide and the assigned human is reciprocal. Each time a human is successfully aided by a Guide, the Guide gains energy. Each time a Spirit Guide reaches out and is unsuccessful or as in this case is rejected by the person being helped, the Guide's energy is sapped. When humans grow and learn through guided assistance, the Spirit Guides benefit as well."

7

I was stunned. This was all so new to me. My curiosity was aroused, so I asked Aleron if I could see more.

He nodded, saying, "Yes, you may. Understanding the course of study to become a Spirit Guide is essential. I will help you all I can."

With that, he motioned for me to follow him, and with one step we were in a different place.

This time the scene was outdoors in a beautiful rural area. The peacefulness of the countryside in the dawn light made me homesick for Derbyshire and the lovely landscapes of England I knew so well. There was a barn with an old wagon nearby. A pitchfork and shovel were propped next to the barn door beside several wooden buckets on the ground. I heard a rooster give its morning crow. Then the scene burst into lively activity.

The farmer, a stout red-faced man, bustled from the barn leading a very pregnant cow. Wiping his brow, he looked concerned.

"Marybelle, Marybelle," I heard him mutter. "What am I going to do with you?"

Then I saw three Guides float along behind the man and his cow. They were luminous with slightly different colors to their radiances. The male Spirit Guide was golden-green. One of the female Guides was a light pink while the other woman Guide glowed white and gold. These shining Beings hovered just behind the man as he led the cow out to pasture.

Once the farmer had closed the gate, he took off her lead and rubbed her forehead with a worried look on his face. Then he did an astonishing thing. Right there in the muddy field, he got down on his knees and clasped his hands in prayer. He wasn't speaking aloud, but I could hear him nonetheless.

Dear God,
Please help my dear Marybelle. She's much too old to be carrying a baby, and she's past her due time. I love her so. I've loved her since the day my dear departed wife gave

her to me. Please help Marybelle. Please don't let her die today. Thank you God. Amen.

As the farmer struggled to his feet, the Guides encircled him and generated a sphere of golden light around him. Miraculously, then the sphere of light divided. The female Guides moved one sphere around the pregnant cow, and the male Guide stood with the farmer in the other golden sphere.

"The farmer has asked for help," said Aleron, "and you see he is receiving it. This is just one small example of what prayer and love can do."

"Will they be all right?" I asked, concerned.

Aleron smiled and replied, "They are in good hands. The farmer and his dear cow are open to receiving help from Spirit, so they will benefit and so will the three Spirit Guides helping them."

Suddenly I heard the sound of hoof beats and saw a horse-drawn carriage move down the lane toward us. The man driving the open cart had a large black hat and a gray beard. He pulled the reins to stop the horse as he drew near the farmer.

"Whoa, there! Whoa! Good morning, Henry. You ready to go?"

"Good morning, Jed. I guess," I heard the farmer say, "though I hate to leave Marybelle. She's so close to giving birth."

"Henry, that's a cow. Cows can do such things for themselves. Come on now. We want to get to town and back before nightfall, don't we?"

"Yes, I guess so," the farmer responded as he took one more look at his Marybelle.

He then hoisted himself up into the seat beside Jed, and they were off down the road. As they departed, I noticed that the male Spirit Guide and another Guide I hadn't seen before were hovering close behind the two men as they traveled along. The two female Guides stayed with the pregnant cow.

One was stroking her nose and the other the side of her distended belly.

The cow let out a bellowing "MOOOO," and paced a little in the direction the farmer had gone.

As we watched, the two beautiful female Spirit Guides tended to that old cow. They increased the brilliance of the light encircling the animal. They stayed close to her as she paced about. Finally old Marybelle carefully let herself down onto the hay pile that was in the corner of the pasture near the gate. It was her time.

The cow's eyes rolled as her belly heaved. The Spirit Guide who radiated pink light took the animal's head in her hands; the cow closed her eyes and seemed to relax. The other golden and white female Guide stroked the stomach until the contractions were akin to regular ripples on a pond.

It was not long before the little one was born. The head and shoulders moved out slowly with the rippling contractions. Then the rest of the calf came out with a sudden whoosh! The pink Guide stayed with the old cow, continuing to stroke her, as the other Guide paid close attention to the newborn.

She scanned the baby with her hands, then glided back a few feet and held her arms out to the calf. The young one lifted its wet head and struggled to stand, which took several tries.

As soon as the newborn was up on all fours, it walked towards its mother. Old Marybelle was tired but lifted her head when her daughter came into view. The two Guides, the mother and calf, all were close together now.

I was amazed to see the circle of golden light increase in brilliance and in size as the old mother cow got to her feet.

"The farmer prayed for help for his cow, and he received it," Aleron shared, nodding toward the scene.

"I've never been able to see Spirit Guides or orbs of light like that," I remarked.

"Not while in a human body. Now you are in spirit form. This gives you access to much more."

Aleron must have seen the puzzled look on my face, so he went on, "Once a Soul enters the human casing or physical body that it has chosen, certain avenues of perception are closed off. It is part of the experience of being human to start from a handicapped place, so to speak, and then learn to open and use these avenues."

All this was so new to me that my mind was awhirl. There's no way to accurately describe the combination of elation and confusion I was experiencing. I still had many questions and wondered if Aleron had the answers.

"I can and will help you," Aleron said, smiling.

I realized that he could read my thoughts with ease.

"Yes, Spirit Guides, Master Guides, Angels—all can read the thoughts and emotions of humans. That is how we know how best to help. That is also why there is the privacy statement in the Spirit Guide Creed."

As I was contemplating this, I noticed that the scene in the farmer's pasture had changed. It was now dusk, and I could hear the horse and cart returning. The reunion of the farmer and his beloved cow made my heart melt with joy. Even the driver in the black hat was moved. As the farmer stroked old Marybelle with one hand and the new calf with the other, Jed tipped his hat to them.

"There! You see, Henry? I told you cows take care of those things all by themselves."

Henry looked up. His ruddy face broke into a smile, as he shook his head no.

"Marybelle had help—the best help. She was watched over by the Angels!"

At that moment, Aleron stood in front of me and put his hands on my shoulders, saying, "It doesn't matter what humans call us as long as they recognize divine help. Henry here knows in his heart that his cow was watched over by Agents of God."

11

"Did I meet God?" I asked. I couldn't help my curiosity. "Was that who brought us together in the Great Hall when I first—died—er—arrived?"

"The hierarchy of Spirit is very complex. In one sense, we are all a part of God, even humans. The Being you met in the center of the Great Hall is a very evolved, very high Spirit—yet not the Creator. There is more for me to show you. Shall we go?"

This time my nod was all it took. The scene changed instantly, and we were back in a classroom. There were hundreds of radiant Beings seated in circular tiers. The teacher in the center was very tall and sparkled and shone with such brilliant light that the sight was wondrous to my eyes. The group began to sing. It was not a hymn from church, the kind of singing with which I was familiar. These Beings were singing tones. The patterns were complex with some of the voices changing notes while others stayed the same. The effect on me was surprising and uplifting. I felt very buoyant and elated.

"What is this, Aleron?"

"One of the many spirit choruses. Their work with tone and light helps refine and energize the Spirit Guides who take part. Remember the golden grandmother Guide we saw trying to help that desperate man? She is here being rejuvenated. She was very weak after that assignment."

"And who is that Being in the center?" I queried, still quite dazzled by her.

"She is one of the Seraphim Angels. They operate on the highest of vibrations, very near the Great Spirit."

"It is all so complex," I mused.

"Complex and beautiful," added Aleron.

"So tell me—even if a Spirit Guide is given a very obstinate and uncooperative human to watch over and even if that human rejects all the help that the Guide offers, there will be no permanent damage to the Spirit Guide, will there?"

"Everything in the Universe is in a continual flow," Aleron answered, "with one constant."

"God?" I guessed.

"Love," Aleron responded, "and God is Love."

With that statement my dear Guide placed his hand on my head, and I felt a surge of love that warmed me and made me tingle from head to foot. At the same time I felt overwhelmed by all I had seen and experienced.

∞ ∞ ∞

I must have lost consciousness, for the next thing I remembered was awaking alone in a small dimly-lit oval compartment and feeling very rested. I was still dazed and a bit disoriented, yet recalled in detail all that I had seen. As I was contemplating my meeting with Aleron and the things he had shown me, I noticed a book on a stand that looked much like the pulpit in the church that I had attended in England.

My inquisitiveness prompted me. Rising from the pallet, I just looked at it. I dared not touch it, for the book glowed with a greenish-white light. The symbols on the page at first made no sense to me. Then either the symbols unscrambled or my mind reoriented itself because I began to understand what was written. There before my eyes was a document signed by me! This startled me so much that I immediately moved closer to examine it more carefully.

I, Darcimon Stillwater, do in these pages proclaim my adhesion to the Universal Will. I understand that the Great Cycle of Life is a Blessing that returns all Spirits to the place of Oneness and Universal Love. I hereby outline those experiences and challenges that I agree to undertake as I begin a new life cycle as a Spirit in human form walking the Earth plane.

I then read a list of specific challenges that I recognized because they had manifested during the toughest times in my last Earth life. As I read, I felt the pain and agony of

13

everything from my first loss as a child when my grandfather died to the helplessness of experiencing the infection and fever that finally claimed my life. The sensations were fleeting, however. As I was reading and feeling all of this, I was assimilating and understanding the value of my last human lifetime.

As I touched the page to turn it, it became even brighter and nearly turned itself so I could continue to read. I recognized lesson after lesson from my last life in England. There were tests of my honesty, my integrity, my ability to love and show compassion. There were tests, too, of my reasoning powers and my instincts. Indeed, I was quite fascinated.

Nonetheless, what I read next was even more intriguing. Beginning after my signature in a different color of ink was an evaluation of my last Earth lifetime. The words startled me for I had no preparation or clues as to how my last Earth life would be valued.

First, there was a series of numbers and each number had a symbol following it. I learned later that these symbols represented planes of activity, levels of learning, and the numbers referred to how many times my Soul had been on each plane. The last number was ninety-two, followed by a circle with a cross in it. This stood for the ninety-two lifetimes I had lived on Earth.

Then came the evaluation. I was surprised at how detailed and thorough it was. It began with my first tests of honesty when I was a child and went year by year, noting every time my Spirit had been subject to trial. After each test was a number; some were in the thousands. The lower numbers sometimes had comments with them. For instance, one day in my last Earth lifetime, a gentleman needing assistance had accosted me. I had done little but offer a few words to the man. The number following this exchange was four-hundred-twenty and the comment was "More help and more compassion was called for. However, the Soul being tested was sick and unable to offer the needed assistance."

I recalled the incident and remembered that I had barely gotten myself home and into bed that day. I had been quite ill.

I was fascinated by this intricate account of my life and thought how useful it would be for human beings to know that such detailed documents are kept. Preachers could reference these records, and merchants could claim honesty and fairness in their transactions, since false dealings would show plainly in these pages. Teachers could use these entries in helping to guide their students.

I wondered why the information in these records was not available to humans. Then I remembered Aleron saying that a Soul entering a human body is like putting on blinders and taking on a handicap.

At the end of pages and pages of evaluations of every deed, every action, every word of significance, there was a final tally and these words:

This Soul has earned passage to a higher level of being and may begin training to become a first tier Spirit Guide.

I lay back down, trying to assimilate all that I had read and learned in the luminous book. A broad perspective of my last life came to me, and I saw in an instant where I had been and where I was going. Still overwhelmed, I rested for quite a while. The softly lit compartment lulled me to sleep.

∞ ∞ ∞

When I came again to consciousness, Aleron was standing by my side and holding his hands over me, palms down. He moved them slowly from above my head and along my spirit body to the space above my feet.

"You are making progress," he informed me. "Your vital energy is slowly rebuilding, and soon you will be ready to make your decision. There is an area about which you have not yet been informed."

I sat up, curious, and asked, "What is it?'

Aleron settled next to me on the soft pallet and answered, "Moving on to study to become a Spirit Guide is a great opportunity for you; you know this."

"Yes."

"It is, however, your choice. The course of training is long and filled with hard work. This is the pathway to take in order to evolve and increase in vibration. You can elect not to set your feet on this path. Other options are available, but they do not necessarily lead in this direction."

"What are these other options?"

Patting my back, Aleron responded, "That is what I am here to tell you."

I turned to face him. I was very interested.

"If you elect not to step to the next higher plane of learning, you will go back to the lower wheel."

"The lower wheel?"

Aleron pointed to the giant glowing volume I had been reading.

"That book is the record of your experiences on the lower wheel of life. You can continue with another Earth life, or you can seek further knowledge on one of the other levels of that wheel. You have learned all you need on this level, but you can choose to go through again to perfect and refine. It's up to you."

"Would I not end up here again with the same offer to go on to be a Spirit Guide?"

"Perhaps. Perhaps not. It all depends on what happens once your Soul goes back into that wheel and how you handle it."

"So I could lose ground. I could lose this opportunity."

"You could."

"Then I must go onward and seize this chance."

"Darci . . . ," Aleron looked at me kindly, "it is my task to make sure you know what you are undertaking if you elect to go on to Spirit Guide training."

"I wish to know."

Standing, Aleron continued, "Very well. Let's go."

What happened next I could only describe as a whirlwind tour. Aleron took me to classroom after classroom, some large and filled with hundreds of beings, some small with only a few. These were not the classrooms I remember from my boyhood in England. These were beautiful, even heavenly. The circular walls and floors glowed, and the students were often seated in luminous disks that changed form as they moved. On several occasions, Aleron and I observed private sessions where a teacher was working closely with just one student. The light in and around these scenes was especially brilliant.

Finally we arrived at a massive hall. I thought it was the place where the Angel Initiates had first brought me, but no. It was even grander with rims or tiers around the outside of the great circular lyceum. These tiers were filled with lighted Beings of many shapes and hues. What I saw in the center was most extraordinary. There was a huge pyramid of brilliant white light. Inside this was a group of Beings in a circle. As Aleron and I looked on, the pyramid of white light became even brighter until we could barely see the Beings inside.

"Watch," said Aleron as he motioned towards the pyramid.

He needn't have prompted me. I could not take my eyes away.

At that moment, the hundreds of beings around the rim of the great hall began to sing. It was no song I had ever heard before, and though it was unfamiliar, it was wondrous! The intricacies of the harmonies and interweaving melodies brought joy into my heart.

I stared into the bright pyramid.

"Was I seeing correctly?" I wondered.

The Beings in the circle inside the pyramid were becoming taller and brighter.

Obviously awed by this spectacle, I asked, "What is all this?"

"This is graduation. Those beings in the center have worked and studied and are now graduating. They are becoming full-fledged Spirit Guides. They will take all they have learned, plus the power being given to them here, and set about helping humans."

"All this to help humans?" I was incredulous.

"Oh yes. All this and more. Most humans do not realize how much assistance from Spirit they have. Of course, from what you have seen since your arrival here, you know that Spirit Guides grow and learn through helping humans."

"So becoming a Spirit Guide is a step up? What comes after being a Spirit Guide?" I couldn't help asking.

Aleron laughed and replied, "You are galloping way ahead of yourself. You have not yet agreed to take this step."

He wiped his eyes and continued, "I will tell you as much as I think you can grasp, for the hierarchy of Spirit is complex. Spirit Guides can become Master Guides, and Master Guides can go on to become Angels. The Angels have their own Hierarchy, each level closer to the Creator. We are all moving to become one with the Creator."

I let out a sigh of amazement.

Aleron continued, "Sometimes the Beings that have moved to higher levels take up work for The Great Spirit on lower levels like Earth."

"What do you mean?"

"Great Earth teachers like the Buddha, the Christ, Mohammed, and the Dalai Lama are all evolved Souls who felt they could best serve the Creator by going to the Earth plane to teach and help humans."

This information caused a sudden expansion of my consciousness. Realizations were clicking into place, and my understanding was quickly increasing. I looked at my Guide. He seemed taller and brighter than when I had first met him.

"Is there anything else I need to know before I decide?" I asked.

Aleron paused a moment before answering. He seemed to be scanning me.

"You know the basics. You have enough information to make your decision. Do you want to undertake the hard work that leads to becoming a Spirit Guide?"

"I think I do. Are there those who try but fail?"

"I do not think that would be you, Darci."

"Does it happen?"

"Everything possible is done to help a struggling student. Most often these trainees just take longer to complete the course. There is much serious talk and much counseling before a student is moved out of the program. It is a fairly rare occurrence."

"What happens to those who drop out?" I asked, wanting information on all possible outcomes.

"Darci, you have determination. You have patience. You have perseverance. You will not fail this course."

"That may be, but I still want to know what happens. Do these Souls who fail go back to the lower wheel?"

"Not directly. There is an interim process. The details of this depend on the status of the individual Soul.

"Are they punished for failing at becoming a Spirit Guide?"

"Never," Aleron responded. "Yet these Souls do lose ground on their journey. Much healing and rejuvenating must be done."

"Hard work and long periods of study do not deter me from stepping onto this path. I am willing to take on all the training I need. My concern is the practice. Once I am a Spirit Guide, I realize the challenges may be great. Will I have you to help me?"

The tall luminous Guide laughed and put his arms around me. I felt a powerful surge of energy.

"You will have all the help you need though it may not be from me. Just as you have been tapped as a candidate for Spirit Guide status, so, too, have I been asked to step to a higher level."

"You have?"

I was taken aback. The possibility that Aleron had a similar choice to make had not entered my mind.

"What are you going to do, Aleron?"

"The decision is easy for me, for I have worked with many Master Guides, and I have long looked forward to the time when I could join them in their work."

"You will become a Master Guide?"

"Yes, after more training and study. I give some of the credit for this great opportunity to you. When you walked the Earth as a human, you were responsive to my input. Whether you remember or not, we worked together and successfully faced your life challenges, and this has helped me get my potential promotion. Thank you, Darci."

"It must have been an unconscious connection, for I don't remember you from my days on Earth."

"Yes, your connection to me and to the guidance I offered was on the subconscious level as it is with most humans. On occasion you felt you had a guardian angel watching over you, which, of course, was me. Overall, you interacted with the Earth plane responsibly and compassionately—with my help."

"Then I thank you, Aleron."

"This is how the universe works best. We help each other even through the boundaries between realms."

"You have no doubt you wish to move on to become a Master Guide?"

"I am much more familiar with all of this, whereas it is new to you. That is why I am taking it slowly with you, Darci. You are being introduced to so much at once. I want to make sure you grasp it all—and understand it. You are doing quite well."

"Will I ever see you again, Aleron?" I asked, feeling a surge of emotion.

"First of all, I will be right here with you until you are well on your way. Second, we are bonded. There will always be a connection of love and trust between us. Soon, however, I will need to move on to my new field of study."

Aleron could see the sadness in my face. He hugged me, and I felt flooded with love.

"Darci, this is not Earth. You are not losing me. You will be so busy with whatever path you choose that you will not miss me."

"I need your help, Aleron."

"You will have all the help you need—though this time it will not come from me. We will see each other again. I know this to be true."

I sighed. Aleron was my only friend in this new and unfamiliar realm.

"I'll stay with you as long as you need me," he smiled.

"I forgot that you can read my thoughts," I replied, smiling back. "I don't want you to stay with me if you are eager to begin your own studies."

"It is my joyful duty to make sure you have safely entered your next phase of learning—whatever that may be. I am in no hurry. There are no deadlines here."

"Knowing that you are embarking on a new course of intensive study gives me the inspiration to begin this for myself. Aleron, I have decided. I want to study to become a Spirit Guide."

As soon as I said these words aloud to my Guide, I saw a brilliant flash of magenta light and found myself alone in a different location. I was a little disoriented at first because the environment was unfamiliar. There were layers of translucent curtains around me, which were undulating slightly.

I did not know what to do, so I spoke aloud, "Where am I? Aleron, where did you go?"

To my utter amazement, I heard his voice. It wasn't coming from anywhere in the room but was coming from right inside my own mind!

"I'm here, Darci. Move through the curtains. Step forward. Go on," I heard him telling me.

I hesitated only briefly, then took a step. The sparkling curtains became much more animated, waving more noticeably and more rhythmically. Also, as I moved forward, the curtains glowed brighter until after about ten steps, I saw an altar.

"Go on. Step up," I heard Aleron's voice in my mind encouraging me. "You must do this on your own. This must be your choice."

Drawing near the altar, which seemed to be made of white marble, I saw a large document. At first it seemed as though this document actually formed the entire top of the altar. Once I was standing right in front, however, I saw that the document was in a golden frame and was exactly the size of the top of the altar. My final step brought me close enough to read the words:

I, Darcimon Stillwater, do freely choose to undertake the courses and studies that will lead me to the initiation of my Spirit into the Sacred Spirit Guide plane. I hereby agree to become a Spirit Guide.

I read this three times, twice to myself and once aloud.

"I agree," I said, and then saw my signature appear on the document.

My journey had begun.

Chapter Two:
My First Tough Class, the Love Tunnel

My training to become a Spirit Guide began slowly and simply. I was placed in a chamber with several other students, and all we did was breathe. I know this sounds strange because as Spirits, we have no physical body, no actual lungs. Taking a spirit breath is different than taking a human breath although they are related. When humans breathe in, they often use their diaphragms to take a deep breath and expand their lungs. Spirits do much the same—the difference being that when a Spirit breathes in, the entire Spirit body expands.

The breath work I was doing with the four other trainees began when an instructor positioned each of us in front of our own individual illuminated screen. We were then shown how to breathe to increase our brilliance and energy. When we did this exercise correctly, the screens before each of us glowed more brightly. In this way, we could monitor our progress and so could the teacher.

This may sound uninteresting, even boring, but it was not. The instructor showed us how to note the subtle changes in our energy fields as they were measured on the screens. The sensations, coupled with the light show I created with my breathing, were certainly engaging enough to keep me absorbed in this activity.

Rest was a part of beginning this new path, too. The five of us in that chamber had all come from different places. We were still in transition from our past experiences. I know I was sometimes disoriented. Operating in spirit form was still very new to me as it was to the others in my group. In essence, we were strengthening our Spirits and raising our energies. The instructor, a golden Being who appeared to be neither male nor female checked on us regularly.

After we had been doing the breathing exercise for a while, I decided to ask the instructor a question. "How long will we be doing this?" I queried as the golden Being was checking the lighted panel before me.

"Before you can begin your studies in earnest, you must be vibrating at a certain frequency. Otherwise, the next lesson will go right by you."

I wanted to ask more, but the golden Being had vanished, so I kept on with the exercise. At least I knew the purpose of it, so I focused on increasing my vibration and resting.

∞ ∞ ∞

The next experience in my training was surprising and quite unusual. I was placed in a whirlpool of energy. The golden Being who had instructed me in the chamber led me through a giant portal. I was still getting used to entryways and, indeed, entire scenes appearing and disappearing. The golden Being said simply that my energy had increased enough for me to be sealed. I had no idea what that meant but trusted the process that I had begun.

Once I went through the portal, I stepped forward, yet there was no floor, so I began falling slowly. Whirling light surrounded me, and I noticed that it was changing colors as I descended. At first, the light was gold. Then as I floated down, it was a glowing orange color, then vibrant red. When I reached the red whirling light, the pace became faster. I seemed to hover in the bright red spinning light for a while. Then a rush of energy filled me from my feet to my head, and I began to rise. I floated slowly upward as the red, then the orange, then the gold light spun around me. This time I kept moving up through golden-green and green light, through blue and violet. As I rose through this funnel, everything seemed to whirl faster and faster until all was a blur.

The purple light was spinning around me at a dizzying rate when suddenly I was launched into a place of peaceful calm where there was nothing but white light. Brilliant sparkling white engulfed me, and I felt incredibly energized yet amazingly peaceful at the same time. I floated there, enjoying the serenity for what seemed to be a long time. I probably could have hovered there indefinitely, but an archway appeared before me, and I knew it was time to move on. I stepped through the arch.

Instantly everything changed. I was finally getting used to the speed at which these changes of location occurred. Now I was in another great hall bustling with activity. There was a high domed ceiling and pillars around the circular perimeter. The activity level was so high that it took me a few breaths to adjust, for I had been going at a much slower pace. I had no idea what to do.

I must have looked quite lost, for a kindly older gentleman came over to me and asked, "Is this your first time at university?"

I nodded, looking him over. He was unique in appearance. His eyes were a startling violet color, and his white beard had crystals woven into it. He wore a purple cap on his head, and his robe was striped lengthwise with different shades of purple. He came closer and took my hand. The minute he touched me, I felt electrified. He led me to a table by one of the pillars and picked up a huge book.

"Here is the information on your first class. Follow me."

He dropped the book in my arms. I was prepared to receive a heavy volume, yet when he placed it in my arms, it was remarkably light. He moved quickly for an elder; I had a hard time keeping up with him. We circled about halfway around the hall until we came to a doorway that I had not noticed before. Still following the elder, I glided through several hallways with glowing walls until we arrived at a circular classroom. Actually, the room was much more like a sphere, for it had a dome ceiling and a concave floor.

The female teacher in the center motioned for us to join her. She was dazzling pink from head to foot with lovely blue eyes and a radiant smile.

"Welcome," she greeted me by clasping both my hands in hers. I felt such a burst of love that it rather overwhelmed me.

Smiling, she continued, "We have been waiting for you."

The elder gentleman in purple put his arm around me and said, "Darci insists on taking his time. He wants to do everything thoroughly."

I was stunned. "How do you know this about me?" I heard myself say.

Both of them laughed and gazed at me with much compassion and love.

The woman spoke first, "Your thoroughness is a good thing. We know much about our incoming students."

Then the elder said, "I must apologize for rushing you out of the Central Hall. It was just that I knew Luanna was waiting for your arrival so she could begin this class. Let me introduce myself. I am your mentor and counselor while you are on this level of learning. I am Sottrol, at your service."

"And as you heard, I am Luanna. Welcome, Darci." The lustrous pink woman put her arm around the elder Spirit as she continued, "Sottrol was my mentor, too, when I arrived. He was a great help to me as I first began my studies. You are fortunate that he is watching over you."

Not to be outdone, Sottrol took Luanna's hand and said, "This beautiful one is an excellent teacher. She will have you well on your way before you know it."

They both laughed again, and this time I joined them. I was glad to be there.

"I'll leave you in her capable hands, but I'll be back," said Sottrol with a wink.

I looked at my new teacher, noticing her kind eyes. Then I turned to ask the elder when he would return, but he had vanished.

"Comings and goings are rather instantaneous around here," I observed.

"You will get more familiar with all of this," Luanna explained with her reassuring smile. "Now that you are here, let us begin. Please make yourself comfortable, Mr. Stillwater," she said, motioning to the lighted benches that were around the rim of this spherical classroom.

I moved to take a seat, and Luanna floated to the center of the classroom. When she arrived at the center point, the entire domed ceiling became much brighter. The other students and I focused on the radiant teacher.

"Dear ones," she began, "you would not be here if you had not given and received much love during your last life experience. Now it is time for you to learn how to raise and refine this experience of love. Here you will learn how to love unconditionally without doubt, without hesitation."

I knew I had heard her correctly. I thought to myself, "How odd. This is a love class."

"It isn't odd at all, Mr. Stillwater," Luanna addressed me. "Unconditional love is the basis for all Spirit Guide work."

"Forgive me. I keep forgetting that you can read my thoughts."

"We teachers can read your thoughts and your feelings, a skill that you will develop as you proceed through this university. Now back to the subject of unconditional love. All of you have come from the lower wheel, most of you from Earth. Perhaps you have not realized it yet—unconditional love is one of the major lessons on that plane. Test after trial after test come to humans to attempt to move them toward loving unconditionally."

A female student across the classroom spoke up, asking, "Isn't unconditional love a given on Earth through parenthood?"

"Very good question," Luanna was quick to say. "The stewardship of parenthood has many challenges. To love unconditionally is one of them, and it is not a 'given' as you put it. Indeed, if you experienced this in your last Earth life, then you are very fortunate.

"Some of you have brought this ability with you from Earth life," she went on. "If so, you will learn to increase and refine it. Others of you will learn from scratch, as it were. Now, do not think for a moment that if you came into this classroom with the experience of loving unconditionally tucked neatly into your soul pack that you are ahead of the others in this class. What we learn here is on an entirely different level."

Luanna looked directly at me and said, "When a Spirit Guide is assigned a human to watch over, this Guide must be able to radiate unconditional love to this human constantly and unshakably. Unconditional love must be your natural mode of operation, your second nature. It must be there, no matter what. I am going to make sure that as Spirit Guides, you always operate with unconditional love. Any more questions?"

She glanced around, then announced, "Then let us begin."

As soon as she spoke those words, a giant cylinder lowered from the dome of the spherical classroom. This cylinder appeared to be made of shiny metal. As it lowered to the spot where Luanna had been standing, she glided up and to the side of it.

Floating around the rim of the classroom, she explained, "This is a true tunnel of love. Its purpose is to measure and help you refine your ability to . . ."

She looked around the class, and many of us said the words "love unconditionally."

She continued, "This tool was developed by the Third Level Angels, and it is a benefit and true blessing to you Spirit Guide trainees. It works this way: you all will be given a situation to which you must respond. This tool that we affectionately call "The Love Tunnel" will rate your automatic response. This device measures your reaction. It shows you how you responded on a love scale and how you need to improve. The miraculous part of this tool is that you can all access it at once. An opening in the cylinder will appear before you. When it does, I want you to move forward and enter."

"All of us in this classroom are going to go into that tube?" asked a male Spirit near me.

"What you see is not all there is to this device. The cylinder is only the entrance."

She paused in her instructions and glided around the classroom, looking carefully at each one of us. It was as though she was sizing us up before we went into the tube.

Then she continued, "Once you enter, you will be given a situation to which you will react. Each circumstance is different and will vary according to your needs as a student. Relax, everyone. You will do this exercise many times, and the tests that you face within this tunnel will vary and increase in difficulty until I am sure that you can respond automatically and consistently with unconditional love.

"After your session today and after each session, I will counsel you. Together we will pinpoint the problem areas that are holding you back from responding as a Spirit Guide would. Let us try this then. Step forward and enter."

As she said this, the shiny metal cylinder increased in size so that the tube came nearer to each of us. Just as Luanna said it would, a door appeared, and I moved toward it. I was a bit apprehensive.

Luanna must have noticed my hesitation because she glided next to me and said, smiling warmly, "This is all about love, Mr. Stillwater. The last thing you want to do is hold back."

I nodded and stepped through the opening.

The door made a whooshing sound as it closed behind me. I felt myself rise as though something or someone was lifting me. The sensation was pleasant, and just as I was relaxing enough to enjoy this feeling and the colored lights that floated by, another doorway opened before me. I stepped through.

Immediately I was hit by a fierce wind. The setting looked like Earth, but it was no place I could identify. The trees were bent nearly horizontal by the force of the gale. I saw a couple trying to make their way in the windstorm. As they moved towards me, I could hear them speak in raised voices to each other.

"God must hate us to put us through this misery," said the woman.

"You stupid woman!" yelled the man. "This proves there is no God. How could a good and loving God abide such ugliness and allow such a wasteland as this to exist?"

"I'm so cold and hungry," moaned the woman. "Please give me what's left of the food."

"We can't stop now, you foolish ass! Keep going!"

"But I cannot go on!" the woman wailed into the wind. "I'm too tired and hungry." And with that, she collapsed.

The man began kicking her and screamed, "Get up! Get up!"

I could not watch this. I hurried over to the couple, put my hand on the man's shoulder and yelled above the roar of the wind, "Stop!"

He was startled and snarled, "Who are you?"

"Don't hurt this poor woman!" I begged, looking into his face. It was dirty and contorted.

"What do you know, Mister? This woman is my wife, and she deserves a beating!"

The woman moaned, and I felt a surge of compassion towards her.

"No one deserves such treatment," I said to the man sternly.

"Maybe you deserve a knock or two, you interfering bastard!"

With that, the man came at me. I moved back as he lunged.

"Got some money, Mister? Got some food for us?"

He came at me again. This time I moved to the other side of his wife. He grabbed a branch that was blowing by and beat his poor huddled wife twice before attacking me. He was disgusting-looking. As he got nearer, I could smell his foul breath. I felt so sorry for the wife of this beast. I had nothing to fight him with, so I raised my hands to protect myself from his ongoing blows. Just as I did this, there was a flash of purple light, and I was in a new location.

I was seated alone before a giant lighted screen. I took a deep breath. I had become so caught up in that windy scene that I had forgotten that it wasn't real. I was still a little dizzy from the wind in my ears, the threat of violence, and then the quick change to this quiet room.

"Things move fast around here," I thought.

"Sometimes they do," I heard Luanna saying to me telepathically, but I did not see her.

An image appeared on the screen, and Luanna said, "Here's how you did, Darci."

On the screen were a dozen or so colored lighted bars that ran vertically. Several were bright; several were dim.

"What does this mean?" I asked aloud.

At that moment, Luanna materialized next to me.

"This was your first time out," she said, placing her hand gently on my head. As before, I felt a rush of love. "Your compassion for the woman in the scene was high."

With her other hand, she pointed to two brightly lit bars on the screen before me. One was shimmering blue, the other a glowing gold. Then she asked me, "Do you recall how you felt about the man?"

"He was a beast!" I blurted as a picture of the man's contorted face flashed in my mind. "I felt repulsed and a bit afraid. He was violent."

Luanna moved her hand from my head to the back of my neck. Electricity shot up my spirit spine.

"We started you with a difficult exercise, Darci. Sottrol insisted upon it. He has predicted that you will be the star student in this group."

"It was difficult," I agreed. "I wanted to help the woman, but I didn't know how, except perhaps to draw away her husband's attention."

Luanna now moved her hand to the base of my spirit spine, and I felt vibrations throughout my entire spirit body.

"First of all, Darci, every lesson in the tunnel is about unconditional love. Many students find it helpful to repeat these two words over and over as they travel in the Love Tunnel to their tests. Secondly, a reaction of compassion is good, and we teachers do want to promote compassionate responses from our students. However, unconditional love was, of course, the response we were looking for here."

"I guess I knew that going in, Luanna. Once in the scene though, the urgency of the situation distracted me."

"You cannot be assigned a human to guide until we know that you will not be distracted by the circumstances surrounding that human or by anything that person does. Your desire to help the woman shows here."

And with that, Luanna touched the bright orange bar on the screen. I realized the other vertical bars were rather faded-looking.

"What are these others that are not so bright?" I asked her.

"I was getting to that." She smiled a little and I could see great compassion in her eyes. "Unconditional love for the woman in the scene is here," she said as she touched a bright pink bar. "It could definitely be stronger. These..." she continued, running her hand along the section of bars that had almost no color. "These relate to how you dealt with the man. You showed no compassion, no desire to help, and no love. In fact, your automatic response of fear and disgust muted this whole section of the graph."

"Love that awful man? Why that's absurd! He treated his wife terribly!"

"Nonetheless, Darci, as a Spirit Guide, you must approach every human with pure unconditional love. That's what this class is all about."

"How?" I asked, totally baffled.

Instead of looking at the screen, Luanna looked directly at me. She turned my shoulders to face her.

"I will tell you. It takes practice. First, know that each and every human has a Soul, a Spirit like you and me. No matter how foul their exterior, no matter how horrible their actions, humans have the potential to be Angels. It is up to us to help encourage them on this path.

"Next, practice detaching yourself. This does not mean to feel nothing or do nothing. It means to step out and look from a spiritual perspective. If you see even the dirtiest, angriest, most foul human as another Spirit who needs your help and guidance, then the next step is to simply love that person."

"I think I see," I replied a bit hesitantly. I was still not sure I could do this.

"I want you to try this exercise again and remember that the purpose is to show those two people unconditional love."

I sighed. I did not really want to go back into the windstorm and face those two lost Souls. Of course, Luanna knew what I was feeling.

"Rest first, dear Darci," she said softly. "When you are ready, simply say you are. The door to the Love Tunnel will open for you."

"I'm not sure I can do this, Luanna. Is there any other help you can give me?"

"Yes. I will make sure you have more to work with. This was a difficult scene for you to start with. Rest now."

∞ ∞ ∞

Almost as soon as I closed my eyes, I felt myself swoon. It was as though I was floating and rotating at once. Just as I was feeling rested and rejuvenated, I felt a tap on my arm. My eyes sprang open and to my surprise, I saw Sottrol.

"My son, my dear Darci, you have much to learn."

My response came slowly as I was still in a relaxed mode, "I'll give you that."

"Remember, Darci, you are in spirit form now. You no longer have a human body to limit you. You needn't fear physical harm because you have no human body, only a spirit body."

When the elder said this, the image of the horrid man coming at me with the tree branch flashed in my mind.

"That man in the wind-scape cannot hurt you. If you ever get the chance to interact directly with any humans, remember that they cannot physically harm you. The threat of violence is just a distraction in these exercises. Even if humans are physically hurt, even killed, their Souls are intact. The Spirit is indestructible. Know this. Take this to heart and know this, Darci."

"How would you have handled that man?" I asked, hoping that now maybe I'd learn what I was supposed to do.

"Simple. Love him. No matter what he says or does, love him and his wife. That is what unconditional love is all about. Love, no matter what."

I sat silent. Sottrol stroked his white beard and pulled a tiny clear crystal from it. He placed it in my palm.

"When you feel this in your hand, you must say to yourself, 'Love is all there is.'"

I took a deep breath and closed my eyes. I thought, "I believe I'm beginning to get it."

Sottrol said, "Good. Then try it again!"

I heard the faint sound of bells, and he was gone.

Still needing a few moments to mull over all that I had just experienced, I used the breathing technique I had learned to strengthen my energy.

When I felt strong and centered, I said, "I am ready to try again."

Amazingly, the shiny metal cylinder instantly appeared before me and a door opened. In I went. The ride was similar though the colored lights that I floated by seemed brighter. When the door opened, I was right back in the wasteland with the wind howling mercilessly.

The exact same scenario played out as it had before. I stepped toward the couple sooner because I remembered that the man was about to kick his wife.

As I moved near to them, I told myself, "Unconditional love. It's all about unconditional love."

Just as the woman collapsed in a heap from hunger and fatigue, I said, "Please remember you and your wife are facing this together. Help one another."

"Who are you?" the man sneered, baring his stained teeth at me. "What business is it of yours?"

I tried to detach and think of all three of us as Spirits.

"We are here to help each other," I said.

"You have some money, Mister?" he snarled. "You have some food we can eat?"

The man was truly menacing.

"Ah . . . well," I stuttered. *I was supposed to love this creature?*

At this point, he grabbed the branch that was flying by and came at me.

"I'll take your money!" he shouted.

At that instant, I felt Sottrol's crystal in my hand, and I remembered he said that no harm could come to me. So I opened my arms wide as if I was about to embrace a long-lost brother.

"I can give you love," I said.

The man looked shocked and dropped the branch, which quickly blew away. The woman uncovered her head and looked up from her crouched position. They both seemed stunned.

"I give you both love," I said louder so as to be heard above the gale.

The purple flash of light signaled the end of the exercise, and I found myself back in the room before the screen with the lighted graph. Both Sottrol and Luanna were there this time. Sottrol smiled and pointed to the colored bars, which were now extremely bright.

"That's more like it!" he said delightedly, moving as if he was dancing a little jig.

"Much better," smiled Luanna. "You learn quickly."

Sottrol and Luanna took the time to explain in detail the graph of lighted colored bars on the large screen. They referred to the room as an evaluation cell and to the screen as the trial results. My ability to show both compassion and unconditional love were charted on the big graph with many subtle nuances recorded there. I was then informed that this first lesson was to be followed by a period of rest and rejuvenation of my energy.

"As Spirits, we do not eat food," Sottrol told me with a sparkle in his eye. "However, we do need to nourish ourselves by replenishing our vital energy."

This, of course, I had learned to do at the very start of my training, and I began to realize the importance of this skill for a Spirit Guide.

As Luanna had explained in class, I entered the Love Tunnel many, many times. On occasion, I would interact with the same scene more than once as happened the first time. This did not occur often, and when it did, I simply wanted to do better. I learned that I could go back and re-enter a test situation with the intention of trying to improve and refine my responses.

After the second round of one of these trials, I said to myself, "If only humans had the chance to go back and do again."

Luanna, who always visited me after each test, appeared next to me the moment I had this thought.

"The Earth plane is very different," she said. "Here we are training you, and the tests can be given again and again. On Earth, the actions of humans set their karma and determine the progress of their Souls."

"No second chances on Earth," I thought. I shook my head, feeling much compassion for all humans, for I had been in an Earth body myself not long ago.

"That's not entirely true," replied Luanna, "for if a Soul has a specific lesson to learn as a human being, and that Soul does not learn it adequately, that same Soul will go through it all again—though probably not until it is time for another Earth lifetime, and the lesson will probably arrive in a different form.

"Also, keep in mind," Luanna continued before I could ask her, "that between Earth lifetimes, this same Soul could be sent to other levels of learning on the lower wheel. The purpose would be to strengthen certain skills, and these skills would then hopefully help the Soul when it comes time to face those same tests again on Earth."

"It's all very complex," I mused.

"And always shifting and changing," added Luanna. "Always moving to balance. That is the Law of Karma."

"Explain karma to me, Luanna."

"You will learn much more about this force as you continue your studies. For now, I will give you the basic definition. Karma is a universal force that always moves to balance."

"And an example would be . . . ?"

"Let's use Earth as the example because the actions that humans take directly affect their karma. If a human does a good deed—is helpful or selfless in action—then the good deed will be returned to this human at some point."

"I never noticed such a force for balance when I walked the Earth, Luanna."

"That's because karma extends far beyond one Earth lifetime. For instance, if a human does something very bad, then this perpetrator will have this same experience happen to him or her. However, it may be several lifetimes further down the road."

"So when bad things happen to certain humans on Earth, this could be karma balancing a negative act from many lifetimes before. Do I have this correct?"

"Basically, yes. That is karma in its essence. Karma is, of course, much more complex, for it involves all the various levels of learning, not just the Earth plane."

"Even the Spirit Guide plane?"

"Oh yes, even the Angels. No Soul, no Spirit escapes the force of karma."

I spent much time in my rest and rejuvenation period contemplating this information. I began to see how I had earned the opportunity to become a Spirit Guide. I had balanced my soul's karma to the point where I could move on in my spirit evolution.

∞ ∞ ∞

Experiences in the Love Tunnel became my life at the Spirit Guide University. I entered the shiny metal cylinder time after time, always confronted by very challenging test situations. Each time I attempted to interact with increased compassion and unconditional love.

In fact, I cultivated the habit of chanting while I was rising up through the silver tube, "I act and interact always with unconditional love."

Each time the door opened and I was thrust into a new test, I tried to keep this chant in my heart and mind. Indeed, I was working towards having this way of acting and reacting become my very nature.

As I tell this story, I need not elaborate on every trial that I faced in the Love Tunnel. However, I do wish to tell about one more test. This is the one I consider my toughest challenge.

Toward the end of my training with Luanna, just as I was finishing my rejuvenation period, I had an unexpected visit from Sottrol. The purple-clad elder manifested beside me, as I was getting ready to enter the Love Tunnel and undergo another test. He didn't say anything at first; he just looked me up and down, nodding as he did so.

"Greetings Sottrol," I said, watching him with interest. "Why do you visit?"

"Just checking your progress, my son. You have been doing well. Luanna tells me you rarely repeat an exercise anymore."

"I haven't for a while. I think I'm getting to the point where I can react automatically with unconditional love."

"Good, good," Sottrol murmured as he circled me. "Listen, Darci. I want you to take a few more minutes and increase your vibration. Please go into this next trial with more focus and more strength."

I nodded to show I understood, and as I did so, Sottrol vanished.

I took my time re-energizing for my next test in the Love Tunnel. In fact, I made sure that my Spirit was brighter and vibrating higher than ever before. As it turns out, I am very glad I did.

The scene before me as the door of the tube opened was one of complete devastation. Never had I witnessed such destruction. All the buildings in view were heaps of rubble or smoldering shells. I could hear wails of agony but could see no one, so with a deep breath, I stepped forward into this horrible scene. My love mantra was going over and over in my head.

First, a mother holding a child ran towards me from one of the burning buildings.

"My baby! My baby!" she cried.

I thought she was referring to the child in her arms. I reached out, radiating as much love as I could, only to have her back away and point in the direction from which she had come.

"Save him! Save my baby!" she screamed.

"I will try!" I told her. "Can I help you?"

"Not me. My son! He's been captured! They'll kill him! Please save him!"

I followed her path through the ashes and rubble to the back of a building that was still smoldering. I could not see or hear any signs of life but sensed a tremendous vacuum. Perhaps I could better describe it as a vortex of negativity.

With each step, I could feel it sucking at my energy field. Despite the smoke, I stopped several times to breathe and increase my vibration.

The first room I entered had no sign of the woman's son. Putrid fumes snaked from scorched beams that still sizzled as I stepped through piles of debris and ash. Bravely, I moved in the direction of the giant black vacuum that I sensed. As I proceeded slowly through the next doorway, I began to hear a whimpering sound amongst the crackles and spits of small fires that were all around.

"Hello. I'm here to help!" I ventured the greeting. "Where are you?"

A piece of ceiling fell close by and startled me. Then I heard muffled sobbing. It seemed to be coming from below, so I looked for stairs to a lower level or basement. I remarked to myself that it was a good thing I was in spirit form and bore no weight. A human might easily break through the charred floorboards.

Just as I came around a sharp corner, I was face to face with two men. Both carried guns, had greasy faces blackened by the smoke, and were wearing dirty torn military garments. The shorter one was wounded. They were sitting, guarding a doorway.

"We heard ya coming," one growled. "You're after the damn boy, aren't ya!"

With that, they both pointed their guns at me; one of them lined me up in his sights and was ready to fire.

"Where is the child?" I asked, putting my hands forward to show I had no weapons. "I've come to help him."

"No you haven't! Don't take us for fools!" barked the wounded man. "You're here to help him escape, and we're not going to let you!"

The other dirty soldier who was ready to pull the trigger stood up and brought the barrel of the gun close to my head, saying, "You're a one of them loyalists, aren't ya! That's why you want him!"

"I've come to help you, too, if I can. I come in love."

"One of those damned religious types—worse yet!" snorted the wounded man, still seated. "You'll be sorry you admitted that. We're wiping you out, too. Don't you know that?" He spat in my direction. "Religious and stupid!"

"Why do you have the boy trapped down there?" I asked, trying to distract them from shooting me, which would end the exercise.

The standing man straightened, lowering the gun a bit as he did so and replied, "We're guarding the boy until our commander arrives." "Then he will kill the Prince himself," bragged the wounded soldier. "And we will see the last heir to that arrogant dynasty perish in a filthy hole, just as it should be!"

"He is only a child," I stalled. "I heard him whimpering. Where is he?"

"Down there," uttered the standing man as he motioned with his chin towards the doorway they were guarding and a shaky stairway that led into the dark. At that very moment, I heard horses.

"The commander is here!" shouted the wounded soldier.

"He can kill ya both. He'll like that," smirked the soldier who had been pointing his gun at me. Just as he said this, he fired it, not at me, but out the window, a signal to those who had just arrived.

Only moments later, a group of five men stomped through the front entrance. One was obviously the leader. He wore a fancy hat with a plume and many medals on his coat. They were all armed. The two soldiers with whom I had been talking snapped to attention.

The commander stepped forward, asking, "You have the Prince?"

"We do, sir—in the cellar. He is still alive as you requested."

"And who is this?" the commander asked, glaring at me.

"Some damn stupid do-gooder who's trying to save the boy. Better kill him too," the soldier growled and spat at me again.

I knew I had to make a move. My energy was being quickly sapped, but I focused on my purpose and said, "What is this all about? Surely you do not want to harm a child!"

"You know nothing, you fool!" bellowed the commander. "You should have saved yourself! You'll pay dearly for your damned insolence!"

"Tell me what is going on," I replied while repeating the chant in my head.

"All the world shall know," the leader boasted as he glowered at me, "and you shall be the first, you contemptuous idiot!"

He paced a little with his arms behind his back as he bragged, "We are ridding the world of the last of the infamous royal family. They have done nothing but take, take, take from the people of this land. We are joining with other forces to purge the country of every member of this royal clan and everyone who supports them. We also move to kill those who follow the old religions. We are now rounding up, interrogating, torturing, and killing all you cursed bastards!"

He turned on his heel and stared at me menacingly as he bragged, "The Queen tried to escape with her two children, but we caught her with one child as we rode in. I slaughtered them myself. See here? Their blood is still fresh on my sleeve. Now I will personally murder this poor stupid boy, the last of whole damned inbred, wasteful, self-indulgent royal clan! Victory is ours!"

My insides quaked as I listened to this speech. My nostrils stung with the stench of their vicious slaughter. I had great compassion for the woman and her children—indeed, for all the victims of this horrendous military purge. Yet I knew I was supposed to love all in the scene, even the bloodthirsty, power-hungry, arrogant commander. I attempted to detach myself, but it was tremendously difficult. The black vacuum of negativity was continuing to deplete my energy. I tried to breathe using the techniques I had learned, but could barely keep ahead of the vortex's draining effect.

I shifted my position slightly so that I could view all the soldiers and the commander, seven in all. Each had a cruel, murderous look in his eyes. Three of them had their guns pointed at me.

"I hear what you say," I began, "and I understand your intent. I am here to help you but not by siding with you in the horrible bloodbath you are perpetrating. I am here to ask you to love all those you say you will kill, love them despite their customs, love them despite their beliefs."

The men couldn't believe what I was saying and stood shocked and silent.

"I will show you how. For even though I find your actions detestable and your attitudes abominable, I send you love."

"He's damned crazy," muttered one of the men behind the commander.

"I am here to help you, to show you the way to unconditional love."

I felt my entire spirit body vibrating with love and compassion, which I channeled out into the scene before me. Looking right into the eyes of the commander, I poured forth as much love energy as I could. He lifted his gun and pointed it at me. I held his gaze and radiated love and compassion to all in that scene. The commander fired. The scene ended in a flash of purple light.

When I next came to consciousness, I was in an evaluation cell that was dimly lit. The giant graph was covered, and Sottrol was seated at the end of the pallet where I lay.

"I failed, didn't I, Sottrol?"

"On the contrary. You did well."

"Nothing I said made any difference in that scene," I sighed. "Those monsters were determined to kill, kill, kill!"

"You still managed to send them love, Darci. That was the key. It didn't matter what they did. It mattered what you did, and you did just fine."

"I feel spent."

"And well you should. That test was the most difficult in the series offered by the tunnel. Not only were you facing a group of men dedicated to hatred and murder, you also faced a very strong negative vortex. This test simulated certain instances on Earth and a few other planes of learning. The negativity centers around a destructive scene such as you just witnessed, and it deepens the tragedy."

I was too exhausted to say anything though I was curious about this phenomenon.

Luanna then arrived. She laid her hand compassionately on my forehead, saying, "Dear Darci, you need much rejuvenation. In fact, we covered the trial results on the graph because the glow was too bright, and we want you to rest now."

I lifted my head and asked in confusion, "Too bright?"

"We can show you if you like," Luanna smiled.

"Yes," I responded. I was anxious to see. I had viewed all my other results right away.

Luanna began to remove the cover, but as she did so the light beaming from underneath blinded me, so I flopped back down on the cot. Luanna let the cover back down over the huge screen.

"Needless to say, you have done well," Luanna remarked with joy as she returned to my side. "You have completed your work with me. Congratulations."

Sottrol now explained, "You have learned well the lesson of unconditional love. All of your tests and the results are recorded in that big book I gave you when we first met. Also, at the end, you will find a bright gold seal that shows you have passed this course, and you have done it with excellence. When you have recuperated, I will meet with you about your next class here at the Spirit Guide University."

Chapter Three:
I Remember Her

During my period of recuperation and rejuvenation, I was not required to be alone. I had a resting cell where I spent much of my time, but I also had access to the hallways, classrooms, and gathering rooms in my area. Sottrol had told me to take my time, relax, and get to know this wing of the great university.

After my first class on unconditional love, I found that I had adapted much better to being in spirit form. My travel from one area to another came more easily. I still could not appear and disappear as Sottrol and Luanna had done so many times in my presence. I could hover though, which is much like treading water but with less motion and less effort. I could also glide in any direction with ease whereas when I first arrived, I was still attempting to walk much as I had done when in a physical body. While I was with other Spirit Guides like Aleron or Sottrol, it was easy to float near them as I followed them, but I had trouble navigating on my own.

After rising from a restful meditative state, I decided to explore as Sottrol had suggested. I moved out of the entrance to my cell, noting the symbols around the door. I floated through several corridors with warmly lit walls. One of these hallways opened into a large domed room with many levels of seating. The place was filled with Spirits like me. Some were talking together; some were reading. I was drawn to a large circular desk in the center, so I approached the two Beings behind the desk.

"Greetings. I am just getting oriented. Can you tell me where I am?"

The taller Spirit, the gentleman with the large book before him, looked me over for a moment and then said, "Welcome. I see you have completed your first round of studies."

"Yes. How did you know?"

"By your level of energy, the rate at which you are vibrating, but if you hadn't just asked me where you were, I would have guessed you were further along in the program."

"So where am I, sir?"

"This is the library, my good man."

"The library?" I questioned, looking around again. "But I see no stacks of books, no shelves. I do see Spirits with books."

The volumes of volumes are not in this room," the tall Guide replied. I noticed that the color of his luminescence was changing from gold to green.

He put his finger up, motioning me to refrain from further talk. He drew nearer to me and said in a lowered tone, "This room is for research and reading. You come here to the center desk, ask for the material you want, and we retrieve it for you. You can then go to that area to read . . ." he continued, pointing to my left "or that area to discuss." He then pointed to my right.

I nodded. A female Spirit glided up beside me to return a large book. The tall librarian thanked her and set the book into a niche that was built into the desk. He placed his hand on the book, and it vanished. He saw my look of astonishment.

"Back to the stacks," he said. I discerned merriment in his eyes. I think he liked surprising newcomers.

"Now, what can I do for you? Oh yes, it's your first time here."

"Yes, I'm resting between classes. I just completed my studies with Luanna."

"The Love Tunnel class, yes, yes. That is a tough course, but it indoctrinates students into the Spirit Guide world. I know what you might like to see."

He placed his hands on a lighted panel that was embedded in the surface of this circular desk as he asked, "How would you like to look over the archives of your past lives?"

"My past lives on Earth?"

"Is that where you were last?

"Yes."

"Your name?"

"Darcimon Stillwater."

I watched him do a dance with his fingers on the lighted panel, which changed colors and made low tones as he moved his hands around on it. He floated back just as a huge book materialized in an oval indentation in the desk.

"There you are, Mr. Stillwater," he said as he bowed a little and he pushed the book toward me. "Just bring it back when you have tired of it, and I shall return it to its proper shelf and level."

I thanked the librarian and glided to a comfortable-looking seat in the reading area. There was a stand for the book, and the chair moved up and down. With my curiosity high, I delved into the records of my 92 lifetimes on Earth.

Some were short, especially the ones in early times. In fact, I had one Earth life that lasted only a few days. The great accomplishment in that incarnation was simply surviving birth. The more interesting lives came later. I was especially fascinated by my life as a healer in Egypt.

The record showed that a great healer who was also astrologer to the king personally instructed me. We were teamed together time and time again because our healing powers increased when we worked as a pair. I read on with interest because in the Egyptian lifetime I fell in love with this gifted woman.

One warm evening when we were sitting together on the banks of the Nile River, I asked her to marry me. She accepted, and we were wed in royal fashion, for she was top advisor to the pharaoh and his family. After the lavish and lengthy ceremony, we went off together on a barge for several days alone, floating down the Nile.

A messenger from the pharaoh interrupted our bliss. We were summoned to return to the palace to help the ruler's young son. Evidently our reputation as healers was great, and the ruler of Egypt would have no others. Of course, we went.

My lovely bride told me we would have many more days and nights together, but that was not to be. Someone in the royal court, jealous of her influence with the king, murdered her less than three years after our marriage. I was heartbroken, as were many who loved her and benefited from her talents and powers.

The records showed a long period of mourning when my Soul was tested again and again. On the anniversary of our wedding, my dear wife came to me in a vision and implored me to continue the work we had begun together. I lived the rest of that Earth life working tirelessly as a healer and teacher. I founded a new healing center in honor of my wife.

I sat back to savor the reading. Of course, it all felt familiar to me. Up to now, I hadn't remembered any of my former Earth experiences, except the life I had lived right before I came there. I found that reading about this incarnation called forth vivid memories from the deepest part of me. Now the knowledge of all my former lifetimes on Earth and on other levels was available to me. I wondered what else I would eventually remember.

∞ ∞ ∞

Although studying to be a Spirit Guide is not a very social activity, I felt the urge to interact with others, so I moved into the conversation area. I was soon drawn to a couple talking near a section of the dome that had a bluish glow.

"Hello, are you studying here?" I began.

Simultaneously they said, "Yes."

The female Spirit was glimmering with pink and gold vertical stripes on her robe, and the male Spirit was incandescent gold with a green stripe down one side of his spirit body.

"Join us," he said.

"Have you been here long?" the female asked as I lowered myself into the seat next to her. I was fascinated by the moving sparkles in her gown.

"I've completed Luanna's tunnel course," I replied, and they both sighed deeply.

"That's the tough beginner course," she informed me. "It took me many, many tries to complete that study."

I was curious and asked, "What are you studying now?"

The male responded, "We are both resting from our level three exams."

The female clarified this, "You've just finished the introductory level or level one. We've just completed level three."

"Have you researched your spirit records?" I asked. My thoughts were still in Egypt.

"Yes," he replied. "Although a little of that reading goes a long way. After all, we've already been through it. I prefer to look ahead."

The female waved her hand and added, "Jono, you know how this library works. Even though all the material is available, we experience reading only that which is currently pertinent to our growth and to our studies here."

I felt a little rush of energy.

"You mean I was meant to access the information about my past Earth life as a healer in Egypt?"

"Oh yes," answered Jono. "There is something or someone significant in there for you. I'm Jono, by the way . . . and this is Kallaray."

"I'm Darci Stillwater. Very pleased to meet you."

"Glad to meet you," smiled Kallaray.

"How do I recognize what in this Egyptian Earth life is significant to me now?"

"Tell us what you read. Maybe we can help you figure this out," offered Jono.

As they sat back, I relayed every colorful detail of that life in Egypt. Strangely, I seemed to come up with more specifics than I had just read in The Great Book.

"It's the woman," said Kallaray as soon as I had finished.

"I agree," said Jono. "She is the significant connection."

"My wife? My dear wife? I may see her again? Study with her? Work with her?" I was overwhelmed with feelings.

"That's my guess," said Jono.

"I know it," said Kallaray as she glided next to me to comfort me. "I can see how moved you are by your memories of her."

"How do I find her?" I asked.

"She could be anywhere," replied Jono. "One thing is for certain. You will meet her again sometime."

"Probably once you become a Spirit Guide, perhaps before," added Kallaray.

This information was a lot for me to assimilate. More images from my Earth life in Egypt bubbled up from deep in my Soul. Jono and Kallaray could see that I was overwhelmed.

"I think you need a little time to yourself," Jono offered. "I hope we've helped."

"Darci . . ." Kallaray put her hand on mine. "You're on a journey. We all are. The dear Soul with whom you were coupled in the Egyptian lifetime and perhaps other lifetimes, too—she is on a journey. We are all progressing up on the spiral path to the Creator. Your two Souls will meet again on this journey, so rejoice. All is well."

With that remark, both of them left me. I did not see where they went, for I was overcome first with emotions, then with questions. My deep longing for this Soul who was my partner so many lifetimes ago surfaced first, then the intense love I felt for her, then the desire to know more.

"Where is she now?" I asked aloud though no one was close by. "How do I find her?"

At that moment, I discovered that spirit teachers can tune in and hear their students whenever they wish, for Sottrol appeared beside me as soon as these words had left my mouth.

"Darci, you are overloading. I can see it in your energy field."

"Yes, I believe I am," I replied, thinking I liked how Sottrol came right to the point.

"Breathe, breathe, my son. I'm here to help."

"What's going on, Sottrol?"

"You are remembering, and for a Spirit, the experience of remembering can be striking and dramatic."

"Why now? And where is she? And when do we . . .?" I asked. The questions tumbled from my mouth.

"Easy, Darci—breathe. I will tell you what you wish to know. It's important for a student, such as yourself to keep in mind the goal of your studies: to give help to the Earth plane and to one human in particular. The Council of Master Guides and Teachers who watch over you and review your progress has decided that now is the time for you to remember your dear soul mate. If all goes well, she will be your assigned human."

"She's on Earth?"

"Not now, but she will be when you are ready."

"Then she is in Spirit! Is she here somewhere? Can I see her?"

"She's going through the twists and turns of learning on the Uranian level of the lower wheel."

I rolled my eyes and asked, "What does that mean?"

"Listen to me! What's important for you to know is that she needs you to complete your studies and become a full-fledged Spirit Guide so you can help her. You must focus, Darci. Focus on your studies. You have been doing well; however, the Council thought a little added motivation might spur you on."

"Is she all right?"

"Of course. All Souls in their essences are all right. She is being tested, and those tests sometimes include suffering. That is the way of things."

"Can I alleviate her suffering in any way?" I asked, feeling a strong pang of compassion as I spoke these words.

"You cannot see her again until you complete your studies."

"Sottrol, I must know more."

"If you wish, I can make available the records of all the lifetimes and experiences you two have shared."

"Yes! Thank you."

"Keep in mind that some of it will not be easy to read."

"I already know that. What could be worse than reading that my beautiful wife was murdered?"

"I just don't want you to get overwhelmed and carried away."

"I'll try, but I cannot promise."

"You can send her love, Darci. No matter where she is, she will receive it in some form. You can do this when you feel overcome."

And with that, Sottrol showed me a stance: feet apart, spine straight, arms clasped above the head. His spirit body changed, and he took the form of a pyramid. He then uttered a low tone and began to glow a brilliant gold. I could tell he was breathing deeply as he glowed brighter and brighter. I could barely see his features or his purple cap and robe.

Other students in the Library began to join me as we marveled at my mentor's magic. It wasn't long before nearly all the Spirits in the room were gathered around, and Sottrol had transformed himself into a pyramid of bright golden light.

There came a flash of white light, and I felt electricity pour through my being. From the gasps around me, I could tell that the other students felt this, too. I blinked in disbelief, for there stood Sottrol as he was before with his white beard and his purple outfit. He had a little twinkle in his eyes.

"Ah, I see I have gathered an audience," he smiled as he turned around, looking every one of us in the eye.

"What was that you did?" asked one fellow across from me.

"You can all do this. You will learn," Sottrol shared, enjoying the awed looks that surrounded him. "The purpose of the power pyramid is to send love, compassion, and healing to another. I just sent this powerful combination of energy to a Soul whom Darci here is very concerned about."

"Did she receive it?" I asked, still a bit stunned by Sottrol's show.

"She received it instantaneously. As soon as I sent it, she felt it."

The students in the circle around us began talking and asking questions. In reply, Sottrol raised his hand and said, "Hush, hush, dear ones. All in good time. I will tell you that this pyramid of power can be accomplished in three easy steps. First, assuming the correct position of the spirit body; second, breathing deeply, which I believe you have all learned, and third—well—ask your individual instructors about the third step. That's all, now. Go back to your reading or whatever."

I came close to the elder and asked, "Why didn't you finish the lesson and give us the third step? I want to know it."

"Because, oh eager one, the third step requires individual supervision. An instructor must be present when this is tried. This is not an exercise that you want to go wrong, believe me."

"I do, Sottrol. Thank you for sending the energy to my wife. You called her my soul mate."

"She is."

"Does she have a name? Can you tell me that much?"

"She has many names, like yourself," replied the elder, looking at me kindly. "Call her Angel."

"Angel?" I wanted to make sure I heard him right. "She's not one, though. You said she is on the lower wheel."

"Ah, Darci—all Souls are potential Angels. You know this. It will be your job to convince her of this fact and set her on the path to becoming a true Angel."

"Angel, my Angel," I said more to myself than to Sottrol. I looked up, and he was gone.

∞ ∞ ∞

I went back to the stand where I had left the book that described my lifetime in Egypt. To my astonishment, the text had changed. The book had different stories now, each one concerning an experience I had had or a lifetime I had shared with my dear Angel. Even though I was a bit spent from all that had transpired, I read the text from the beginning. I couldn't help myself; I had to know more.

The first story was set in primitive times and revolved around a clan that lived in the woods and caves. The book described a mating ceremony between Angel and me; however, in this scenario, I was the young female and Angel was the male. Our wrists were tied together with vines, and water was sprinkled over us. We were officially coupled and our union blessed by the clan. Though the book did not offer much detail on this Earth life, it did describe one other experience, and I began to see why I felt so much for this Soul called Angel.

The words before me painted a picture of a dark moonless night, the sky bright with stars. There was a mountain with a cave, a waterfall, and a sacred fire circle near its base.

A small group of primitive people were seated around the sacred fire, me among them incarnated as the young female and Angel as the young male. I was pregnant, and the gathering was in honor of the unborn child. In one section of the circle, which faced directly east, there was a white stone with several items around it, including feathers, berries, and a carved stick.

The book did not give much detail on the ceremony because great thumping and rustling sounds in the nearby brush interrupted the group. The people knew a predator was approaching, so they quickly retreated to the cave—all but Angel. This brave Soul was determined to protect his clan and especially his pregnant wife.

Taking a branch and lighting it in the fire, he moved towards the sounds in the brush. As soon as he took two steps in this direction, a giant bear broke through the briars. The beast eyed the young man as a potential meal and began to circle.

Meanwhile, others were restraining me. I wanted to rush to my husband's aid though I wasn't sure how I could help. The huge bear got about half way around the fire while the young man was backing up, his eyes fixed upon it. As we watched from the entrance to the cave, my husband, who was now standing over the altar in the east, picked up the white stone.

He spoke something into this rock and took a step towards the bear. The creature leapt forward. The young man hurled the rock, hitting the beast right between the eyes and knocking it unconscious. The other clan members then rushed out to finish the killing. There was celebration, for the gift of the bear meant much food for the clan and a warm hide for my baby and me.

I pondered this story, my mind filling in the pictures, the details, for I had been there. The memory was imprinted in my Soul. Even though it was not written in the big book, I recalled the birth of that baby. I remembered how attentive my husband had been and how joyous I felt wrapped in that bearskin holding our newborn.

Now I was exhausted. The memory of birthing a child in a cave many millennia ago was all I could take in right then, especially since I had already experienced quite a lot in the Library. Even though I wanted to continue to read, I returned the book to the circular desk with the understanding that I could come back and read more.

∞ ∞ ∞

My rest was deep, for I was thoroughly spent. However, I was restless because images from my life in Egypt and from my days with the ancient cave clan kept rolling through my mind. In my heart, a longing had been awakened. I now knew I had a partner, a soul mate, one whose spirit journey was akin to mine. I had always considered patience one of my attributes, but I restlessly yearned for a reunion of my Angel and me.

In fact, I was imagining how and where this might occur when Sottrol joined me in my rejuvenation cell.

"You're all fired up, my son," he said as he sat on the end of my bed. "Your memories are returning like the floodwaters in an Earth spring."

"I can't help myself."

"Yes, yes, I know. This is not surprising, for yours is one of the great partnerships of all time."

I sat up and begged, "Tell me more."

Sottrol laughed, saying, "You will know all—every detail—soon enough."

His face then became serious as he told me, "Two things are important here: first, that you are inspired and motivated by your connection to the Soul called Angel; second, that you are not distracted from your path and your particular studies."

"What's next for me?" I asked the elder.

"Your next class is on non-judgment, Darci. I think you need a bit more rest before you begin."

"I feel ready," I answered, wanting to get on with it.

"I know, I know," Sottrol consoled me, putting his magical hand on my shoulder. I felt a rush of electricity.

"Focus on your breathing and the rejuvenation of your energy," he instructed. "I will be back to check on you soon."

The elder vanished into sparkling mist. With a sigh, I realized that the only way I would be reunited with Angel was through pursuing my studies, so I did as Sottrol suggested and launched into a series of breathing exercises designed to raise my energy level. I'm not sure how long I worked on this.

I went back and forth between resting and doing these exercises for what seemed like a long while.

Sottrol eventually reappeared with a cloak in his arms.

"For you," he said, motioning for me to take it.

The robe was rich purple and had silver sparkles woven into it. Up until now, my spirit body had appeared clad in the dress of the early 1800s, the clothes I was wearing in my last life when I was buried.

"It's time you look like a Spirit Guide-in-Training," said Sottrol, appearing pleased with himself. "This garment has been designed especially for you."

"Thank you."

The robe seemed to put itself on me as I reached out and touched it.

"Yes, just right," Sottrol smiled, his eyes glistening. "Now you are truly ready to begin your next class. Follow me."

Surprisingly, wearing the robe seemed to facilitate my movements. Instead of following behind Sottrol as he floated through the illuminated hallways, I was able to keep up with him and glided along by his side.

It wasn't long before we reached a classroom that I had not seen before. This room had a blue hue to it. It was circular like all the rooms I had seen in this university. However, this particular one had a raised portion in the center. It rose and descended smoothly like a well-proportioned hill. Around this center hill were floating oval seats, many of them filled with spirit students like me. The domed ceiling had many different-colored circular lights within it. I was marveling at this splendid classroom when a very tall male Spirit approached. I sensed instantly that he was my new instructor.

Sottrol made the introductions.

"Beminer, this is Darci Stillwater, the new student I told you about. Darci, this is Beminer Shovan, your new teacher."

"A pleasure, sir," I said, gazing in awe at this vibrant Spirit instructor.

"Mr. Stillwater," he said, nodding at me.

He had layers of varying shades of blue, and I couldn't tell if these layers were a part of his robe or his aura. His eyes were bright piercing blue, and he wore a blue and silver cap. Even his skin appeared to have a blue tint to it. His hair was silver, and although he was without a beard, he wore his medium-length hair in many small braids. I was quite taken by the sight of him.

Beminer motioned for me to join the others in the floating chairs. Sottrol, of course, had disappeared, so I glided to an empty seat and took a deep breath. The teacher moved effortlessly to the top of the smooth glassy hill in the center of the room. As he did so, he seemed to increase in size. His robe extended much lower than before so that it nearly covered the hill. He appeared gigantic.

Beminer rotated, looking us over before he began. The seats in the classroom were all occupied now. There were about twenty of us.

"Your studies here are a privilege—a privilege you have earned. Now through these studies, you earn your right to be a Spirit Guide. I am here to teach you one of the most important lessons you will face.

"When a Spirit Guide is assigned a human to watch over and help, the Guide must follow a Spirit Guide Creed. Each class you take is a step towards making this creed a part of your very being. Once it is a part of you, then you will automatically act and react according to it. Only then can you take on the guardianship of a human being.

"This creed I speak of—it's not something you learn by memorization. You learn it through practice, practice, practice. On level one, you met challenges and learned how to react with unconditional love. That is the first part—indeed, the basis of the Spirit Guide Creed. Here on level two, I will teach you about judging—in particular, *not* judging."

Beminer twirled around on his perch. He made the motions of sprinkling something, but I did not see anything.

Suddenly, right before me, a thin book appeared. The same thing happened to all the students. The books hovered in front of us.

Beminer raised his voice a bit as he clearly said, "Yes, reach out and take them. Take them! They are learning tools. You have each just received a file that contains detailed descriptions of every test you faced in the Love Tunnel during your last class. I want you to go through this file and note every time you were judgmental. Judging yourself and others has become second nature to many of you, so much so that you don't even know you are doing it. Step one is recognizing this behavior."

A student on the other side of the circular classroom spoke up, "How detailed do you want us to be?"

Beminer did not hesitate as he responded, "I want every judgmental word, every single adjective you used in a judgmental way, every judgmental thought noted. Be thorough."

He continued, "When the third level Angels developed the tunnel, they incorporated a way to record and measure your levels of judging others. All Souls are equal in the eyes of The Great Spirit. Even though a human may dress a certain way or act a certain way, this human is equal to every other human, or any other Soul for that matter, and must be viewed this way by you. Now, even though the exercises in the tunnel are simulated and do not affect the universal balance, they are excellent indicators of how much you judge yourself and others.

"The goal of this class is for you to get to the point where you can view and interact with all life without judging any of it. I'll tell you one thing right now. Humans love this about their Spirit Guides. Humans will make mistakes again and again. You must be able love them and not judge them no matter what they choose to do. Once humans know you will not judge their thoughts, words, and actions, they are more likely to trust you and heed your guidance.

"Make no mistake. This is a cornerstone in the Spirit Guide teachings. You must master this no matter how long you stay in my class, so let's begin."

We all started reading our files from the tunnel class. As we did so, Beminer gave one more instruction, "Every time you think you were judgmental in those trials, make a mark with the first finger of your left hand. Go on."

I didn't know what he meant exactly, but I went ahead with the reading. In my first test in the tunnel, I had met that foul, wretched man, so there were plenty of places where I judged his appearance, his actions, even his odor. I did as Beminer had instructed and placed my left index finger on the page next to the description of the first time I saw the man.

To my astonishment, when I touched the page, the writing that narrated my judging the man lit up! The letters turned from dark blue to red, and there was a yellow glow behind them. The description of that first experience in the tunnel had many passages that showed how judgmental I had been. Even my discussion with Luanna and Sottrol afterwards was filled with judgmental words. I called the man a "beast" among other things. Before I knew it, much of this first part of the file was lit and written in red.

Beminer appeared next to me to see how I was doing and said, "Yes. Good, Mr. Stillwater. Keep going."

So I pressed on. I was distraught when I realized just how judgmental I had been most of the time. It seemed as though I was always evaluating how someone looked or acted. Since we had all endured many tests in the tunnel, this exercise in recognizing judgmental behavior took a long time. Finally, I had finished going through the file once and was starting over again when Beminer spoke to the students.

"Now that you have scrutinized these files, I want you to do it again," Beminer announced to the class.

I heard a few gasps around the classroom.

"The judgmental behavior you have recognized will be described in red with yellow light, as you have seen."

He paused as he rotated, eyeing his new students as he continued, "Any judgmental behavior you missed—any you did not highlight the first time through—will appear in bright purple letters with a green highlight. Go through again and see how you did."

Laboriously, we all went through the text again. I had done fairly well recognizing and noting the judgments I had made. I had missed a few, and as Beminer indicated, they were now in bright purple with a glowing green light behind them. Near the end of this exercise, I was remarking to myself that this was the longest class I had ever been in when Beminer came up beside me.

"Judging my class are you, Mr. Stillwater?" he asked.

I was at a loss for words.

"Mr. Stillwater here thinks my class is the longest class he has ever been in," Beminer announced.

I cringed a bit. I had forgotten again that these spirit teachers could read thoughts.

"I'm glad you had that thought, Mr. Stillwater, because it is an example of how making judgments is a behavior that is ingrained into your very beings. My job is to help you rise above this way of acting and never dally in it again! Can it be done?"

Beminer seemed to hear the thoughts of another student.

He looked at one male student near me and said in an encouraging voice, "Of course, Mr. Esterville, of course it can be done. Many have done it before you. In fact, you have all taken the very first step by recognizing your judgmental ways."

He further instructed us, "Between now and the next time this class meets, I want you to work on raising your vibrations higher. Use the breathing techniques you were taught. That is all for now."

∞　∞　∞

Back in my rejuvenation cell, I did more breathwork, but I also thought about the new class. At first I firmly held the view that evaluating oneself and others was natural behavior. Then after several series of breathing exercises, I began to realize that judging may be natural for humans but not for Spirit Guides. I pondered what I had learned in the first class and came to the conclusion that a Guide could not judge the actions of another and at the same time love that person unconditionally.

By the time the next class with Beminer reconvened, I was determined to get this lesson learned and learned well. I found it was not easy.

Beminer told story after story about the process of judgment and the evolution of it on the Earth plane and other levels on the lower wheel.

At the end of each tale, he would always say, "This is not acceptable on The Spirit Guide plane."

Beminer related one very long and detailed story about humans' view of judgment day. He referred to the Bible and other texts that are considered sacred on Earth. As he was concluding this part of the lecture, his talk took a surprising turn.

He began, "Most Souls who are experiencing lifetimes on the lower wheel do not understand the Law of Karma. For that reason, they invented judgment day—a day when a Soul goes before the Creator and is taken to task for all misdeeds and failures—and also rewarded for virtuous behavior. As I have explained, this view evolved over time because the Souls operating on the lower rings of the spiral do not usually see the overview that shows karma as the balancing force in the universe. It is not a judging force; it is a *balancing force*. These Souls on the lower wheel, such as humans who have free will and can choose how to act and react, are constantly tipping the scales out of balance. Yet the great force of karma continually works to bring everything into balance. The result is a cosmic dance with everything in flux."

Beminer continued, "What's important to understand here, class, is that when a Soul passes from, say, the Earth plane—

I'm using Earth as an example because most of you were there during your last lifetimes—this Soul is not brought before a jury of Saints or Angels or before God to be judged. No! You remember your passing, don't you?"

He paused until he had looked every one of us in the eye.

"Well, don't you?" he queried. "Wasn't your welcome here wondrous? Weren't you greeted by loving Beings who cared for you and helped you in every way?"

I thought back to the band of Angel Initiates who had greeted me, encircled me, and cared for me.

"Yes, of course," Beminer continued, reading my thoughts and probably the thoughts of others.

"The Law of Karma applies throughout the universe. However, on the Spirit Guide plane and those levels that are higher, all beings exist in a state of balance. All actions are taken with unconditional love. Nothing is done selfishly or wantonly to upset this glorious balance. That is why it is so important for you to not only learn these lessons but also to make them a part of you. None of the teachers at this university can allow students to move on if there are any doubts about their behavior."

Beminer continued to explain, "The saying 'You reap what you sow' is sometimes quoted on Earth. Humans do have some idea about karma, but they do not understand the overall influence of this force. Humans cannot usually see that karma works over the span of many lifetimes and on many planes of experience. Because humans rarely see past the Earth life they are living, they cannot grasp the vastness and the power of karma. It is not the Creator who is judging them. Oh no. The Creator loves and embraces us all. It is karma that brings situations and circumstances that may seem like great judgments from beyond, but which are actually counterweights to balance actions previously taken. Is everyone following me here?" he asked.

The class was quiet. I saw a few nods.

"Many Souls continue learning on the lower end of the spiral because they must have experiences that bring their personal karma into balance."

Once Beminer said this, my thoughts strayed to Angel. I wondered if this was the reason she was still reincarnating on the lower wheel. I caught Beminer's eye and realized he was reading my thoughts again. This time, however, he did not stop to share my ponderings with the other students.

Beminer continued, "So to become a Spirit Guide, you must completely eliminate judgmental behavior from your Being. I now offer you the keys to opening that door of learning. There are three keys: detachment, compassion, and unconditional love—with unconditional love being the most useful. I know you have been listening to me talk for quite a while, so I am going to vary the lesson by showing some examples."

With that, Beminer moved off his podium-hill, and right before my eyes, the hill changed shape and became a concave platform. The lights embedded in the ceiling of the dome suddenly sent down beams of different colored light. These rays spun around, dancing and interweaving. I had never seen anything like it. The light show slowed, and two characters appeared on the stage, a man and a woman, both dressed very simply. The man was angry, and the woman was crying.

"You betrayed me!" he yelled, pointing his finger at her face.

"I'm sorry," she sobbed.

"I feel nothing but hatred and loathing towards you now!" He nearly spat these words.

"You left me alone for so long," she cried. "I thought you had abandoned me!"

"I can no longer trust you," said the man.

"You broke your promises to me!" The woman now pointed at him and shouted, "You vowed to love me and care for me, but you left!"

The players stopped and Beminer addressed the class as he floated around the rim of the stage.

"It's a scene that has been played out so many times," said the teacher. "Now I ask you, 'Who is right in this situation?'"

A female student spoke, "Why, the woman is. The man broke his vows!"

A male student stood and retorted, "Not at all. She is the betrayer here!"

I saw what our teacher was up to, but before I had a chance to offer my comments, Beminer rose onto the stage and joined the two actors.

He said first to the female student while motioning toward the man on stage, "Where is your compassion for him?"

Then extending his arm towards the woman on stage, he spoke to the male student, "And, sir, where is your compassion for her?"

He circled the room with his long blue robes floating behind him as he urged the students, "Detach! Detach yourselves. Then look with compassionate eyes, and send love, unconditional love, from your heart. These two represent beings who have both made mistakes."

Beminer continued, "When you have guardianship of a human, that human will make mistakes aplenty! Do not judge! Detach, show compassion, and send unconditional love. This is how Spirit Guides react and relate to the humans to whom they are assigned. You will be watching many scenes like this when you begin interacting with the Earth plane. It is important that you never, ever judge humans, no matter what they do. Is this becoming clear, class?"

I don't know about the others, but Beminer's lessons were clear to me. I could see how difficult it could be to give up the behavior of judging others, but I was determined to do it.

∞ ∞ ∞

Between classes, Beminer always had us do the breathing exercises to raise our vibrations. It wasn't until the fourth class that I found out why. The students were seated, watching another drama on the concave stage. These little plays were always designed to stir our emotions, and this one was no different.

This time an elderly woman in ill health was asking her son to do something he didn't want to do. In fact, it went against his very nature. He was wracked by guilt and resentment as the old woman tried to manipulate him.

Every time we watched such an exchange, we were supposed to practice detaching and then sending compassion and love. I found that the highly emotional subject matter distracted me from automatically reacting as our teacher had instructed. Also, I suspected that the floating oval chairs in which we sat had some sort of measuring device in them that informed Beminer of our inner emotional responses to these scenes.

At the conclusion of this play, Beminer came over, stood by me, and asked the class, "Mr. Stillwater here has been doing his out-of-class assignments. How do I know? Look at his vibration. Can anyone see how bright his energy field is? For those of you who do not yet see energy patterns, you will learn.

"Every time you leave my class, I ask you to do the breathing exercises. Why? Because the higher your vibration, the easier it is for you to detach. . . ."

He looked around the class, motioning with his hand. A number of us finished his sentence ". . . and show compassion and unconditional love."

"You have to be able to do this every single time, or you do not move on from my class," the teacher said sternly.

"You, you, you, and you," Beminer said, pointing at me and three others. "You four are ready for your personalized challenges. Enter the Power Booths, please. The rest of you stay here."

He walked over to an area of the circular wall that had four arched doors. I hadn't noticed them before. Perhaps they weren't lit up as they were now. The four of us that Beminer had chosen moved to the doors. They opened automatically, and we each entered one.

I did not hesitate. I was ready for something new and was certain that I would not be harmed. At first, the Power Booth was brightly lit. Then slowly the lighted walls and ceiling dimmed. I used the time to breathe to increase my energy further.

It was a while before anything happened. I was patient. A semi-circular seat emerged from the wall of the Power Booth, so I took that as a sign to sit.

After a while, the Power Booth was completely dark. This was unusual for since I had been in spirit form, there always seemed to be something glowing somewhere. I breathed deeply a few more times.

Then suddenly and very unexpectedly the entire side of the Power Booth across from me seemed to drop away! I found myself hovering over the Earth at night. I could see a silver river winding through the moonlit landscape and gasped as I looked up and saw the night sky. I realized how much I missed the Earth and all its beauty, especially the starry sky-scape.

I didn't have long to admire the view because I found myself sliding down towards the ground. There was a farmyard with haystacks and a small house in the distance. I heard screams.

A young woman in tattered clothing ran from the house. Her face was tear-stained and filled with agony. She hid behind one of the haystacks, threw herself into the hay, and sobbed quietly. She was trembling.

I felt much compassion for her. She seemed very distraught.

Only moments later, a man emerged from the little house. He was big and burly. His pants were unfastened, his shirt was open, and he had a stick of some kind in his hand.

"You naughty wench!" he shouted. "You come here and obey me!"

I could see the young woman freeze with fear. I thought she had stopped breathing.

"I'll find you. You know I will!" called the big man as he approached. "You cannot escape your wifely duties. Come, you must do what I say!"

He was heading right toward the pile of hay where the young woman was trying to hide. My heart went out to her. She reminded me of my dear Angel.

When he was about to discover her, she jumped out from behind the haystack and fell to her knees begging,. "Please don't hurt me! Please! Husbands are supposed to love their wives!" She broke into sobs.

The big man cracked the stick on the ground next to her, and she jumped.

"Stop your blubbering and serve your husband!"

With that, he grabbed her hair and pulled her up until her face was in front of his massive chest and demanded, "You do what you're supposed to do, or I lay this stick across your back!"

The woman was shaking and seemed unable to respond.

"I want it now!" the man bellowed as he pushed her face down in the hay.

What happened next I can only describe as a brutal rape. The woman struggled a bit at first. It was obvious to me that she was in pain. Her face was buried in the straw so she could barely breathe.

As I observed this, I forgot I was in a classroom booth. I forgot the lessons Beminer had repeated over and over. My emotions were surging.

I was angry with the man, and before I knew it I said, "You brute! Stop! You're killing her!"

They couldn't hear me. I could not become a part of the action as I had done in the Love Tunnel. My part was as observer only.

The brutality continued. The big man picked up his wife who was now limp but alive. I could see blood running down her legs. He threw her back on the hay face-up and ripped her already shredded clothing. I couldn't bear to watch anymore. How could I help?

Then a rush of energy swept over me, and I realized that I had been judging the scene and especially judging the man. I took a few deep breaths and tried to use the three keys. First, I detached myself from the ongoing rape, which was not easy. Next, I let compassion flow. It came easily for the poor woman. It was difficult for me to feel compassion for the man at first. Then, amazingly, it overflowed. Finally, remembering my instruction in the Love Tunnel, I radiated unconditional love to the pair. The violence stopped immediately. The man took his wife in his arms and smoothed her hair. He told her he loved her and never wanted to hurt her.

The scene before me dimmed, and I was again in darkness. Slowly the walls and ceiling of the Power Booth became luminous as they were before. My test was over.

When the arched doorway opened, I was not in Beminer's classroom but back in my rejuvenation cell. I was glad for that and lay down to rest and reflect.

∞ ∞ ∞

My studies with Beminer were long. He did as he said he would. He made sure that I was free of the behavior of judging before I left his class and moved on. This took listening to many lectures, seeing many plays, and taking many journeys in the traveling booth.

"Practice, practice, practice!" Beminer would say to us.

I grasped that changing one's way of automatically reacting takes time and practice, so I threw myself into making this change.

Finally another student and I were called aside by Beminer after class.

"You two are very close to completing this course," he told us, his blue eyes more luminous than ever. "You have actually moved through quite quickly."

He paused, then continued, "I know it seems long to you."

He nodded toward the other student, a female, and I guessed he was reading her thoughts and was responding. He continued, "You have done well. There is only one more hurdle, one more test for you to pass. Successful completion of this exam will insure your graduation from my class."

The other student and I looked at each other, then at Beminer.

"I'm ready," I said.

"I am also," she replied.

"Very well. Take these seats if you will."

Beminer led us to another section of his circular classroom. There against the wall were two seats unlike any I had ever seen. They had very tall backs, ornate arm rests, and lighted oval seats. They looked like cosmic thrones. The chairs had just materialized in the room, for I hadn't noticed them before.

"Go on! Sit!" Beminer motioned for us to move to the thrones. "Take a few minutes to breathe, then say you are ready and the exam will begin."

The classroom went dark except for a glow around the thrones and us. Beminer was no longer in sight. The two of us sat there for a while doing our breathing exercises, then I heard the female student say, "I am ready."

There was a low noise that got louder, followed by what sounded like a clap of thunder. The chair she was sitting in dropped through the floor out of sight! This rattled me a little, so I took extra time preparing with deep breaths.

Finally I said, "I am ready."

I immediately felt a trembling in the chair and heard the low noise as before. When the loud thunderous clap occurred, the chair moved quickly as though I was sliding down a chute. The rapid descent was designed to disorient—at least that's what it did to me. When the chair and I plunked down, the landing was gentle. I did not recognize where I was. There was a thick mist all around, and I could see nothing.

Slowly the mists lifted a bit, and I found myself on the throne in a great stone circle. My chair and I were in the place of one of the giant stones. It was odd, looking up at these huge pillars and then realizing I was sitting where one of these great stones should be.

From between the tall stones across from me came a line of people. They approached through the mist slowly, almost reverently, staying in line. Once the first man in line reached the center of the circle, they all stopped and began chanting. At first I couldn't understand any of it; then it became clear.

"The time of judgment has arrived," they chanted. "We stand before you to be judged. Be merciful. Oh please, show us mercy!"

I was completely surprised. Here was a group of people waiting for me to issue judgments, the very thing I had been studying not to do! The first man in line stepped forward alone. He walked up to me, putting his arms forward, palms up.

"Sir, I have sinned aplenty. I have lied, cheated, and stolen from my neighbor. I agree to accept your judgment and any punishment you wish to give me. Please be merciful."

My mind was in a whirl. First, I am taught not to judge, then I am asked to do so? This seemed senseless. Then I reminded myself that this was my final exam, and I told myself not to be fooled by appearances.

"I am here to be judged. Please have mercy!" cried the man.

I breathed deeply and detached. I radiated compassion to this man and said, "I do not judge you. I give you unconditional love."

As soon as I said this, the man vanished, and another stepped forward.

"I am here to be judged. I lied to my family, I cheated my brother, and I cut the hands off a man I saw touching my wife. My heart is dark with anger and hatred. I accept your judgment and the punishment you choose. Please have mercy!"

The man went down on his knees, and I did as I had done before. I took a deep breath, detached, sent compassion to the fellow, and said, "I do not judge you. I give you unconditional love."

This repeated over and over with each person confessing crimes that were worse than the one before. Some of the descriptions were truly grisly, but I remembered my lessons and remained detached and compassionate. I answered the same way to each of those who came before me, making sure that I did actually send compassion and love as I said those words.

This went on and on with more figures emerging from the mist until I was dealing with those who confessed the darkest, cruelest acts. It took all my concentration to remain detached and compassionate, but I did.

Finally a big muscular man stepped before me. He had a huge bushy beard and arms the size of tree trunks.

"I have killed many people," he grunted. "I have maimed even more. No one is the same when I'm finished with them!"

This man was different. He didn't ask for mercy. He was boasting.

"No one messes with me," he muttered, then said louder, "Not even you!"

He lurched forward at me and grabbed my neck. The sensation was very odd. It seemed as if he were strangling me, but I didn't feel it. My breathing was constricted, however, so I was confused for a moment. As he began kicking me, I realized I had to work fast. The man's grip on my throat made it impossible for me to speak, so I used my heart and mind.

My heart sent him compassion, and my mind said, "I do not judge you. I send you unconditional love."

Instantly the scene dissolved into phosphorescent light. I was still sitting on the throne, but all around me were sparkles of gold and white. The mist had turned from gray to light pink, and I felt the chair slowly rising.

Before long, Beminer appeared before me. He still wore his multi-layered blue robes, yet he did not seem as tall.

"That's because you are taller, Darci," Beminer said, patting me on the shoulder. "You have completed my class, which is a difficult one. You are ready to move on with your studies. You have my blessing."

He took a strand of glowing beads from around his neck and put them around mine. I seemed to vibrate faster once they were in place.

Beminer laid both his hands on my shoulders and said, "Bless you, Darcimon Stillwater," and he was gone.

The pink mist cleared to reveal the door to my rejuvenation cell. I entered, ready for a long rest.

Chapter Four:
The Deepening

My rest was long and satisfying. I felt as though I had really made progress by completing Beminer's class. My spirit Being was changing and becoming more purified. My vibration was definitely higher, and I moved about with more ease. I could see that the two classes I finished had done more than just teach me how to refine my behavior. They had helped me actually alter my essence.

During Beminer's class, I had focused on learning and practicing the lessons of detaching from judgment and doing the breathing exercises to increase my vibration. The class was difficult for me, so I did not do much else.

Now that I was once again in a rejuvenation period between classes, I decided to return to the Library. My curiosity was high regarding my past, present, and future relationships with the Soul called Angel. Ever since I had read about our lifetime together in Egypt, I thought about her. Now I had the opportunity to further explore this partnership. Sottrol had told me that Angel was my soul mate. I wanted to know what that meant.

As soon as I entered the large main chamber of the Library, I noticed that a different Spirit was behind the circular desk—a female with a very classic look. Her hair appeared braided and piled on her head like a Greek goddess. She was large by both height and breadth. Her voluminous robe was striped with pinks and lavenders.

"Hello and congratulations," she greeted me in a jolly fashion. "You're looking well."

"Thank you," I said, a little surprised. Everyone on this plane seemed to know more about me than I knew about him or her.

"You are glittering and glowing, Sir. I can tell you've just graduated. Level two, was it?"

Yes, Beminer's class."

"Oh, he's a tough taskmaster. You've obviously thrived under his tutelage. What can I do for you?"

I explained about the magical book I was reading during my last rest period and told her how the text had changed while it was on the reading stand.

"That's a normal occurrence in this Library," she informed me. "The reference books will show you whatever you need to know and understand at that moment."

"Yes. However, I want to know more about my soul mate. That's what I was reading the last time I was here."

"I'll do what I can, Mr. . . . ?"

"Stillwater. Darcimon Stillwater."

She proceeded to move her fingers around on the panel behind the desk. It seemed like a complicated procedure.

A short while later, a large book materialized in one of the notches in the desk. I recognized the cover from the last time I was there. I thanked the woman as I took the heavy volume.

I found a comfortable seat and book stand in a relatively private section of the reading area. My hands trembled as I opened the book. The words jumped off the page into my heart.

The landscape described was covered in snow and ice. I quickly realized that the setting was somewhere in the far north in a primitive time. There I was, a young man dressed in seal skins and huddling with my very pregnant young wife in a small hut built of ice. Two older women were there and an older man. They had come to help with the birth.

I read the passage very carefully, going back over certain sentences. The pregnant woman was not my dear soul mate. In fact, Angel was nowhere in this scene. I sighed and read on.

The winds whipped around this little bungalow of ice as the birth began. My young wife was wide-eyed as this was her first child. The two elder women seemed concerned about her. They talked to me at length about how my wife had been ill while I was away hunting. They said she might not have the strength to survive this birth.

The labor went on for an entire day. My poor wife grew weaker. I held her hand and sang to her. I wanted to take her place.

The elder man said, "Talk to the baby. Sing to the baby. Tell it to come out."

I made up a welcoming song for the one being born and sang it over and over. The three elders smiled and joined in. The birth was hard.

As I was reading, I began to recall how I felt at the time. As before, the details of the lifetime began pouring out of me as I read the account of it. I remember how stressful the situation was and how anxious I felt. The midwives were very busy talking to my wife, wiping her brow as they did so. The elder gentleman kept feeding the fire in the center of the hut. He sang and chanted.

I watched in wonder, as the young one emerged, slimy and wet. One midwife wrapped the baby girl and handed her to me. As I looked into the infant's eyes, I recognized her. My new daughter was Angel!

The elder women now focused on my wife who was exhausted and very weak. They tried to give her water, then broth, but she could not raise her head. Even with help, she barely drank anything.

Holding our new daughter, I sat by my wife's side, but she passed away only hours later. I had never felt such a strange combination of grief and joy. There in my arms was this darling precious child who seemed so magical and who filled me with joy. Yet there lay my poor wife who had given up her life in childbirth.

In those ancient tribal times, there was much support from others in the extended family. The text described briefly how aunts, uncles, and other members of the tribe helped me care for and raise my daughter.

There was one more detailed story about my incarnation with Angel in this frozen land.

It was a clear day with sun glinting off the snowy landscape. My daughter was eleven years old, and I was taking her on her first hunting trip. The women of the tribe did not often hunt. This was mostly the job of men although a few tribeswomen were excellent hunters, especially when it came to small game. The men usually went in groups to harvest a seal or perhaps a polar bear. This excursion was a special trip for Angel to learn how to hunt. She had been begging me since she was four years old. She said over and over that she wanted to be a great hunter like me. Indeed, I was in my prime as a provider for the tribe. Angel had been born when I was seventeen. Now I was larger, stronger, and more accurate with my spear.

So off we went with a sled carrying a few provisions. We planned to be away for only one night, but that is not what happened. I took my eager daughter to a location where I knew the fishing would be good. My plan was to begin by teaching her how to spear the big fish. She already knew how to clean and cook them.

It was a beautiful day, sunny and calm. We chatted as we walked along on our primitive snowshoes. I was pulling the sled as Angel asked me question after question.

Arriving at the fishing spot in late afternoon, we dug a shelter near the river. The snow was powdery, and we made fast work of sculpting our home for the night. Angel was so anxious to try the new spear I had made for her that I agreed to take her to one of my favorite fishing spots, a place where I had always had success. We came upon a bend in the river marked by two large boulders. I showed Angel how to watch for the fish. I taught her how to aim because the water warped what we were seeing.

The fish were there and I speared one. Angel followed my lead, plunging her spear into the water. She got one just above the tail and was ecstatic. We fished until dark. We had caught more than we could eat, so we buried the surplus in the snow next to our shelter and cooked two for dinner. Angel's dark eyes sparkled as she ate her first catch. She smiled and laughed. We enjoyed the starry sky until we felt the fatigue of the day and climbed into our shelter, which was layered with hides.

Sounds from outside our snow shelter woke first Angel, then me. I wrapped myself in a bear hide and climbed out to take a look. A polar bear was digging up our stash of fish. I had my spear in my hand since I had placed it next to the entrance in case of such an occurrence, but I was sleepy and therefore a bit slow. The bear was big and hungry. I was willing to let her take our fish.

Angel poked her head out, saw the bear, and made a sound halfway between a scream and a yelp. The bear looked at us. We had been upwind so it had not noticed us until then.

The huge creature came closer. Perhaps it was the hide I was wrapped in—I do not know. The bear stood on her hind legs and then lunged at me, clawing my leg.

Angel grabbed her spear and shouted, "Go! Go, bear! Leave my father!"

The bear, now seeing two of us and two spears, retreated, taking a few fish in her mouth.

The damage to my leg was serious. The flesh had been torn in several places by the bear's claws, and I was bleeding. I dragged myself back into the shelter leaving a trail of blood. Angel rekindled the fire and cleansed my wounds. Pain was beginning to make me delirious, so Angel insisted that I lie back and let her help me.

She had seen some of the tribeswomen dress wounds but had not yet done it herself. That little girl sat up the rest of the night feeding the fire and bravely standing guard, protecting her wounded father.

On the dawning of the next day, Angel crawled up next to me in the shelter and said, "Father, there is a storm coming. I can see it in the west."

If I had not been injured, we could have probably made it back to our tribe and home before the storm arrived. As it was, I didn't know how we were going to travel. I could put no weight on my wounded leg. We were low on fuel for the fire, and the bear had taken our fish.

"We will have to ride out the storm here," I told my daughter. "Perhaps when it has passed, we will be able to journey back."

Angel looked concerned and said, "You need the help of the medicine woman. We must go home."

"We are better off here until after the storm," I assured her, taking her hand and squeezing it. "Can you spear us two more fish? We'd best eat now and then prepare for bad weather."

Although she was concerned about leaving me, Angel took her new spear and went back to the spot on the river where we had fished the day before. She returned after a while with four fish.

"I will cook them all. We will have extra to get us through the blizzard."

She rekindled the embers and cooked the fish. We had brought very little with us, so I lay there going over in my mind how we could best prepare for the approaching bad weather. I couldn't think beyond that.

The winds came in the afternoon. Angel had banked the shelter to the west and north as I had instructed. We then huddled together and listened to the storm howl. Angel held on to me for warmth and comfort. Her dark eyes grew large as she heard the winds attack our little shelter.

I had been caught by storms before when I was out on hunting trips, but this was all new to my daughter. I slept more than Angel did. The wounds in my leg throbbed, so I went in and out of consciousness. Every time I opened my eyes, Angel was looking at me.

"Sleep, little one," I whispered. "We can go nowhere, and nothing will be out there now that will harm us—not in this weather."

The storm continued all night and into the next day. It wasn't until the following afternoon that the winds finally died down. Angel dug her way out of the shelter and surveyed the scene.

"New snow up past my knees, Father," she reported as she scrambled back into the shelter, "and clear skies to the west."

Then a look of concern crossed her face as she asked, "If you cannot walk, how will we make it back home?"

I had been thinking about this, so I was ready with a response, "Do you think you can pull me on the sled?"

"But you will not fit on that little sled!"

"We can tie on two of these hides." I had worked this out. "We'll make an extension that I can lie on."

"I'll try to pull you, Father. I want to go home."

Angel was becoming quite skilled at spearing fish. She caught several more and used the last of our fuel to cook them. We spent another night, planning to leave the next morning at first light.

When dawn broke, I instructed her on how to lash the hides to the sled, and she did so. Then I dragged myself onto the extension with a prayer on my lips that Angel could pull the sled and me. She put on her little snowshoes and gave me a smile.

"I'll get you home, Father."

We had easily made the journey in one day's light to that fishing spot, but now the pace was much slower. Angel was strong for her age, but she couldn't pull all the weight and keep our usual speed. She also needed to rest at regular intervals. I knew we would have to camp overnight again.

As the sun hung low in the west, the little one looked very tired. I told my daughter that we had better stop and make ourselves a shelter for the night.

"We are too far to make it home," she sighed.

"We'll make it back tomorrow. You have done well. You need to rest and so do I."

I still could not stand and without my help, building a snow shelter for the night would be difficult. Angel was exhausted, too, but went about following my directions as best she could. Just as she was helping me into the dugout, we heard dogs.

There in the distance was a team of four dogs pulling a sled. Two members of the tribe had come looking for us. The men were hunting partners of mine.

They inspected my wound and thought it best to travel at night to get us home. They patted Angel on the back and told her that she had saved my life. It was true.

The two men then tucked me into the big sled and Angel into the small sled. Off we went under a brilliant night sky. I remember watching dancing streaks of light on the horizon before I fell into a deep slumber. Angel slept on the way home, too. Poor little one was completely spent.

In time my wounds healed though there were scars from the bear's claws. I made a song about my daughter's courage and bravery. She eventually became a primary hunter for the tribe.

After reading this account, I sat back in my chair and reflected on the two primitive lifetimes described in the big book. Both times Angel had faced a bear in order to protect me.

"Is this a pattern?" I wondered. "What is the significance of the bear in all of this?"

I heard a faint whooshing sound, and my mentor Sottrol was seated beside me. It seemed he had materialized himself and a chair to sit in.

"The bear is the Earth way of testing courage," he said, leaning toward me. "Angel passed both tests."

"She saved me twice."

"I know. And you will have the opportunity to help her once you become a Spirit Guide."

"Where is she now? Can I see her?" I had been greatly moved by reading about this lifetime. I wanted to talk to her about it, to thank her.

"That is not possible just yet," said Sottrol as he put his hand on mine. "You must focus on your studies so that you will be ready to help her when the time comes."

"Then what is next? I want to know."

Sottrol chuckled and replied, "I have come to fetch you. Come. Return the book. I want to introduce you to your new instructor."

∞　∞　∞

We left the Library by an exit I had not used before. This was unfamiliar territory, so I stayed close to Sottrol as we glided through several lighted passageways. There was quite a bit of activity in these halls. We passed many Spirits on their way to and from somewhere.

After several turns, which I tried to memorize, we arrived at a great portal. Much about this university was grand, but this archway was spectacular. It stood very high, was lit from within, and had moving sparkles of different colors on and around it. It was alive with energy!

Sottrol and I floated through the arch into a cavernous room. From where we entered, the floor was far below us and the ceiling high above us. The room was a huge sphere with incredible ornate detail everywhere I looked.

"This is one of the oldest sections of the university," Sottrol explained. "You will be taking your next class in this wing."

With that, he glided up to a balcony across from us. I followed. There were several Spirits at a table. Each had a large book.

"Mr. Darcimon Stillwater," Sottrol announced to the Being in the center, a very luminous female Spirit.

"Mr. Stillwater. We have been expecting you. Welcome to The Deepening."

She had a lovely bell-like timbre to her voice. I wanted to ask about that. I also wanted to ask about The Deepening, but Sottrol quickly escorted me away once my name had been added to the register.

We circled around the spherical room. The beauty of it awed me. There were circular panels that glowed, each trimmed exquisitely. Anyone who saw me would know it was my first time there because of the way I gawked and stared.

Because I was so fascinated by my surroundings, I did not look where I was going, and I bumped into another Being. Although I was just getting used to my spirit form, this had not happened before. It was an odd sensation—this colliding of energetic bodies. Some sparking occurred along with a buzzing sound.

Apologizing to the Spirit, I said, "I'm sorry. This is my first time . . . ," but my words trailed off, for I was face to face with a magnificent Spirit.

She was glorious, shimmering white with lavender and blue sparkles. Her hair was white, braided and pulled back from her face. Her eyes were piercing violet and spoke of deep wisdom she had gained from experience.

"Ah, my son," she said, nodding and smiling, "you have jostled me but not upset me."

She then shook her entire spirit body slightly, much as I had seen birds do.

"There, back in balance. Please do the same, for I have made an indentation in your energy field."

It was true; I felt unbalanced.

"What did you do just then?" I asked. "How can I do it?"

By that time Sottrol had returned to my side and said, "Not paying attention, Darci? Never mind. Here, try this."

He positioned himself on one side of me, the splendid white and lavender Guide placed herself on the other, and they shook me. It wasn't like shaking a human body. The movements were faster and more even. I felt an electric charge pass through me from one Guide to the other. My head became extremely clear, and I felt very well.

"Thank you, Sottrol," said the resplendent female Guide. "Is this the new student you were speaking to me about?"

"Yes, this is Darcimon Stillwater. Darci, meet Chalherine Contivica. She is Chancellor of this wing of the university."

"Darci," Chalherine softly replied, extending her hand towards me and nodding.

I was speechless, so Sottrol gave me a little shove.

"Very pleased to meet you," I managed to say, clasping her offered hand. Again I felt an electric buzzing.

Sottrol explained, smiling, "He's awed by the splendor. He will adjust."

"My being your tutor is no accident," the radiant woman spoke to both of us. "There has been a fluctuation in the third continuum which gives me the opportunity to tutor a new student. I believe Darci here is that student."

Sottrol's face lit up with delight as he responded, "This is what I hoped for! You'll find he is dedicated and learns quickly. Chalherine, thank you very much. If I can be of any help at all . . ."

"I'll take it from here, Sottrol."

Chalherine floated up to me so that her eyes looked directly into mine. The sensation was incredible—as if she were pouring molten lava deep into me. I shuddered, knowing that I was at the mercy of this powerful elder Guide. I wasn't sure I was ready.

"You are ready," Chalherine answered, reading my thoughts. "You are just new and inexperienced. This will change. Follow me."

I glanced around for Sottrol who seemed like an old friend at this point, but he had vanished.

"Come with me," said Chalherine, taking my arm and pulling me through a circular doorway that had symbols all around it. We glided down what seemed like a slight incline to a somewhat smaller spherical room with many circular doors. Everything was glowing in a rich gold color.

"This is where my students stay," Chalherine explained, "and here is your chamber."

She pointed to a series of symbols outside of one of the circular doorways. They were the same symbols that had been over the door of my rejuvenation cell.

"These are the signs for your Soul," Chalherine explained, moving her hand over them, "and this is now your space, your home."

"Thank you," I said quietly. I was still in awe of my new teacher.

"I will give you time to adjust. I shall return soon, and we will begin our work." She vanished in a flurry of silent scintilla.

∞ ∞ ∞

My rejuvenation cell had been small and simple with nothing more than a cot and a door. This chamber was larger and had several pallets, each in a different location and at a different level. The area was made up of two oval rooms. One end of the chamber had very low light while the other glowed bright gold. There were also several pairs of seats at different levels, and near these were niches or small alcoves that were empty now but were the right size for a book or two.

I needed to rest and assimilate—not just this move to a new abode but also the reading I had done about Angel and me. I was exhilarated by all the input but frazzled by it, too. I needed to bring myself into balance. Gravitating to the low-lit area, I lay down and proceeded to do my breathing exercises, which were becoming second nature.

It was quite a while before Chalherine returned. I was thinking about how busy she must be when suddenly there appeared a sphere of brilliant white light just inside the entrance to my chamber, and Chalherine materialized.

"Darci Stillwater," she addressed me.

I stood up and responded, "Yes, Chancellor Contivica."

"Please call me Chalherine. It is the name I prefer. Darci, I have come to tutor you in The Deepening. I have several assistants who will help in your schooling. Sottrol was right to bring you to my attention. You have drive, passion, and determination—attributes I require in my students."

"Chalherine, what is 'The Deepening'?"

The radiant elder motioned for me to sit with her on the curved bench by the doorway as she elucidated, "Level three of your studies to become a Spirit Guide is also known as 'The Deepening.' Here you will hone your skills. There are many things a student must master in order to become a Spirit Guide. You have learned two important basics: non-judgment and unconditional love."

I nodded, eager to learn what was in store.

"Level three is about developing skills that you will use constantly as a Spirit Guide."

"Skills? I'm not sure what you mean."

"Telepathy is one. You know how we teachers have been able to read your thoughts? You will learn to do this. Spirit vision is another skill that is essential. You will learn to see and read energy fields."

"The energy fields around humans?" I questioned, becoming quite excited now.

"Yes, the energy in and around everything. The Universe is made of energy. You will see this. There is more. There is toning, which is akin to chanting but even more powerful, and, of course, there is healing, a very useful skill and one that you will need frequently when you begin interacting with the Earth plane."

"Where do we start?"

"The reason this course is called 'The Deepening' is because that is what you will experience, the deepening of your spirit power. Acquiring the skills is a part of this process of deepening . . . and you start here."

She rose and went to a place on the wall of my chamber. There was a symbol that looked like a stick drawing of a bird with no legs or a tipped infinity sign with one loop larger and a little beak on the smaller loop. Chalherine saw my interest in the symbol.

"You enter here," she shared, pointing to the beak.

"Then deepen to here," she continued, indicating the smaller loop.

"Then deepen all the way to here," she said, moving her finger to the larger loop.

Next she placed her hands, palms down, on either side of the symbol, and an oval doorway appeared.

"This is your Power Booth, Darci. I want you to enter here at regular intervals. To assist you, I have set this doorway so it will appear when it is time for you to enter. You can use this whenever you want as well. Just place your hands on either side of the symbol as I did."

She continued before I could ask anything, "Once in the Power Booth, begin by breathing as you have been previously instructed, then quicken and deepen your breaths like this."

She demonstrated a new breathing technique and then had me do it. It took a couple of tries for me to learn it.

"That's it," Chalherine said, placing her hands on either side of my face. Her eyes penetrated deep into my Being.

"Your first assignment is to begin using this Power Booth. Do not fear. I can monitor your progress. I will return if you need help."

I did not want to show hesitation in front of my new teacher, so in I went. As soon as I did so, the door slid closed behind me and disappeared.

The interior of the Power Booth was dimly lit, so I looked around. There were no seats. In fact, there was only room to stand. The walls were curved, and I felt as if I were a yolk inside an egg. Along these curved walls were ornate panels that ran vertically.

The booth vibrated, first a little, then more. I had the distinct impression that it was rotating as well. The vibration became steady, and my mind flashed to the occasion when Sottrol and Chalherine were shaking me because this experience seemed similar. I surmised that the Power Booth was bringing my energy field into a balanced state and made a mental note to ask Chalherine about this.

The vibrating continued for a while. When it stopped, my head was clear, and I felt exhilarated. This was a very good thing because what happened next could have been frightening if I hadn't been feeling so great.

The bottom of the Power Booth opened, and I dropped down. Previously, I had learned to hover and float with my spirit body, but I was taken by surprise so I fell. It was a short drop, almost as though I had slipped neatly into a slot.

It was a tight fit. I couldn't move. Not long ago, a situation like this would have scared me, for I never enjoyed being restrained. This time though I felt secure and trusted the process I had begun.

Soon I understood why I had to keep my spirit body so still. Small but very intense rays of light came from a source I could not see and penetrated me. They were aimed at my head about eye level. I could feel these powerful beams and could tell by the sensation that rays were penetrating my head from above as well. I also sensed that I was moving slowly forward, and as I did so, the piercing rays changed color, first gold, then white, then blue-white, then magenta, then gold again. Except for the fact that I was unable to move at all, I was not uncomfortable.

I decided to notice as much as I could. I found the most interesting observations were looking into my own spirit body. The pattern of light rays continued outside me. Inside me, things were shifting. This is very difficult to describe. I can only say that it seemed as if these beams of light were redrawing my inner landscape, altering my inner pathways.

I had a vision of a trip I had taken with my father when I was a boy during my most recent Earth lifetime. We were riding in a carriage coming back home from London. I was watching the scenery go by and saw a road that led through a stone archway. There were huge trees beside the arched gateway and flowers at its base.

"Let's go through there," I begged, pointing to the arch. "Please, that's the way I want to go!"

Of course, back in that lifetime, father said no, that we had to stay on the road towards home.

In this vision, however, we took the road through the stone archway and down a thickly wooded lane. The trees parted to show a spectacular building that looked like a large temple with golden spires, rows and rows of steps, and a reflecting pool in front.

I saw me as a little boy jump from the carriage and run to the pool. I had always loved to play in the water. When I peered into the pond, I gasped, for I saw myself not as a boy, but as a Being of Light!

I was shimmering and shining like the Angel Initiates who had met me when I first passed over. My head was especially bright. I looked again and saw rings of light pulsing from my spirit body. I was overwhelmed and found myself trembling.

Amazingly, then I heard Chalherine's voice inside my own head saying, "That is enough for now."

I felt my body free up, and a tall oval door opened before me. I was back in my chamber.

Since I was still trembling and also a bit disoriented, I asked aloud, "Chalherine, what is happening to me?"

I heard her voice inside my head again.

She said, "Rest, rest dear Darci. I shall visit you shortly."

She did not really need to tell me to rest, for I felt very fatigued, and I knew instinctively that's what I should do. As I lay down, I noticed that my spirit body tingled, and I felt more buoyant, more effervescent.

∞ ∞ ∞

Chalherine returned as she said she would. Just as I sat up, refreshed from my rest, she appeared seated next to me. I was surprised by her sudden manifestation and her intense luminosity, so I jumped a little.

"Sorry. You startled me."

"That's all right, Darci," she smiled. "You will get used to this, and one day you will also travel in this way."

"Chalherine, I heard you speak to me. I heard your voice inside my head!"

"And well you should," she replied. "Here's why. The Power Booth starts by helping you increase your telepathic abilities. This is done by elevating the vibrations here and here." She pointed to the spot between her eyes and to the top of her head.

"Already you know that you have thoughts that others can read. This has happened several times since you began your classes here. Am I correct?"

I nodded.

"Now you, too, can read the thoughts of others. Try it."

I wasn't sure what I was supposed to do. I sat there.

I kept wondering how to go about reading her thoughts when Chalherine said aloud, "You're trying too hard. Take a deep breath."

I took several. Just as I was inhaling on the fourth breath, I heard Chalherine's voice inside my head saying, "How did you like your reflection in the pool?"

I looked at her. She smiled, and I heard her voice say, "I thought you looked beautifully radiant."

She was still smiling. Her lips weren't moving.

"You just asked me about my reflection in the pool," I said aloud.

"Yes, Darci," she spoke aloud, "your telepathic communication center is activated."

"How did you know about my vision of the temple with the golden spires and the pool?"

"Because my telepathic abilities are highly developed."

"Can I send a message to you?"

"Yes."

"Can I send a message to anyone?"

"Of course. The intended recipient may not be able to hear it if her telepathic center is not fired up."

In my own head, I thought of Angel and about sending her a message.

Chalherine said, "Not yet, Darci. Please just focus on your studies. You and Angel will eventually have plenty of communication. Come now; let's practice speaking to each other with our minds."

As I nodded, I heard Chalherine's voice in my head saying, "I know you love Angel. She loves you, too. She just does not remember right now."

I began to speak aloud, but Chalherine put her finger to my lips, and I took a deep breath that was also a sigh.

I thought, "My dear Angel. Where is she? Why doesn't she remember me?"

Chalherine answered by projecting another thought to me, "You did not think of her during your last Earth life. She is now as you were then, completely involved in an experience on one of the levels on the lower spiral."

"When can I see her?" I thought back.

"Once you are a Spirit Guide" came the reply into my mind.

I realized that my teacher and I were conversing telepathically, so I said a little "Ah" aloud.

"Yes, you have done well," responded Chalherine, also aloud.

"I want you to meet one of my assistants who will also tutor you."

She gestured to her left side, but there was no one there. A second later, a shimmering Being manifested. At first I could not discern anything but hoops of light, intertwined and rotating. I watched as a face emerged from the brilliant display. I could not tell if this Being was male or female.

"It doesn't matter," Chalherine said softly.

My eyes were fixed in fascination as a Spirit Being took shape right before me. The rotating hoops of light curved and altered until a slender glowing figure was standing before us.

"Hello, Hespahba," Chalherine greeted the Being. "Meet Darci Stillwater."

Hespahba bowed and then spoke to Chalherine, "He has an abundance of blue, doesn't he?"

Chalherine must have caught the quizzical look on my face because she laughed and said to me, "Hespahba's specialty is reading energy fields. Yours is quite blue."

"Vibrant blue," stated the newly arrived Spirit, "with a spiraling center pattern. Have you just come from the Power Booth?"

Chalherine and I said, "Yes" together.

Then she added, "But you knew that. Well, why don't you take over here? Darci has enough spunk left in him for a lesson from you."

Hespahba moved in front of me while Chalherine floated to the side. This tutor was exotic looking—slim, bald, and wearing a tight body suit instead of the usual robe. This Guide's brilliant almond eyes and sweet voice indicated that she was a female, yet her spirit body's appearance was that of a young male.

"I prefer not to be identified with either gender," the Spirit said. "Besides, my look has nothing to do with our work together. Shall we begin?"

"Yes, Hespahba," I replied, bowing a little.

My new tutor rose to the top of my chamber and put on a display for me. First, the Guide appeared to be in a shiny purple body suit, then a gold suit, then golden-green, then white. The colors faded from one to the other as the Guide hovered above me. Then Hespahba twirled and turned into a sphere of brilliant white light which changed into a sphere of pink and blue swirls. I was fascinated, but I couldn't see how this was a lesson or how it related to my studies and me. The display ended with Hespahba spinning and touching down on one toe with a mischievous smile and a wink.

"Now you try it," the tutor said.

A burst of laughter followed as the Guide beheld the stunned look on my face.

"I am here to teach you how to read energy patterns," said the tutor as he/she moved to a spot directly in front of me. "The light show I just put on for you was designed to interest and entertain you."

Hespahba sat down across from me where Chalherine had been and began, "Reading energy patterns is actually a different way of seeing. It is seeing not with your eyes but with your very Soul."

"Seeing with my Soul?" I replied, confused.

"Yes, absolutely. It is actually sensing with your Soul, and you can interpret that into images," Hespahba explained but could see that I didn't get it.

"Your time in the Power Booth will help you increase your personal vibration. The higher your personal vibration, the easier it will be for you to do this."

"Do what?" I questioned, not sure at all at what I was supposed to be learning here.

"Sensing or seeing with your Soul is part of activating the telepathic centers in your spirit body. Perhaps after another visit to the Power Booth, you will better grasp what I am here to teach you."

The Being before me could sense some apprehension on my part and encouraged me, saying, "Darci, the experience will be different this time and, indeed, every time you set foot in the Power Booth. I'll return after you have used the Power Booth again."

And with that, the strange and humorous Guide disappeared. Chalherine was also gone. There was nothing for me to do but enter the Booth once again.

∞ ∞ ∞

Hespahba was right. When I stepped into the Power Booth, everything was different. The walls though still curved were white and very smooth. I saw no circles or panels or ornate decorations.

I reached out and touched the smooth glowing walls. My hand left a blue print. This surprised me. I tried placing my other hand on the white wall, and it left a lighter blue print. When I touched the wall with both hands at the same time, the Booth seemed to begin to rotate and rise, first slowly, then faster and faster.

The twirling got to the point where it was a dizzying experience for me. Perhaps the purpose was to disorient me because that was what happened. Everything around me changed. The booth with its smooth alabaster walls no longer existed.

I was somehow on a garden pathway with a hedge row on my right and blue sage on my left. It seemed as though I was back on Earth, but I knew that couldn't be.

I followed the path into a wooded glen. About a dozen steps into the forest something very odd occurred. I hit an invisible wall. I bumped into an energy field that I could not see, but it was very much there because I could not step forward. It was blocking me. I could see the path, the trees, the little brook, but I could not reach them because of this wall of energy.

"What do I do now?" I wondered.

"Sit and observe," I heard in my mind. It was Chalherine's voice.

I noticed a small wooden bench by the side of the path, so I sat there and looked at the scene. At first it seemed like a pleasant forest lane like many I had walked on Earth.

The words "Breathe and detach" floated into my head from my teacher, so I did.

I sat quietly doing the breathing exercises I had learned. It was a while before I noticed anything. Eventually I saw that the trees and shrubs and even the brook had an eerie glow around them. The glow slowly became more visible until each plant had its own visible energy field.

Then I saw mist—at least that's what I thought it was. The mist hung over the pathway at the very point where I had encountered the impassable energy field. It was not a moving, swirling mist; instead, it had a marbled appearance.

Very slowly the mist began to glow until it became a luminous orange color. Suddenly it ignited and turned into flames! I was awestruck, for the red-orange blaze reached high above the path.

In my head I heard Chalherine's instruction, "Walk through the wall of fire."

"What?!" I said aloud. I didn't want to do it. Being burned by fire was a fear I'd had in my last lifetime.

"Face the flames, Darci," I heard Chalherine again. "Walk through the wall of fire."

I couldn't just keep sitting there, especially with my teacher urging me on, so I rose and faced the strange flames. They were very bright, but they did not radiate heat.

I took a deep breath and stepped forward, expecting either to hit a wall or be singed to a crisp. Instead, I entered an area of dancing vertical lights. Bright pulsing rays of different colors came up from below me and soared high above me. I could not see their origins or their destinations.

"Walk to the spot, stand, and breathe, Darci. Breathe!" I heard Chalherine's words in my head.

I realized I was so stunned that my breathing had become shallow. As I made a conscious effort to breathe deeply, I saw a ring of glowing embers before me. I knew this must be the spot Chalherine was referring to. I stepped into the center of the circle and took another deep breath. I heard a low tone, then another in harmony with it, then another.

Suddenly a vertical ray shot up through the circle of embers and through me! It was a ray of bright red-violet light that made my spirit body buzz and tingle as it passed through me. This seemed to last a moment or two. It was difficult for me to tell. In the quiet period that followed, I breathed deeply and listened to the chorus of low tones around me.

Just as quickly as the first, a second ray zoomed up through the circle and through me. This ray was a golden-orange color that made me feel warm and a little woozy. Following this came more tones, higher ones, and a ray of pure yellow. This one seemed very electric as it passed through me. The dance of vertical rays continued around me.

As I experienced the penetration of the next ray, which was emerald green, I flashed to the incarnation in Egypt. I saw Angel and me in a giant temple with triangular windows. Each window had a different colored light ray passing through it. We were moving a patient from resting on a pallet in red light to green light. We stood at either end of the ailing child so that the green rays, too, covered us. We chanted. I held the boy's ankles while Angel held her hands on his head. The image was gone as soon as the green ray stopped pulsing through me.

Blue was next, then lavender. Each had a different effect on me. Finally, I was bathed in white light. This seemed to be the strongest ray of all, for my spirit body shuddered as it vibrated up through me.

Just when I thought the experience was nearly over, the whole process happened again. All in all, I went through the series of light rays four times. Each time the rays seemed more powerful than before.

The marbled mist closed in on me, and I could see nothing. I did not try to find my way out of it because I was still overcome with vibrations from the colored rays. I was patient. I stood and breathed and said a little prayer.

Soon an oval door appeared in the mist and then opened for me. I stepped through the doorway into my chamber.

I felt like a new being. I can only describe it as being akin to the exhilaration I felt after swimming or even bathing back on Earth though many times greater. I was tingling. Every part of my spirit body was alive with vibration.

I sat on one of the benches in my chamber and tried to assimilate my latest experience in the Power Booth. I did not have long to ponder, for both Chalherine and Hespahba glided towards me out of nowhere.

"Look at the difference!" Hespahba exclaimed.

Chalherine looked pleased and put her hand on my shoulder. I felt a rush of love.

"Darci, you heard me and followed my suggestions, and you got the most you could out of that experience. That's all we teachers can ask of our students. You have done well."

Hespahba knelt and took my feet. The tutor held one of my heels in each hand as if he/she was weighing them and said, "Better—but still a ways to go."

"You can try the first part of the lesson," Chalherine addressed us both and then vanished in a swirl of sparkling light.

Hespahba came close to me, lining up our spirit bodies. The Guide's eyes were peering right into mine. He/she then spoke slowly as though I were writing down each word.

He began, "All the Universe is energy. Even when you walked the Earth in a carbon-based body, everything was energy. Seeing the energy patterns around and within all things is an important skill for a Spirit Guide. Reading the energy patterns is the best way to accurately evaluate any situation. It is an important tool."

The tutor stepped back and asked, "Do you understand this?"

"Yes," I answered.

Hespahba continued, "There are many masks, many illusions on the lower wheel. They are there for numerous reasons. Overall, the lower spiral is the place where Souls face their most basic challenges. If you are to really help a human, you must be able to see through the illusions to the true essence of a situation. Each human has challenges to meet and tasks to accomplish. Unless you can accurately evaluate the situation on Earth, or on any level for that matter, you will not be able to assist in the most appropriate way—understand?"

"Yes, I do."

"You must be able to see through all the outer layers, the masks, and perceive the true energetic patterns that are driving the situation. My task is to teach you how to do this."

"Thank you, Hespahba."

"You can thank me once I have taught you this skill. It does not come easily to everyone. The first step is for you to practice seeing the energy fields. This can be confusing when there are many, and they overlap and intermingle. Let's begin simply. Here is a flowering gardenia."

As he/she said this, a gardenia plant in full bloom appeared next to us.

"Sit with this floral Being. Ask the plant to show you its energy field. This is your homework. I shall return," he said, and with that, the Guide was gone, leaving me with a fragrant new friend.

I wondered if either Chalherine or Hespahba knew that gardenias were a favorite of mine. During my last Earth life, our family had a gardener who took excellent care of the grounds. This man loved flowering plants and would try to have something in bloom the year round. As a boy, I remember following the incredible magical fragrance of the gardenias in search of the source.

So I sat with the plant not knowing what to do. I recalled Hespahba saying to befriend the plant, so I touched one of the leaves and said, "Greetings. I am here to learn from you."

At first nothing happened, but I was content to enjoy the lovely aroma and look at the delicate blossoms. I did not know what else to do. Finally, I had a breakthrough when I narrowed my eyes and peered through my lashes. The plant seemed brighter when I did that. Also, it seemed to be glowing a little when I tried observing the plant out of the corner of my eye. I saw a very distinct ring of light around it. This ring was faint at first, but each time I looked, it became brighter until I was able to see it while staring straight at the gardenia.

A childhood memory from my last Earth life came surging into my heart and mind. I saw myself as a little boy racing into the sun-lit conservatory, running up to a gardenia in full bloom and embracing it because of its beautiful smell. I then picked one of the blossoms for my mother.

She hugged me, thanked me, and placed the flower in her hair. I was overcome with love for her, love for that moment in time, and love for the gardenia that sat before me.

I let my love pour into the plant, and the plant responded! It glowed with a bright white-gold light. I didn't have to look at it sideways or squint. I could definitely see the light radiating from the plant. This inspired me to emit even more love for this little plant, and it again responded by glowing even brighter. There was no doubt about it. The plant had an energy field around it, and I could clearly see it.

I wondered if this technique worked in all situations. If I sent love and compassion, would I automatically tune in to the energy patterns? Was it that straightforward? My questions would have to wait. I could tell it was time for me to rest.

∞　∞　∞

When I awoke, I was surprised to see a cat sitting where the plant had been. It was a striped orange colored cat, and it was licking its paws. I liked all kinds of animals and had a special fondness for felines. I remembered how important they were during my lifetime in Egypt. Cats were considered sacred and were often looked to for signs and omens. Angel and I had cared for several cats, one very much like this cat that sat before me.

"Hello cat," I addressed it. "Welcome to my chamber. What have you to teach me?"

The cat looked at me and then went back to cleaning itself. I smiled because the animal was so like the one I'd known and loved in Egypt. That old cat had kept me company and brought me comfort after my dear Angel had been taken from me.

I felt a surge of love for that cat, and as soon as I experienced this, the cat across from me looked at me and blinked. I saw a halo of light around the feline. I rubbed my eyes and looked again. The energy field was there, even brighter than before. I could distinguish layers in the aura and areas that were brighter than others.

The cat jumped down from its perch and came over to me, rubbing along my robe. I petted the creature, still observing the rings of light, which were especially visible around its head. I picked it up to pet it, and the cat purred. Its energy field glowed even brighter when I did this.

I enjoyed my feline companion and wondered if it could stay. Except for interaction with my teachers, I didn't have many exchanges with other beings. I was pondering how much I missed socializing with others when Hespahba entered the chamber—this time through the door at one end.

"Greetings, Darci," the tutor announced, bowing slightly.

I bowed back.

"You are a good student. You learn quickly. Yes, the cat can stay if you wish. I have another exercise for you that you may enjoy. Come. I'll show you how to return to the Library from here."

Hespahba appeared this time in a silver body suit with red trim around the neck and wrists. He/she literally shimmered as we floated through the maze of hallways. The tutor spoke to me as we glided along.

"I want you to spend some time observing other Beings, and the Library is a good place for this because they sit and read or talk."

"I want you to memorize this route. Your assignment is to travel to the Library at least four times and observe. Please make notes on what you see."

We had reached the entrance to the Library's great room, but before we entered, Hespahba had more to say.

"Take notes as soon as you enter. Then increase your energy using the breathing techniques. Look again and observe. If there are differences, write them down. Here."

Out of nowhere, the tutor produced a ledger with what appeared to be blank pages. He/she also handed me a quill pen much like the one I had used to write my sister when I lived in England during my last Earth life. I was a bit surprised because although I had seen many books since my arrival here, I had not seen anyone write in one.

Hespahba motioned for me to take the items and then nodded for me to enter the Library. I thanked him and went in. There was an oval chair available at the edge of the reading section, so I sat there.

My first impulse was to go to the circular desk and ask for the book that described my lifetimes with Angel. I knew there was much more to read, much more to know, and I was hungry for the information. Every time I read about a lifetime we had shared, I relived it and felt closer to her.

As Hespahba had suggested, I made a few notes in the ledger about the Beings around me in the reading area. They had one thing in common: they were all absorbed in what they were reading, and I could understand that.

I began thinking about what I had read in this Library and how it affected me, how it moved me. The first time I was in this room, I read about the lifetime I shared with Angel in Egypt. Once again I became overwhelmed with first images, then emotions.

Every detail of the night I proposed to Angel came into my heart and mind. I saw us sitting together on the banks of the Nile, quite spent after cooperating on a very complex healing session. I remembered how nervous I was and how my passion for this woman drove me to speak. Then I saw her face in the moonlight, her eyes afire. I saw her smile when she agreed to be my wife. I sighed deeply when I recalled the sweetness of our embrace.

A hand on my shoulder interrupted my memory, and I looked around to see Sottrol. His eyes penetrated me as he shook his head.

"Dreaming about Angel?"

I nodded.

"I must say that in all the time I have taught, tutored, and mentored, I have rarely encountered such depth of passion. I'm afraid this may be interfering with your studies."

"I'm sorry," I apologized. "I first remembered Angel in this Library. The memories that come to me as I sit here are very powerful."

"I have an idea," Sottrol said, winking. He went to the circular desk and ordered a book, which appeared right away. He took the large volume and motioned for me to follow him.

"Come with me," Sottrol said.

We moved through a maze of glowing corridors until we got to what looked like a large porthole. It opened for us and we entered. There wasn't much in this space—just a circular chair, a book stand, and a screen.

Sottrol began, "Here we are. Now, Darci, instead of having your memories of Angel distract you from your studies, let's use them to help you learn. I have your attention now, don't I? Here is the giant book which describes all the lifetimes you have shared with Angel."

He placed the large book on the stand and indicated that I should sit.

Then he continued, "This screen reflects energy patterns only. When you look at your reflection in this screen, you will see the energy you are emitting—the color, the shape, the intensity. This screen shows you the type of vision you must develop in order to be a Spirit Guide."

"But I don't see anything."

"Hold on, Darci. I must give you instructions. Then I will have the Regent activate this cubicle. Once I leave, the room will dim. Stand in front of the screen and observe your energy field. Make notes, too, as your tutor asked. Then sit and read. When the words on the page disappear, stand again before the screen and observe your energy field. Notice the changes in detail. Make notes. Return again to read. You'll find that the words have reappeared on the pages. They will be there until it is time for you to once again look and evaluate your energy field. Take this at your own pace. I expect that you will move right along with this exercise."

"Why is that, Sottrol?"

"You will be reading about Angel," he smiled, "and you will be astounded by the changes in your energetic patterns. This energy mirror is very accurate and very vivid. You will be here for a while, Darci, so breathe deeply, relax, and learn. Your passion and your love for your soul mate will teach you."

Chapter Five:
Passion is My Teacher

Once Sottrol set me on this new course of using the screen that reflects energy patterns, everything changed. For one thing, I now incorporated into my studies the very activity that I yearned to do—namely, read about my former lifetimes with Angel. I could enthusiastically launch into doing this with no guilt or fear of distraction and could examine the relationships through the patterns on the screen. Best of all, it was a way for me to reach out and feel closer to my soul mate. Indeed, Sottrol had said that my connection with Angel and my love for her was going to teach me.

Once Sottrol left, the room dimmed, and the energy screen that made up one wall came alive. I stood before the screen and observed the light show.

"This is my energy pattern?" I wondered to myself.

I saw a patch of gold light surrounded by varying hues of blue. I moved a little to the right, then to the left, to see if the pattern on the screen would follow my movements. This did occur but not exactly like the mirrors I had used on Earth. The energy field on the screen floated gently from one side to the other as I moved.

"So I guess this is me," I concluded. I took the ledger that Hespahba had given to me and wrote these observations. Now I could begin to read.

As happened before, the text in this great book had changed since the last time I read from it. This time not only had the words become different, so had the layout and the color of the pages. Now they were a golden color and the words themselves were written in script.

The scene described was a desert village. The houses, the streets, the landscape were all the color of sand. There I was, a little dark-skinned boy, running down the street with thick sandals on my feet and loose pants that came to my knees. I was probably about eight or nine years old, and I was looking for someone or something.

I was yelling, "Astara! Astara!"

An elderly woman blocked me by holding out her walking stick as I tried to run by her. I screeched to a halt.

"Who are you searching for?" she asked.

"My little sister," came my breathless answer. "Astara is lost!"

"There are children playing by the well. Perhaps she is there," offered the old woman. "Find her soon, lad," she continued. "I can tell the wind is picking up. There'll be a mighty sand storm by dusk."

I raced off in the direction of the well. My sister loved playing in the water, so I thought the elder woman might be right. When I reached the well, there were about a dozen children playing in the wet sand.

I watched as a woman drew up a gourd of water. The children begged her to sprinkle some on them. She did, and the little ones jumped and giggled and squealed with laughter. I did not see my sister there, so I asked two little girls that were near me.

"Have you seen Astara?"

They looked around quickly.

One replied, "Oh . . . she was here."

The other one said, "She got very wet. Maybe she went home."

I thanked them, but I knew Astara wasn't at home for I had just come from there. My mother was upset with me because I had let my little sister out of my sight while we were out buying the day's produce for our family.

The wind was noticeably stronger now, and I remembered what the elder woman had said. Soon sand would be blowing through the streets, buffeting and blinding those who were not inside some kind of shelter. I knew what sand storms were like.

I had been on a journey with my father. We were on our way home from a neighboring village and were caught in a sudden storm. We wrapped ourselves with every piece of clothing we had, including the blankets and parcels that we were transporting. This was the first time I had been exposed to such weather, and it frightened me. The sand stung my skin and my eyes and got into my mouth. Once my father had covered us, he held me and told me to be still. We huddled together for hours as the wind whipped around us. We were buried in the sand, fast becoming a part of the landscape when the storm finally passed. We were able to dig out and continue our journey.

I was thinking about this experience as I searched the streets for my sister. She was so young. She wouldn't know what to do in a sand storm.

I searched every street in the desert village, going back through the market twice. The vendors were taking down their temporary booths and packing away their goods.

I called, "Astara! Astara!" and asked over and over if anyone had seen my little sister, but no one had.

Panic was setting in as I felt the sand stinging my bare legs. I couldn't go back home without her, so I bravely set out for the loop. This was a little oasis or garden spot not far from the edge of the village. Travelers often stopped there because there was a bathing pool and a fair amount of shade from some tall palm trees. The road from the village went out to this small oasis and looped around it, crossing the major travel route. I knew this was a favorite spot for my little sister, but she had never attempted the walk on her own.

"She is still little," I thought. "Only six—but where else can she be? I've looked everywhere in the village twice! I even knocked on the doors of other families that we know!"

The walk to the loop was easy on a calm pleasant day, but this day it was a struggle. The wind was gaining strength, and I had to lean into it and keep my head down. It took me longer than I thought, but I made it. I slid down into the pocket that had been carved out for the pool. Some of the trees were helping to protect the little oasis. I was glad to crouch down and finally be out of the direct gale, for the wind was whipping fiercely across the desert now.

As I was catching my breath, I wondered if Astara had wandered out here before the weather turned so fierce. I didn't see anyone else; however, the blowing sand reduced visibility. I thought I knew my sister, but maybe I was wrong. Perhaps she wasn't here at all.

Just then, through the howling of the wind and the sound of the swirling sand, I heard something. I couldn't tell what it was. It sounded like a bird, but I knew no birds would be out in this storm. I slid down closer to the pool of water that was agitated by the wind. I crawled in the direction of the sound. My instincts told me to keep going even though the storm was becoming worse, and my father had taught me to find the most protected spot, stay put, and wait it out.

Slowly I crept around the edge of the pool that was being directly hit by the wind. I was nearly blinded by flying sand. I don't know how, but I distinctly heard a little cry over the sound of the wind. I pulled myself along on my elbows with my head down. Sand was in my eyes, my mouth, my nose. I rolled around a small hill, hoping to find a more sheltered spot on the other side and landed on a small huddled child—my sister Astara.

It was my Angel.

Astara's face was streaked with tears, and she wailed when she saw me.

"Eber! Eber! I knew you'd come to save me! Oh, Eber!"

She threw her little arms around me and sobbed. I could see she had taken a fall. Her legs were scraped and bleeding. My arms were bleeding, too, from the burn of crawling over the rocks and sand. We were a sorry pair.

Once I had held her for a few moments, I evaluated our situation. We needed to relocate and ride out the storm in the safest spot we could find. I knew there was a shelter that was sometimes used by travelers, but it was on the other edge of the pool. I wasn't sure we could make it.

We had to try. Sometimes these storms blew for days. We would die if we stayed where we were.

"We have to move!" I raised my voice above the wind.

"I'll try," came her reply though I could see that she was scared.

I bundled little Astara in the wrap that she had and put my arms around her. Slowly we walked forward into the wind.

"Keep your head down!" I shouted, pushing her head down with my hand. "Walk!"

We had to stop several times. My heart was racing. The whipping grains of sand bit into my skin. The stinging sensation was hard to bear, but I focused on my little sister. Keeping her safe and getting us to shelter were my only goals at that moment in time.

It was a tremendous struggle, but we finally reached the hut. Even this shelter was being invaded by the sand storm. I chose the most protected corner. There was a jug with some water in it, some mats to lie on, and some cloths for washing. I cleaned my sister's wounds. Her legs were badly scraped, and one gash was still bleeding. I didn't know much about bandaging although I had seen my mother do it. I ripped a cloth into strips, wet one strip, and tied it around the deep gash. Once I got her settled down on one of the mats, I tended to my own cuts, scrapes, and burns.

The storm howled all night long. I didn't sleep much; neither did she. We sat crouched together, holding each other. Sometimes Astara would squeeze my hand when a big burst of wind came through. When dawn broke, the wind subsided, and we began to think about how hungry we were.

I ventured out of the hut to see if there was anything at all I could scrounge for food. The sand had covered everything. Even the tall palm trees were standing with sand drifts partway up their trunks.

My sister and I were about to start back to the village when the wind picked up, and once again sand rained against the shelter. Astara was brave. I could tell the cuts and gashes on her legs hurt her. One in particular was quite red and beginning to swell.

Because I was very concerned about her, I made the courageous decision to go for help. I got myself primed, ready to step back into the sand storm, and fight my way back to the village, but little Astara would not let me go. She insisted she would follow me if I left her there. Knowing that would mean her death, I did not leave.

Instead, we sat hungry and hurt, trying to keep our spirits up. We made up songs about the storm, about the shelter, about the village, about ourselves.

We played a game where I would say, "Astara, here is your magic carpet. Where would you like to fly today?" and she would choose a destination.

Finally at dusk the wind abated, but we were so tired we fell asleep. I was holding my little sister.

We were awakened by noises in the night, the sounds of villagers searching for us. Soon there were torches in our faces. I remember the fire was blinding as our worried parents examined us. The search party was very relieved to find us alive though we must have looked tattered and dirty.

The group that found us had brought a large drag, one that both Astara and I could lie on. Our father and another man pulled us back along the loop road to the village and home.

It took me over a week to recover though Astara's healing took longer. Because the gash on her leg was infected, she had an especially hard time and couldn't walk for well over a moon cycle. During that time, I kept her company. We even made up a song about our adventure.

My father took me aside and told me that I had done well to find my sister and get us both to shelter. He said that I had saved Astara's life.

Once I had read that sentence in the giant book of lifetimes, the words on the page disappeared. I knew it was time to use the energy screen, so I closed the book and stood before it. What I expected to see was not there. Before me were two life-sized figures. They became clearer, and I recognized the image of Angel and I incarnated as Astara and Eber. There we were as the two desert children holding hands. The detail in the picture was amazing. I could look right into the eyes of the images on the screen. I saw true affection there and much love between these siblings.

Then Angel's image faded, and my image changed. Instead of the dark-skinned boy, I beheld a pattern of vertical beams of light. They danced and flickered, first in varying shades of gold, then green and gold, then green and blue. A pulsing circle of bright pink light was in the center of this light show.

As the colors on the screen dimmed, I took the ledger and noted everything I had seen on the screen in as much detail as I could. At the end, I wrote, "At least in this lifetime, it was I who cared for and saved my soul mate."

I opened the book to read more, but the pages were still blank. This puzzled me though I felt a little tired, so I rested and assimilated the essence of the desert lifetime I had just read about, including the images I had viewed on the energy screen.

∞ ∞ ∞

I am not sure how long I was in this meditative state, but a visitor roused me. I must have instinctively felt a presence because my eyes popped open to find Hespahba hovering near the ceiling. The tutor, seeing my eyes open, floated down and stood before me. This Guide, more than any other I had met, seemed to like to stand very close to me.

The tutor's eyes were right in front of mine as I heard the voice say, "Here you are, Darcimon Stillwater. I have located you."

"Hespahba, yes, I am here."

"Chalherine wondered where you were. You are under our tutelage, you know."

"Sottrol . . . ," I began to explain.

Putting a finger over my mouth, the androgynous Guide chuckled.

"You needn't explain. Sottrol is one of the wise elders at this University and has held almost every position here. Now he is advisor to all areas. He has taken a liking to you, Darci, and says your connection to the Soul named Angel is the best learning tool we have, so let's use it."

Hespahba floated back and twirled around, his turquoise body suit with silver trim sparkling.

The tutor again came close to me and continued, "At first I wasn't sure I agreed with Sottrol, but now I do. I have seen the results of this first use of the screen, and they are quite positive."

"You've read what I wrote?"

"That ledger is designed so that I can read whatever you write as you write it. A good tutor keeps close track of his/her student. I ask only that you take plenty of time with your evaluations and descriptions. The more details you note, the better. Now I shall go and leave you to your studies."

The Guide floated up and vanished through the ceiling of the room. I wondered if someday I might be able to do that.

I took some deep breaths and stretched my spirit body a bit. Then with some anticipation I opened the book. Words had returned to the pages, which now had a rose-colored glow to them.

The setting was Rome during the time the great empire was being built. I saw myself as a young man who was studying hard. My goal was to become a scribe for the Roman Senate.

My father, however, wanted me to have military experience, so I became a soldier. Because of my skills as a writer, I soon became an assistant to one of the military leaders. This General was on a mission to Sicily in order to secure the island as a Roman stronghold. The ruler of Sicily was in the process of negotiating with Rome and wanted to maintain his rule of the island nation and keep peace. He especially did not want to be replaced by a governor hand-picked by the Roman authorities. This king was convinced that Sicily was much better off if he, a native, kept control, so he was looking for ways to compromise.

The trip to Sicily with the General and his entourage was my first adventure away from the city of Rome. I was asked to go because some sort of peace agreement with Sicily was in the works, and my job was to document the negotiations and draw up the accord.

I read on as the book described how I was captivated by the place as soon as I arrived on Sicilian shores. The sun was warm, and a soft breeze brought alluring fragrances from the land.

Our delegation of eight was shown to our quarters on the estate of the Sicilian ruler. Servants brought us fruit and bathed our feet while musicians played. Although my father was very well-to-do and a member of the Roman Senate, I had never been treated so lavishly.

That evening there was a banquet to honor our visit. It was apparent to me that the Sicilian King was intent on making a positive impression. The table was long and overflowing with food of all kinds. We were introduced to the ruler's wife and the heads of the most prominent families on this island nation.

My training had taught me to observe details, so I noticed the mannerisms and the expressions of our host and hostess as they introduced us to the others at the table. I was sure that the King had met with these Lords before our arrival, and together they had planned a strategy. I hoped it was a peaceful one.

After a fitful night in a strange bed trying to digest food that was unfamiliar to my system, I rose at first light to stroll around the grounds. Walking out to the side of the estate that faced the sea and the rising sun, I felt somehow strangely attracted to this island though I did not know why. This was a beautiful place. knew I did not want to see any harm come to Sicily or its residents.

As I walked toward the main house, an elegant mansion, I saw a young woman on the verandah. The first rays of sunrise glinted in her hair and brought out red highlights. I climbed the steps and walked toward her. She was facing the rising sun holding some books in her arms. She was young, probably in her late teens, and dressed in a flowing pink robe with rose and silver trim. This young woman was a vision, and I who had never before been speechless could not find any words to say.

She did not see me at first because I was coming from behind her. Then she heard my footsteps and turned. Perhaps my Soul knew of lifetimes we had previously shared because something deep inside me stirred and recognized her as soon as I saw her eyes.

She smiled shyly, clutching the books to her chest, and said, "Hello."

I bowed my head as a greeting, still speechless. My heart was racing.

"You are one of our visitors," she said, taking a step towards me. "I can see by your dress that you are a Roman soldier."

"Yes," I managed to say. Now I had a giddy feeling. Heat pulsed up my chest and neck into my cheeks.

"I hope you find your accommodations comfortable."

"Yes, I do."

I swallowed, bowed again, offered my hand, and said, "I am Alger Matticus, Scribe to the General."

I looked up at her as she tipped her head toward me but did not clasp my hand. Our eyes met, and we held the gaze. My stomach felt as if it had dropped off a cliff.

"Greetings, Alger Matticus."

As she said my name, I felt as if my whole body followed my stomach off that cliff.

"I am Yulanna Carlotta. My father is your host, the King."

"So pleased to meet you," I uttered, my voice cracking, and then cleared my throat.

"Forgive me. I must go. My tutor is waiting."

She gracefully lifted the skirt of her dress in order to walk down the steps.

I was dumbstruck. I had never experienced this reaction to anyone or anything before. As I sat on the marble bench by the railing of the verandah and tried to regain my composure, I ran a number of possibilities through my head.

"Was it sleep deprivation?" I asked myself. "No, I had been without sleep before. Was it the unfamiliar food? Perhaps there was some strange effect, but I hadn't eaten anything since the night before. Was it the location? It was truly beautiful there, and the place did have a touch of magic to it." But after I thought all this through, I concluded that the presence of the young woman triggered my surprising response.

At this point in my reading, I sat back and closed my eyes. As had happened before when I read from The Great Book of Lifetimes, once an incarnation was described in the pages, many more details of that lifetime flooded back into my memory. It was as though the book was a gateway to experiencing the rich landscapes of my former lives. I sat there with my hand on the giant pages, smiling.

Now as I looked back to those few precious moments on that verandah, I knew exactly what had happened. I had met my soul mate, Angel, and had been reunited with the partner who had saved my life in primitive times. Later I had saved hers. Once again, I was in the presence of the Soul whom I had grown to love deeply. From my vantage point in Spirit, I could see how the attraction, the affection, and the love lasted from one lifetime to the next.

But as the young Roman scholar and soldier, I did not have that perspective, so I was confused about my reactions.

As that young man, it took me a while to get my feet under me and return to my quarters.

I thought some food might help, but I wasn't hungry. I knew there was an important meeting later that morning, so I forced down a few morsels.

All through the briefing with the General and his aides and also at the meeting with the King and several of the Lords, I had to discipline myself to concentrate on the business at hand. More than once, I found my thoughts straying to that sunrise meeting with Yulanna Carlotta.

That day seemed to last forever. After the midday meal, we returned to our quarters for a siesta. It was quite warm outside, and I was glad to take off my formal military garb and rest. Of course, my thoughts were of the evening to come and the possibility of spending some time with the Princess.

As the afternoon cooled, I walked along the shore. I loved the sea, the sound and the smell of it. Except for my voyage to Sicily, I had not been near the ocean very much. I wondered if Yulanna Carlotta's eyes were so beautiful and deep because she gazed out at the sea every day.

The dinner that evening was another formal affair. There were a few new faces, a Lord and Lady who hadn't been at the previous dinner, and, of course, Yulanna Carlotta. She sat next to her mother across and about halfway down the long table from me. She said nothing during the entire meal.

I looked at her often but tried not to stare. Her long hair was braided, and some of it was looped on the back of her head. Her dress was light blue-green with silver. She wore a thin silver band like a crown and looked very much like a princess.

The Queen noticed that I often glanced in their direction. She addressed me during a pause in the conversation, saying, "Alger Matticus, tell me of your family."

"My father is a member of the Roman Senate, your Majesty. My mother is a skilled and educated Lady. I have a younger brother and sister. We live in Rome."

The Queen seemed satisfied with my response. I noticed Yulanna Carlotta had stopped eating and paid close attention to my answer.

The dinner was over far too quickly. I watched Yulanna Carlotta as she left with her mother. She turned and our eyes met. Once again, I had a falling sensation. In fact, I had to steady myself by grabbing the edge of the table.

There was one more day of negotiations. The General was insisting on a certain number of Roman soldiers being stationed at strategic points on the Sicilian shore. The King was balking, but he would have to agree to something in order to avoid a complete takeover by the Romans. Finally, the two leaders reached a compromise, and the General informed us we would be returning to Rome right away.

I had much work to do, many scrolls to prepare. In fact, I was still working on them during the return voyage. Focusing on my duties helped keep me from thinking about Yulanna Carlotta. Every once in a while though I would look up from my work and visualize her. Such daydreams always ended with the wish to see her again.

Once I returned home, I was allowed time with my family. My father sat me down and asked me to tell him every detail of the negotiations. He inspected the scrolls that were going to be presented to the Senate.

"Good work, son," he remarked, nodding with approval. "You have done well. Did you enjoy the trip?"

"It was beautiful there, Father."

"Yes, and a very important country for Rome to have access to for strategic purposes."

"I understand that. Will any harm come to this island or to its residents?"

"No one can predict what will be. The Sicilians are better off with the Roman soldiers on their shores, especially if they are invaded by sea."

"I hope there is no war there."

"You really liked the place! What is this I see? You are flushed! What is going on, son?"

"It has been a long journey, and I have worked hard. I need rest. That is all."

My father excused me, and I went to my suite of rooms to rest. Yulanna Carlotta's face, her voice, her figure were always in my heart and mind. My chums at school had talked about being lovesick. I thought this must be what I was experiencing, for I wasn't hungry, didn't want to see anyone, and did not leave my area of the villa for over a day.

Finally, my mother came to me.

"You are not well, Alger," she said, feeling my brow. "I believe you have brought an illness from this foreign land."

My father presented the scrolls I had prepared to the Senate and arranged sick leave for me. I lay delirious with fever for nearly a week. My mother sat with me much of the time. On the seventh day, my fever broke and I sat up in bed with some clarity of mind. My mother brought me hot broth and smiled, seeing I was better.

"Who is Yulanna Carlotta?" she asked, sitting next to me, then checking my forehead and cheeks with her hand.

She saw my surprised look and continued, "You murmured her name while you were down with fever. You even called it out once while I was sitting by you. Who is she?"

"The Princess of Sicilia."

"You met her?"

"Very briefly, mother. Yet there was a strong connection."

"There must have been. Tell me about her."

I proceeded to relate to my mother all there was to tell. I even included some of my reactions and feelings. She nodded and smiled a little as she listened. Later that day my father paid me a visit.

"You are looking much better, my son. Your mother was quite worried when your fever was high. Ah, but you are young and strong. I have good news. The Senate approved the agreement with Sicilia. Your hard work is much appreciated by all involved."

He hesitated, shifting in his seat by my bed. "I wish to ask you about a more delicate matter . . . er . . . the King's daughter."

My heart began racing, and I could feel a flush of warmth move up my body, reddening my face. My father noticed.

"You are of marriageable age, Alger. Up until now, you have focused on your studies and your military training. It is time you considered taking a wife."

Now it was my turn to shift uncomfortably.

"If it were possible to interest the King in betrothing his eldest daughter to you, would you be interested?"

My eyes grew wide. I couldn't speak. I thought my heart would jump out of my body and race away. My father stood up and began pacing as he talked.

"The agreement between Sicilia and Roma is a fragile one. The King has made a solid alliance with all the Lords in his island kingdom. They could amass enough troops between them to keep us from setting up our strategic outposts."

"They have agreed to let Roma do this."

"On those scrolls, son, yes. Word has it that this does not mean much to the King and his company of Lords. Roma cannot be distracted by skirmishes with Sicilia. It is much better if this island is absorbed into the Roman fold in a non-combative way. It is my feeling that if the King's daughter was married to a Roman of high rank and lived in Rome, there would be much less contention and more trust between Roma and Sicilia."

I was starting to see the picture and was overwhelmed. It was possible that political maneuvering could bring Yulanna Carlotta straight into my arms.

"Would you be willing to pursue such a match?" my father asked with a half-smile on his face.

"As long as it is Yulanna Carlotta, the King's eldest daughter. She is the one, Father."

"Very well," he nodded. "I shall proceed."

"Can I help? Should I not talk to her or at least to her father?"

"Not right now. Let me go through formal channels first. I will let you know if you can aid in this matter." He strode off with a bounce in his step.

Things changed for me almost immediately. I was transferred from the General's entourage to the Senate chambers and was made Second Scribe. My duties mostly involved copying scrolls though I also spent time learning the elaborate filing system.

About a month later, my father came to me and asked me to write a letter professing my affection for the King's daughter. This was to be delivered with an official decree of peace between Roma and Sicilia. I set to work right away on the missive. It took me many long hours, for I wanted it to be perfect.

When it was done, I was pleased. I especially liked the section where I asked the King to show his daughter the letter so that she would know the depths of my passion.

Then came the months of waiting. I asked every other day about word from Sicilia, but none came. I became downhearted. Finally, four full months after I had written the letter to the King came the reply. It was very official-looking with the royal seal on it. I trembled as I opened it. My family was with me. I took a deep breath as my future was on this scroll.

The King said no. He said his daughter was too young to leave her home and live in the big city of Rome. I was broken-hearted. My father sat me down and reminded me that perhaps the ruler had said no for other reasons, political reasons that were not mentioned in the reply.

"Son, do you really care for this woman?"

"No person, woman or man, has ever affected me the way Yulanna Carlotta has," I said firmly, almost shouting the words.

My father was silent for a few moments. Then he said, "Let me see what I can do."

During the following months, I threw myself into my work. I thought of Yulanna Carlotta every day, mostly at sunrise as I was preparing for my daily duties. On the anniversary of my voyage to Sicilia, I went to my father and told him that my love for the Princess had grown. I asked permission to write again to the King. He did not give it right away. My interest in the King's daughter was a political matter as far as the Senate was concerned. For me, it was all about love.

Two days later, my father sat with me and asked me what I would do if the situation with Yulanna Carlotta did not work out. I had been thinking about this constantly.

"I will move to Sicilia. I will live there and court her. Even if she will not have me, at least I will be near her."

Seeing it was hopeless, my father sighed. He and my mother had hosted several social events for my benefit over the last few months. They had invited the best families in Rome, especially those with eligible daughters. I enjoyed these events and the light social interaction although nothing happened that compared to what I had experienced during that short exchange with Yulanna Carlotta. How could I think about taking another wife when no one moved me as deeply as she? I was committed to the Princess and was willing to leave my home, my family, my position as second Scribe—all for her.

Father put his hand on my shoulder, "Write your letter, son—this time to the Princess. Tell her how you feel. Let's hope the Queen sees it."

So I wrote. I was good at letters, for I had written many for the General and the members of the Senate. This one took me longer than any other I had penned because it had to be absolutely perfect. It had to bring Yulanna Carlotta to me.

After many tries, I decided a simple, straightforward, honest approach was best.

I wrote:

Dear Princess Yulanna Carlotta,

> *You have been in my heart and my mind since the morning we met on the verandah of your home. My affection for you has grown stronger with the passing months. You are the only one I wish to spend my life with. I wish to marry you, and I will wait patiently until you are ready. I can promise you devotion, fidelity, and deep and abiding love. My position in Rome is such that I can offer you all the comforts you now have and more. I will care for you, love you, and cherish you all the days that I live and beyond. Please take these words to heart and say you will become my wife.*

With sincerity and affection,

Alger Matticus,
Second Scribe to the Roman Senate

When finished, I held the letter over my heart and radiated as much love as I could into it. One day soon it would be in Yulanna Carlotta's hands.

Once the letter was sent, it was difficult for me not to imagine what might be taking place. I found myself indulging in endless fantasies, especially as I sat in the Senate Chambers when the debates were tedious and boring. I held much hope in my heart that the connection I felt with Yulanna Carlotta was mutual.

Of course, looking at the situation from the spirit side as I was reading in The Great Book of Lifetimes, Yulanna Carlotta and I were soul mates. The bonds between us were deep and transcended the boundaries of one Earth incarnation.

According to the book, Yulanna Carlotta dreamed of me, fantasized about seeing me again, and even drew pictures of me. We were connecting on a soul level even though we were at a distance on the Earth plane.

The first letter I wrote to the King never reached her. Her father saw it as a political ploy and discussed it with his Council of Lords but not with Yulanna Carlotta. He did not even mention it to the Queen until much later. By that time, the refusal had already been sent.

The Queen decided to withhold telling her eldest daughter about my first letter and instead talked to the King.

"Yulanna Carlotta has confided that she loves this young Roman," she told her husband.

The ruler paced, his girth shaking, and bellowed, "What's done is done! I cannot go back on what I have decided. It would make me look weak."

"What about your daughter's happiness?"

"She will get over it."

"She hasn't yet. I doubt she ever will. Have you considered that this pairing might be right? Perhaps they are fated to be together."

"Fate, bah! It's all political posturing on the part of the Romans."

"I don't think so, dear. I think the boy is sincere."

"Too late now, Mother. That's my final word."

"Let's compromise. We will let it stand for now. If another opportunity comes to unite these two young people, let's consider it."

My second letter was addressed to the Princess herself. It was given to the King first, who opened it in the presence of the Queen. He sighed.

"Well, Mother, you were right. This boy seems very sincere. He certainly is persistent."

"This letter beautifully written. Tell me, wouldn't you be proud to have such a man become your son?"

The King shrugged.

"This letter is meant for Yulanna Carlotta," said the Queen, "and I am going to give it to her."

"Then you two will write to this Roman, and there will be no stopping this! I must confer with my Council of Lords first."

"You will do no such thing! This may be a matter of state to you, but it is a matter of the heart to these young people, and I intend to honor that."

"But we cannot ignore the political ramifications, Mother. They are great indeed."

"If fate means for these two to be united, then fate means for us to befriend the Romans. That is how I see it." And off went the Queen with my letter to Yulanna Carlotta.

The book then tenderly described the scene in Yulanna Carlotta's bedroom when the Queen handed the young woman my letter. She read it and clasped it to her heart, just as I had done before I sent it. Joyful tears overflowed her dark eyes.

Her smile was wide as she murmured, "Alger! It was meant to be!"

The King was right. There was no stopping our union now. Yulanna Carlotta went to see her father soon after reading my missive.

The King embraced his daughter with a sadness that only a father feels when losing his eldest child as he stated, "There is much to consider, Yulanna Carlotta. However, I will do what I can to clear the way for you and Alger."

And so it was. The answer from the King was written and sent.

It said:

The King of Sicilia is pleased to grant Alger Matticus, Scribe and Scholar, permission to wed his eldest daughter Yulanna Carlotta. The messenger who carries this letter has been briefed as to the wishes of our family and has been given the authority to meet with the family of Matticus to make the arrangements for the wedding.

There was a warm breeze blowing from the south on the day I received this joyous news. I read the letter several times before totally grasping its meaning. Then I felt as if I were levitating off the ground. My heart thumped wildly, and I let out a yell because I could not contain the joy I felt.

The messenger, a very formal man with gray hair and a mustache, stepped back so as not to be injured as I spun around wildly, waving my arms in delight. Tears of joy ran down my cheeks as I threw my arms around the man who was trying to maintain his composure.

The wedding was planned, and we were married in Roma with much pomp and ceremony. Because Yulanna Carlotta was going to be wed on foreign shores, her father insisted on many things. He drew up his demands on scroll after scroll and sent messenger after messenger to our villa. My mother got to the point where she rolled her eyes every time a new message from the King arrived.

At first, both the King and the Queen were going to accompany their daughter to Rome for the wedding, but that changed. I later learned from my wife that the King had dreamed that he was assassinated en route, and he took that as a sign not to go. Instead, he insisted that Yulanna Carlotta have the most splendid procession Rome had ever seen. The entire journey from the ship into the city was to be a parade in honor of our union. The King spared no expense.

This was the first time I had seen Yulanna Carlotta since our brief meetings well over a year before. I was seated with my family and members of the Senate in a spacious balcony overlooking the parade route. The book did not describe this, but I remembered how restless and anxious I felt. It was difficult for me to sit still and wait for the procession to reach the city. As the groom I was duty-bound to be in the seat of honor. Otherwise, I would have run out from the city to greet my beloved Yulanna Carlotta.

It was a bright sunny day. Word came that the ship had docked the previous evening. We expected the arrival of the

Princess and her entourage at midday. Indeed, just as the sun was at its height, I heard the sound of several conch shells being blown. The sounds overlapped to make ebbing and surging tones, much like the surf.

My heart galloped up into my throat as I saw blinding flashes coming from the direction of the procession. First came many soldiers marching in line. There were Roman soldiers escorting the Princess and Sicilian soldiers protecting her. Then came Yulanna Carlotta's attendants dressed in their finest garb and holding baskets filled with flowers, which they distributed to the onlookers.

My eyes grew wide. The rumors were true. There was a giant beast in the procession, an elephant decorated with colorful cloth and jewels. A dark-skinned man rode the beast and threw coins to the crowd. More soldiers and more attendants came by, and then finally I saw my wife-to-be.

The sight blinded me. She wore a gown that was covered with small discs that reflected light, so that she appeared as a shining goddess. She was riding in an elaborately decorated open cart drawn by four handsome steeds and was surrounded with flowers. All this was incredibly spectacular.

The citizens of Rome were awed by this display. Personally, I would have preferred that the Princess arrive quietly and that our first meeting on Roman soil be private. This was not possible, and I knew it. Our marriage represented the friendly alliance of neighboring states, and as such, it had to be properly celebrated.

The wedding took place in the great open hall that led to the Senate Chamber. The citizens of Rome crowded onto the steps and peered around the pillars as the Magistrate went through the formalities needed to make us officially husband and wife.

I could not take my eyes off the lovely woman standing beside me. She didn't need the sparkling reflecting gown, for she had natural radiance and beauty. Her long hair was braided and wound around her head like a crown and jewels had been placed in the braids. Her gown shimmered with many rainbow colors, but her eyes moved me the most. I looked into them as the Magistrate's voice droned on, and again I had that feeling of falling off a cliff.

She smiled shyly, and I knew my cheeks were becoming red. We were so lost in looking at each other that we had to be told twice to hold hands.

I cannot accurately describe the feelings I experienced when I first touched her hand. A whirlwind tore through me, and I heard a whooshing sound in my ears. The echoes of our many lifetimes together resounded in our hearts. Deep in my Soul I felt that she and I were being reunited, and indeed we were.

∞   ∞   ∞

Our marriage faced its share of challenges. Dear Yulanna Carlotta was always a little homesick. She missed her walks by the sea, so we journeyed often to the shore.

Our first child was born a year to the day after our marriage. He was healthy and had Yulanna Carlotta's eyes. Her second pregnancy was complicated by a fever, and that child was stillborn.

The heartbreak we both felt was tremendous, so to help her heal, I took my wife and our young son back to Sicily for a visit. There she recovered her strength and her love of life though it was difficult for her when it came time to return to Rome.

We had two more children, both girls. I eventually became a Senator and sometimes became entangled in the politics of the time. I could always count on Yulanna Carlotta to have a level head and impeccable intuition when it came to making choices, whether they were domestic or professional.

Our life was rich. Our children gave us both challenges and joy. We lived to be elders and advisors. Yulanna Carlotta even taught the young women of the city some of her knowledge of plants and gardening.

The book then went on to tell of a scenario that moved the very essence of my Soul. There we were: two respected elders with our children grown. Yulanna Carlotta caught a chill while out in damp weather showing a young friend how to water leeks while transplanting them. I could see she was not well, so I brought hot broth to warm her, and I held her as she drank it.

Looking up at me she said quietly, "Alger, you know there is more than this."

I did not understand at first. "More?"

"Our union—it does not stop when our bodies do. We will meet again somewhere, sometime."

"Hush, now. No talk of dying."

"I love you, my dear husband. I think I loved you before that moment on the verandah when I looked into your eyes. My Soul loves your Soul."

I responded in a whisper, "My love for you is deeper than the oceans and will last longer than all time."

She smiled and closed her eyes. I held her all night long. Her Soul passed at sunrise at the very moment of the day when we had first met. I wept openly, but I could feel her love surrounding me. I held her for hours before I called the servants. I did not want to let her go—my Angel, my dear Angel.

I was so absorbed in reading this that I had been transported to that moment in my past life. Therefore, I was taken aback when suddenly all the words disappeared from the pages of The Great Book. I closed my eyes and sat there. I knew I was supposed to stand and view the screen, but I was overcome with emotion and couldn't move.

"Look . . . look, Darci," Chalherine's words came into my head. Hearing them prompted me to stand.

The screen glowed, then showed many bright flashing colors. Two figures became clear as the flickering subsided. There we stood, Angel and me as Yulanna Carlotta and Alger. We appeared there just as we were in our prime as husband and wife. The two images on the screen turned, looked at one another, and embraced. Then the female figure collapsed into the arms of the man. I gasped as I sensed my heart swell. I felt as if I were losing Angel all over again.

The figures on the screen became absorbed into an incredible light show. In the center was a circle of bright red surrounded by a larger ring of brilliant pink. This was pulsing against a backdrop of vertical rays, which danced and flickered. These rays began as a series of blue lights, then changed to luminous gold and white. Next, the vertical rays swirled and became part of the circular pattern so I saw a vibrant red center with a wide ring of deep pink light, then a halo of sparkling gold, then bright white light making the outer ring. Everything on the screen vibrated and glowed.

As the colors on the screen faded, I set about noting every detail of what I had seen. I tried to describe every phase, every aspect of how the pictures on the screen had changed. It was a good exercise for me because it kept me from being overcome with emotion and immobilized. Reliving that incarnation in Rome had a powerful effect on me. My feelings had been surging so strongly that I was exhausted.

There was no place to lie down in the viewing room, so I rested as best I could in the reading chair. Images of my lifetime in Rome kept passing through my mind. More and more details emerged. I could tell that I was beginning to connect fully with my own memories of this lifetime.

"Take heart, Darci. You two shall be reunited," Chalherine's voice came from above. I looked up and saw her floating near the ceiling. She glided down and stood next to me, putting her hands on my shoulder.

"You need time to assimilate this experience. Would you like to return to your chamber to rest?"

I sighed. "I probably need to— but I want to keep this book. It is my link to Angel and all that we have shared."

Chalherine smiled and put her hands on my head. This soothed me and I felt lighter.

"It is true that from the standpoint of the Guides, Master Guides, and Angels, your bonds with the Soul called Angel are some of the strongest that exist between Beings. Yours is a love story known to many. That is why we teachers decided to employ your memories and your strong connection to Angel as tools to help you learn. Right now the lesson is seeing energy fields."

"That's what I was viewing on the screen, right? My energy field?"

"Yes. Notice how different it appeared after your first reading, then after your second."

"Very different."

"The screen was reflecting your energy field as it is now, so you see how much it changed from one reading to the next."

"I do."

"When a Spirit Guide watches over a human, reading that human's energy pattern is the best way to access how that individual is doing. You can see emotions, stress, illness, even unresolved karma in the energy field."

"What was the red glow in the center of my energy pattern?"

"Passionate love, Darci. The pink is devotion and compassionate love."

"There is so much to learn."

"Rest is what you need, Mr. Stillwater. Do not be concerned. I will reserve this room for you and take good care of this book. Follow me."

She picked up The Great Book of Lifetimes and floated out the door, which opened automatically as she approached it.

I stayed close behind her. I tried to memorize the route back to my chamber, but it was full of turns. We seemed to be going up as well. Once back in the chamber, I asked Chalherine the one question I really wanted answered.

"Where is Angel now? Why can't I see her?"

"She is immersed in an experience. She is focused on what she needs to do right now and doesn't have time to do anything else. Send her love, Darci, for she needs it. Know that she will receive it though she probably won't connect it with you right now."

"Why not if we are so bonded?"

"Because where she is, she has blinders on. That is to say, she can only see aspects of her present circumstance. It is the same when any Soul enters a human body. Nothing is remembered of the lifetimes and experiences that came before."

"So she will receive my love. Will this help her?"

"Yes, love always helps. Now rest. Take your time. One of us will fetch you when it is time for you to continue your studies." She disappeared, leaving a luminescent mist that lingered for a short while.

∞ ∞ ∞

I did as she suggested and stretched out to rest. I wondered if I would need so much recuperation time once I was a true Spirit Guide. My rest was deep, but not without passing images from the lifetime in Rome. It seemed that once again reading The Great Book of Lifetimes opened the door to my own memories. Perhaps I could better phrase this. Reading the book opened the floodgates. Memories poured into my mind, bringing feelings of elation. I opened my eyes slightly and noticed a pink glow around me.

As I lay there, I recalled what Chalherine had said, that no matter where Angel was, no matter what she was doing, I could send her love and this would help her. So I took my blissful emotions and visualized putting them in a sphere of pink light. I also radiated much love into this sparkling pink sphere until the image was brilliant and luminous in my mind.

I then said, "Please take this gift of love to my dear Angel wherever she is. May it lift her spirits. May it help her no matter what she is doing. May she know deep in her Soul that I am here and that I care about and love her."

Once I sent this off to Angel with a prayer in my heart, I rested well.

∞ ∞ ∞

My next visitor was the unusual-looking androgynous Guide, Hespahba. He/she once again was hovering near the ceiling, this time singing with an angelic voice:

Love abounds. Love meanders
Through all lifetimes far and near.
Bonds of Love, Soul Connectors,
Blissful ties bring deep Love here.

The tutor floated down to sit next to me. He/she scanned me, then sat back and nodded.

"You are remembering her now."

"Angel?"

"I can see by your energy field. It is saturated with love."

"Yes, I feel it. This is not enough, Hespahba! I want to see Angel now. I want to know where she is. I want to help her."

For the first time, I saw real compassion in the tutor's eyes.

"I do understand your desire. It would do neither of you any good to unite you too soon. The circumstances must be just right."

"May I look in on her?"

"Then you will want to help her."

"What's wrong with that?"

"Angel, like all Souls, needs certain experiences. If you interrupt her flow, she may not learn important lessons that will enable her to move on."

"I wish only to help her."

"Then continue your studies. Be happy. At least you can enjoy reading about your many lives together."

"I guess. I wish I could do more."

"We can add another step to your current exercise. You must begin seeing energy fields without the assistance of the screen. The screen is only a tool to help you. You need to do this on your own."

"If only I could see Angel now, I could read her energy patterns. I know I could."

"That may be, yet it is not possible to set that up right now."

I didn't push the Guide further on this, though I made a promise to myself that I would persevere and find my way to wherever my dear Angel was. I realized the tutor could read my thoughts.

"Be that as it may, Darci, let's continue with the lesson. I am going to take you back to the room with the screen. Continue as you have been doing with one added step. After you read, view the screen and make notes, sit in the dim light and try to see the energy patterns on your own. You were beginning to do so after your last round of reading."

"I did see a pink glow around me. It disappeared."

"No it didn't. Your ability to see it is what vanished."

"Do you have any tips or instructions that would help?"

"After making your notes, go into meditation and remember to breathe deeply. That restful yet fully conscious state is the best place to begin viewing energy fields. Come, let's go. I have another student who needs attention."

Hespahba literally flew to the door of my study chamber. I was a bit slower, so the tutor waited for me just outside.

The viewing room seemed larger to me, and I wondered if it was the same place. The Great Book was on the reading stand, and all seemed ready. Hespahba did one last thing. The Guide put one hand on my back and one hand on the back of my head. Then the tutor pushed up with the higher hand and down with the lower hand. I felt a strange, very rapid vibration running through my spirit body. I turned around to ask my tutor about this, but Hespahba was gone.

One deep breath later, the room was activated as the lights dimmed.

I began by letting the screen scan my energy field. My aura was light pink with vertical blue rays. I noted this down in the ledger and opened The Great Book of Lifetimes. The pages were tinted blue this time.

To my surprise, the setting was ancient Mongolia. This was a part of the Earth that I thought I knew very little about. I was soon to think differently.

I saw myself tall, assured, and dressed in a red robe with gold trim. As a traveler and a trader, I had employed several young men to shift the goods and pull the cart with the merchandise. The wooden pallet on wheels served as a mobile store.

Goods would be piled high upon entering a village. The residents would gather around and pick through what I brought, choosing what they wished and paying me or trading with me. Payment came in many forms, and sometimes the cart would also be piled high with different items upon leaving a village.

One chilly, blustery day I was on the road with two of my employees when we were suddenly surrounded by a band of thieves. There were at least a dozen tattered, dirty robbers, some with soiled cloths tied over their faces for disguise. We could not fight our way out of it, so I tried to bargain with them.

The leader of the gang laughed, "Why should we barter when we can easily take all you have?"

As the leader taunted me, my two assistants without a signal from me drew their swords and began to fight. The skirmish didn't last long. I barely had my own sword drawn when I saw that both of my men had been slain. They had injured only one of the robbers, the small one with the slight build. At sword point, the gang absconded with my cart of goods, and I was left alone. They even took my sword.

I wandered in the direction of the nearest village, downhearted and a little shaken but unhurt. Suddenly I began seeing drops of blood on the path, then heard muffled whimpering sounds. Around a steep corner, I found the injured robber by the roadside.

Something urged me to draw closer. I was cautious, for the thief might still be armed. I stood over the frail form. There was no weapon. The soft sobs sounded like those of a female. I used my foot to roll the wounded body over and gasped. There lay a beautiful young woman dressed in men's clothes. She was dirty . . . injured . . . scared. Even though she had been one of the gang that had robbed me, my heart went out to her.

"They abandoned me," she sobbed. "I cannot walk."

I saw that her thigh was bleeding. The wound had not been cared for at all as the robbers were in a hurry to move on. She was suffering. I could not let her lie there and die. Besides, I felt attracted to and almost mesmerized by this young woman.

Of course, as I was reading this, I knew that our Soul to Soul connection was drawing me closer to the wounded female. It was Angel.

Night was approaching. I located a sheltered spot by a small waterfall that was not too far from the trail and carried the woman to it. She was weak and limp and did not protest. Perhaps she, too, felt the soul connection between us.

The wound was deep. I shredded the bottom of my robe to make a bandage to stop the bleeding. I made a nest of leaves and laid her in it. She was unconscious now.

I had no food, but I did have two bags of tea in my pocket that the thieves hadn't found. Although I had access to water, I had no way to heat it, so in the twilight, I walked along the running stream. Luck was with us, or perhaps our Spirit Guides were helping. I found an old metal bowl that someone had left by the brook. I kept bits of flint in my shoe, so before long had a small fire going with water boiling for tea.

I propped up the young woman to get her to drink some hot liquid. She was delirious. After a few sips though, she seemed to focus more. Then she drank the tea as if she hadn't had anything in her stomach for days, which may very well have been the case. She looked up at me with thankful eyes.

"Good," she said between sips. Once she had drunk her fill, she handed the bowl to me, wincing as she moved.

"That injury is serious," I said to her. "I do not think you can travel."

"That is why the others left me," she said, looking so forlorn. "Why do you help me? We robbed you of everything. Why did you not leave me to die?"

I had no answer.

"I could not," I said and left it at that.

I helped her move nearer to the fire. In the light from the flames, I unwrapped her wound and examined it more closely.

"I am going to try to clean this," I told her. "Now that we have some boiled water, I want to wash this and rebind it."

Her lower lip trembled as she replied, "You are so kind to me. I know not what to say but thank you, compassionate stranger."

I didn't sleep that night—just sat and kept the fire going, thinking all the while about what had happened. Watching the young woman sleep, I pondered what to do. I had lost my livelihood and taken on an injured woman. I marveled over how much my life had changed in one day.

Just after dawn, I heard a caravan on the trail not far from where we were. I climbed up onto a rock to see if the oncomers were friendly and was relieved to recognize one of the men at the front of the group of travelers. He was a hired guard. Those who wished to travel long distances often paid such men to protect them for the length of their journey. I climbed down and approached them, my hand raised.

"Jin Ya!" I greeted my acquaintance.

"Mihlo!" he replied, walking over to me as the others kept going. "Mihlo, what has happened to you?"

"A gang of robbers killed my men and took everything I had."

"Join us. We will get you safely to the next village, or you can go with us all the way to Chunduh."

"I cannot although your offer is appreciated. I have a wounded woman with me. We need food. Can you spare any?"

"A woman? Have you taken a wife since we last saw each other?"

"No, no. It is a long story. She cannot walk. Her wound is serious."

At that moment Jin Ya put up his hand as a signal to stop the caravan. He turned and talked with a gentleman who was well-dressed and seemed to be the head of this group of travelers.

"I am escorting this family to their new home in Chunduh. There is room in one of the carts to lay this injured woman. We can at least get you to the next village where you will have food and shelter."

I thanked him and the head of the traveling family. It took me a few minutes to put out the fire and carry the young woman back to the trail. Fever had her in its grip, and she was incoherent.

For part of the trip, I walked with my friend Jin Ya. The rest of the time I sat in the cart with the wounded woman. She reached out and touched my hand. I took hers and held it. As we were jounced and jostled over the rough road, I began to feel strangely connected to this woman. Fate had brought us together in a most unusual way.

We reached the nearest village by nightfall. The caravan camped just beyond the town. I knew this place. It was on my usual trade route, so I visited twice a year.

There was a modest common house, a place where people came together for meetings, celebrations, and ceremonies. Since this was a small village with no inn for travelers, I asked one of the town leaders if I could stay in the common house as I had done before. Once he agreed, I asked about the whereabouts of a medicine person. He said there wasn't one, but that there was an elder who knew about herbs and healing.

Jin Ya had been generous. He had left me with a large parcel of food, a robe, and some blankets. I gave thanks for his kindness. Once I had the wounded woman settled in the corner of the common house near the fire, I went to fetch the elder I had been told about. I was very concerned about the young woman. I did not want her to die.

The elder was an odd old woman who had long white hair tied back with a twist of vine. I saw a sparkle in her eyes as I told her how worried I was about the woman.

"Your wife?"

"No."

"Your sweetheart then?"

"I don't even know her name. I came upon her by the roadside and could not leave her there to die."

I did not say that she had been one of the gang who had robbed me. That didn't seem to matter anymore.

The old woman began by bathing the poor young woman's face and neck with cool water to help ease the fever. I watched as she worked. As the dirt and blood were washed away from the woman's face, her natural beauty shone through. My heart surged as a chord of recognition was struck deep inside me. My Soul was stirred by hers.

Then the elder carefully undid the bandage I had put on and used a tea made from pungent herbs to clean the gash. The young woman shuddered and shivered. I tried to comfort her by holding her hand and by gently rubbing her arm.

"This is bad," said the old woman. "Goes to the bone. Nothing broken, but this will take a long time to heal if she does not die of fever first." The gash was swollen and an angry red color, contrasting with her pale skin.

"I need more herbs," said the elder. "Go! Go fetch them. I will clean her, change her clothes. These dirty rags she is wearing are not helping."

Following the old woman's directions to her home, I collected several bunches of herbs that were hanging near her door as she had instructed me. When I returned to the common house, I stood in shock. The young woman was lying completely naked as the old one carefully bathed her. I was a young man, well-traveled, but I had never seen the entire body of a woman unclothed. She was beautiful. She still had gentle curves although she was quite thin from scrounging for food day to day as she roved with that gang of bandits. She had some bruises, too, on her upper arms.

"This one was mistreated," said the elder, "and went hungry a lot. She's better off now. You will not hurt her."

I looked on as the old woman whispered to the young one to turn onto her side so that the bathing could continue. I was caught up in watching this when the elder hissed at me.

"You want to help her? Don't just sit there gawking. Shred those herbs. Put them in here." She pointed to a pot nearby.

"We get her to drink some—maybe the fever will come down."

As I broke up pieces of bark and crumbled leaves, I couldn't take my eyes off the young woman. I found myself wanting to touch her and was surprised at my arousal.

Once the brew was ready, I held up her head as the elder tried to get her to drink some of the potion. We were not too successful at first, for the woman was semi-conscious.

"Come now," I encouraged her. "I want you to live. Drink, please."

My words seemed to help, and she began taking the liquid.

The old woman nodded and said, "Good. She listens to you."

We wrapped the injured one in blankets. I offered some of the food I had been given to the old woman to thank her.

"I'll take some millet, my favorite, and not easily gotten here."

I gave her the satchel of grain.

139

"I will go now. You watch her. Give her more broth in a while. Keep her brow cool with water. I will return tomorrow to redress the wound."

Even though I was very tired, for I hadn't really slept since the robbery, I sat with the young woman all night. After successfully getting her to sip some herbal broth, I allowed myself to nod into a dreamlike state.

I'm not sure if it was a vision or a dream. I saw a golden light around this woman. She sat up, shining brilliantly, then stood and walked over to me. She placed her glowing hands on my face, and I felt a rush of love.

"You are kind and compassionate," said the vision. "You have helped a stranger who has turned out to be your Angel."

She then hugged me and her light surrounded me. Feeling ecstatic, I stood to fully embrace her.

At that point, I fell from my seated position, which jarred me awake. I shook my head to clear it.

The dream was strong. I looked at the sleeping woman, and in the pre-dawn light, there was a golden glow around her. I rubbed my eyes. It was definitely there. I cooled her brow again, then lay down, putting my arms around her. As that young man in that place and time, I did not know what the vision meant. I did know that this woman was special to me, that our meeting was no accident.

The first rays of sun woke me. I scrambled up to prod the fire to life. I wanted to have hot water ready for the old woman's arrival. The injured one was still burning with fever, so I tried to cool her down by mopping her brow. The elder arrived with more bark and more herbs. She set about making medicine while I applied cool cloths to the young woman's head.

"Not enough," said the old one. "Take the blankets away. Cool the whole body."

My hands trembled as I unwrapped her, revealing her beautiful body. I quickly set about cooling her neck, arms, and torso so that the old woman wouldn't shout at me for gawking.

"Will she live?" I asked the elder, remembering my vision.

"Don't know. Another day, maybe two, we'll know. Can you stay and care for her?"

"I have nothing else at all in my life to do," I answered, realizing once again how much my life had changed in just one day.

During that entire day I stayed by the side of that young woman. I did not think she would survive to see the sunset. She burned with fever. Every once in a while she opened her eyes, and I could see they were glassy and unfocused. She cried out a few times, almost as if she were being attacked or tortured. I tried to comfort her with words and by holding her hand. I continued to tend her as the elder had shown me.

I will not say that I took pleasure in running a cool cloth over her body, but the task was not at all unpleasant. As I cooled her neck, I wondered why I had not thought about taking a wife.

There were a few girls I had fancied back in my village when I was a boy. Once I began traveling and became a merchant, I had no home of my own and no need or desire for a wife. I met many women in my travels but interacted with them only briefly. Some of the boys I hired to help me would romance the village women as we passed through town, but a one-night, one-time experience never appealed to me. Now that all my merchandise and my cart had been stolen, perhaps it was time to consider another way of life.

By the time the old woman returned that night, I had memorized every mark, every curve, and every angle of that young woman's body. I was mystified by a lopsided X mark on the back of her right leg. I showed it to the elder.

"Is this a birthmark?"

"Don't think so. She's been branded."

"Branded?"

"Mark made with hot metal. Psssssssss! Burned into the skin."

"That's horrible! Who would do that to such a beautiful girl?"

"Mark means she belongs to somebody or some gang maybe. Outlaws sometimes do that to a new member. I've seen it before."

As I cooled her torso, I wondered how she had become mixed up with those bandits. I wanted to hear her tell me. I wanted her to wake up.

The old woman looked at me, saying, "You do a good job. If she lives, she has you to thank."

The elder had prepared me some food. She told me to sleep, and she would tend the injured one. I was hungry and exhausted, so I ate and slept.

My dreams were vivid and unsettling. In one, I was on the trail once again facing robbers. In another, I was a boy back in my village, taking a little girl as a wife. The third dream was heart-wrenching for in it I held this beautiful young woman as her Soul passed from her body. She died in my arms. I awoke from this dream with a start and sat up.

"Is she dead?"

"On the contrary," said the elder. "I believe the fever has broken. The wound looks better, too. She'll sleep for a while yet."

On the evening of the second day a full moon hung in the sky. With the patient sleeping comfortably, I stretched my legs a bit by walking around the village. When I returned, the elder was gone, and the young woman was lying propped up on one arm, looking dazed but awake.

"Where am I?" she asked as I entered.

I moved quickly to her side and looked into her eyes. They were clear, not glassy as before. I felt her brow. The fever had gone.

"Who are you?" she asked.

"Don't you remember? I found you by the roadside. I've been caring for you for three days."

"Three days? No, I don't remember. We had set up an ambush for a wealthy merchant. There was a fight. I was cut and couldn't walk."

Then her expression clouded, and she mumbled, "They left me."

"They left you, but I found you. What is your name?"

"What do you want with me?" she asked, pulling back.

"Nothing. I've been caring for you with the help of an old woman from the village."

"I don't know you."

"Obviously I will not harm you."

She seemed to relax a little bit but didn't say any more. At that moment, the elder arrived with hot porridge made from the millet I had given her.

"Thought you might be awake. Good. The full moon brings you back."

The old one looked at me and said, "You . . . Shoo! Go look at moonlight on the pond. I'll feed her."

So I left. After days of doing nothing but caring for this injured woman, I thought I'd receive some thanks, but she was almost hostile. I stared at the ripples on the village pond. The water seemed alive in the moonlight. The current moved like molten gold.

Feeling lost, I sighed. I knew I had to begin my life over but wasn't sure where to start. I had entertained the thought that the new beginning might be with this woman, but now I didn't know if this was even a remote possibility.

When I returned, the young woman was sitting wrapped in a blanket. She had a rosy look about her, and she smiled just a little.

The old woman shoved a bowl of porridge into my hands and said, "Some for you, too. Eat. Talk. I'll go now." And off she went with her funny hobbled walk.

Saying nothing, I sat and began eating. The woman watched me. She was looking me over as if she were seeing me for the first time.

Finally she spoke, "The old one told me what you did for me. Part of me is grateful. Part of me wishes you had left me there to die."

I put down the bowl and asked in confusion, "Why? You are young and beautiful."

"I am marked! I belong to a . . ." Her voice trailed off.

"A gang of robbers," I finished her sentence.

Her eyes grew wide. "How did you know? Did you see the mark?"

"Yes. Then the old woman told me what it meant. But you no longer belong to them or anyone. They left you to die. You are free to do as you wish."

The woman's eyes filled with tears as she answered, "Free? So free I have nothing. Where shall I go? What shall I do? No one will want a marked woman."

I came over and sat beside her. With two fingers I touched her chin and raised her face towards mine.

"I, too, have nothing," I said. "I, too, have nowhere to go. I would be honored to have you join me wherever we go from here."

"But the mark."

"It means nothing to me."

She sat silent for a while.

Feeling my heart pounding, I wondered if hers was doing the same.

"I am Soliya. Who are you? Why are you here with no place to go?"

"Mihlo, at your service," I responded, bowing a little and smiling. "I am the merchant that your gang of thieves robbed."

She gasped and drew back from me.

I waved my hand, saying, "I will not hurt you. You have already suffered so much."

She came closer and said in a whisper, "You must be an extraordinary man. Such a man I never met."

"I am a normal man. If I am extraordinary, then it was finding you that made me so."

We talked the whole night until dawn. She told me of her childhood and her parents' death. At age fourteen she and her older brother left their home and set out to find a better life. At one point in their travels, they were confronted by a bunch of ruffians and beaten. Their few possessions had been taken. Soliya was heart-broken because the thugs took a bracelet that had belonged to her mother. Her brother befriended some men in the next town. They were rivals of the ruffians who had attacked Soliya and himself, so he made an alliance with them.

"My brother knew that this gang he had befriended was larger and more ruthless, so he thought they could attack the others and reclaim our treasures, especially Mama's bracelet. That isn't what happened. They forced us to work for them. We slaved—doing everything, cooking, washing and mending, even bathing them. My brother protected me from the others in this gang.

Soon though, he joined their ranks as a thief. He convinced me to learn to use a sword so that I could come with them as they roved the highways looking for wealthy travelers to rob. He gave me lessons in sword play, including how to stay light on my feet and how to kill. The others in the gang laughed at me until I defeated one of their best swordsmen. I used a trick my brother taught me. I tripped him."

She giggled. It was wonderful to see the spark in her eyes. Then her face became serious.

"Once I had this man on the ground with my sword at his throat, the leader grabbed me. They held me down and marked me with a hot iron from the fire. I became one of them. Times were hard. We often had no food. Then sometimes we would rob a caravan and have too much to eat so some of it spoiled. It was not the life I wanted, but it was all I had."

Darkness passed over her face as she continued, "My brother was killed two moons ago. We ambushed a caravan that looked unprotected, but the guards were in the rear and fended off the attack. My brother was cut down right on the trail. I could not help him. We were driven off, and he died there."

She cried quietly for a few minutes. I put my hand on hers to offer comfort.

"I miss him. He was my only family."

I nodded for her to go on.

"Without my brother to stand between me and the other gang members, I had to fend for myself. The men knew I was good with my sword, so they were wary, but I was a woman and a desirable target," she said remembering, then shook her head and burst out crying.

Once she had composed herself, she continued, "One of the gang surprised me by the river. I had put my sword down to wash my hands and face. He came up behind me and grabbed my shoulders, forcing me down. I struggled. He held me so hard it hurt. Finally, I kicked him with all my strength right where my brother had shown me. He fell into the water moaning. That was just a few days ago."

"I saw the bruises on your arms."

"You saw? How?"

"I've been caring for you, bathing you," I explained and could feel myself flush as I saw her look down shyly. "I was cooling your body to bring down your fever. The old one showed me how."

She quickly changed the subject. "You saved my life, and now you want us to stay with each other? To start over together?"

"Fate has brought us together and besides . . ." I hesitated, thinking I might sound foolish to her. "I have a sense that we are special to each other. You do not have to decide now. You cannot travel. You must rest and heal."

For one week more we stayed there. Soliya gained strength every day. Several times I visited the elder and did some chores for her. I liked this village and asked Soliya if she wanted to stay. A troubled look came over her face.

"Too close to my old gang. If they knew I was alive, they would kidnap me or kill me. That mark on my leg means I am theirs for life."

"The whole village knows we are here by now. It is no secret," I said.

She looked frightened and responded, "Word will get to the band of thieves; I know it will. They have someone in each village in this area who gives them news. That's how they find out about travelers and caravans."

"Do you know who it is in this town?"

"I've been trying to remember. It may be the wheelsmith. The gang would give him carts and wagons that they stole in exchange for news."

A pang hit my heart. I had been chatting with the wheelsmith the day before, inquiring about a cart for our travels.

"As of yesterday, he knew about you, about us. Are you sure it's him?"

"Yes, I think so. There aren't many villages that have their own wheelsmith. We'd better leave now." She pulled herself up, using the walking stick I had found for her but fell back down.

"We won't get far without a cart," I said, sitting next to her and putting my arms around her. "We are safe here. Your old gang wouldn't raid this village just to find you, would they? Aren't they mostly focused on robbing travelers?"

She sighed and shuddered a little and replied, "They are unpredictable. They do as they wish. We must assume that they know I am here. I am not sure what they will do."

I pulled her close to me and felt her melt in my arms. I kissed her neck and then her face.

"We have just found each other, Soliya. No one, not these robbers, not anyone can part us. We were meant to be together."

"I have never known a man like you. My brother protected me, but you—you saved my life, nursed me, cared for me, bathed me, fed me, tended my wounds. There surely is not another like you anywhere in the land."

We kissed and passion raged through me like an out-of-control fire. She let out a sigh as I held her tight against me.

"Let us ask the elder who in this village can bestow the blessing of marriage upon us. Are you willing? Will you be my wife?"

She dropped her head, answering, "Mihlo, surely you will regret taking a marked woman in marriage."

I held her face in my hands and replied tenderly, "Never, ever will I be sorry for loving you. Please say you will bond with me in marriage."

"Yes. It is what I want, too. Nowhere will I find a finer man."

"Or one who loves you more."

That evening the elder brought the village leader who performed such ceremonies. The ritual was simple and involved pledges of love and fidelity, the binding of our left hands together with flowering vine, and the drinking of an herbal potion from a ceremonial cup.

The old woman looked on, prompting us to do this and that at the proper time. She had brought us wedding gifts: a new dress for Soliya and a new robe for me.

"These belonged to my family, and now I give them to you. Good fortune be with you."

Our bonds were strong; I could feel it. Our connections were deep. Universes rolled past me as I held her and loved her. We were transported to a place reached only when two Souls merge in unconditional love.

We spent two more blissful days in the common house, but then Soliya became very restless.

"We must go. We must leave here. I have a strong feeling that the robbers may try to find me."

"Are you sure? Why would they bother? They left you by the roadside."

"True. But I know who they are and what they've done. That makes me dangerous to them. Let's leave tonight. The moon is new. We shall have its waxing light to travel by."

I wasn't sure I wanted to leave and asked, "Are we not safer here than out on the highway?"

"They know where I am if we remain here. At least on the road we have a chance."

I could see she was serious and would be uncomfortable staying any longer. Our journey would be slow without a cart, for Soliya still limped and needed a walking stick.

There were three roads leading from this village. We chose the smallest steepest path, figuring it was least likely to be patrolled by the bandits. We didn't yet have a destination. Fate had brought us this far; fate would bring us the next step.

In the rosy twilight, we slowly climbed out of the valley where the village sat. We rested atop a large rock and looked back down at the huts and houses below us. We had told no one we were leaving. We hoped this would give us some lead time.

Once the crescent moon set, it was quite dark. Soliya was already tired, so we found a sheltered spot and held each other until first light. When I opened my eyes, Soliya was looking into them.

She kissed me and said softly, "I love you, Mihlo. I am happy to be your wife."

We began our day's journey. We moved slowly, and because we had no weapons, we listened carefully for sounds ahead or behind us on the trail. At one point we heard a cart and some voices, so we hid in the brush by the roadside. The travelers passed us, and we resumed our journey.

We spent the evening by a stream and waterfall, not unlike the place I first cared for Soliya after I found her. We washed in the stream, then made a bed of leaves and celebrated our marriage with much passion and joy. We slept soundly, planning to travel again at dawn.

The sound of the stream and waterfall masked the noises from the roadway. Just as we were preparing to begin our day's journey, we heard voices and scuffling sounds coming towards us.

What happened next made me shudder and ache as I read the account in The Great Book. The gang of robbers had found us. They had tracked us and spotted where we left the trail. They crashed through the brush and surrounded us before we could escape. The leader grabbed Soliya and shook her.

"You belong to us. You come with us now!"

"No!" she shouted, standing up to him. "I am married now. I belong with my husband. I am no longer one of you."

I jumped to her side and held her tight. "Leave us. We do you no harm. We have no swords to fight you. Let us go!"

The other thieves jeered and shouted. The leader looked around and then ran us through with his sword, both of us with one angry thrust. We died there in each other's arms.

The words disappeared from the page, so I closed the book. I was immobilized with emotions. I took a deep breath and forced myself to stand before the screen.

At first, I saw a swirling mass of gray with darker and lighter areas. Then I saw two figures lying with their arms around each other. As the image became clearer, I saw myself as Mihlo and Angel as Soliya, lying there slain by the robber's sword. Behind the image were vertical bars of red and gray. Then the screen showed two lighted figures rising from the intertwined bodies. These figures were brilliant gold with whirling pink circles in their mid-sections. The background turned brilliant white—so bright that I could barely look at the screen.

I collapsed back into the oval seat, overwhelmed and exhausted. Vibrating intensely, I felt dizzy. I closed my eyes to steady myself, and at that moment, I felt a hand on each of my shoulders. Sottrol and Chalherine were standing on either side of me. They had much compassion in their eyes.

Sottrol began. "We know that was difficult for you. We can see by your aura that you are quite shaken."

"We've come to help," said Chalherine. "Stand between us."

They positioned me so that Sottrol faced my left side and Chalherine my right.

"Breathe, Darci," Sottrol prompted. "Close your eyes. Breathe. Now open them slowly."

I took my time and did as instructed. As I opened my eyes just a little, I was taken aback by what I saw. Horizontal stripes of flickering light, red then orange, encircled me. My eyes automatically popped open, and the image persisted though not as brightly.

"Darci," Chalherine spoke now, "breathe and focus on your love for Angel and the joy you felt once you passed over together. Listen. This is important. You were in each other's arms as you both moved through the veil between worlds. See it."

I closed my eyes again and saw Angel and me embracing, floating together as luminous golden Spirits with pulsing pink hearts. I felt a surge of joy.

"Now . . . open your eyes slowly," said Sottrol.

As I did so, I saw vertical rays of brilliant gold and pink light around me. The beams danced and vibrated, fading only slightly as I fully opened my eyes.

"You're getting it," said Chalherine. "It is often hardest to see your own energy field. Most students learn by observing others."

Sottrol interjected, "Emotions intensify energy patterns, so we thought in your case . . ."

Chalherine took over, ". . . you would learn best by intensifying your emotions through memories of Angel, then examining your own aura."

"All is well, Darci." Sottrol patted me on the shoulder. "You have done well here."

The Chancellor smiled and added, "Sottrol and I will discuss what's next for you since you are on your own special path of learning. For now, we shall escort you to your chamber for some well-earned rest."

Chapter Six:
A Pocket of Karmic Trouble

While resting in my chamber, I thought about how fortunate I was to have the two fine elders, Sottrol and Chalherine, as teachers. I felt confident that they would choose the best path of learning for me. Whatever they decided, I knew I would push ahead with determination, for that was the only way I could see Angel again.

This was a longer rest period than I had experienced between any of my other lessons. I had much time to reflect on what I had read and remembered. The lifetime in Rome was one I often pondered because there were many pleasant memories.

Ours was an incredible love story. The fact that in Mongolia we met, fell in love, and married in only a few weeks is just one example. I remember that despite the danger, I had no doubts in my heart that I wanted to marry Soliya. Several times I wondered what life would have been for us if we had not been killed together only days after we were wed. I was going over this again in my mind when Sottrol entered my chamber.

"Darci," he said sitting next to me, "you need a Spirit Guide perspective on this." The elder put his arm around me. "I have watched you go over and over your brief time with Soliya. You are missing the most important part, the very reason for your sharing of that lifetime."

I was puzzled. "Tell me, Sottrol."

"The experience in Mongolia brought out your compassion and your ability to forgive. However, the most significant part of that lifetime was your dying together in each other's arms, indeed, dying by the same sword. You passed over from the Earth plane to the other side intertwined. Even when you two were on the spirit side, you would not be parted.

It took much love and much debriefing to separate you. I've never seen two Souls so enmeshed, so determined to stay together."

The old one pulled a small crystal from his beard, held it up and looked through it as he talked.

"Birth—when a Soul officially enters the Earth plane—and death are two very sensitive and significant times for a Being. An imprint is made each time a Soul passes to or from the Earth. The circumstances surrounding death are especially important, for whatever is in the heart and mind of the one passing will be a part of that imprint. In many, many lifetimes your love of Angel has been in your heart when you died."

My mentor looked at me with compassion in his eyes and continued, "When one human helps the Soul of another human to pass, a bond is formed. This is true even if they are strangers. In the Mongolian lifetime that you just reviewed, there existed the possibility that you would care for Soliya but that she would die from her original wound. That alone would have strengthened your bond. However, the stage was set, so to speak, for a higher purpose. You two fulfilled it by coming together of your own free will and falling in love.

"Darci, you shone especially bright in that incarnation because of your ability to give compassion and forgiveness to a person who had robbed you. Even though you have been pondering what your lives might have been if you had not been slain that day, you and Angel fulfilled your purpose, your Soul Contracts. You did this by bravely facing those murderous robbers and then passing from Earth, holding each other with love in your hearts."

"Oh yes, our Soul Contracts," I remembered.

"Yours was written differently than hers. For you, open-mindedness that you attained through your travels, plus, forgiveness, compassion, and unconditional love were all lessons. For Angel, courage, the will to live, resilience, and unconditional love were written in her contract. By loving each other, by standing up to those robbers together, and by

154

dying together, you both actually did quite well as far as your soul growth. When you two passed over from Mongolia, your bond was so strong even the Angel Initiates who greet the newly arrived could not separate you. As I look at you now, Darci, I see how you long for your dear Angel."

"I know the time is not yet right, but I do wish to see her wherever she is. I have this sense that she needs me."

"Oh, indeed she does. She has gotten herself into a mess and is trying to work herself out of it, but she needs help."

I felt a pang in my spirit heart when Sottrol told me this and begged, "Please—let me help her. Angel!" I called out to her, "What can I do?"

"You are doing the very best thing you can—working towards becoming a Spirit Guide."

"How long will it take, Sottrol? Angel needs me now; I can feel it."

"Hush now, dear Darci," my mentor tried to soothe me. "Angel has her own spirit path and her own experiences to endure. She has to pass through her current phase before she will be ready for you to contact her. This gives you time to prepare."

"What sort of trouble is she in? I must know. I'll think of nothing else unless you tell me."

"You will discover all you need to know as you continue your studies."

"Then what is next? Let's get on with it."

"You are still in Chalherine's wing of the university. She is the one to usher you into your next round of studies. You need a bit more rest. Then Chalherine will visit and show you."

Sottrol could see I was a bit disappointed as he said, "Continue enjoying your memories and remember that you can send Angel love and prayers. They do help."

After Sottrol hugged me and departed, I sat quietly and pictured Angel in all the lifetimes I had read about and remembered. My heart was overflowing with love for this

Soul. Instead of using my energy in wishing to see her, I used it to send her my love. I prayed for her over and over and sent her all the love I could muster, which was a great deal indeed.

Although I felt rested and ready to continue my training, I had to wait for Chalherine. It was not easy, but I realized that patience was something a Spirit Guide must possess in abundance.

∞ ∞ ∞

Eventually Chalherine arrived with Hespahba.

"My apologies, Darci," she began as she floated towards me. "I know you are anxious to continue your studies. I wanted to clear my schedule so I could work with you personally."

She turned to Hespahba and asked him/her to fetch something, so the tutor departed.

"Your next step is a big one, Darci. I want to be sure you are ready. Stand here."

I did as she directed.

Circling me, she looked me up and down.

"Describe your energy field to me," she said.

I took a deep breath and thought of Angel. As I felt my heart swell, I opened my eyes slightly and saw pink and gold.

"My aura is pink in the center, then gold, with a little blue on the edge."

Chalherine circled me again.

"Picture your wife's death in Rome. Go through that day in your mind."

This was difficult for me, for it made me sad and always increased my longing to be with Angel. I did as I was asked though it took me a while.

"Now describe your energy field to me."

I peered through my eyelashes to see a red and gray wave pattern moving horizontally around me. I told her in detail what I saw.

"Good. You've done well once again. Sit. Relax. We have much to discuss."

Hespahba returned with what looked like a large wooden box.

"Thank you," Chalherine nodded to the tutor. "Go on. I know you have a student waiting."

Once the androgynous Guide departed, Chalherine moved close to me on the bench and took my hands in hers. My entire spirit body felt as if it were levitating.

"Now that you have mastered unconditional love, learned not to judge, and have had some success reading energy fields, it is time for you to understand more about karma."

I listened intently. There were so many things that I didn't understand though I wanted to.

"Karma is simple and complex at the same time," Chalherine began. "It is complex in the way it plays itself out over the span of many lifetimes; however, it is simple because it is a force which always moves to balance. Let me begin where Sottrol left off. He told me he explained the imprints that are made on the Soul at birth and at death."

"Please say again," I requested for I wished to have further clarification of this phenomenon.

"The imprint at birth is partially determined by the environment the Soul enters, but it is mostly set by the Spirit Contract, which, of course, is made before birth. Therefore, we Spirit Guides can assist in setting up the contract and the resulting imprint. Death and its imprint are an entirely different story. Humans have control of that. All humans have free will. They are still subject to the great cycles, but they can act and react as they choose. How humans elect to live their lives is a factor in the death imprint. For instance, if a human led a very compassionate lifetime but died violently, both would show on the imprint."

"Where does karma come in?" I asked before I got too lost.

"I was just about to say that when we Guides assist in planning an Earth incarnation and when we help in writing that contract, we have to take karma into account. Karma moves everything to balance. We Guides help the individual see how best to balance the soul's experience. Once a Soul has been born onto Earth, the force of karma works through the contract to move that person towards the experiences needed. It's far more complicated than that, of course. Humans have free will, so most make choices that throw them out of balance in new ways."

"I think I follow, Chalherine. It is quite complex."

She laughed and replied, "Oh, Darci, we have only scratched the surface here. You must know that a solid understanding of the principle of karma is essential for a Spirit Guide. Only with such knowledge can you proceed to truly help a human."

"You're talking about Angel. I want to help Angel," I said, getting a bit excited because I saw how the study of karma could apply.

Chalherine continued, "Yes. Before you see where Angel is and what has happened in the evolution of her Soul, you must understand karma. I want to start you off with the big picture because it is easy to get lost in details and examples. I'll try to describe this as simply as possible.

"Each of us, every Soul, is a gem from the ultimate crown jewel, the Creator. We are all still connected to the Great One though we appear to navigate separately. The goal, the purpose, of every Soul is to return to the Creator and once again become a part of that crown jewel."

"Are there Souls who have returned to the Source?" I asked.

"Yes, the first one to do so elected to leave again to show others how to find their way home. That Soul was known on Earth as Jesus.

"In order to reunite with The Great Spirit, a Soul must be in perfect balance—this after experiencing a myriad of lessons and challenges. The irony is that these lessons and challenges more often than not tip the Soul even further out of balance. It takes a conscious effort on the part of a human being to stop this see-saw and focus on what is important. That's what Spirit Guides do—help humans see through the illusions of life on Earth to what is important for their Souls. Your understanding of karma is the foundation upon which you will base the rest of your skills as a Spirit Guide. You will grasp your human's karmic situation . . ."

"Angel!" I interjected. "I'm going to be helping Angel!"

"Very well. Right from the start here we'll say, 'Angel's' karmic situation.' You will understand it, evaluate it, and do all you can to show Angel the way to conscious awareness. Once you help her understand what is important to her Soul, you can guide her more easily towards a more balanced karmic state.

"Remember, Darci," Chalherine held up her index finger. "Karma is very complex. Do you recall how on Earth every flower was just a little different, each snowflake different from every other snowflake?"

"Yes, I guess so."

"Every karmic situation is a little different, and just like the snowflake in a temperature change, karmic circumstances change constantly. The Universe is in continual motion, and karma, the force of balance, is at the center."

Chalherine paused to see if I understood.

I nodded.

"I'm getting the idea. However, I want to make sure I understand the basics. Karma is a natural force in the Universe in the way gravity is a natural force on Earth. Karma pulls towards balance the way gravity pulls towards ground."

"Close enough," Chalherine smiled. "Karma is different from gravity in that it applies to the entire universe and is in constant motion."

"I'm still confused about the imprints though. I understand karma affects these imprints, but what are they?"

"Let's start with the Soul. The Soul is a spark of the Creator, a little piece of The Great Spirit. The Soul is a unique form of energy because it has consciousness. The inner spark that is the basis of the Soul remains constant, but the energy around it changes—sometimes so much that it nearly obscures that divine spark. As you know from your study of auras, energy patterns shift and change. The imprints last much longer."

"These are imprints on the energy patterns of a Spirit?"

"A Spirit, a Soul, a human. If a baby were tattooed at birth, that marking would last the lifetime of that human. It might change a little, but the basics of that mark would stay until death when the physical body was discarded by the Soul. The imprints we are talking about are more complex but similar. When humans are born, they are tattooed cosmically. The imprint is made on their energy field, and the Soul must work with that imprint until death."

"Can a human learn about the imprint or read it somehow?"

"There are clues. The astrological natal chart offers the most straightforward information on both the birth imprint and the Soul Contract. These two are connected, of course."

"The imprint at birth is based on the Soul Contract?"

"Partially, yes. You're getting it."

"What about the imprint at death? How long does that last?"

"That depends on how evolved the Soul is. If the Soul continues to learn on the lower spiral, the death imprint continues until another birth and a new imprint is made. You, Darci, stepped up and out of the lower spiral when you chose to become a Spirit Guide. The death imprint from your last Earth life was lessened in stages and finally erased completely in the Power Booth."

"Ah, so that's what was happening to me."

"Your energetic pattern was being cleansed and elevated. Are you grasping all of this?"

"I think so. How will I know Angel's karmic situation?"

"You always bring it back to Angel, don't you? First, research. You can read the records of Angel's experiences to see what challenges she has faced and how she has endured."

"I've been doing that."

"You've been reading about your shared lifetimes. You have been incarnated during the same time periods on Earth quite often but not every time. There is more for you to learn about Angel if you are to assist her as a Spirit Guide. Evaluating her energy field, especially her current imprint, will tell you a great deal."

"I want to learn to read imprints, Chalherine."

"To learn to read imprints, you'll have to journey to Earth as an understudy to a working Spirit Guide. The death imprints are on record. They are factors when a Soul is formulating a new contract."

"You mentioned that before. The imprint at death must be taken into account. Can you give me an example?"

"Yes. If a human dies in fear, then fear dominates the death imprint and will most certainly be listed as one of the challenges in that soul's next contract. It's not always that simple, but you get the idea."

"I do."

"When working with a human being, you must be able to clearly read both the shifting energy patterns in the aura and the more stable birth imprint."

"Angel was an astrologer in Egypt. She would understand the concept of a Soul Contract."

"Your Angel has gained much wisdom and knowledge through many lifetimes."

"Why am I here and not her? I would have thought she would be ahead of me at this University. She was my teacher in Egypt."

"Always remember that the entire picture is extremely complex and always shifting, especially on the lower wheel. The Spirit Guide plane and those above it are more stable."

161

"What shifted for Angel? Why is she there and not here?"

"You will find out. Now I have an exercise for you." Chalherine turned to the large box that Hespahba had brought. She touched the top, and the lid detached, levitated, and disappeared.

"This truly is a land of magic," I thought to myself.

"It's all energy," said Chalherine, once again reading my thoughts. "Here are the records of four Souls. Their karma is intertwined, yet each has its own spirit path. Study these, Darci. See if you can follow the force of karma through the experiences of these four Souls."

"Are these Souls real, Chalherine?"

"No, they are examples used for study. In reality, situations are more complex. This is an exercise to see if you understand karma. There are five ledgers, one for each Soul, and one that contains an exam I wish you to take when you are ready. Any questions?"

"Not about this exercise. Thank you for your time and attention, Chalherine."

"We Guides are looking to you and Angel to accomplish many great and blessed things." With that intriguing statement, she vanished into a breathtaking incandescent mist.

Anxious to get on with my studies, I reached into the box. I had a feeling of urgency pulling at me. Angel was in trouble and needed my help. I had to do everything I could to reach her.

The five ledgers were colored differently. I determined right away that the gold one on the bottom was the exam. Blue, green, brown, and purple ledgers each described the evolution of a particular Soul. I read through, then forced myself to read them again. Perhaps because I knew that these were study examples, I was less interested. After reading the exciting accounts of my various lifetimes with Angel, these seemed tame and unimportant. Still, I tried to focus and learn what these example texts were trying to teach me.

Hespahba returned to collect the exam. I had long since finished and was resting, contemplating how my choices and my karmic situations had brought me out of the lower wheel. Hespahba could read my thoughts and offered the following.

"Darci Stillwater, you chose to act and react from a place of deep compassion. You chose to love unconditionally in trying situations. Soon you will know all."

Then in an instant the tutor was out the door and gone.

∞ ∞ ∞

I did not have long to wait this time. Chalherine and an assistant entered my chamber. The radiant teacher seemed to glow ever brighter. The Guide with her was female, had long dark braids, and a robe with pink, lavender, and silver panels.

"Darci, this is Wachena. She is my assistant and another of the tutors."

We nodded a greeting at each other while Chalherine continued.

"It is obvious that you are most focused and do best when learning through your experiences with Angel. We have decided it is time for you to study Angel's karmic situation. There is no better example for you."

Chalherine sat down beside me while Wachena stood by her.

"There are a few things I must tell you in preparation. In order for a Soul to make the journey back to the Source, the Creator, that entity must be whole and complete. That is to say, that Being must have endured the myriad of experiences offered on every level of the spiral. This includes being a Spirit Guide, a Master Guide, an Angel, an Archangel, but also all experiences on the lower wheel. Many Souls find it difficult to rise above the lower spiral.

"On the lower levels of learning, Earth offers physical, material, and emotional challenges. Every Soul must experience it all: being healthy and being ill, being with family and being without, being wealthy and being poor, being well-fed and being hungry. Do you see?"

"I think so." I wondered where all this was leading. Wachena seemed a bit restless. She was twisting one of her silver bracelets.

"You recall your Roman lifetime," Chalherine continued, "a life full of wealth, luxury, fine food, beautiful clothing, a lovely home . . ."

"Yes, I remember it well."

"You and Angel also shared times of poverty as part of your souls' growth."

"When we lived in Mongolia?" I offered.

"Poverty was not the focus of that Earth life. It's time for you to learn about the lifetime that was one of your poverty experiences. Wachena is my newest assistant. She is known for her compassion and deep understanding and will help you through this next phase because it will not be easy for you. I've arranged for you to have The Great Book of Lifetimes here in your chamber. I want you to be comfortable and at ease when you relive these Earth lifetimes. Wachena will hold you in a circle of light and compassion as you read and experience what The Great Book shows. She is to remain, for I do not want you to be alone. Wachena is here not just to monitor you and your reactions; she is here to comfort you and help you keep a spirit perspective."

The door to my chamber vanished. Sottrol entered carrying the giant book, and the door reappeared behind him. He placed the large volume on a reading stand, which I hadn't noticed before.

"Dear Darci," he said, coming towards me, "Chalherine and I believe you are ready for this. We will give you all the assistance you need."

"What could be so terrible?" I heard myself say.

Smiling a little and touching my back gently, Chalherine said, "All will be healed in light and love, Darci—and you will do the healing."

"Whenever in doubt," Sottrol offered, "just say
is well' because it is, and saying this will help you
that."

The two elder Guides then stood on either sid ᴗᵣ ᴍe.
Sottrol pulled me gently to a standing position. Silently they
encircled me with their arms. I felt as if I were being infused
with energy and love. It was a very exhilarating experience,
but I still had a troubled feeling in my heart.

I spoke aloud, "All is well."

Sottrol nodded. Chalherine smiled compassionately, and
the two of them disappeared leaving a fine effulgent mist that
lingered.

Up to this point, Wachena had not spoken. Once the
elders had departed, we looked at each other. She appeared
calmer now and was moving her lips as though she were
saying a silent prayer. Her braids were wound with silver
thread. Her eyes were deep, dark, and reminded me of the eyes
of a deer. Certainly she had a very gentle air about her.

I heard her take a breath and she spoke, "Mr. Stillwater,
you may begin whenever you are ready."

"Thank you. I will, Wachena."

I wondered about having someone watch as I was reading.
Wachena knew my thoughts and reassured me.

"I will sit in meditation with my eyes closed. This is the
best way for me to hold the energy for you."

She then sat on one of the upper benches, crossed her legs,
and closed her eyes.

I turned to The Great Book. It opened on its own, the
pages flipping over until a dark blue page with gold writing
appeared. I sat and read.

The location was Europe in the Middle Ages in the valley
between France and Germany. I was a female, born third in a
family of ten, with two older brothers. As the eldest daughter,
many household responsibilities were handed to me at a very
young age. I saw myself at the age of seven scrubbing the
walls of the hovel we called home. My parents were not old

but looked tired and stooped over from work. My father worked in the fields, and my mother did mending and sewing. It was a hard life with few pleasures.

One spring morning when I was fifteen, I was outside washing clothes in a tub. I had learned to find enjoyment in little things and was watching the sun glint off the water in the washtub. I liked how the drops sparkled when I splashed.

After I hung the clothes, I returned to empty the tub and found flowers floating in the water. Not just a few: the entire surface was blooming. I looked around but saw no one close by. This puzzled me and I thought about it over and over as I did my chores.

Keeping fresh water in the house was the biggest task because it was so heavy to carry. My brothers were in charge of hauling the water, but the oldest boy had broken his ankle and could not work, so I was recruited. My other older brother and I toted as many buckets as we could carry to the brook.

The boys had dug a hole in the streambed to make it easier to lower the buckets and fill them. My job was to wash all the dirt and slime from the pails so that the water we carried back would be truly clean and fit for drinking. As I finished scrubbing each bucket, my brother would fill it and haul it to the hut. When I had cleaned the last pail, I told my brother that I wanted to stay by the stream for a few minutes and wash my face, hands and feet. He shrugged and left, loaded down with the last two buckets splashing over with water.

I untied my rough goat-hide shoes and slowly immersed my feet in the cold brook. I couldn't help kicking and splashing and watching the sun glisten on the drops as they flew. I was enjoying my play so thoroughly that I didn't hear the footsteps until they were right behind me. I jumped a little, turned, and looked up to see a tall young man smiling at me.

"You love the water I see," he began, "so do I. There is a beautiful spot just a bit further downstream. I visit there often. Would you like to see it?"

He offered his hand to help me up, and I took it.

"I am Gabriel. You are Marie, am I right?"

I nodded, reaching for my shoes.

"I have seen you, Gabriel. You live in the village."

"On the far side. I am an apprentice to the metal smith."

"Do you come often to this side of the village?" I was noticing his dark lashes and the angular lines in his face.

"This stream is one of my favorite places, so I come here whenever I can. Look," he said, pointing to a bend in the brook where there was a grassy hill and rise in the stream bank. "This is a wonderful place to sit and watch the water, the birds, the sky. Can you stay for a moment?"

I wanted to. This boy seemed kind, and I was glad for a break from my chores. We sat silently for a while, enjoying the sun and the sound of the stream.

"I often see you when I come this way," he began. "I . . . I think you are beautiful."

No one had ever told me that, so I didn't know what to say.

He continued, "I left you some flowers to bring joy to your day. You deserve happiness. I want us to be friends, Marie . . . maybe more."

"More?"

"Now that I am learning a trade, I can think about taking a wife."

I was speechless and suddenly became very shy. I knew what it meant to be married. I knew what being a wife was all about from watching my mother. I guess I always knew I would follow in her footsteps, for there was nothing else for a girl to do in this valley.

I looked at this man who would take me as his wife. He was attractive to me. He was long and lean. His face showed strength of character, and his arms showed physical strength. He was, indeed, Angel incarnated this time as a man. We were about to be paired again.

We were married on the longest day of the year. The ceremony was held in the village church. The celebration afterwards was modest. Gabriel's parents had died, and my parents couldn't afford much.

Gabriel's house was smaller and much emptier than my family home. It needed cleaning, so even before we lay in our marriage bed together, I set about cleaning the sleeping area. My new husband had other ideas and grabbed me around the waist as I was shaking out the bedcovers.

"You must learn to play!" he said, kissing me everywhere he could reach.

I was young and had no experience, but our soul connection was strong and our love flowed as naturally as that stream.

Our first child was born the following spring, a boy we named Raphael. Gabriel worked hard and looked forward to becoming the metal smith in the village. Our life was simple but good.

The expression of our love for each other resulted in eight children in eleven years. During this time, Gabriel had several disappointments involving his work. Another of the metal smith's apprentices took over that business. Gabriel tried many jobs in order to continue to provide for our family, each job harder than the next.

I tried to comfort my husband as he toiled at jobs he didn't like, jobs he was not good at, and jobs that lessened his self-confidence. Because of the lack of suitable work, we left our village and moved to a neighboring town where Gabriel found employment fixing wheels. We located a small house with barely enough room for all of us. I was lonely without my family close by, but the children kept me very busy, so I didn't have time to miss my brothers and sisters.

One evening in late winter, I was making a stew with our new baby in my arms. Our eldest son Raphael was eleven, nearly twelve. I had reprimanded him earlier in the day for mercilessly teasing his younger brother. The house was too small for rough play, and the older boys had accidentally hurt one of the toddlers. My nerves were frayed by the time darkness fell. I awaited Gabriel's return, which always lifted my spirits.

Gabriel was a good father, a kind father. He spent Sundays with the children and me although during the week he worked so hard he didn't have much energy to spare for family matters.

This winter evening, my husband looked particularly tired when he came through the door. We were all waiting for him in the large front room that served as a cooking and dining area. Gabriel stood at the entrance, looked around, and our eyes met. Something was wrong. I could see it in his face. I could feel it as soon as he walked through the door.

"I had a disagreement with the wheelmaster," he began, softly at first. "He asked me to do something impractical—in fact, nearly impossible. I have much training in working with metals, but he would not listen to me."

His voice was louder now. "I told him I was trying to help, and if he took my suggestions, he would benefit. Instead, he fired me!"

My heart sank. The baby began to cry. One of the older children asked if we could move back home now, and Raphael began taunting his father.

"Father lost another job!" came the boy's singsong voice. "Father is a failure! Father is a failure!"

Gabriel lost his temper. He kicked the boy, and the pointed toe of his boot wounded Raphael in the side. Our son's eyes rolled back in his head as he collapsed.

Gabriel was instantly sorry.

We all rushed to the boy's side. Blood was coming from his nose and mouth. I was horrified and quite beside myself with worry.

Gabriel stood over Raphael saying, "Son, I am so sorry!"

Finally, I had enough presence of mind to put my nine-year-old daughter in charge of feeding the other children. My husband wrapped the boy in a blanket, I took the baby, and we literally ran through the town to the doctor's house.

That night was the longest night of my life. Gabriel and I took turns sitting by our eldest son and looking in on the other children.

The doctor was kind but did not hold out much hope. He told us there were internal injuries that he could do nothing about. Raphael died at dawn.

From that moment on, my dear husband was a broken man. He put a curse on his right leg, the leg that had kicked and killed his son. He grieved and blamed himself endlessly.

I forgave him. I had much compassion in my heart for this poor suffering Soul. Gabriel, the man I had married, the husband that I knew and loved, was lost to me. His guilt and his grief overtook him, and he became a mere shadow of the man he had been.

The family had no choice. With Gabriel so debilitated, I made arrangements to move back to our old village. I needed help and turned to my brothers and sisters. I had lost both a son and a husband on that blustery winter's night.

We lived on the charity of our home village. My siblings made sure we always had food, and sometimes they or my nieces or nephews would help, so we survived.

I missed Gabriel so much. His body was there, but his mind and Spirit had retreated to a dark place. I tried every day to reach him, but he shunned me and everyone else. He sat day after day with his head in his hands. He barely ate. Once I saw him beating his right leg with a stick.

Friends stopped by to see him. The priest who married us made a special visit. No one could get through to him. I tried putting our beautiful new daughter in his lap. He had always loved holding our babies, but he pushed her away, saying he would only hurt her. He sank deeper and deeper into depression.

Gabriel wasted away slowly over the next four years. When at last he was weak and bedridden, I knew the end was near, so I sat with him as much as I could.

When I brought him soup or tea, he would whisper, "Go away. I do not deserve your attention."

One peaceful spring evening, I sat holding his hand. He looked almost like a skeleton. The children were quiet, most of them asleep. I began talking softly to him. I reminisced about life before the death of Raphael. I recalled in detail all the joyous times.

"Gabriel, I have long ago forgiven you for losing your temper and kicking our son in anger. For quite a while, I could not forgive you for withdrawing from us. I have missed you terribly, and every day I have prayed for your recovery. Now I want you to know I forgive you everything. I love you. I have loved you since we met long ago by the stream. I love you now, Gabriel. I love you now."

As I said these words, his hand went limp, and I knew he was gone.

Now all the grief that I had hidden and suppressed for the past four years came pouring out. I wailed. I threw myself on Gabriel's frail lifeless body and sobbed until dawn.

Reading the account of this lifetime was like reliving it. I found myself filled with feelings of sorrow as I read the last few paragraphs. My hands were trembling, and my heart cried out for poor Angel. As Gabriel, she died in a mire of grief, self-pity, self-loathing, and self-defamation. I was overcome with emotions and found myself sobbing aloud, much as I had done when Gabriel's troubled Soul finally departed.

"Angel, dear Angel," I cried.

Compassion for her swelled within me until it flowed from me as though I was the source of a great waterfall. I opened my eyes a little and was shocked to see streams of green and gold light radiating from me.

Then I felt gentle spirit hands on my shoulders. It was Wachena standing behind me. With her touch, I experienced a deep cleansing of the grief. I watched in amazement as the rays of light changed to pure gold. I breathed deeply and sighed.

The lovely tutor came around and sat before me. She took my hands and looked into my eyes.

"You love this Soul very, very much. I can see that."

"Angel," I said. It sounded like a sob.

"You have endured much together," continued Wachena. "This particular Earth life was extremely hard for both of you, but for Angel it was ruinous."

"Yes." My voice was barely a whisper. I was still caught up in my feelings.

"Darci, you realize that her reaction to the death of your son was her choice. As Gabriel, she chose to curse her leg. She chose to place blame on her limb and waste away in grief."

"That one rash action changed everything in our lives," I said in a whisper as the enormity of this experience began to set in.

"It changed Angel's karmic situation," said the tutor. "She still has not recovered."

"Oh no!"

"You will help her find her way out of the deep dark karmic pocket she is in. Let's begin with a spirit perspective on the incident. Gabriel's angry reaction to your son's taunting had tragic results. Keep in mind that even though he reacted this way, he never intended to hurt the boy. Intent is the first thing to assess when dealing with a situation where one human harms another."

I found myself defending my mate.

"He was frustrated and overcome with worry for the well-being of our family. He must have been mulling over the loss of the job on his walk home. He must have been questioning his decision to move our family to that town. He must have felt terrible when he had to walk through that door and tell us the news."

"Yes, so the violent physical reaction when he kicked your son was a simple venting mechanism. He was angry, but there was no malice involved."

"I see that."

I was starting to feel a little better, but the image of the spirit of my dear Angel in the devastated and wasted body of that broken man sent shivers through me.

Wachena continued, "It is true that Angel as your husband Gabriel threw her karmic situation way out of balance with that one rash action. However, Gabriel's subsequent choices are what got Angel into deep, long-lasting trouble."

"What do you mean?"

"Gabriel could have handled the tragedy differently. Of course he was sorry. Of course, he was overwhelmed by the fact that he caused his son's death. This was a natural reaction, but he went overboard. He basically chose to abandon you and his seven other children to wallow in self-pity and grief. This choice brought a very serious karmic situation to bear for this Soul. The violent act, as horrible as it was, did not get Angel where she is today. The choices made afterward are what dug Angel into a deep well of karmic trouble."

"Where is Angel now? Has she made progress in balancing this out?"

"You will see."

"Gabriel's choices were harmful to his Soul, to Angel," I spoke softly. "He became a burden to the family. He was like a sick child. He had to be fed and tended to. I remember how much I missed having the help and companionship of my husband. It was as if he died when Raphael died. He was never the same, and it broke my heart to see him waste away."

"Gabriel had free will and could have reacted differently. For one thing, he could have forgiven himself for the angry thoughtless act that resulted in your son's death. That might have taken some time, but if he had reached that point, he could have begun to function as a husband and a father."

"He never forgave himself—never," I remembered. "He cursed his leg over and over. I saw him sit and beat his leg and weep."

"It is time for you to see the imprint Gabriel made upon his passing."

Wachena turned the book around on the stand and opened it to a page near the back. My eyes grew wide with astonishment, for there on a dark gray page was a faint outline of the husband I had once known! There was Gabriel, emaciated, just as he had been on his death bed. Everything on the page was dark, except a tiny pink circle near his mid-section and a blood-red outline that extended from his right hip all the way around his right leg.

"What is this red line?" I asked Wachena, pointing to the leg.

"The curse Gabriel put on his limb is part of the death imprint."

"And the pink circle?"

"That is what was left of his Soul."

"Angel!" I cried out. "That's all there was of Angel after that lifetime? That tiny glow of pink? After all she had been in those many previous lifetimes, that's all that was left?"

"That shows the condition of Angel's Soul just as it departed from Gabriel's body."

"My poor Angel!"

"Remember, on Earth humans have free will. Choices are what got your Angel into the trouble she is in."

"How can I help her, Wachena?"

"Continue your studies. There is more for you to know about Angel's karma. After this very dark death imprint was made and Angel passed once again into the spirit realm, she began her long road to recovering from this devastating Earth lifetime."

"What happened next?"

"She was greeted by the Angel Initiates and brought immediately to a love bath where she soaked for a very long time. The death imprint was strong, however, and stayed. Her Spirit Guide at the time went to the Master Guides for help. They agreed that several more births and deaths on the Earth plane were needed to completely rid Angel of this debilitating imprint."

"So she got stuck on the lower wheel for a few more rounds."

"She needs you, Darci. She needs you as her Spirit Guide. We think you are the only one who can reach through the veil between worlds and touch her."

"Is that possible?" I was astounded.

"Oh yes, though few humans know exactly what is happening. In Earth history, in literature, and in religious texts there are numerous references to Spirit Guide activity though 'Spirit Guide' is not a term that is often used. Instead, you find the words 'guardian angel.'"

"I can be Angel's guardian angel?!" I smiled at the idea.

"There is more for you to understand, Darci. You must see the big picture—that is, where the Earth plane and humanity are in their evolutions."

"Go on." I was fascinated.

"Earth is a level of experience for the Soul; it is a learning place. The quality of the experiences available on Earth is changing. Humanity is nearing a time of rapid change and an opportunity to take an evolutionary leap, as it were."

"Is this predetermined?"

"To some extent, yes. Earth is part of an interlocking network of giant cycles, and the time is coming soon for events on Earth to be accelerated and new opportunities presented. The details of how this plays out are in the hands of those Souls incarnated on the Earth at the time. Humans have free will within the context of these giant cycles."

"Spirit Guides can also play a part, can we not?" I felt myself becoming excited by this prospect.

"Only through interaction with a human. You as a Spirit Guide cannot physically participate or change anything. You can, however, influence a human to take action. Indeed, this is what Spirit Guides do—guide their assigned humans to right action."

"Where was Angel's Spirit Guide when she was incarnated as Gabriel?"

"Right by the man's side, but Gabriel was not open to receiving help from the assigned Guide or from anyone."

I thought back to one of the first scenes I was shown when I was asked to decide whether or not to become a Spirit Guide. Aleron had shown me a man rejecting help from his Spirit Guide.

"How do I get through to Angel to help her?"

"You will learn. She must be open to your contact. The bond between you is very strong. We believe that if any two Souls can connect through the veil between worlds, you two can. This is why you and Angel have been selected for a special assignment."

"A special what? I thought I was going to help her with her karmic situation."

"You can do both. The opportunities for you and Angel are very great. You must study and prepare yourself, Darci. You want to be ready when the time is right."

"What is next then?" I wanted to move on. I again felt a sense of urgency.

"Before you see where Angel is now, you must familiarize yourself with the most recent lifetime that you both shared."

"There was another shared lifetime after we were Gabriel and Marie?"

"Yes, and it is time you knew the details of that life. Let me do a cleansing on your energy before you begin."

The tutor circled me with her arms extended. She floated around me several times, and with each pass I felt calmer. Using the Spirit breathing exercises, I eventually became more centered and ready for whatever was next.

∞ ∞ ∞

Wachena opened the book and returned to her position on a bench above me.

"I will sit as I did before while you read."

This time I was in India, born as a male. My home was the city of Bombay. The book described my birth into a large family. I was the youngest son, so received much attention from my siblings and my mother. My father was a rug merchant. He spent his days in the marketplace where he had a large stand. Our home was filled with beautiful carpets. My two uncles ran the rug-making business. They employed many people, including some of my sisters and brothers.

As a boy I spent much time in the market. It was noisy and dusty but full of color and excitement. I would run errands for my father or sit in the shade of his shop and watch the activity around me.

When I was sixteen, I was officially employed by my father to deliver rugs or help customers carry them to their homes. One of my first deliveries was to a school teacher near the marketplace. I knew this teacher because he had tutored some of my brothers. It was a good thing I was young and strong for I had to carry the heavy rug up many stairs to the home of the teacher.

Arriving at the door, I called out for someone to open it, "Carpet man! Your rug is here!"

I listened and heard a faint response, "Push the door open and come in."

I did so and entered an empty room.

"Hello? Where do you want your rug?"

"Here," came the voice, so I followed the sound and entered a room that overlooked the street and one end of the market. A beautiful young woman was sitting on a bed by the window. She was just my age and had radiant skin and lovely dark eyes.

"The rug goes here," She pointed to the floor of that room. "Please roll it out for me."

She watched me quietly and nodded when I was done. I wanted to stay and talk to her, but I did not know what to say, so once I had unrolled the carpet, I left.

Whenever I passed through that end of the market, I would look up and see her in the window watching life go by. I wondered why she never came down to walk around. Why did she stay up in that room day after day?

One busy morning in the market, I got my answer. I saw the teacher pulling a little cart. In it was his beautiful doe-eyed daughter holding onto the sides. It bumped and jiggled through the streets. She laughed as it wound its way through the crooked aisles of the market.

The teacher stopped at a stand near my family's rug business, so I bravely approached. Just as I was about to say hello to the young woman, her father turned and saw me.

"You are Hari Kanoum."

"Yes sir. I delivered your carpet to you."

"Your family does good work. It is a fine rug. I know your father and your brothers."

He saw me looking at his daughter.

"This is Shalia, my only child, my jewel."

Shalia bowed her head shyly. When the introduction was made, she glanced up at me briefly. Our eyes met for an instant, and I felt a tingling rush go through me. It was Angel; my Soul recognized her Soul.

"May I take Shalia into my father's shop and show her around?" I asked her father eagerly.

Shalia's head sank lower as her father refused.

"That is not possible. My daughter remains in the cart and stays with me."

The man who had been friendly a moment before turned cold and quickly departed, pulling the cart and his daughter away from me.

I was puzzled by this reaction. After all, I was just trying to make friends with a young woman who seemed to need company.

Between customers I asked my father about the teacher and his daughter.

"I will tell you about them, Son," he said. "You will then appreciate your family that much more."

My father explained that Shalia's mother had died in childbirth and that Shalia was crippled. He didn't know exactly what was wrong; he just knew she couldn't walk.

"Her father is very protective of her," he continued, "for she is all he has. As I understand it, the girl looks much like her mother. As far as I know, he keeps his daughter at home while he is working, and when he goes out like today, he never allows her out of his sight."

At that moment, a customer entered the shop, so my father did not say more.

The face of the beautiful young woman haunted me. Since I had already been to her living quarters to deliver a carpet, I knew the way. I found myself walking to that end of the market so I could glance up at her window. It was as though some mysterious force within me was guiding me. I'd often see her there looking out the window. Each time I'd see her, my heart would do a little leap in my chest.

One morning I walked up the stairs and knocked.

"Hello . . . Shalia?"

"Yes?"

"It is Hari. May I visit?"

There was no reply. I tried again.

"Shalia, I've brought you some fresh fruit from the market. May I come in?"

"Hari? The carpet boy?"

"Yes. Please, Shalia. I just want to say hello. I will not stay if you do not want me to."

Silence.

Then I heard, "Come in."

I knew how to find her. I had dressed up a little for the visit.

She had a comb in her hand as I entered.

Our eyes met, and I felt that same rush, only stronger—so strong, in fact, I had a buzzing in my ears.

"Here," I said, handing her the fruit.

I sat on the carpet by her bed and said, "It is very fresh."

"Thank you, Hari," she said shyly.

"Do you sit here all day? Do you do nothing else?"

She looked away, embarrassed.

"Shalia, I know you cannot walk. My father told me."

She took a breath, still looking out the window. Then she turned towards me. She was beautiful though a little pale.

"As you know, my father is a teacher. He spends time tutoring me so unlike many girls, I can read and write. This helps make up for the fact that I cannot walk."

I had an idea.

"I'd like to visit again, and we can read to each other. My reading isn't all it should be. You can help me. We can help each other."

"My father can tutor you."

I moved a little closer, "It's you I want to see, Shalia. I want to spend time with you."

I thought I saw her blush.

"I . . . I 'm not sure my father would approve. He might be angry that I let you in to see me today."

"May I get you something? Some water?" I asked, changing the subject.

She smiled. "You are kind. You could fill my water pitcher for me."

The pitcher was not yet empty, but I fulfilled her request. I used my knife to cut the fruit that I had brought and handed pieces to her.

"I will ask your father if you wish. That is . . . if you would like me to come back."

"No!" she said quickly and then put her hand over her mouth to stifle a giggle.

"I mean yes, I'd like you to visit again, but let me ask my father. I know how to approach him."

With the possibility of future visits in mind, I stayed only a little while that first day. I could have sat with Shalia for hours. I felt so drawn to her, so alive in her presence.

Two days later, Shalia's father came into the carpet shop.

He cornered me, looked me over sternly, and asked, "You wish to court my daughter?"

"Sir . . . I . . . I wish only to visit her. She can help me with my reading . . . and she could use the company."

His face softened a little as he replied, "Yes, that is what she said. I do sometimes worry about her when I am gone long hours in the day."

He was silent for a moment, shifting his weight. He eyed me again and said, "There are two days each week when I travel to the other edge of the city to teach. You may look in on my Shalia on those days. If I hear of you misbehaving or mistreating her, I will have your hide."

"I would never do anything to harm her. Thank you, sir. Thank you."

He turned on his heel and left.

My regular visits to Shalia began a few days later. I spent much time preparing myself before I went to her quarters. I entered carrying a book that I liked and a pomegranate. The sight of her stunned me. She looked even lovelier than before. She was dressed in pink with a soft scarf over her shoulders and wore silver bracelets. Her legs were covered as always.

Shalia, too, had chosen a book, so I read to her from mine, and she to me from hers. It was fun. I dissected the pomegranate and fed it to her. We talked and laughed, and before we knew it, the sun was setting.

On days when I was not scheduled for a visit, I would find excuses to walk through the end of the market where I could see her window. If I saw her sitting there, I would wave and smile. Once I even did a little jig, which made her laugh.

After two months and well over a dozen visits, I came to Shalia's room to find her crying. My heart went out to her, and I knelt by her bed.

"What is wrong?"

She sobbed and would not talk for a long while. I rubbed her arm and softly urged her to tell me what had upset her so.

"A dream," she finally said. "A dream of you and me."

"What was this dream?" I was very curious, for I also had dreams of the two of us.

She hesitated, then looked up at me with watery eyes. "You and I, Hari . . . you and I were . . . together . . . you know, husband and wife."

"That is a beautiful dream. Why are you crying?"

"Because it is not possible. It cannot be. I am crippled. I cannot be a wife to you or any man."

"That's not true, Shalia." I tried to comfort her.

"I am not worthy of you, Hari. Leave me. I cannot let myself love you."

I could not go, especially since she had put the words "love" and "you" together. I took a breath. I decided to be brave.

"It is too late, Shalia, and you know it. We already love each other."

She looked at me with wide tearful eyes. "You love me?"

"Yes."

Her head dropped. She fell over on the bed, muffling her sobs in the blanket.

I was bold. I sat on the bed next to her. I rubbed her back gently.

She slowly stopped crying and relaxed under my touch.

I felt compassion, then strong feelings of love for her flowed through me. I looked at her graceful arms and her lovely neck. She was a small but very beautiful young woman. I was touching her for the first time, and I will admit that this aroused my passion.

She could tell because she turned over and looked up at me. Her face was rosy, and I wondered if she felt as I did.

"I do not care that you cannot walk, Shalia. I love you."

She reached up and put her hand on my face and replied, "Such a man I never met. Such a man I never knew existed."

I leaned over as I pulled her to me and kissed her first on the cheek, then on the lips. I thought my head would spin off and fly through the window with the rest of my body following.

She sighed deeply, and I let myself down to lie on the bed next to her.

"Let me love you, Shalia," I whispered.

She was silent but held my hand, moving her fingers so that our fingertips touched. It was electric.

That day flew by. All we did was lie and hold each other, yet our time together was over before I knew it.

The three days until my next visit went slowly. I tried to keep myself busy, but my heart and mind were with Shalia in that little room overlooking the market. I did not know what would happen when I saw her again. All I knew was that I lived for the day.

I rose before dawn on the day I was to return to see her. I walked through the streets of Bombay at first light. I wanted to bring her something special that day, something to show her I really loved her. I went all the way to the sea, which was on the other side of the city. The fishermen were preparing their nets and loading their boats. As the sun rose behind me illuminating the seascape, I followed the shoreline. My eyes caught a glimmer of pink, so I investigated. It was a large shell, which had the colors of beautiful Shalia, the light bronze of her skin, the pink of her dress and her cheeks, the white of her smile. I washed my treasure in the sea and headed back towards the market.

When I walked below Shalia's window, I did not see her there. I rushed up the stairs and knocked with the shell under my arm. I heard no reply, so I knocked again with more force. It was still quiet, so I slowly opened the door and entered.

Shalia was asleep on her bed. She looked so peaceful and lovely in her lime green sari and her pink scarf.

I was a little early for our visit and, wishing not to disturb her, I sat on the end of the bed and took her usual place at the window. I wanted to see the street from her perch, see the world through her eyes. This window was Shalia's world.

Even on the rare occasion when her father took her out in the cart, they never went much beyond the view that she had from that window. I wondered if Shalia had ever seen the sea. When I turned to look at her, she was lying there watching me.

"Good morning," I said, surprised that she had not said a word.

"Hari," she said and then smiled and continued, "what is that?"

"A gift for you, a shell I found on the shore."

She turned it over and over in her delicate hands. "It is lovely. I shall cherish it. You are so kind to me."

"Has your father taken you to the sea? It is a wondrous sight."

She sighed, running ran her hand over the smooth part of the shell.

"It is too far for him to pull the cart. He travels to that area to teach, so he doesn't care to make extra trips."

"I have a favorite story about the sea," she said, reaching for a book. She sat and read to me with the shell on her lap.

Since my last visit when Shalia was crying and I comforted her and kissed her, I had thought of touching her again. Indeed, I thought of little else. As she read to me, I realized how much she aroused my passion, and I yearned to express it. The reading and talking were fun, but I wanted to hold her, to do everything a husband would do, so when she finished reading the story, I got down on my knees by the bed and clasped my hands in supplication.

"I must tell you how much I love you, Shalia. I want to see you every day. I want to be your husband. Will you be my wife? Please?"

Her eyes widened and her mouth dropped open. She remained speechless for a few torturous moments.

Then her eyes filled with tears as she murmured, "We settled this, Hari. I am no use to any man. I am crippled."

"It does not matter to me. I love you."

"Think about it, will you? I cannot cook or keep house.

I cannot care for any children we might have. I am useless—good for nothing!"

"Nonsense!" I nearly shouted. "You are a warm, wonderful, intelligent, beautiful woman. We can work all of that out if you love me, too."

She hung her head and wiped her eyes. "My world is very small. For many years I saw only my father. He realized I was much too sheltered, so he bought the cart. He said I needed sunshine and more contact with people. Then you came to my door and became a part of my little world."

She paused, then looked right into my eyes. "Of course I love you, Hari."

Our Souls connected, and I felt my body burn with fiery passion. I took her hand, but she withdrew it.

"You and your visits are everything to me—but it is because I love you that I must refuse your affections. I cannot burden you with a useless crippled wife. I cannot do that to you."

"We can find a way past it," I insisted. "We will find a way!"

"You have not seen my leg."

"It doesn't matter, Shalia. It's you I care about, not your limb."

She looked me in the eyes for a long time. It seemed she was trying to decide something. She turned away and sighed.

"Shalia, let me talk to your father. I want to marry you."

She jerked around toward me and said, "Hari, you will do no such thing. I will show you why. You may never return, but I shall show you."

She slowly pulled up the soft green gown to reveal a lovely foot and a shapely ankle. This was her left leg. No right leg could be seen. She stopped, shut her eyes, and with a little scowl, lifted the dress.

I admit I did utter a small gasp, for I had never seen anything like it. Her right leg was shriveled and dark. It was misshapen as if it had been beaten over and over. Even the skin was rough and scaly. This limb was as ugly as the rest of her was beautiful. I swallowed hard. I felt a little dizzy and nauseated. She pulled her dress back down over her deformity.

"Good-bye, Hari."

I couldn't move. I couldn't talk. I was repulsed, and my reaction surprised me. The sight of that shriveled leg had touched something deep inside me. I inhaled and exhaled slowly, feeling my disgust turn to compassion. I wondered why such a beautiful girl had to endure this horrible malformation.

My compassion for her swelled and overflowed as I said, "Oh Shalia, I am so sorry. I wish I could make you a brand new leg. Then you could have a happy life."

"Dear Hari, you are the only one who has seen my . . . my leg besides Father and the midwives who delivered me."

"I am glad you showed me. A husband should know all about his wife."

"What?" She was the one who was shocked now. "You still talk of marriage after you have seen how damaged I am?"

"I love you more."

She began weeping.

I sat next to her and put my arm around her. I asked her, "Why do you cry? Our love is a reason to celebrate!"

"My heart bursts with joy. I cannot help myself," she sobbed.

I held her close as clouds thickened outside the window. I could tell there was going to be a midday rainstorm. We began kissing as the first rumbles of thunder rolled in from the sea. She was as passionate as I was and touched me as though she had done it many times in her imagination. She ran her hands over my chest, my back, then kissed my neck and shoulders.

As the rain poured and the lightning flashed, we explored each other's bodies. I was a young man with many older brothers, so I knew how to approach a woman. She was delicate and sweet, much like the mango once you peel the outer layer. This beautiful young woman opened to me like a dewy morning flower, and I expressed all the feelings that had been building inside since I first saw her. Although this was all new to her, she relaxed and let me guide her. There was something happening that was much deeper than just our physical contact. I felt as if I were reuniting with a long-lost love, someone I was literally driven to be with. My exuberant passion flowed into her, and she sighed as she too felt that at last we were together.

We held each other silently as we listened to the sound of the rain pouring on the street and the market below. With her breath upon my chest, I felt a deep, soul-stirring connection. I knew it was right for me to love her, to be with her, to marry her.

The rain ended and an exhilarating fresh smell hung in the air over the city.

I felt wonderful as I stretched. Shalia smiled.

"Hari, you'd better go. Father will return soon now that the rain has stopped."

I knelt again by her bed, "It's like we are already married, Shalia. That was our wedding, our melding into one. We must now formally marry in front of your father and my family. Then we can be together always."

"I never thought I would ever marry. I thought my life would be always with my father."

"You wish to marry me, don't you?"

She looked away. I saw tears filling her eyes once again, so I sat by her and held her. I smoothed her lovely long hair and said softly, "No matter what you thought before and no matter what your doubts are, you must let me love you and take you as my wife. There is no other path for us."

She wiped her eyes, responding softly, "Go, Hari."

I did not want to leave her, but I was not yet ready to face her father.

"Shalia must be sure about what she wants," I thought to myself as I headed home. "If she truly wants me, she will convince her father, and we shall marry."

When I visited, Shalia always kept her deformed leg covered with her skirt or wrapped in a blanket or cloth. Even when she relaxed under my loving intimate caresses, she would not let me touch her crippled leg. This added a slight awkwardness to the usual spontaneity of making love. As we lay in each other's arms at the end of an afternoon, I asked if I could look at her all over. It was true, I was curious to see her leg again, but I also wanted Shalia to be comfortable with my seeing all of her.

"No, Hari. Not today. It is getting late and you must go. I want to rest before Father returns."

A few days later, I went to talk to Shalia's father. It was dinnertime when I knocked. He opened the door, told me that they were eating, and tried to shut it, but I wedged my body against the jamb so he could not.

"Please, sir, hear me out. Your daughter's happiness is at stake."

He could see that I was not going to leave, so with a rather grim look on his face, he nodded for me to enter. Shalia was sitting at a small table that had one candle on it. There were plates of food half-eaten. Her eyes danced in the candlelight, but she didn't speak. She looked so lovely I couldn't take my eyes off of her. My heart ached, for I longed to run to her and enfold her in my arms.

"Say your piece and let us be," her father said gruffly.

Perhaps I was a bit too dramatic, but I felt this was my only chance, so I threw myself down on my knees and clasped my hands.

"I love Shalia with all my heart, with all of me. I beg you, please, allow me to take her as my wife."

"Oh, Hari." I heard Shalia whisper.

Her father walked over and stood right in front of me. "Foolish boy! Stupid boy! What do you know of love?"

"I know I love your daughter."

"Bah! I'll tell you what love is. Love is taking care of her, preparing her meals, bathing her, helping her dress, cleaning the house, teaching her, tending her when she is ill. My daughter cannot do these things for herself."

"I realize that, sir . . . of course, I do. I would be honored to . . ."

"To what? Take a woman that must be cared for like a child?" His voice softened a little. "Hari, you are a bright young man. Surely you can see that a marriage to my daughter would burden you with endless responsibilities. You need a wife like your brothers have, a wife who can serve you, cook for you, tend your children. Shalia can do none of those things."

"I don't care about that, sir. Listen to me. I love her. I believe she loves me. We can make a life together."

"Out of the question. Shalia is all the family I have. She remains with me. You have spoken your piece. Now go!"

"Shalia, tell him it is what you desire!" I reached towards her. Her eyes were filled with tears.

"Leave us to our dinner, young man," growled her father.

But I could not go. When her father stood, grabbing me to force me out the door, Shalia finally spoke, "Father, wait! Hari is a good man. He is kind and compassionate. I believe he loves me."

She hesitated, then said, "I love him."

Her father let me go than stomped back and forth between the two of us ranting, "There can be no wedding! A marriage is impossible! My daughter stays here with me, and you are forbidden to see her! Out! Out now!"

I retreated toward the door as he came at me. Looking at Shalia, I saw tears streaming down her face. She nodded at me, a signal that I should go, so I left.

Although I was discouraged, I held a spark of hope because I knew she loved me.

I didn't know how to let go of my love for Shalia. In fact, it grew more intense as time passed. Every day I would walk to her window and wave to her, throw her kisses and try to make her smile. A few times I wrote in the dirt with my sandal "I love you."

One day about a month later, she was not at the window. I raced up the stairs and banged on the door.

"Shalia! Shalia! Are you all right?"

There was no answer, and I never saw her in the window again.

The last time I saw my sweet Shalia was on a gloomy day a few weeks after she had disappeared from her window perch. I was working in my father's carpet store when I saw Shalia's father pulling the cart through the streets. He was nearly running, shooing people out of the way as he guided the cart over bumps and around obstacles. I ran and caught up with them. Shalia was lying in the cart looking terribly ill. Her eyes were glazed with fever. At first her father did not see me, so I trotted alongside. She looked very pale. I lifted her hand; it was limp. I think she did recognize me for I saw her lips move. At that point, her father saw me and stopped the cart.

"Away! Away from my daughter! You have brought this on! It is your fault! She has been pining away for you and now she is ill. Go! I must get her to the doctor."

"Let me help. I can pull faster than you."

I didn't let him say no. Grabbing the handles of the cart, I yelled, "Show me the way."

Then I pulled, bouncing and weaving through the crowded streets until we reached a large building. Her father was leaning over to pick her up when I scooped her out of the cart.

"Lead the way. I'll carry her."

She was weak and feverish but came to consciousness in my arms. It was as if my presence revived her. She was so frail. I was very worried. My heart was overflowing with compassion and love for this beautiful Soul. As I placed her gently on the cot in the doctor's clinic, she moved her lips again, so I knelt by her side and put my head on her chest.

I heard her say softly, "Another time, Hari. We will be together another lifetime."

She died there with me close by. Her father was beside himself with grief.

I tried to comfort him, but my own heart was breaking. I felt that if Shalia and I had been allowed to marry, she would not have wasted away and become so ill. I did not express this, however. She was gone, and there was nothing that could be done.

The narration of this lifetime closed with a paragraph about how I then decided that there would be no other love for me, so I took vows and became a dedicated monk. I lived the rest of that life in spiritual service.

I closed the book, once again overwhelmed with emotion. Wachena was there to assist me. She put her hand on my shoulder, and I immediately felt a bit better.

"Take a breath, Darci," she urged. "I know it was difficult for you to relive that."

"Help me, Wachena. Help me understand."

"You must view this lifetime from a spirit perspective. Remember Gabriel's death imprint?"

"I do."

"Look at Shalia's birth imprint."

Wachena opened the book to the back and turned it towards me. Before me on a page of light pink was a circle with rings. Each ring had a number of symbols. Behind this graph was the faint outline of a human body. Instead of the right leg, there was a thin line that ended above the place where the ankle would have been.

"Shalia's shriveled leg." I said, pointing to the line.

"Gabriel's cursed leg," Wachena added. "You recall how the curse that Gabriel put on his own right leg showed on the death imprint. This is how the curse was taken into account when Angel reincarnated as Shalia."

"Wachena, I never believed in curses, but I see that this did happen."

"It was not the curse, but the thought of it that Gabriel held strongly in his heart and mind that carried over through death into the next lifetime for Angel."

"Poor Angel. What she has had to endure!"

"She is moving to balance her karmic situation. The deformity she experienced as Shalia helped to neutralize the damage done by Gabriel's decisions."

"Angel has had so many lives on Earth. She is experienced and wise. I cannot believe she got herself into this."

"Let me remind you, Darci, that when a Soul is incarnated into a human body, that Spirit does not consciously remember any of the former lifetimes. Humans are programmed to focus on the Earth experience. Sometimes, as in Gabriel's case, the circumstances overwhelm the Soul, and harmful choices are made."

"I'm glad I was there to help Angel both times. I wish I could have done more."

"You did everything you could as Marie and as Hari. You showed love, loyalty, and an immense amount of compassion. Angel is very fortunate that you care so much about her. Let's look at Shalia's death imprint."

Wachena flipped a page in The Great Book, and I stared at a golden page with a pink circle in the center. The outline of Shalia's frail frame was there in blue, including a single line representing her crippled leg. There was, however, a pink glow around that line. Wachena pointed to it.

"You see here, Darci, the healing has begun. The fact that you were in Shalia's life that you loved her and expressed that love to her helped her."

"How, exactly?"

"Even though she was a beautiful young woman, the ugly deformed leg kept her self-esteem low. Your love helped her love herself, so when she passed over, the healing of the cursed limb began."

"I could have done more!

If she had lived, I could have loved her longer and helped her more!"

Wachena looked at me with compassion.

"Shalia was frail to begin with. Her health was never good. In the brief time that you knew her and loved her, you accomplished all that could be done during that lifetime."

"Is that why she died so young?"

"Although it is not quite that simple, yes. Your two Spirits came together and experienced deep healing love. This was stated in both your Soul Contracts, and you both fulfilled what was written. That is why as Hari you gave your life in spiritual service after Shalia's death. Your Soul had accomplished what it came to the Earth plane to do."

"But I didn't die once the contract was fulfilled."

"No. Hari was healthy, strong, and vigorous. You used those extra years to refine your character. Your choices have been very good for the evolution of your Soul. That is why you are here studying to become a Spirit Guide."

"I lived another lifetime on Earth without Angel?"

"Yes, the life just previous to your entering Spirit Guide training."

Wachena smiled and replied, "You'd think that you would go from the monastery directly to Spirit Guide University, wouldn't you? Believe it or not, you had to be separated from Angel for one lifetime. When you died as Hari, you still held your love for Shalia deep in your heart."

"It was in my death imprint."

"Yes. You had to undergo another Earth life to get you to a more neutral place. We wanted you to make the choice to become a Spirit Guide without the conscious influence of your strong bonds to Angel."

"Yet almost as soon as I began my studies, I found her, and all the memories and experiences came flooding back to me."

"That was as it should be.

Now that you are on the path to becoming a Spirit Guide, you may have access to all the information about your and Angel's past experiences."

"I want to know everything, Wachena. If I am to help Angel, wherever she is, I must know everything about her."

Wachena closed The Great Book and put her hand on mine, which brought a very comforting feeling.

"You must rest and assimilate all that you have learned."

"I am fine. I wish to continue. If, indeed, I have lived ninety-two Earth lifetimes, then I have read about only a handful. How many lifetimes have I shared with Angel?"

Wachena sat back and looked me over as if she were scanning me. She didn't speak for a while, and I used that time to shift my gaze. By narrowing my eyes, I could see rings of luminous pink light pulsing from Wachena. Then I noticed the golden light around my own spirit hand.

"Well over half your Earth lifetimes were lived with Angel close to you," she finally responded.

"Unless I can see where Angel is right now . . . then I wish to read more about the lives we have shared on Earth."

"Two things must happen before you see Angel now. One is that she must move from her current level of learning to be born once again on Earth. If you are ready at this point, then as a Spirit Guide in training, you can look in on her . . . as long as you are in the company of a more experienced Guide. Two, you must refine your energy field further, for you are a long way from where it needs to be."

"I don't seem to be able to appear and disappear or move through ceilings and doors like some of the other Guides."

"It all becomes second nature after a while," Wachena smiled again. "You will not be able to graduate to an apprenticeship until your energy is further increased and purified."

"Can I be an apprentice to Angel's next Spirit Guide?" I asked eagerly.

"I can see that this would motivate you.

Your request will be considered."

"Then what is next? I am ready."

"You must rest. Please. Relax. I shall soon return."

She bowed and floated backwards towards the door and exited.

∞ ∞ ∞

The Great Book was still there, but the words had disappeared from all the pages except a few near the beginning. I took this to mean I could read these pages, so I did.

The book described an American Indian village on the edge of the plains at the foot of the mountains. I saw myself as a native girl in a deerskin dress walking to a stream to fetch water. I sat down and peered into a tranquil pool. In the twilight, I saw my face, dark eyes, and dark hair. Suddenly I heard the voice of an elder behind me.

"Bring water," said the elder. The old woman set down two more gourds.

"Time to put away childhood and begin your medicine studies," she said. Her dark beady eyes pierced into me. "Time to focus on learning."

This was the first time the elder had ever spoken to me. She was one of the group of medicine people, the healers of the tribe. Usually they were silent except in ceremonies and healings.

I blushed and hung my head. I had been taught not to speak to these powerful elders.

"I have decided to take you as student. You have possible talent as a healer. Soon we will know."

She pointed toward the camp so I walked in that direction carrying the water. When I stopped and looked back, she was gone.

The very next day my mother woke me at first light and gave me a new dress to wear. She wove my hair into little plaits, then took my hand.

"We are going to old Bear Woman. You will be her student. She has much to teach you."

Mother led me by the hand to the old woman's teepee, which was on the far side of the settlement.

Inside was dark, and I noticed the pungent smell of herbs. The old medicine woman sat cross-legged on the other side of the teepee. She motioned for me to sit opposite her. As my eyes adjusted to the dark, I saw bundles of herbs hanging from the poles and stacks of grasses around the edge of the circular abode.

"You will listen, little Morning Sky. What I teach you, you learn. It will stay with you in your Soul for all time. In your spirit walk, you will heal many."

According to The Great Book, Bear Woman taught me to heal with plants and with energy. I assisted her and other medicine people from our large tribe when they did healings. There was always something to do: a baby to birth or tend, a child with a scrape, a hunter with a wound.

A young brave named Little Elk had been hunting with his father and brother when a mother bear protecting her cubs had wounded him. Little Elk was carried back to camp on a drag. He was brought immediately to the medicine teepee.

My heart leaped when I saw the handsome young brave lying on the drag, blood all over him. He opened his eyes, saw me, and reached out. I felt a warm flush go through me

As Bear Woman cleaned the wound, I watched carefully. Even though I had seen many things since studying with her, I was horrified by the gashes and hanging skin on poor Little Elk. When at last he was tended to, bandaged, and resting, the old healer turned to me. There was a glint in her eye.

"Morning Sky, you stay. Watch him. See if fever comes."

She pointed first to me, then to the wounded young man, then to me. "You two have a bond. You are the best one to heal him. Practice what I have taught you."

So I sat by Little Elk's side. I sang healing songs and shook Bear Woman's rattle over him. I moved my hands above him as the old woman had shown me and prayed to the Great Spirit to spare this young man.

Bear Woman came into the medicine teepee at dawn to find me asleep beside Little Elk. She smiled a little crooked smile as she poked me with her foot.

"Good job. No fever. Boy will be back on his leg soon."

My dedication to learning the healing ways of our tribe increased with Little Elk to tend. I rarely left his side. He did not like being injured, and I had to watch him or he would try to get up and move around before his wounds were healed enough.

Bear Woman said to tell him stories, so I did. I told him tales of the medicine tent, the births I had tended, the injuries, the illnesses, the deaths. When I ran out of those tales, I made up stories. One day, I got Little Elk laughing really hard with the story of a buffalo that fell in love with a prairie chicken.

"That would never work!" he gasped between laughs. "Much better when it is two like you and me."

When I looked away shyly, he touched my arm.

"You're a good woman, a beautiful woman. I want you to be my woman."

I looked him straight in the eye. His eyes were sincere and drew me in. I felt my Soul and his Soul rolling and tumbling in a cosmic dance. I began to tremble as the bottom dropped out of my stomach. There was a loud tone in my head as my Soul recognized his. He was Angel.

Little Elk grabbed my hand and asked if I was all right. I couldn't answer. My mouth was open, but there were no words. He moved closer and put his arm around me. Now my insides were quivering, and my eyes watered. He drew me to him and held me. No words were needed.

Bear Woman found us rocking gently back and forth in this embrace.

"Morning Sky is a good healer. She sure put the spark back in Little Elk."

To keep Little Elk busy while he healed, Bear Woman told him to carve a walking stick. When he finished it, he rolled it over and over in his hands. I admired it and pointed to the parts that I liked.

"Time to stand," he said, planting the beautiful stick next to him. He pulled himself up and smiled. "Walk with me to the stream."

I thought it best to do this in case he fell or reopened one of his wounds. It was a beautiful late spring day. The air was sweet, and many birds sang to us as we walked slowly towards the brook. When we got to the pool, some children were playing there.

"That was us not long ago," said Little Elk nodding toward the scampering children. "Now we are grown and must make our contribution to the tribe."

I looked at him. He was staring at me with a serious and very earnest look.

"My father and grandfather and all my brothers are hunters," he continued. "One day I was to be Great Elk, most famous of all the hunters and warriors. But now, that is not my path."

He looked down and poked a stone by the water's edge with his stick. Then he looked into my eyes with such intensity I stopped breathing as my heart pounded.

"You have opened my eyes to my true path, Morning Sky. I am going to study to be a healer, too. Bear Woman agrees that I am called to it. She said the mother bear brought me into the medicine teepee so that I could know this. I begin my training with tomorrow's sunrise."

I exhaled, my heart fluttering with joy. Little Elk and I would be learning together. The young man took a very deep breath and moved closer to me.

"We can be partners," he said softly. "We can work together to help and to heal."

He brought his face close to mine. "We can join together for life and make our own family.

Would you like that, my beautiful sunrise? Will you be my wife?"

As I nodded yes, he embraced me, and I experienced tumbling exhilaration, feeling as if we were linked for all time.

Little Elk worked hard at learning the healing techniques of the tribe. He studied with the oldest and wisest of the medicine men.

In autumn, we were married. Before our wedding ceremony, Little Elk went through an initiation changing his name to Night Sky Fire. This made his new path as a healer official.

We had four children, three who lived to be adults and take their places in the tribe.

One spring evening when we were tribal elders and had apprentices of our own, we sat by the river bank and watched the sky. There were dancing streaks of color and a fiery glow towards the north.

"Night Sky Fire," I said pointing to the northern lights. "Your name sake."

"It is a sign," said my beloved husband. "Great Spirit calls me home."

"No! We may be old, but we have much more we can do here!"

"You forget, my sweet sunrise, I am older than you. I have been hearing the owl speak to me." He looked at me with kindness and much love in his eyes and continued, "There is nothing to fear. We have served our people well. Great Spirit will unite us once again."

I held him close. We had shared everything, and I could not imagine going on without my dear husband. I knew his old injury pained him, and it was becoming more difficult for him to get around.

He stayed for the summer, continuing to teach and train his students, but on a chilly autumn night, the northern lights called him home. He passed away in my arms as we slept together. His Spirit had departed peacefully.

Morning sun crept into our teepee to find me rocking my husband's lifeless body. I wept, but in my heart I knew we would be together again, for we had lived a good life of service, and our Souls had bonded through our work and through our love.

As I finished reading the last paragraph, all the words on the page disappeared. Once again I was very moved by the memory of holding Angel as she passed from Earth life. I knew it was time for me to rest and assimilate.

I closed The Great Book and stretched. Now I did feel the need for rejuvenation. I also felt myself vibrating with a warm, even energy. I narrowed my eyes and saw beautiful waves of pink light evenly spaced, radiating from my spirit body. My love for Angel was manifesting in my energy field once again.

I lay down and contemplated all I had learned. I wondered why The Great Book had shown me that last lifetime, for it predated our lifetime in the Middle Ages, our lifetime in India, and perhaps even our lifetime in Egypt.

Chalherine's voice came into my head. This surprised me though it probably shouldn't have. I knew all Spirit Guides in training were closely monitored.

"You have been shown Angel's karmic situation," Chalherine told me telepathically. "Now you are receiving details on what skills you have acquired and what you two have accomplished together. You can see from this American Indian lifetime that you two became powerful healers. Your time together in Egypt showed you to be masterful healers, especially when you worked together. We wanted you to see part of the positive side of your bond with Angel. You two have earned the ability to communicate with each other and to heal powerfully through your soul connection. Remember this, Darci. Now rest."

I breathed deeply and smiled. I knew in my heart that no matter what deep dark karmic situation Angel had gotten herself into, we could get her out of it by working together.

∞ ∞ ∞

When I awoke, Sottrol was sitting across from me. White light emanated from him in pulsing, sparkling rings. I remember thinking that he seemed brighter than ever.

"That's because of you, Darci," he informed me telepathically. "When our students do well, we also thrive."

Sitting up, I turned to face him. "What is next, Sottrol? Another class? An exercise I must complete? I want to get on with this."

My voice rose in volume, as my passion flowed, "Angel needs my help, Sottrol! I know now the severity of the trouble she is in! Saving her Soul is worth every effort! My beautiful Angel! Please, let me see her. Let me help her. I must help her!"

After inhaling deeply, I spoke in a quieter tone, "You know me, Sottrol. I want to focus on this. I want to devote myself fully to becoming a Spirit Guide so that I may help my dear Angel."

The mentor glided to my side and rested a hand on my shoulder. Serenity filled me.

"Darci, you must rest and strengthen yourself, for the path ahead is long and arduous. I will tell you this. Angel has just been born on the Earth plane. Her Soul once again inhabits a human body. She is now but a newborn babe. If all goes well, you will see her before long."

My heart thrummed with excitement at the thought of such a reunion. My entire spirit body vibrated with love for Angel.

"Good, good, Darci," Sottrol smiled. "That is an excellent response. Do you see your aura? It glows like the Earth's sun."

I looked down and saw white and gold light swirling around my hands and bright pink and gold radiance pulsing from my chest.

"I do, Sottrol. I see."

"You have learned your lessons well. You excelled in your classes with Luanna and Beminer, and although you have taken a different path than most of our students here at university, you are learning rapidly. Chalherine told me she believes that you have grasped the meaning of karma and you understand the death and birth imprints used for humans. I can see for myself that you read auras. In our estimation, you have successfully completed your classes at Spirit Guide University."

I nodded, my thoughts still on Angel.

"What you need now is patience and rest."

I sighed.

"I know you are anxious to meet Angel. Know that she is being watched over right now by an excellent Spirit Guide."

I stood. "But Sottrol. I am to be her Guide!"

He placed his hands on my shoulder and without effort caused me to sit.

"Darci, you know you are not yet ready."

"I want to be ready," I cried. "What can I do?"

"Assimilate all the lessons you have learned so far. Make sure they are a natural part of your very Being. And rest."

He looked me in the eyes. "I am serious, Darci. Take care and rest. Go back over anything and everything. You cannot move on until Chalherine and I know for certain that you are ready. The most recent life experiences you read about have affected you greatly. Rest and assimilate—and know that you are doing well. If anyone can complete the training to become a Spirit Guide in record time, it will be you, Darci."

With those words, he turned and stepped into a funnel of radiant white light, which spun and lifted out of sight.

I sat for a while with my head in my hands, knowing I had no choice but to be patient and wait for the next challenge to arrive. I would follow the elder's advice. I would go back over every lesson, every experience. I would do whatever was necessary to become a Spirit Guide and be with Angel again.

Chapter Seven:
Mountains and Valleys Unite

Trust is important when studying to become a Spirit Guide. I learned to trust my teachers and to follow their instructions. Chalherine and Sottrol visited me separately, then again together. It seemed to me that my studies were stalled. I had been resting and assimilating for a while and was anxious to move forward. A sense of urgency nagged at me often. I knew that my dear soul mate Angel was in deep karmic trouble, and I desperately wanted to help her. I had been told that I could do nothing at present except continue my studies, so I used my free time praying for her. In fact, I was sending prayers and light to Angel when Sottrol and Chalherine entered my chamber.

"Ah, at last I can go on with my training," I said to myself, remembering mid-thought that the two elders could telepathically hear me thinking.

"A bit antsy to get on with it, are we, Darci?" Sottrol said as he hugged me.

Chalherine, too, embraced me, and between the two of them, I received a burst of energy that lifted me off the floor.

"We want to be certain how best to proceed with your studies," Chalherine began. "By your own decisions and reactions, you have taken yourself onto your own innovative path of learning. This will work only if we are sure you are getting everything you need."

"And more," added Sottrol.

"You began your Spirit Guide training like the other students," Chalherine continued. "However, once you came into my wing of the university, you seemed to strike out on your own. Your studies on karma were completely different from those of the other trainees."

Sottrol winked at me adding, "You finished them sooner, too, Darci. You are well motivated."

Chalherine smiled, and I relaxed a little.

"If all my students had such a strong bond with another Soul still on the lower spiral, then perhaps they would progress as you have," she said. "Sottrol and I have been contemplating and discussing how best to proceed in your case. Your passion and dedication have taken you onto a truly unique path of learning."

"What have I left to learn?"

I thought knowing that would be a good place to start.

Chalherine moved her hands up and down, palms facing me as if measuring something.

"You must increase and refine your energy, Darci. It has to be to a specific level and quality before you can become an apprentice."

"Lots of time in the Power Booth," Sottrol clarified. "You've chosen to read rather than spend much time in the Booth."

I realized that I had shied away from using that unpredictable and powerful tool.

"So now I must make up for it? Is that what you are saying?" I asked.

Chalherine put her hand on my shoulder and replied, "You did some of this energy work as you were reacquainting yourself with your past lifetimes. Love is what it's all about, Darci, and you have an abundance of love for the Soul we call Angel. Your love for her and the compassion that you feel for her have already raised your personal energy level quite a bit."

Sottrol stepped closer and continued, "We have come up with a program for you that we think you will like—one for one."

"One what?" I questioned, not following.

Chalherine, motioning towards the door of the Power Booth, clarified, "One session in the Booth, one lifetime from

The Great Book. Then back to the Power Booth, then another reading."

"We will keep an eye on you, Darci," Sottrol reassured me patting my arm. "You did so well with your studies of karma that we decided to keep utilizing The Great Book of Lifetimes. Most of the students who started when you did haven't yet seen a death or a birth imprint. You have experienced how they work in an intimate and personal way."

"I am motivated. I know I must get to the point where I can help Angel."

"And so you shall, Mr. Stillwater," said Chalherine as she bowed a little and floated towards the ceiling.

Just as she disappeared, Sottrol spoke.

"There are no short cuts here. Be aware of that. You must meet every high standard for a practicing Spirit Guide. I brought you the Spirit Guide Creed. Since you are not in class with the others, do as they do. Speak it often. Perhaps you could repeat it before you sit to read in The Great Book."

He handed me a scroll edged in gold.

"But for now, the Power Booth awaits you," Sottrol said as he bowed his head and vanished.

The deep breath I took came out more like a sigh. It was true—I had not chosen to enter the Power Booth very often after my first time. The element of uncertainty put me off. I never knew what would happen to me once I stepped through that opening. I told myself that I had to trust the elders and the process. I reminded myself that I had always felt better following the time spent in the Power Booth.

Standing before the symbol that showed where the door was located, I stated, "This is for you, Angel, for you and for me."

I placed my hands on either side of the symbol, and before I had a chance to say a prayer or even take a breath, the oval door appeared, and I was literally sucked in through the opening.

I fell as if I had been blown off a cliff.

The falling sensation was not unpleasant, yet I could not help feeling uneasy. As I plummeted, lights were flashing all around me. At first, they were green and white, then magenta and white, then purple and white, then gold.

When the golden lights danced around me, a strange thing occurred. My fall slowed, and I found myself suspended. The dazzling golden lights around me intensified until I was nearly blinded by their brilliance.

I found I could hover and maneuver a little. As I moved towards the lights on one side of me, I heard a great tone; when I moved away, it stopped. After floating for a while, it occurred to me that perhaps I needed to move into the rays of gold and vibrate with the tone.

"Trust," I told myself. "Trust the Power Booth."

I followed my intuition and moved into the brilliant flashing gold light to one side. The tone began again and vibrated through me. It became louder as I floated there. Suddenly it stopped, and I was propelled back into the center.

Next I picked the opposite direction and moved into the sparkling golden light. This time the tone was higher, and the vibrations I felt were faster. The same thing happened. The tone ceased after a while, and I was jettisoned back to the center.

All in all, I entered the golden curtain of glittering luminescence eight times. After the eighth exit, purple rays that provided a calm, steady, violet light immediately surrounded me. This was a relief after all the bright flashing gold. The violet light also brought a buoyant feeling.

I felt myself rise up higher and higher in this field of purple light. I then heard a whirring sound and found myself moving through the familiar oval doorway into my chamber. I was vibrating all over at a very high rate. Sitting on one of the benches, I took note of how I felt. I had a sense of something within me dissolving, yet I was exhilarated at the same time. This mystified me.

It wasn't long after I returned to my chamber that Sottrol stopped in to check on me. He made his usual instantaneous arrival as he manifested on the bench across from where I was resting.

"A few more sessions like that one, lad, and you will be on your way."

"Hello, Sottrol. I'm doing well?"

"Fine, just fine. See for yourself."

I closed my eyes, then opened them to slits and was surprised by the intensity of the golden light I saw emanating from my spirit body.

"I will not stay long," continued the elder. "Please remember to repeat the Spirit Guide Creed before you open The Great Book."

He sat quietly and studied me for a moment or two, then vanished.

∞ ∞ ∞

Unrolling the scroll he had given me earlier, I read aloud the creed I had heard spoken in a classroom shortly after my arrival.

As Spirit Guides, we walk in light. We come to the Earth plane to help and to heal, to guide, and to love. We work always from the highest vibration of uncompromising, unconditional love. We never judge humans. We do not frighten or scare anyone. We stay close to the humans we watch over, stepping back when they request privacy. We use all our resources as Spirit Guides to help and to heal.

A full-fledged Spirit Guide—that's what I wanted to be— that was my goal. With that in mind, I opened The Great Book of Lifetimes, wondering what it had to show me this time.

The words on the page took me to a tropical setting in the Americas. The air was steamy and rich with fragrances from the surrounding flora. There I was, a young man running along a path. I could hear my feet hitting the dirt as I ran. I was on a mission for the village healer who wanted some bark from a certain tree. My mother was ill and needed medicine from this bark, so I hurried to the spot where I knew there was such a tree. The path followed a vibrant stream that rolled down from the mountains.

Soon the sound of a waterfall reached my ears, and I knew I was near my destination. I stopped short because I also heard the voices of women talking and laughing. I slowed my pace and approached the waterfall quietly, ducking behind some bushes.

The pool at the base of the waterfall was filled with women. There were a dozen or so females: two elders, two mothers with babies, several pregnant women and other women of varying ages. They were bathing, some splashing in the pool and some on the rocks enjoying the midday sun as it filtered through the lush vegetation.

I could not help watching from the bushes, for I had never seen such a sight. In this warm climate, no one wore much clothing, but these women were completely naked. They were all relaxed and enjoying the pool.

I crouched, peering through the bushes for a while as any man might when I felt two hands clamp onto my shoulders. I was pulled roughly backwards and fell hard upon my back. I looked up to see a young woman standing over me holding a spear right at my throat. She glared at me fiercely. I put my hands up, moving the point of the spear away.

She stepped on my hair and spat at me, "Intruder!"

I could tell from her dress and dialect that she was from a tribe that lived on the other side of the mountain. I had visited there once with my uncle.

"No!" I sputtered, trying to catch my breath. "I am here on a special mission for Xetico, our healer."

She bent down putting her spear at my throat. In a sudden move, I grabbed the shaft and pulled her off her feet. We tumbled over one another. The spear fell into the brush. Since

I was bigger, I ended up pinning her down, my knees on her legs, my hands holding down her arms. We were face-to-face.

Time stopped. Everything stopped as our eyes met and held. I pressed down firmly so she couldn't move, yet she was affecting me with her eyes. They dove deep into me and made my stomach quiver. Then my groin seemed to come alive with fire. I felt dizzy but kept my tight hold on her.

Our eyes continued to pierce each other's Souls as we both breathed heavily from the scuffle. I knew her. My Soul knew her. It was Angel.

She was beautiful, strong, and lean with her dark hair braided with golden grasses. She wore a kind of woven tunic that covered her torso. I wished for a moment that I had spied her naked in the pool with the others.

"I must gather medicine," I told her, still holding her down. "I came to collect bark. My mother is ill."

"You came upon a private sacred ritual for the women of our tribe, which no man is allowed to see."

"It was an accident that I saw this. I mean you no harm."

"Then let me up!" She struggled, but I held her even tighter.

"You must promise to let me collect the medicine bark and be on my way."

"Yes, yes. Just go quickly and do not look again at the women in the pool."

I continued to hold her down.

"There is something else I want," I said boldly.

She tried to kick, but I had her legs pinned.

"What is it?" she hissed.

"I want to visit you where you live."

"No! That cannot be!"

"I will not let you up until you say yes." I blew in her face.

"I have too many brothers. They will not let you near our hut. I will meet you here."

"When?"

"At sunset and moonrise—when mother moon is full and round."

"Promise me. Swear a solemn oath, for I will come."

"I promise. Two sunsets from now. I am called Nunzah."

"I am Zontyl. Meet you here in two sunsets."

Once I took a few pieces of the medicinal bark, I made the trip home quickly, as it was all downhill. My people lived on the flat lands below the mountain and grew corn in the fertile soil. My father was a member of the council of leaders, and as his son I had various duties, such as helping to oversee the planting, cultivation, and harvest. I had started in the fields as a boy, so I knew every aspect of the job.

Nunzah's people, the mountain tribes, were much different. They foraged and hunted for their food. Many in my clan looked down on them as savages. It was true our village had more sophisticated houses and gathering places, including a circular arena for ceremonies; however, I was fascinated by the mountain people and had been ever since I visited them as a boy. Now I had a rendezvous with one of them and couldn't help being excited by the prospect.

Two days hence, I made sure my work was done early so I could take my time climbing through the forest. I arrived first and enjoyed a swim and then dozed on a flat rock by the pool.

Out of nowhere a great wave of water splashed upon me. It was Nunzah waking me. She had come to meet me.

We swam for a while in the twilight. Finally we crawled out of the pool and lay on the rock in the humid night air.

"You are a good swimmer," I started the conversation.

"You are not bad either—for a boy from the lowlands," she retorted.

"Have you been to my village?"

"No, and I don't care to go."

"Why? It is beautiful, especially when the fields are full."

"Your people do not like us," she said defensively. "I know this. I have heard the talk from the others in my clan."

"I like you. We are different, but that can be good.

210

What do you do for your tribe?"

"I hunt with my brothers."

"You are a woman. Your tribe has women hunters?"

She took a moment, then answered, "I want to be like my brothers. It is true that as a girl, I was made to go wild gathering with the women—but now I hunt."

"What have you killed?"

She dropped her head a little. "Well—nothing yet. I have just been given permission to hunt with my brothers. I've gone out twice, but so far they have brought down all the game."

I moved a little closer to her on the rock and said, "You protect the tribeswomen. I know that for look how you pounced on me!"

She replied, looking at me seriously. "I should have killed you for gazing upon our sacred women's ritual. You must never tell anyone what you saw, or you will place yourself in danger."

"You could not harm me, Nunzah. We have a link—a connection. I was dreaming of it when you found me lying on this rock."

She sat silent for a moment, sighed softly, and replied, "I really don't know what my life will be, Zontyl. I do not fit in with my brothers though I try. I do not wish to have the life of a woman in my tribe. It is hard work from first light to last— except for the sacred ceremonies like the one you saw."

"You are beautiful, strong, smart, and quick. You can do what you like. Why not visit my people? We all work hard in my village, too, but we also have time for fun."

"I will be ridiculed by your people."

"Not if you are with me."

She would not agree to come but did not say no, so I moved on to other topics. We talked about our childhood, our families, and our favorite things. Then I began talking about my future.

We were both lying on our backs, staring at the stars when I mentioned having many children.

She scrambled to a seated position and looked at me.

"Have you ever seen a child being born?"

"No, but I have seen the pregnant women of your tribe and how beautiful they are."

She splashed some water at me. "I told you not to speak of seeing that sacred ceremony!"

"You are the only one I can talk to about it. Have you thought of having a child? You are old enough."

"I have seen childbirth, and it frightens me. That is my fate unless I do something extraordinary—like become the best hunter our tribe has ever seen."

"My mother said she loved having every one of her children. She said the sky god came and held her hand when I was born."

"Humph!"

Now it was my turn to splash water on her. Before long, we were showering each other until we were soaking wet once again. Grabbing her shoulders, I rolled with her off the rock into the pool. I pulled her under and kissed her. We surfaced, gasping. She kicked water in my face.

"You are very bold, Zontyl," she sputtered. "I should kill you for doing that!"

I laughed heartily and kicked water back at her.

"Big talk, but you are not meant to be a hunter, a killer of life. You are meant to be with me. Together we will make life."

She dove below the surface, grabbed me at the waist and pulled me under. I wrapped my legs around her and kissed her again.

"You are really asking for it," she cried when we came up for air.

"Asking for what? For you? Yes! I am asking for you! Come to my village with me, Nunzah."

"No!"

"You can meet my family."

"No!"

"You would be my honored guest."

"No!"

"You will sit at the head of the table and enjoy a great feast of corn."

"Corn?"

"Yes. I help grow it. The harvest is near, and you can have all you want."

She swam to the rock, pulled herself out of the pool, and sat with her legs in the water. I could see her wet skin glistening in the moonlight.

"I have had corn only twice when our people traded for it. It was the most heavenly food I ever ate—and you grow it?"

I swam to her and rested my arms on her legs.

"Please, please come to the corn harvest celebration with me. It is only a moon away. I promise you can have all you want, and you can take some back to your people."

She sat silently as I fingered her wet braids.

"Please, Nunzah. You will come as my guest."

"All right. I'll come."

My heart leapt with joy. I pulled her back into the pool and kissed her again. This time she relaxed and kissed me back.

"Zontyl, I must return to my tribe well before first light. If my brothers realize I have been away all this time, they will question me and force me to tell them where I have been."

"You must find a way to spend at least a day with me during the harvest festival. You agreed to come."

"I will try. It may be that once I visit you, I will not be able to return to my people though I hope that will not be the case."

We planned to meet at that very spot a week later, but she did not arrive. She knew the harvest festival was on the next full moon, so on the eve of the event, I returned to the waterfall hoping that this time she would meet me there. I was very tired, for I had been working hard bringing in the crop and preparing for the festivities. I fell asleep by the pool as the sun was setting.

Nunzah arrived in a panic, sure that her brothers were on her trail. She bolted forward down the mountain path with me at her heels. I noticed she was wearing several travel satchels. When we stopped to rest, she confessed that she had left her home.

A sad look came over her face as she sighed, "I tried— but I do not fit in. I do not want to end up like my mother working, working, working for her husband and children with no time for anything else. Yet I cannot keep up with my brothers and the other the men on the hunt. I must strike out and try something new."

At that moment we heard voices and footsteps on the trail. We lay flat on the moss and peered through the ferns. Three large men with spears ran by us and continued down the trail. Nunzah told me the men were her brothers, so we climbed into a large tree and hid. The rain obscured our footprints.

Her brothers came by twice more—once down the path, then up again.

At first light we descended and literally ran down the mountain, stopping only once for a drink at a spring by the path. The sun was two hours up by the time we arrived in my village, which was alive with activity. The corn festival was that day, and the feast was being prepared.

Nunzah's eyes were wide as we walked through the streets. We were quite a sight after being rained on, spending the night in a tree, and then running for our lives. Those who passed us nodded at me and stared at Nunzah. It was obvious she was from the mountains.

I headed directly to my family's complex, one of the larger homes in this thriving village. My mother and sisters were busy preparing food. Everything stopped when I appeared in the doorway with Nunzah. There was an awkward moment. Then my mother motioned for me and my guest to follow her. She had recovered from her illness but still needed rest. She appeared to be tired as she sat us down in one of the more private rooms.

"Zontyl, what have you done?"

"Mother, this is my friend Nunzah."

"Hello, Nunzah. Do your people know you are here with my son?"

Nunzah looked at me, her eyes wide with apprehension.

"Nunzah has left her people, Mother. She is my guest. I want her to stay."

"This is serious business, my son. We do not want trouble with the mountain people. The girl must go back."

Nunzah stood up, pleading, "No! No, please. I wanted to leave my people. It was my idea, not Zontyl's. I don't mean to bring you trouble. I will move on."

Now I stood, grabbing the young woman's shoulders and told her, "No! You can't leave here. We just found each other. You must stay! Please stay!"

Mother sighed and answered, "We'll discuss this later. Nunzah, is it? You'll stay for the feast. You look as if you could use some food. I will send one of my daughters to help bathe and dress you."

I washed and donned my festival clothes. I was excited to show Nunzah how good life could be in this village.

The feast was due to start when the sun was highest in the sky. I was helping set the last of the giant torches for the evening celebration when I saw my sister approaching with a stunning young woman. It was Nunzah.

I was so awed by the sight that I dropped the torch pole on my foot. The two girls laughed.

Every time I had seen Nunzah before, she had been streaked with dirt or soaking wet. This was a new look for her that made me blink my eyes. My sisters had bathed her and combed out her hair. She wore one of my sister's ankle-length tunics, and she had a lovely rosy glow about her. I was overwhelmed. I walked over to them and grasped Nunzah's hands.

She squeezed back hard and said under her breath, "Zontyl, I don't know anyone here but you, so do not leave me again!"

Throughout the entire festival, Nunzah stayed by my side. I delighted in showing her everything. She enjoyed the feast, though she was too excited to eat much. She especially loved the torch lit chanting and singing in the ceremonial circle.

We were both so exhausted from the day's festivities and our sleepless night in the tree that we drifted away from the activity to find a place to rest. I took her to a grassy spot at the edge of the village. We lay down and admired the night sky.

"Thank you, Zontyl," said Nunzah, stifling a yawn. "If I die tomorrow, I will be happy because I have been a part of all this."

We slept until dawn, wrapped in each other's arms and dreams.

Feast day was over and I had responsibilities to tend to. The harvest had to be stored and seeds saved. Nunzah would not leave my side, so I let her help. I talked about cultivation as a good way of life.

I was showing Nunzah how we choose our seeds when my sister ran up to us saying that three mountain men had arrived at our village. They were looking for Nunzah, and although she wanted to face them to avoid trouble for our village, I wouldn't let her. My sister shoved us into one of the huts where the corn was stored. Only moments later we heard heavy footsteps and the voices of Nunzah's brothers.

Nunzah and I sat wrapped in each other's arms trying to make ourselves invisible behind the mounds of corn. She was trembling. It was not easy for me to sit still. I wanted to jump up and face these men, but for Nunzah's sake, I did not.

We could hear them talking to several of the villagers, including my sister.

I had gotten used to Nunzah's dialect, so I could make out some but not all of what the men were saying. I heard the words "chief" and "promised" and "shame on the family."

I looked at Nunzah, and tears streaked her face. This shocked me because she had always seemed so tough. As her brothers moved away from our hiding spot, I held her head and rocked her.

"What is this? Why the tears?"

She hung her head. A sob escaped as she explained, "I did not tell you every reason I wish to leave my people. I did not lie to you. I just did not tell you all."

"Tell me now."

"Yes. You will hear it from the other villagers. My father is the leader. He is the chief."

"You never mentioned your father."

"That's because as chief, he has planned my destiny. He gave me as a peace settlement to a warrior from a neighboring mountain tribe. There was a dispute over a hunting area. My father and his advisors want good relations with this tribe, so they see my marriage to this fierce warrior as a way of achieving this. I pleaded with my father not to bargain me away. I did everything I could to show him that I would not fit the role of wife to this frightening man. He is not like you, Zontyl. This warrior is cruel. I know he would abuse me."

"How do you know?"

"He asked to see me during the negotiations. He walked around me, looking me up and down like a piece of game he had just killed. He pulled my hair—hard. He poked my stomach until it hurt. I would rather die than put myself at the mercy of this man!"

"How could your father give you to a man like that?"

"Father is the leader and must be concerned with the entire tribe. He told me that I could be most useful to my people by becoming this warrior's wife. He said I would bring shame on my people if I did not mate with this horrible man. Oh, Zontyl, this warrior is coarse and crude. He has evil in his eyes and on his breath!"

My mind was reeling. I was holding a tribal princess promised to a fierce warrior of another tribe. Picturing the two mountain tribes joining forces and attacking our village made me shudder.

"We must go before the Council," I told her. "I want you to stay, but it is not up to me. The Council will decide if you can join our people."

A meeting was called at my father's request. I spoke on behalf of Nunzah. Several of the villagers who had talked with her brothers also spoke. Finally my father asked Nunzah to say what was in her heart. The young woman stood bravely before the Council and dozens of onlookers. She spoke slowly so all could understand her.

"I have never in my life known such kindness as has been shown to me by this man, Zontyl—and by all of you. I would like nothing better than to join your village. However, I do not want to bring trouble or danger to your peaceful settlement. I wish to do all I can to help your community, not harm it."

I was proud of Nunzah. She spoke well. We sat holding hands as the Council discussed her. My father offered a solution.

"Let us negotiate with this woman's father. Let us bring him corn and try to find a way to settle this."

There was more discussion, especially about the savage tribe that Nunzah had been promised to. Finally I stood, indicating I wished to speak.

"You all know me. You know my family. You know how hard I work for this village. You know how I love it here. My happiness rests on having this woman, this tribal princess, as my wife."

I heard a gasp from Nunzah. We had never talked of marriage. I glanced at her and saw that her cheeks were flushed.

The Council members asked us to step outside while they made their decision, so Nunzah and I walked under the night sky. We didn't speak for a while. Then we started to talk at the same time. We laughed as I nodded for her to go on.

"You never asked me to be your wife."

"I know. I want that though. I think I have loved you since our first scuffle by the waterfall."

"I'm not sure I want to be any man's wife."

I stopped walking and stood in front of her. I took her face in my hands and looked deep into her eyes.

"We have a connection, Nunzah—a connection written in the stars—written in our Souls. You cannot deny this."

"If I were to marry any man . . ."

I interrupted her by putting my lips on hers. It took a moment, but she kissed me back. It felt as if we were standing in a bolt of lightning. Electricity soared through us. No more words were needed.

The Council elected to send an envoy to her father with a gift of corn. Several days later, he returned with a list of what the old chief wanted for his daughter. My family agreed to the terms, and Nunzah was officially welcomed into our village. We were married just after the crop was planted—such a hopeful time. I remember the green shoots poking up from the ground. They seemed to be singing, "Happy day, joyful day!"

It was the custom to have a great feast when there was a wedding. The celebration lasted well into the night. We were given a modest hut that had belonged to one of the elders who had passed on. We returned to our new home while the village chanted and sang to us.

My new wife was radiant. She wore a crown of flowers, a necklace of flowers, and flowers around her ankles. I was removing these decorations as the celebration continued outside our new home. Nunzah drew me close to her.

"I would do this for no one but you," she whispered in my ear.

We found ourselves often uniting in love, and when the corn stood shoulder-high in the fields, my beautiful Nunzah was pregnant. As the corn grew, so did her belly and so did her fears of childbirth.

Nunzah grew bigger and moved more slowly. I spent as much time with her as I could. My sisters visited her when I was busy. One humid misty morning, I left early to meet with my father and some of the village planners so Nunzah was alone. Just as we were ending our discussion, my sister ran to me.

"Where's Nunzah?" she asked, looking worried.

A pang struck my heart and stomach at once.

"She's not at home?"

"I can't find her."

Trying not to panic, we searched for my wife whose time to give birth was coming very soon. One of the hunters joined the search and spotted some footprints leading from our hut to the nearby woods. There were at least three sets of fresh tracks.

"Someone has taken her," the hunter informed us. "See this mark? Here they are dragging her." He walked a few steps. "Here they pick her up and carry her."

I was buzzing head to foot with panic, fear, and worry. I could barely move.

"They can't have gone far," said my father. "Let's gather a search party—quickly!"

He grabbed my arm, "Son, who could have done this?"

I couldn't answer. I was terrified for my beautiful Nunzah.

The hunter said, "Warriors from the mountain tribes. At least that's the way they are heading."

"Nunzah's people wouldn't take her," I finally spat out the words. "They came to our wedding. They approved the match!"

The hunter examined scuffle marks by the door of the hut, "She resisted. You can see where she dug in her heels."

"Gather the men," ordered my father.

We decided to head first to Nunzah's people. A group of eight of us arrived by nightfall. Her family was unaware of the abduction. Her father, the chief, looked troubled but said nothing. Her mother, a sweet little woman with beautiful eyes, took me aside. She grasped my wrist and squeezed it hard.

"I knew no good would come of this," she said.

"Our marriage?"

"No, no. His lies!" She nodded towards the chief who sat with a scowl on his face. "I will tell you this because he will not. My daughter's life and the life of your child depend on you finding her!"

"Who took her? Do you know?"

She crouched and pulled me down next to her.

"Meletmuc!" She almost spit the name. "The warrior from our neighboring tribe, the one to whom my daughter was first promised. My oh-so-smart husband saw that he could receive many material things from your family in exchange for Nunzah. I saw she would be happier and much better off with you. The problem was how to escape the pact that my husband had already made with Meletmuc."

"I wondered about that. What did the chief do?"

"He lied. He said she died. He told that fierce warrior an outright lie, and now we are experiencing the consequences. My poor Nunzah with her time so near."

"What will he do to her?" I was wild with worry.

"I do not know." The elder woman shook her head. "He must have found out she was alive and living in your village. I want to go with you on your search, but I would only slow you down. Take one of the healers with you. Nunzah and her baby may need him."

Two of Nunzah's brothers, a healer, and another hunter joined our ranks, so now we were twelve. They knew the way to the camp where Meletmuc had probably taken my wife.

We left at first light and approached at dusk. Nunzah's brother told us to stay hidden and quiet while he scouted the area. He said he would try to find where in the camp they were holding her.

I sat feeling very helpless, my heart crying out for my poor wife. She was terrified enough about enduring childbirth; now she was also at the mercy of a man she feared. I prayed to the sky god and to the gods of the Earth.

I began weeping. My compassion for Nunzah flowed.

Then, as I sat in the brush outside that primitive camp, I had a vision. I saw a tall lighted being, an apparition, standing before me. The figure was so bright that I could not make out any features or details. The being held out its arms, and I felt a wave of peace flow over me. The lighted figure then glided away and into the enemy camp. It rose up and hovered over a hut on the far side. I knew instantly that my beloved Nunzah was there. The luminous being continued to float as I went to the other men.

"I know where she is! Let's go!" I called in a hoarse whisper.

The tone of my voice must have convinced them, for several followed me as I moved quietly through the woods toward the hut on the far side. It was not easy. The terrain was steep, but I moved as quickly as I could on the slope.

The hut was crudely built. It had no windows, but there were spaces between the sticks that made the walls. There was a small fire in front of this hut, as there were before several of the others. This particular hut had more activity. There was a warrior guard at the front by the fire. Another warrior entered as I watched.

"Meletmuc," Nunzah's brother nodded towards the man.

He was big and looked very menacing. I heard his agitated voice coming from that little hut, and I couldn't stand it! I crawled towards the hut, signaling for the others to stay back. My heart sank into the pit of my stomach when I peeked through the opening between the sticks. There lay my wife. Her mouth was bound with reeds. Her hands were above her head, lashed to a pole with vines. Meletmuc stood over her shouting. I understood most of what he said. He went on and on about how he had been deceived and humiliated, how he wanted revenge and justice.

Horror overtook me as I saw the angry warrior take a knife and cut away Nunzah's clothing. I could see the tears rolling from her eyes.

He ran the flat of his crude knife over her belly, then straddled her.

I was about to leap in and stop him though it most certainly would have meant my death when the other members of our rescue party entered the camp from the far side causing a distraction. Meletmuc spit on my poor wife and left to see who was entering his camp. The guard followed him.

Immediately I sneaked into the hut and cut Nunzah's bonds with my knife. She was dirty and scared but unhurt. She was so glad to see me that she threw her arms around me, weeping.

The healer and another hunter were waiting for us, and we moved as fast as we could away from the camp and into the deep woods. In Nunzah's condition, she could not run. The terrain was too steep and rocky for me to continue to carry her. She put her arm around my shoulders and, as a team, we made our way up the slope.

The two others went before us. Both men were from Nunzah's tribe, so they knew the mountain. Nothing was said. We followed them up and up for what seemed like hours. Nunzah was panting and holding very tightly to me. She moaned, and I felt warm liquid pour down the outside of my leg.

"The baby!" she gasped. "The baby comes now. The water is the sign."

I signaled to the others. The healer saw what was happening.

"We are very near a cave that will be safe," he said. "Not in Meletmuc's territory. Come!"

We struggled on. Nunzah was sweating and her eyes were wide. At long last, we reached the small cave. The other two men dragged brush in front of the opening while I tried to make my wife comfortable.

I removed my tunic so that she would have something to lie on. We sat in the darkness. I could hear her breathing heavily, moaning slightly.

The hunter stood guard while the healer joined us. Our child would soon be born.

In those dark hours before dawn, Nunzah endured the waves of pain that come before childbirth. We had no water, but the healer brought her a certain kind of leaf to chew on. As first light entered the small cave, I was able to discern the outline of my wife's body and watch as the natural process of birth overtook her. The healer paid close attention to her. He and the other man from Nunzah's tribe had gathered some large soft leaves and made a place for her to deliver. I was astounded by the phenomenon, for I had never seen a body contract in such intense rhythms before.

Nunzah didn't cry out—perhaps out of fear of being found—but she did moan. I held her in my arms as much as I could. Restless and continually shifting positions, she was wet with sweat and acted like an animal in pain. I wanted to ease her discomfort. I felt so helpless.

As the first rays of the sun filtered through the forest, her breathing became very fast, and the healer indicated that the baby was about to arrive. I never knew a human body could do what my wife's body did at that moment. She groaned and opened. A round slimy head appeared. Clutching onto me, she grunted and pushed, then moaned long and low as the baby slid out into the hands of the healer.

Nunzah collapsed in my arms as the healer set about cleaning the child's face. I could see that we had a son and watched in amazement as the man severed the cord between my wife and the child. The healer then sent the hunter to find water. We tried to clean up mother and baby as best we could. Our new son seemed fine. He didn't cry, almost as if he knew we were in hiding.

We stayed there that entire day. The hunter brought us fruit and large leaves filled with water. Nunzah was weak and tired. She was bruised and had raw red marks on her wrists from being tied up. I sat so she could lean against me and hold our son. She closed her eyes and let him nurse.

Finally, she looked at peace.

The hunter informed us that there had been a battle at the camp after we escaped. Some people on both sides had been killed. The remainder of the rescue team had fled back to Nunzah's people, but he said we shouldn't go there because Meletmuc was looking for us and expected us to go that way.

Although it was much further away, we decided to try to make it to my village, which was large and well-protected. This would not be easy. In fact, once we began our journey, I wondered if we might have been better off staying in the cave.

Nunzah was still frightened and shaky from her ordeal, and the baby needed constant tending. I could not believe how often something was either going in or coming out of the little one. We stopped often to rest and let Nunzah feed the child. The journey would take days at this pace. We knew Meletmuc was searching for us but we did not speak of it. Nunzah was very brave. It was a challenge to care for a newborn on the run.

On the fourth day we came to the floor of the valley but were still very far from my village. We located a spring and camped there. The hunter caught two fat birds, and for the first time we built a small fire. Nourishment was essential, for we were all becoming weak with hunger.

It took two more days to skirt the base of the hills and reach my village. When we arrived, there was much hugging and sobbing and cooing over the baby. We learned that Meletmuc's warriors had been there the day before but had left when they found that no one had seen us.

My family prepared a feast to thank the two members of Nunzah's tribe who had helped us. I thanked the sky gods and all the gods of the Earth for our safe return. My father took me aside while the others were eating.

"This is not over, son. Meletmuc is a man determined to get revenge."

"Can we ease his grudge with gifts?" I asked.

My father looked worried.

"We can try. I fear our messengers to him may be killed. One of Nunzah's brothers was slain at the camp the night you escaped."

This saddened me. I knew my wife would grieve when she heard.

"Can we fend off an attack?" I asked him.

He shook his head and answered, "I don't know."

My father called a meeting of the Council. He explained details of the situation. Nunzah and I were there to answer questions. The members of the Council decided to send our finest hunters and fighters to Meletmuc with gifts. They would be the ones best able to defend themselves if the fierce warrior rejected our offer of peace. Nunzah stood and declared she did not want to see any more deaths occur. Two days later the envoys were sent to Meletmuc. Nunzah and I prayed that they would be successful, and their efforts would bring an end to the madness.

The day after they left, I was sitting holding my new son, marveling at his tiny fingers and toes. It was evening, and a passing shower brought a sweet smell to the air. Nunzah sat beside me.

"I received help from the Great Beyond when I came to Meletmuc's camp searching for you," I told her.

"What do you mean?" She asked as the baby began to fuss, so Nunzah took him to nurse.

"An illuminated being appeared to me as I prayed, waiting in the brush outside the camp. The entity was as bright as the sun and very tall. It showed me exactly where you were!"

"No one else saw this being?"

"No one else mentioned it. As far as I know, only I saw it. From this experience, I know our prayers are heard, so take heart."

I learned later that the group of the best hunters and fighters from our village found Meletmuc's camp empty. That was because the warriors were already on their way to our village. Perhaps Meletmuc knew somehow that the village's best protectors were away and decided to attack. In the absence of moonlight, the warriors snuck close to the settlement.

Just before first light when all was still and quiet, they attacked, yelling and carrying torches. Several village guards were awake and ready, but they could not do much against the horde. Our home was one of the first set ablaze.

Nunzah and I ran with the baby to the brush on the outskirts and watched horrified and helpless as the village was nearly destroyed. Eight of our people were killed, and the village suffered much damage. Our stores of corn were looted, and the storage huts burned.

Even though I had escaped without my knife or spear, I joined the battle with a long pole. We managed to kill one warrior and capture one. By the time the sun shone through the mist and smoke, it was over. Meletmuc and his men had exacted their revenge. Nunzah was still in the brush, rocking back and forth with the baby in her arms. Her tears dripped onto the child. We embraced, sobbing. Although we were glad to be alive, we grieved over the devastation of our peaceful village.

Father sent the son of one of the Council members, a boy who was known to run very fast, to tell our envoys what had happened. Two days later, the remaining members of the Council were meeting when the men who had gone on the peace mission returned.

They walked into the meeting holding Meletmuc's spear! The story was told that these brave hunters and fighters were on their way home after finding no one in Meletmuc's camp when they got the message from the runner. Turning around, they set up an ambush. Meletmuc and half his men had been killed. The threat was over.

Because of this news, the Council elected to rebuild the settlement. There was still enough seed to plant a new crop. There was much work to do, and even though she had a baby on her back, Nunzah toiled in the fields planting corn. She was often so tired at night that I would find her asleep with the baby nursing at her breast.

"You must not drive yourself so hard," I told her one evening after I had awakened her with kisses.

"I must," she said sleepily. "It is because of me that all the deaths and destruction occurred."

"Is that what you think?" I drew her and our son into my arms and held them close to me. "None of this was your fault."

"It was my choice to leave my people and marry you."

"No, Nunzah. Your father made a bad deal promising you to Meletmuc and then lying to that war monger saying you were dead. If anything, blame him!"

"I can blame no one but myself. Many lives would have been saved if I had just gone with Meletmuc in the first place."

"Stop!" I raised my voice, and the baby began to cry. Nunzah stroked his little head and got him feeding again.

"You mustn't think that way, Nunzah," I said quietly. "You would have been miserable. You would have been forced to bear that monster's children. You probably would have died. Now he is gone and the nightmare is over. We must look forward, not back."

She didn't say anymore, but I could see her heart was heavy.

Months passed. The corn stood again in the fields, and the village was slowly being restored. My sisters loved their little nephew, and every few days they would take him for the evening so that Nunzah and I could be alone together.

On one particularly beautiful evening, we walked to our favorite grassy meadow. As we lay under the stars, I noticed a little frown on my wife's beautiful face.

"There is something you can do to help my people—our people," I said to her.

Nunzah's face brightened immediately, "I will gladly do anything."

"You can give me a daughter. We do have to repopulate."

She laughed, rolled on her side and punched me playfully.

I grabbed her shoulders and pulled her on top of me. Our second child was conceived that night.

Another harvest came, and the village was back to normal. When planting time arrived again, Nunzah was large with child. She insisted on helping with the planting by bringing water to all who sowed the seeds. On one of her trips from the spring with a heavy clay pot of water, she fainted in the hot sun. A few minutes passed before anyone found her. As we carried her to our hut, her water broke. She was suffering from heat stroke as she went into labor. My mother and sisters buzzed around, cooling her body with wet leaves, trying to get her to drink, preparing for the baby's arrival.

Nunzah lay with her head in my lap, squeezing both my hands as pain rolled through her. She seemed to get weaker as the labor progressed. My mother, who had attended many births, looked worried.

The labor lasted well into the night. Nunzah became delirious, shouting, "No, no!" as each wave of pain swept through her body.

Our daughter was born in the dark before the dawn at just the time Meletmuc and his men had attacked our village. The baby was small but healthy.

Nunzah, however, was not well. I tried to get her to hold the baby, but she was weak and still delirious. I lay holding Nunzah, talking to her, caressing her, but she slipped slowly away and died at dusk of the same day she birthed our daughter. As I lay sobbing, holding my wife's lifeless body, a bright white light appeared over us. I stared at it with my eyes squinted and saw two illuminated figures close together.

I heard Nunzah's voice clearly say, "I love you, Zontyl. I will never be far away, and we shall be together again."

The story ended there as the words disappeared from The Great Book of Lifetimes. I closed the book and sat back. I was vibrating with emotion and could see the patterns of light around me. There were layers of cream, purple, yellow, peach, and pink light undulating in thin waves.

I needed some perspective on what I had just read, so I asked for help simply by sending off a thought to the elders. I knew entering the Power Booth was next for me but wanted to talk about what I had read and get the spirit view. Why did The Great Book show me this lifetime, and why did the narrative stop with Angel's death?

Chalherine and Wachena entered my chamber through the door. They glided over to me and hugged me, Wachena first, then the elder. I could feel the difference in their energy. Wachena's embraces made me feel very peaceful whereas Chalherine's hugs electrified me. They sat on either side examining my energy field. Chalherine placed her hand on my solar plexus, and I felt a powerful jolt.

"Now we can talk," she said looking at me kindly. "That was a very significant lifetime you just reviewed."

She nodded at Wachena who moved to a seated position on the floor before me and took my spirit feet in her lap. My surging emotions and jangling vibrations seemed to steady a bit when she did this.

Chalherine continued, "You can see that you and Angel faced danger, death, and birth as a team. Your Soul Contracts specified these challenges. In general, you both did well, showing bravery, wisdom, compassion, a desire for peace, and abiding love for each other. Let's examine the problem areas of this Earth lifetime. Two were guilt and blame."

Wachena must have sensed the pang I felt in my heart. She calmed me by wrapping her arms around my legs as Chalherine continued.

"I will begin with Angel. As Nunzah, she never stopped feeling guilty about the deaths in Meletmuc's camp and the burning and killings in your village. No matter what you said to her, she carried that guilt like a heavy pot of water until it broke her. As you probably gathered from reading about this incarnation, Nunzah kept her emotions deep inside her for the most part. The guilt ate away at her until she was too weak to survive childbirth. Her death imprint was steeped in guilt."

Chalherine flipped open The Great Book to the back and showed me the death imprint. There was a faint outline of Nunzah's body on a gray background. There were bars of black across the image. The only color on the page was a gold circle surrounded with pink in the body's mid-section.

"Her love for you remained," Chalherine said, pointing to the pink and gold. "Because guilt was so strong in her death imprint, she returned to Earth in a different incarnation with a Soul Contract that stated she must deal again with guilt."

I sat forward. "Gabriel! She came back as Gabriel to experience guilt!"

"Yes, though there were experiences on other levels where Angel tackled this. Now for you as Zontyl, the issue was blame. You intuitively felt your wife's burden of guilt though she spoke of it rarely. You wished to blame the others in this scenario. In your grief after Nunzah died, you spent weeks saying, "If only I had . . ." and "I wish I had . . . If only I had gone to Meletmuc when Nunzah's father changed his mind and gave her to me. I wish I had told Meletmuc the truth man-to-man. Then he could not say he was deceived. If only I had thought to do this. I wish I had done this.

"So in the end when you passed from that lifetime, you carried some of the blame but still held others responsible. By the time you died as Zontyl, you were an elder. Your son was a member of the Council, and you had ten grandchildren. Much of the sting of losing Nunzah at such a young age was lessened by the passing of time and by the joy of having children and grandchildren. You told many stories about Nunzah to them. You often felt her Spirit near you though you never stopped missing her physical presence."

Chalherine flipped over a page of The Great Book and said, "Here is your death imprint as Zontyl."

There I was, an old man with much pink and gold in my torso area and a few gray bars across the head and groin.

"In order to balance the lifetime as Zontyl, you came back to the Earth plane to work on issues of laying blame and taking responsibility. It was an incarnation without Angel."

Again a pang went through me. Wachena stood up and walked behind the reading chair where I was seated. She put her spirit hands on my head, and I felt better.

"It is Angel's karma you are studying here, Darci. You can see how her vitality, strength, wit and wisdom were overshadowed by remorse. The guilt-ridden emotions increased within her until they overwhelmed her, and she surrendered to them."

"My poor Angel."

"At least as Nunzah she remained a contributing member of your village. In fact, she overcompensated by working far too hard to help out, which also contributed to her death."

"I told her so often not to push herself! I could not stop her. I'd turn around, and she would be doing some strenuous task. 'Oh, Angel, you drove yourself to exhaustion!'"

"Her bravery and dedication and her love for you and her children are noted in Nunzah's death imprint, yet all of that is secondary to the overriding feelings of guilt she held within her at death."

"Chalherine, she didn't do any better as Gabriel!"

"No, I'm sorry to say. As that broken man, Angel spiraled downward adding self-loathing and self-pity to the burden of guilt."

"She made progress as Shalia. How is she doing now?"

"You will see for yourself soon enough. I want to point out that as Zontyl you had a strong connection to Spirit Guides."

"Was it my Guide who showed me where Meletmuc was holding Nunzah?"

"Yes, and it was Nunzah's Guide you saw with her just after she died. You have had psychic talent in many of your Earth lives."

"Did this help get me to where I am today as a Spirit Guide-in-Training?"

"It did. Your perseverance, your love of the Earth, your integrity, and your insistence on truth all helped make you a candidate for this university. Any more questions?"

"How soon will I be able to help Angel? When can I see her? Will I be able to touch her as you and Wachena touch me?"

"Slow down, Darci!" Chalherine laughed. "One step at a time, and the next step for you is the Power Booth. I want to see your Spirit vibration increased tenfold by the time we are finished here."

I sighed. I could tell much work still lay ahead of me before I could reconnect with Angel.

"Oh, it may not be as long as you think," Chalherine answered my thought." "And Darci . . ."

"Yes?"

"Try to enjoy the Power Booth."

With that, she and Wachena drifted backwards away from me and vanished in a lovely sparkling mist.

I sat for a while, absorbing all I had heard and read. It was difficult for me to accept that the love and passion I felt for Angel couldn't open and heal her heart when she was Nunzah. I told myself that I was very busy as one of the village leaders and was often distracted. Yet my quiet times with Nunzah were my favorite times.

Why did I not see her distress? Why did I not fully comprehend her burden and act to relieve it? I promised myself that, if I ever got to be Angel's Spirit Guide, I would be sensitive to her every trouble, her every challenge, her every need.

∞ ∞ ∞

It took a while before I was ready to stand in front of the symbol on the wall of my chamber and open the door to the Power Booth. Once I did place my hands on either side of the symbol, the oval door instantly appeared, opened, and sucked me in.

This time the forces in the Power Booth spun me counter-clockwise. Everything was a blur of lights. Just when I was so disoriented and dizzy that I thought I would lose consciousness, I slid into a seat with a very straight back. The seat seemed to remain stationary as everything moved around it and me. I remembered Chalherine's parting words, urging me to try to enjoy the Power Booth, so I breathed deeply and surrendered to the process.

Immediately a great low tone vibrated through me as I was bathed in magenta light. An image flashed into my mind. I saw the tone and the light becoming one with my spirit body. I opened myself up and absorbed them both, taking in as much as I could.

The chair began to spin as the tone subsided, and the light changed to a bright peach color. When the chair stopped moving, a slightly higher tone resonated through me. As before, I consciously opened myself to the colored light and the tone, letting them penetrate my spirit body.

After a while the chair spun again but faster, and when it stopped, I heard a higher tone and was penetrated this time by brilliant yellow light. This process continued with each tone becoming slightly higher and the colors progressing to emerald, turquoise, deep blue and violet.

Then the chair spun one final time, and I was bathed in bright white light. The tones went up and down from lowest to highest, then back down to lowest then up again as I sat absorbing the luminescent white light. Suddenly I felt something grab me under the arms and lift me as the chair fell away.

Whatever had pulled me up disappeared, and I found myself floating in the field of white light. My spirit body hovered in an upright position. The light around me was so bright I couldn't discern much though I could make out individual beams of white light. Discovering that my entire spirit body, especially my spine, vibrated even faster when I glided into one of the beams, I chose to spend a long time floating in these vertical white rays.

I began to feel as if I was dissolving into the white light when an oval opening manifested, and I was propelled through it. I found myself back in my chamber hovering above the floor. I was pulsating at such a high rate that I thought I would never be able to calm down. That was not the case, however.

I glided to my favorite resting spot and gracefully lowered myself onto the pallet. I felt good, energized, yet peaceful. I lay there with my entire energy field vibrating intensely and drifted off, losing consciousness for what was probably a long while.

∞ ∞ ∞

Upon awakening, I was surprised to find that my chamber was very dimly lit. In fact, I noticed that my aura was the brightest thing in the room as it glowed with aluminiferous golden light.

Then I saw a shaft of light illuminating The Great Book of Lifetimes, which lay open on the book stand. Floating my newly energized spirit body over to the giant tome, I settled into the reading chair. There were no words on the pages, and this mystified me until I remembered what Sottrol had asked me to do.

I took one deep breath and recited aloud the Spirit Guide Creed. After I added a silent prayer for Angel, the words appeared on the pages of The Great Book. I eagerly began reading.

The setting was Manchuria long ago. The story described an exodus of people, carts, and animals caused by severe flooding in the river valleys. These were not the usual seasonal floods. The valleys had become a chain of lakes, and entire villages had to relocate to higher ground.

I was a boy of eleven, a member of one of the displaced families.

My job was to herd the goats as the refugees snaked slowly up the mountain.

I had many brothers and sisters, and each of us had our work to do, even out on the trail. The journey was slow and arduous. I was certain that I had the hardest job of all because the goats were uncooperative, running off in all directions to search for tidbits of greenery to chew. The weather made traveling that much more difficult. The rains continued off and on day and night. Everything was wet or damp. In the evening when we stopped to camp, eat, and sleep, it was nearly impossible to get a fire going.

One man in the group of travelers had a way with fire. He was called on each evening to employ his magic and start the cook fires. I was fascinated by this wizard and watched closely as he struck two stones together to produce sparks. This man was older than my father and wore clothing that was different from those the other villagers wore. I took to following him, trying to herd the goats close to his path. It didn't take long for him to catch onto my interest in him.

"Yong Shu Win!" he called to me, "I am Raffa. Pleased to meet you."

I bowed but said nothing. I had been taught not to speak to adults unless they requested that I do so.

"I have an idea that might help you with your goats," he said. His eyes had a lively sparkle. "Let's cut branches of your goats' favorite food and use them to keep the goats on the trail.

Raffa helped me cut some succulent branches that would keep the goats interested in staying near me. It worked well.

That night as Raffa started the evening fire, I came close to watch. I saw him take dry straw out of a pocket in his robe along with the two special rocks. He used his cape to block blowing mist as he set about starting a flame. He had picked the most sheltered spot he could find. Even so, everything was wet, and getting a flame wasn't easy. I marveled at Raffa's expertise. It was as if the flame were a shy old friend that he had to coax into his company.

Once the cook fires were lit, Raffa sat with his back against a great rock and motioned for me to sit near him.

"In times of change, it is the wise and grateful man who benefits," Raffa told me. "If you are thankful for all you have, then you will experience abundance. If you are wise and generous, then the bounty will increase ten-fold."

"I have very little, Raffa—just these clothes, my stick, and the goats, which belong to my family. The flood took everything else."

"You have your life, you have your family, and you have food." Raffa nodded toward the cooking fires where the big kettles were being filled with root vegetables and set to boil.

At that moment, a kettle of boiling water tipped and splashed hot water in our direction. The scalding water hit Raffa on the arm and leg. It spattered on my face and chest. I was further away, so the boiling droplets only sprinkled on me, but I could see that Raffa was burned. He quickly turned away from the others, removing his cape and robe.

"Get me cold water!" he cried hoarsely. I ran to the far side of the cooking area and filled a cup.

When I returned, Raffa had moved behind a shrub and was laying wet leaves on his arm. He poured the cold water I brought him onto the leaves then drank the rest. He lifted his underdress, and I could see red splotches on his leg, so I went to fetch more cold water. As I watched him put wet leaves on the leg burns, I noticed he had strange marks on his upper arms. They were a series of v-shaped scars very evenly spaced, obviously made very carefully and purposefully. I wanted to ask the wizard man about them but held my tongue.

Two more days of strenuous journeying brought us to a pass with steep slopes on either side. We camped at the entrance, and as usual, I tried to be close to Raffa as he lit the evening fires.

"Only one fire tonight," he told those in charge of cooking. "We may have to move quickly," Raffa told them.

"We must keep our presence here brief. Any smoke we make may put us in danger."

My eyes grew wide, and I shifted my seat closer to the fire starter.

"What is it, Raffa?" I asked, my heart thumping.

"I know this place," he said. "It is a pass used often by the roving hunters of the mountains. They would like to eat your goats!"

"Will they kill us?"

"They live very differently from you and your family. They may not like so many people from the flooded valleys encroaching upon their territory. I will go talk to your father and the heads of the other families."

After dinner, I was very restless. One of the goats was nibbling a bush that marked a small trail off the major route through the pass. On an impulse, I hiked along the little path in the bright moonlight. After our camp was no longer in sight, I heard the thumping of feet on the trail ahead of me.

I hid in the bushes near the path and tried to keep the goat quiet. The footsteps came closer and my heart leapt about in my chest. I saw three primitive warriors moving quickly along the trail. The three mountain savages moved past me and paused on the bluff overlooking our camp.

"How can I warn my family?" I thought, terrified with fear.

As the musky-smelling men walked back up the path, the goat betrayed my hiding spot, and I was captured. My heart sank as the savages marched my goat and me up the trail and away from my family and the life that I knew.

We walked along the steep rocky path for a long time until we reached a curve in the trail. Around it was a flat field where these primitive people made their home. There was a large fire in the center. On one side, several women were cooking. They had meat on spits and were poking around in the coals where roots were roasting.

The three men took me past the fire to the back of the level area. As my eyes adjusted to the darkness, I saw the opening of a cave. A group of these savages sat just inside the entrance. My captors shoved me into the center of this group and started talking, telling of what they had seen.

I looked around at the faces. Several were elders, both male and female. The rest were warriors like the men who had captured me. They had the same style of dress, the same weapons, and the same odor. I looked into the eyes of the elders, hoping to stir their compassion. I did not want to be killed and perhaps even eaten by these barbarians.

There was much discussion, none of which I understood. My legs were weary, and finally I sank down next to an elder woman. She whispered something to me, but again I had no idea what she said.

The men talked more heatedly until most of them jumped up shouting, "Aga Rah!"

They took their weapons and left the camp. I feared for my family and the other travelers in our group. Just as I was considering escape to warn my people, the elder woman took my hand and led me into the cave. Showing me a bed made of soft grasses, she patted the area indicating I should lie there.

Exhaustion took over. I slept soundly

At dawn the warriors returned. With much noise and clamor, they marched into the camp with more goats, supplies from our carts, and two captives. One was Raffa. I ran to him and threw my arms around him. He held me close.

"You are all right then, Yong Shu. Good. Good."

"What happened, Raffa? My family—are they dead?"

"I don't know. Some were killed. Some escaped. We were captured."

It was at that moment that I noticed Raffa's hands were not tied. I tugged on Raffa's robe.

"Can you speak their language?"

"Yes, enough to be understood. That is why they didn't bind my wrists.

I told them in their own tongue that I would come with them peacefully. It probably saved my life."

The other captive was bound. He yelled and spit at the warriors and was killed right in front of us. I held on to Raffa and wept.

"Do what I say, and that will not happen to us," whispered Raffa.

The two of us sat waiting for the next event, which turned out to be food. A woman with a girl by her side brought us roasted roots and water. The girl seemed about my age, maybe older.

"Not too many children here in this camp," Raffa observed. "These people may want to adopt you."

"No!"

Raffa looked at me very seriously and explained, "You have a new life now, Yong Shu. Your home, your family, your old life is gone. You must adapt so you can survive."

Even though I was hungry, I pouted, ignoring the food before me. In my heart, I knew the old man was right, but I wasn't ready to accept it.

"Eat," urged Raffa. "They feed us. That means they think we are worth something."

Once in a while, one of the men would walk by and bark something at us. Finally I asked Raffa what they were saying.

"Oh, different things," Raffa replied. "Trespassers, invaders, migrants—one fellow called us fools."

"How do you know their language?"

"During my many years on Earth, I have traveled a great deal. I spent part of my youth in these mountains."

"You chose to journey here and visit these savages?"

"I came with my father. He was born near here. He taught me his native tongue and showed me the customs of these people."

"You are one of them, Raffa!"

"My father was."

Soon after this discussion, we were taken to the cave and made to stand before a large group of warriors and elders. Finally, after standing there on display for what seemed like hours, Raffa spoke to the group. I could see by their faces that they were fascinated by his words. Once he finished, two men moved us back outside the cave so the group could continue discussing our fate.

"What did you tell them, Raffa?"

"Words that will hopefully save our lives, little Shu."

"What exactly?"

We sat down near the fire. There was a light misty rain in the air, so Raffa covered me with his cape.

"First I told them of my bloodline and how I was related to them. Then I told them of my travels and my talents. If they find me interesting and useful, they will not kill me."

"What about me?"

"I asked them to spare you. I said you were strong and brave and had a way with goats."

I groaned.

Raffa's smile doubled the wrinkles on his face. He continued, "I also pointed out how few children they had and that you might be a welcome addition to their camp."

"You mean I'd have to stay here? Join them? Become one of them? I don't understand anything they're saying—and those violent men scare me!" I began to whimper.

"Now don't let our captors see your weakness. Do not worry. I will teach you all I know so that you can communicate and survive."

Right away, Raffa taught me the words for food, water, and sleep. This helped take my mind off the loss of my family and my old life. From that day on, the old man tutored me. He gave me language lessons, culture lessons, and lessons on life in general.

I had been put on goat duty and was instructed to stay in sight with the herd. This wasn't easy, but I managed using the trick Raffa had shown me on the trail. One morning weeks after our capture I noticed that one of the big female goats was missing. I told the woman at the cook fire that the goat was gone.

She said for me to wait while she called her daughter to go with me. I guessed that they still didn't trust me. This girl, the one who brought us food the first night we arrived, was the only female near my age in the camp. She had deep dark eyes and long straight hair.

"I am Hoh Nu," she said as we hiked up the path. "You can call me Nua."

"You can call me Shu."

We searched and found the goat, who had wandered away to deliver her baby. Nua helped me with the birth, and we were friends from that day on. Her duties centered on feeding everyone. I showed her how to get milk from the mother goat, and she learned to do it, but she blushed. Because of my knowledge, goat's milk and goat's cheese were added to the diet of these primitive people.

Months passed. Raffa and I were slowly accepted into this group. One evening while we were seated near the fire eating, I asked both Raffa and Nua why there were so few children in the camp. Nua sat silently, looking at her food. Raffa chewed for a moment, then swallowed and spoke.

"There was a great illness that took nearly all the children. This happened when you were just a baby, Hoh Nu. Your father told me that he and your mother took you way up into the high mountain ridges to keep you from becoming ill."

The old man took another bite and chewed slowly as he said, "There are not many women of childbearing age either."

"I noticed that the camp was filled mostly with men," I said.

Nua went to get more food as Raffa continued, "There was an attack on this camp when Hoh Nu was about six. The attacking tribe captured or killed most of the women. I've heard this story from several of the men. The warriors were lured from the village so the women were not well protected.

At least, that's what they tell me. Nua is valuable to the future of these people. She will be expected to bear many children."

I looked at Nua standing by the fire. She was thin and wiry. Her straight black hair hung to her waist. I wondered if she knew what was expected of her.

Raffa nodded at her, saying, "She likes you. Do you like her?"

"She's my friend. No, Raffa, I don't think of her as a wife. She's just a pal."

"You are both young. This will change."

Several years passed, and change did come. Nua blossomed into a beautiful young woman. I was taught to hunt and was allowed to carry a knife.

Raffa sat often with the elders when they discussed important matters. One full moon night, the elders met in the cave, and Raffa asked me to join them. I was glad I was able to understand what was said.

One of the old men began speaking, "We elders look to the future. Many of us wish to see grandchildren and great grandchildren. Only a few of our people can give us these future generations. One of them, Hoh Nu, is ready to begin serving her people in this way."

The old man nodded toward Raffa, then looked at me and then said, "This man says you want to make babies with Hoh Nu."

I was speechless. I glanced at Raffa who was smiling.

The elder continued, "Many men want Hoh Nu. Any of our warriors can father children with this girl, but fire-starter says you would be best. You tell us why."

I reddened. I stuttered. I looked at Raffa for help. He strode over to my side and put his arm around me.

"Can you not see he has no words to express his devotion to the young woman? He is overcome with love and finds it hard to speak."

I was overcome. That part was true—overcome by surprise. I was not yet fifteen and thought more about hunting

and animals than about women. There was no question that I
liked Hoh Nu and considered her my friend. I did not want to
see her in the clutches of one of the smelly, blood-thirsty
warriors. I wondered how Nua felt about the matchmaking.
The group was quiet, and all were staring at me, so I stood up
straight and took a deep breath.

"Will Hoh Nu have me?"

The old men in the group chuckled, and the old women
nodded.

One of the female elders spoke, "It is as I have said. If we
want Hoh Nu to thrive and give us many children, she must be
happy. She must like her mate and be willing, even
enthusiastic."

The elder who had spoken first said, "Then let us hear
from the young woman whose future we debate."

I sat with Raffa opposite the elders as someone went to
fetch Nua. The old fire starter leaned over and whispered in
my ear, "I hope you don't mind that I spoke on your behalf. I
have had a vision, you see, and my instincts told me to act
upon it."

"A vision? About me?"

"You and your friend Hoh Nu. I will tell you later. Here
comes the lovely Nua now."

It was a good thing I was seated because when Nua
entered the cave circle and stood before the elders, I felt as if I
were falling head first down a mountainside. I had never seen
Nua look like this before. Her hair was pinned in a spiral on
her head, and she wore a long slim robe that showed her figure.
She was a woman!

"She—she looks so—so different," I stuttered under my
breath.

Raffa smiled and said, "She has just undergone the
initiation into womanhood for her fifteenth birthday. That is
why there is talk about mating her. According to their
customs, she is now ready."

The elder who seemed to be running the meeting addressed the young woman, "Now that you have come of age, you must select a mate and begin a family. Many warriors have approached us and asked for you. We wish to know who you choose."

"May I see them?" Nua asked quietly.

The elder motioned for the men to step forward.

From the back of the circle came six men, all much older than me. Although I had grown tall, I was still skinny and lanky. These warriors were muscular and strong. If the elders made us fight, any one of them could beat me.

Raffa took my arm and shoved me towards the other men with the command, "Go!"

So I stood next to these six huge men and felt small and a little foolish. I looked at Nua, and she was staring right at me. Our eyes locked, and I felt myself being drawn into her Soul. A myriad of emotions swept through me as our Spirits recognized each other. I experienced a surge of passion for this young woman, who I now knew must be my mate. It was indeed my Angel.

There was a loud buzzing sound in my ears. I realized the elders were talking amongst themselves, smiling and nodding.

Nua stood there, silent, blushing.

I looked at Raffa, and he made a little motion, pointing at my groin. My passion was showing.

Raffa jumped to my rescue. With a huge smile on his face, he put his arm around me and confirmed, "You can see for yourself; this young man has the desire and the ability to partner this young woman. Here is your proof! He will be a fine mate. What say you?"

The elders nodded their approval.

"What say you, Hoh Nu?"

"I have long wanted Yong Shu. May I have him now?"

There was laughter and clapping. Even the other warriors, as fierce as they looked, slapped me on the back and congratulated me.

One pointed to the thin hide I wore from my waist down and told me my body had good timing.

The elders arranged a bonding ceremony for Nua and me. They wasted no time setting the event for the next full moon, which was only a few days away.

Nua was busy receiving instruction from the elders and from her family.

I spent the time with Raffa.

"I'm not sure I am ready for this," I told my old friend.

"Nonsense. You showed everyone you are ready. Besides—I know this to be as the universe wishes. I have seen it."

"Tell me about the vision you had."

"I was sitting overlooking the pass where your family was killed years ago. A great bird landed on a rock nearby. The bird had a strange white glow around it. I thought it might be the Spirit of one of those who died in the pass, so I asked the bird what it had come to tell me. It danced on the rock for a few minutes and left some droppings. It hopped about some more, cawed, and flew away. I immediately went to the rock to examine the droppings. There was the whole story of the exodus of your people, the near extinction of Nua's people, and the union that would bring both people together to start a new clan."

"You saw all that in some bird droppings?"

"I sat and looked at the sky for confirmation. I saw again in the cloud patterns the melding of the two peoples through the union of you and Hoh Nu. It is a lofty purpose you have, my boy. Your bloodline from the cultured valleys of this land and her bloodline from the primitive hills can unite to make a new people, stronger, wiser, and more resilient. Look to this purpose and enjoy fulfilling your duty. Do you need any—er—fatherly advice?"

"You have been like a father to me, Raffa. You have protected me and watched over me. Now you help me set my feet on the path of my destiny once again."

I hesitated and then asked, "Is it like animals? My mother told me birth for people is much the same as birth for animals. Is that true with—making the babies, too? I have seen animals mating."

"Similar, little Shu. With humans it is gentler, more loving, and more varied. Allow your instincts to guide you. Your body will know what to do. It certainly did at that meeting the other day."

We both laughed. I knew I would never live down that moment, but if it won me Nua, then I didn't care.

I approached our mating ceremony with much anticipation. Raffa informed me of the basics of the ritual. The elders prepared a special wedding bed for us deep in the recesses of the cave. There was never much privacy in this primitive camp, but the old ones knew that successful mating came from time together without distraction.

The weather was warm on the day of our marriage ritual. Two elder men and Raffa prepared me. I wore very little, only a lightweight hide around my waist. They rubbed a chalky substance on my shoulders and cut my hair quite short. Raffa talked to me as this was taking place.

"Yong Shu, you are a brave man. You have seen much in your young life. You now have the opportunity to go through the initiation into adulthood as a part of the rituals today. If you choose to do this, you will show your courage and strength, and you will win the respect of these people."

"You did not mention this before. What is involved?"

"The elders spoke to me about it this morning. It is a ritual I experienced when I came to the mountains with my father."

He pulled off his robe, and I saw the v-marks on his shoulders.

He explained, "They were made when I was a boy your age. They signify my brave arrival into manhood. I am not allowed to tell you more."

I swallowed hard.

Body scarring was something I hadn't bargained for. I felt very close to this old man, and I could see how undergoing this ritual might make me an official part of his family.

"Do you recommend I experience this?"

"It is your choice, of course. I will say the ritual changed my life for the better."

I looked at the other two elders who nodded and pulled aside their garments to show similar markings. I sighed. This was already going to be a big day for me, so I elected to undergo the initiation.

The V-marks on my shoulders were made with a heated blade. My eyes were tearing from the pain, but I did not cry out. By the time the last of the sixteen blade marks were made, the men were chanting so loud my ears hurt, too.

I saw a flash of white light and found myself floating in the air above the canyon. Two large birds of a unique golden color circled above me. The two birds melded into one that turned into a tree. I watched as the tree sent down long roots into the Earth and branches high up, up, up into the sky. Then the tree burst into bloom with different flowers on every branch. In every blossom was the face of a child. I looked from flower to flower from face to face until everything went white.

I found myself back in the circle. The men had stopped chanting. Raffa and the elder were each holding one of my arms. My shoulders felt on fire, and my head was swimming.

"You are all right, Yong Shu," said Raffa softly. "I believe you had yourself a vision."

The other men left slowly, one by one. Raffa and the old man stayed with me. I was still a bit unsteady, and my body was in shock.

The elder nodded at the fire starter, and Raffa began applying wet leaves to my burns. The leaves were soaked in a sticky substance that brought some relief from the pain.

"You did well," Raffa noted, squeezing my hand.

"I can no longer call you Little Shu. You have become a man. These people will honor you today."

The three of us made our way down to the camp where Raffa carefully put fresh leaves on my burns. I lay and rested with my wise old friend next to me. After a while, I related my vision to him.

"You have now seen your destiny for yourself, Yong Shu. The two golden birds are you and Nua, uniting to make a new family tree. Many generations will spring from your fruitful union."

"I don't know how fruitful I can be tonight with these burns, Raffa."

My friend looked at me compassionately, replying, "You were very brave to go through this today. Hoh Nu has been told and will be prepared to care for your burns. Do not worry. I believe your passion for each other will carry you."

The bonding ritual was to take place at sunset and moonrise just outside the entrance to the cave. The women began to sing very sweetly in high contrast to the chanting the men had done for me earlier in the day. As the females sang, Hoh Nu emerged from the cave and joined me in the circle. She was glowing. Her long hair was twisted with vines and flowers. She had flowers on her wrists and ankles and around her waist. Her eyes sparkled as she took her place next to me in the circle.

I forgot about my pain. I felt exhilarated and buoyant. My heart swelled with joy.

The elders took turns speaking. I didn't hear much of it, especially after they asked Nua and me to join hands. We simply got lost in each other's eyes. I saw tears rolling down Nua's face as she smiled at me.

The entire group sang to us as we were pronounced officially bonded. The feasting began with much cheering and laughing.

I had no appetite, and my new wife did not seem interested in food either. We sat together in a fog, watching the others celebrate. As the moon rose higher in the sky, I began to feel the fatigue of the day set in. The burns on my shoulders began to hurt, and the pain made me very uncomfortable.

Raffa must have been keeping an eye on me. He walked over to us and said we should retire to our private area. One of the elder women joined Raffa, and the four of us entered the cave. The fire starter brought fresh leaves for my wounds while the old woman brought water and some food from the feast. They only stayed long enough to make sure we were settled. Then they left. Raffa smiled and winked as he turned to go.

Finally Nua and I were alone. I realized the last time we were alone together was years ago when we helped that mother goat birth her kid. Nua's eyes were full of compassion.

"You cannot know how upset I was when mother told me you were going through the passage initiation today! Let me put those fresh leaves on you. Dear Shu, does it hurt?"

"Yes, but I'll be fine."

"At least I had a chance to heal before our bonding," she said, gently layering the cool wet leaves on my burns.

"You? But I see no marks on your shoulders."

"Women receive the ritual blade on a different part of their body."

My heart jumped, and I asked, "Where? Nua, where did they scar you?"

She looked at me shyly. She slowly pulled up her robe. I gasped when I saw the burned v-marks on the inside of both her thighs.

"How you must have suffered, my Nua!"

"It is true that I could not walk for days. I am fine now. You, however, will have to be careful for a while until these burns scab and heal."

As she applied the last of the leaves, she kissed my neck. I have to admit I winced because her hand was still on my sore shoulder.

"I'm sorry, Shu."

"No. I'm sorry. I guess I shouldn't have undergone the passage ritual today."

"I wouldn't have chosen it for you, but it was today or never. The two ceremonies have to be in the order that you did them. It is our custom."

"I'm glad to be alone with you."

"They will leave us alone for as long as we want. Neither of us has to do our chores!"

"Our duty to your people is different now."

"Our people, Shu. Lie back and relax. I will stay away from those wounded shoulders of yours. I'll rub your feet."

No one had ever massaged my feet before. Nua's hands were strong and firm. I moaned and sighed and took deep breaths as the stress of the day poured out of me. Anyone listening would have thought we were making love, but alas, Nua's therapeutic touch relaxed me into a deep sleep.

After we rested, I lovingly removed the wedding decorations from my new wife. Raffa was right. My passion burned much hotter than the wounds on my shoulders. At last I beheld the whole of my beautiful wife and realized what a prize I had been given.

We went days without saying a word, never leaving the private part of the cave that had been assigned to us. Water and fresh food were left outside our private area. We explored every hill and valley of each other's bodies as our Souls conversed.

On the fourth or fifth night after our bonding ceremony, I waited for the rest of the camp to settle into a deep sleep. I then took Nua's hand, and we walked past sleeping men and women out of the depths of the cave into the starry night. We both breathed in the sweet night air as I lead Nua to the big rock where we had first talked the day we had helped the mother goat with the birth of her kid.

She climbed up onto the rock and stretched her arms out to the stars. I scrambled up next to her and wound my arms tightly around her waist.

Starlight reflected in her dark hair and made her look like an angel.

"Our people expect me to birth many babies," she said quietly. "I would like you to be there at every birth though that is not the custom."

"We shall make new customs then," I told her.

Months passed. The season of the cold winds came and went. The season of the rains came and went. When the warm weather returned, Nua was heavy with child.

The elders were not been receptive to the idea of my participation in the birth. They tried to keep me away, but Nua sent messages to my heart, so I knew her time had come. She stubbornly held back, refusing to deliver, insisting that I be by her side. The elders finally agreed to let me be there. That day my beautiful young wife delivered twin girls.

Raffa smiled at us, "The elders—all the people—are so delighted that they will now want you at all her births, Yong Shu."

Nua looked up and said emphatically, "Oh, yes. I insist."

"A new generation, a new family—and new customs," I added.

The pages of The Great Book of Lifetimes went blank. I was so caught up in the story that this took me by surprise. As I sat staring at the empty pages, I noticed that my spirit body was buzzing and tingling.

I looked up to see shimmering rays of pink light radiating from me. The luminescence varied from a deep rose to a lush pink to a light pink to bright white. Looking down, I saw magenta, purple, and deep red colors pulsing in my core. I knew by how I felt that the recounting of this Earth incarnation affected me greatly. The colors in my energy field confirmed it.

∞　∞　∞

I sat for a while in a blissful state going over in my mind all I had read. With my eyes closed, I held the image of beautiful Nua on the big rock with the starlight in her hair. She was my Angel.

"She is your partner through time," I heard the familiar voice of my mentor, Sottrol, say. He had somehow silently appeared beside me.

I smiled saying, "Hello, Sottrol."

I looked again at the blank pages, then closed The Great Book and glanced back. My heart jumped, for there was Raffa sitting where Sottrol had been!

"Raffa?" I questioned, rubbing my eyes and looking again.

"At last you recognize me," said the elder as I saw Sottrol once more.

"Sottrol, I thought you were Raffa for a minute."

"You are more than caught up in the story of your incarnation in Manchuria. You saw correctly. I am—or was—Raffa, your old friend and mentor from that lifetime. It was long ago—and was my last incarnations on Earth."

"You were Raffa?"

"Yes, and if you were ready, The Great Book of Lifetimes would show you other revelations."

"Like what? Give me an example."

"For instance, one of your first-born daughters from your incarnation as Yong Shu became your mother in your incarnation as Alger Matticus in Rome."

"Why am I not ready to learn these things?"

"You would get lost in the complexities. What is important now is for you to focus on what each incarnation is telling you. This last reading, for example, showed you—what?"

It took me a minute to gather my thoughts. I was taken aback by the fact that Sottrol had been Raffa.

"Take your time," said the elder. "Your analysis of each incarnation is very important in your learning process."

A few breaths later, I mentioned some ideas.

"Nua and I could read each other's thoughts and feel each other's feelings, so Angel and I developed a telepathic way of communicating in that lifetime."

"Yes. There's more."

"We learned tolerance—no—appreciation for another culture, and we eventually blended those two cultures through our union."

"Very good, Darci. The truth is that you as Yong Shu and Angel as Hoh Nu are the ancient ancestors of many of the humans who now reside in that part of China. Bonds between Souls are strengthened every time birth and death are shared. Was there anything else you learned from reading about this incarnation?"

"Let's see—I was glad to have you—er—Raffa there. You helped me move through grieving over the loss of my family and my old life. You helped me adapt and survive."

"Being flexible and adaptable are two very important traits for a Spirit Guide, for you never know what crazy choices humans may make. You have to be ready to go along and try to help no matter what they do."

"What about Angel?"

"She came into that incarnation with strong intuitive powers. She recognized you as her mate almost as soon as you were captured and brought to her camp. Her intuition strengthened, especially when it came to you. Also, she showed courage and dedication to her people. There is still one important factor you have not yet mentioned."

"My ability with goats?"

Sottrol laughed and replied, "It's true—you have been good with animals since that lifetime. No, I was speaking of your love for each other. It deepened into a fierce passion in that lifetime."

"What happened to Nua and Shu?"

"If you took the time, you would probably recall that you fathered sixteen children with Nua. You had much help from the rest of the tribe in caring for and raising them. They were communal children. I stayed on the scene long enough to see several more births. I remember watching you and Nua sitting together, lost in each other as the children played around you."

"I miss Angel. Every time I read about another lifetime we shared, I miss her more. I want to see her, Sottrol. I want to be close to her. I want to be connected with her again," I pleaded.

"So it shall be. Patience, my dear Darci, patience. I do come with news. You have now completed the foundation program at the university. Congratulations! You are well on your way. Now it is time to test your skills and knowledge in the field. Because of recent events, Chalherine and I, as well as some of the Master Guides and teachers, are recommending that you begin your Spirit Guide apprenticeship on Earth in the company of a full-fledged Spirit Guide."

"Will I see Angel?"

"That is the reason we are arranging this."

My entire spirit body began vibrating wildly. Huge vertical rushes of energy pulsed through me. Finally, I was to see Angel!

"Easy, Darci. You must take one more long session in the Power Booth to increase your aura's vibration as much as possible. Then you will meet with Chalherine and the Spirit Guide currently watching over Angel."

"You said that she's on Earth now."

"A child on the Earth plane, yes."

My vibrating spirit body was radiating circles of bright pink light that were pulsing from me in luminescent waves.

"Your vibration is already quite high. I can see we were right in choosing this path for you, Darci. Through your exploration of these Earth lifetimes with Angel, you have learned about karma and have increased the intensity of your energy field. The Power Booth will help you refine your energy further and raise it to an even higher and purer state."

I looked at the old wizard and said, "Thank you, Sottrol.

Thank you for helping me when I was Shu and you were Raffa—and thank you for helping me now."

"My pleasure, Darci. You are well on your way to becoming a Spirit Guide in your own right."

"Will you wait for me while I am in the Power Booth?"

"I will be here when you step out of it," the elder assured me.

Without wasting a moment, I strode to the wall and placed my hands on either side of the symbol. As before, the opening appeared, and I was propelled into it instantly.

Instead of falling, this time I rose gently, surrounded by golden-green light. It was difficult for me to tell down from up, but I believe I was rotated so that I was lying horizontally on a disc of brilliant gold.

The disc began spinning, slowly at first, then faster and faster until I was whirling at a very high speed. This went on for almost too long. Just when I thought I was going to lose consciousness, the disc dropped away and I was floating, suspended in a field of different colored rays of light.

I managed to move myself into what I surmised was an upright position. As I did so, I was drawn into a greenish-blue beam of light, which felt very good. It calmed me and eliminated all residual dizziness. A beautiful low tone vibrated gently through me. I floated there for a long time, then moved to the next ray which was violet. Another tone sounded as I hovered there for a time. All in all, I bathed in a dozen different rays. I simply floated from one to the next, trusting that this was the best course of action.

After immersing myself in every colored ray, I heard the tinkling of tiny bells. A gigantic, bright, white figure appeared before me. I knew instantly that I was in the presence of an Archangel. The Being was so luminous that I could barely look at it.

Great arms pulled me in, and I was embraced and engulfed in pure white light. The sensation was extraordinary. I was exhilarated beyond anything I had ever experienced before, yet

I felt calm and peaceful at the same time. I hovered in this state of bliss for a long while, seeing nothing around me but brilliant white light. Eventually, the door to my chamber appeared before me, and I glided through it.

Sottrol was standing on the other side awaiting my return. He gathered me in his arms and hugged me for a long time.

"It is a rare occasion when an Archangel visits the university. You have attracted their interest, Darci. Your mission must be very important. We will all learn more at the meeting. For now—rest. I shall sit by you."

Although I had many questions, I thanked my old friend and stretched out for much needed repose. However, my mind raced with so many thoughts of Angel: "Sottrol had told me that she is now a child on Earth, but where is she? What are her circumstances? What will happen when I see her? Will she see me? Will she recognize me?"

The wizard chuckled, "Patience, Darci. You will know all soon enough."

With those words, he put his hand on my head. The whirring in my mind subsided. I took a deep breath, settled down, and slid into a deep sleep.

Chapter Eight:
The Electric Reunion

When I awoke in my chamber at the Spirit Guide University, my mentor Sottrol was standing next to me moving his hands, palms down, slowly back and forth above me.

"Ah, Darci, just checking your energy field," he said, his smile enhancing the twinkle in his eyes and the sparkling crystals in his white beard. You have slept long. When you become a full-fledged Spirit Guide, you will no longer need extended periods of rest."

"How am I doing?" I asked rubbing my eyes.

"You are ready," the wise old wizard said, winking at me. "What you have been requesting for so long is about to unfold."

My mind instantly whirled with anticipation. I was to finally see her again, my long lost mate, my partner, my Soul love, my Angel.

"Let's go!" I cried, springing to my feet, which caused Sottrol to rise quickly upward and hover above me.

"Easy, my boy."

He floated down and looked me in the eyes saying, "One step at a time."

"But I've taken so many steps! I've tried to be patient, but you said . . ."

"Yes, I know, but first we must attend a meeting of The Elevated Council where you will be introduced to Angel's current Spirit Guide and learn about your mission."

"My mission?"

"Yours and Angel's. Come with me," he said as he placed his hand on my back, which instantly calmed me. We floated side-by-side out of my chamber and through the glowing hallway.

The meeting was held in a beautiful circular room with large prisms around the circumference and a great lighted domed ceiling covered with crystals. The room shimmered with white and gold light. I was awed by its majesty as soon as Sottrol led me through the arched doorway. In the center was a large bench, shaped like a horseshoe. In the space between the ends of the bench was a single oval seat.

The bench was already full of Beings. I recognized Chalherine and Wachena, but there were four others I didn't know. Chalherine smiled and motioned for me to sit in the single seat while Sottrol joined her and the others on the horseshoe bench.

I looked around the circle at those who would decide my fate. Directly across from me sitting in the curve of the bench was an American Indian man who wore more paint than clothing. He had broad shoulders, and many feathers were braided into his hair. He stared at me with a very serious expression. Next to him on his left was an elder with a closely-cropped white beard who wore a bright purple and blue-striped robe with the hood up over his head. The female Being next to him was extraordinary because her figure was translucent. She was wrapped in pastel veils, and everything about her seemed in flux except her eyes, which were bright green and fixed upon me. The Being closest to me on my right was a tiny man. His suit twinkled with rainbow colors as he moved. He had short ginger-colored hair with a beard and mustache to match. Nothing was said for a few minutes while I looked at these seven unusual Beings, and they all looked at me.

Sottrol, who was sitting on the end of the bench to my left, stood up.

"Allow me to make the introductions," he began. "Darci Stillwater, meet The Elevated Council. Chalherine and Wachena you know. Next to you is Chilliwon Mac."

As Sottrol announced his name, the little man in the sparkling suit stood up on the bench and bowed to me. I nodded respectfully back to him.

"Mac, as we call him, is the Spirit Guide who has come from the ranks of elves. He now oversees all communications between Spirit Guides and humans, a big job for a little man."

"He does it very well," Chalherine added.

Sottrol continued, "Next to Mac is Esther, a Master Guide. She oversees the relationships between Souls, and she has many Spirit Guides with her name who work in the field to help humans with relationships."

As Sottrol talked about Esther, her eyes glittered like emeralds and seemed to zoom in very close to mine.

"Next, meet the Master Guide Arcillis. He heads a group of Master Guides who have designed your mission, Darci."

The elder Guide removed his hood and nodded towards me. I was astounded because his head was covered with crystals, which sparkled in the rarefied light and dazzled my eyes.

"Finally, this is Syd Manyfeathers. He is Angel's current Spirit Guide. Now that the introductions have been made, let us begin."

I was concerned that no one was watching over Angel at that moment, but I did not want to talk out of turn.

Sottrol continued, "We have gathered to evaluate the status of both Darci and Angel to see how best to proceed. Arcillis, please begin by outlining the mission we have chosen for these two Souls."

Arcillis stood. He was very tall and had a commanding presence. When he spoke, his voice had a bell-like timbre.

"Earth is one generation away from a potential evolutionary leap. Because of a gift from the Creator, humans will have the opportunity to use more of their conscious minds. This will enable them to communicate directly with their Spirit Guides. Whereas sporadic contact has occurred through the ages, humans will soon be able to converse with their Spirit Guides on a regular basis. Darci, we would like you and Angel to be leaders in this movement to awareness."

I sat stunned, thinking, "Angel and I were being asked to lead a new phase in the evolution of humanity?!"

Esther then spoke. Her voice also had a gentle ringing sound to it. "Because of your strong bonds with Angel, you two have been selected for this mission. It will not be easy. However, you will have much help from the spirit side."

Mac then jumped up again and stood on the bench. He talked excitedly, using his hands to gesture.

"We chose you from thousands of couples because you two have communicated so well in many Earth incarnations. This time, you will lead the way for other humans by communicating with each other through the Great Veil between worlds. If all goes well, you will teach others how to do this, too!"

The little man hopped around with joy as sparkles seemed to fly off his suit.

I was becoming very excited, too. I was thrilled that Angel and I had been selected for such an important mission.

Syd Manyfeathers then stood, and all went quiet. He bowed his head and spoke slowly in a language that I did not understand.

When he finished, he looked directly at me. His dark eyes pierced my heart as he explained, "That was a prayer for Angel. She suffers much on the Earth plane. I come to ask that her Soul be brought home."

My insides quivered as my heart swelled with compassion. How I wanted Angel to be there with me.

Sottrol spoke next, "Angel has just reentered the Earth plane. She still has Earth work to do. Her karma remains unbalanced. I must ask—if we bring her home now, will she be ready to partner Darci on this mission?"

Chalherine rose and crossed over to talk with Arcillis and Esther. I could not hear what was said.

When she returned to her seat on the horseshoe, she looked at me and spoke with a smile, "We can arrange this for the benefit of all. Angel will have to work especially hard.

With you to help her, Darci, we believe she will be fine. Manyfeathers, you are authorized to take Darci with you. He is now officially a Guide-in-Training and your apprentice until Angel passes from the Earth plane. We all agree that this must happen soon. We shall reconvene when Angel is ready to join us."

All the Beings stood, so I did as well.

Wachena walked over to me and took my hands. I felt a rush of strength flow through me. Each of these powerful Guides did the same.

Manyfeathers was last. Instead of grasping my hands as the others had done, he placed his hands on my shoulders. Instead of a surge of strength, I felt overwhelmed with compassion, which rolled into a deep longing to be with Angel.

"You are ready to come with me," said the Indian Guide.

We didn't go far. Near the arched entry to the meeting room was a stand with a large book on it. Syd Manyfeathers opened the book to the back without even looking. On the left page was Angel's death imprint from her lifetime as Shalia, the incarnation before her current one; I recognized it instantly. On the right page was a birth imprint, one I hadn't seen. It was a circular graph with many symbols, most of them at the bottom of the chart.

Manyfeathers explained, "Angel arrived once again on the Earth plane in 1899. She was born into a male body in Livorno, Italy. Her parents named her Anthony. With hope for a better life, the family left on a ship bound for the United States in 1901. Both parents died during the voyage. Angel, or little Tony as the toddler was called, was placed in an orphanage in Brooklyn, New York. The boy is now nearly eight. What you see when we visit may disturb you. Remember, you can do nothing to change the situation, but you can send love and compassion to anyone we see. Are you ready to travel?"

"I want to see Angel," I said, surprised by the intensity in my voice.

"That's all I've wanted since I remembered her. Yes, let's go."

I followed Manyfeathers through curved and winding hallways. This area was not familiar to me. We came to a giant circular entrance that was long enough to be considered a tunnel. Soothing blue and green lights illuminated the path as we proceeded through this extended doorway into a giant chamber.

The room was a perfect sphere. We entered and immediately began to float to the other side. I looked around, trying to take in as much as I could. The sphere was covered with panels. Most were lighted ovals, but some were shiny domes while others were circular pockets. Each one was large enough to be a doorway.

Manyfeathers knew right where he was going and wasted no time. He glided to an oval panel that had a radiant emerald glow. As he placed his hands on either side, we were both drawn through the opening into a field of green light. Manyfeathers put his arm around me to keep me with him as we sailed along a corridor. The green light faded to blue-gray, and I noticed many figures below us walking slowly along this strange passageway. I wanted to ask where this place was, but we were traveling much too fast to exchange words.

After a while, I began noticing openings in the corridor. Some looked like portholes, some like doorways, and some like entrances to other passageways. Eventually Syd Manyfeathers took me through one of the larger doorways, and we were instantly lost in clouds.

"Clouds!" I thought, trying not to get too excited. "This must be Earth!"

As soon as I saw the clouds part and the beautiful star-filled night sky stretch out above us, I knew I was right. We had returned to Earth.

After floating over a wide river that shimmered in the starlight, Manyfeathers led me to a grassy field by the riverbank and motioned for me to sit there with him.

"Just want to make sure you are all right," he said. "Sometimes the first trip to the lower wheel causes dizziness and disorientation."

"I'm fine," I assured him, as I noticed that my spirit body was trembling a bit. "If I'm anxious at all, it's because I am finally going to see Angel."

"She won't see you."

"She'll know I'm there."

"Of course, I'll take you to her. That's why we're here. I want to prepare you. What we see here may unsettle you."

"Angel and I have been through so much together. Wherever she is, whatever her current circumstance, she is my partner. I must be with her."

"Remember how she got stuck on this lower spiral?"

"I do. I was there when she was Gabriel who wasted his life away in self-pity. I was there when she was the frail, crippled Shalia."

"She is still attempting to balance her karma here, Darci. She came back to Earth destined to be orphaned."

"Surely this experience will pay for that one instant when Gabriel lost his temper, kicked, and fatally wounded his son."

"It's far more complicated than that. As you look upon this scene, remember that she is in the process of paying her karmic debt."

"Manyfeathers, the Master Guides were concerned that Angel might not be ready to return to Spirit."

"If we take her too soon from this lifetime, she will still have Earth karma to resolve. This must then be addressed in her next Earth lifetime."

"But we shall be together then. I will help her!"

The Native Guide looked at me. He stared into my eyes for what seemed like a long time.

Finally he spoke, "Nothing is so decided. If you do work together, you will be on one side of the Great Veil between worlds, and she will be on the other. It will not be easy."

I felt my heart swell as I said, "I believe in the strength of the bonds between us. I love her and she loves me. We can do whatever is necessary."

"Then let's go."

We stood and gazed at the river for a minute or two. I said a silent prayer and believe he did the same. The American Indian man stood behind me and once again put his hands on my shoulders.

"Take a step forward," he instructed.

I did so and felt myself gliding downward. The entire scene changed as soon as I moved. Instead of sliding towards the river, Manyfeathers and I were passing through the roof of an old brick building. From the noises around us, I could tell we were in a city. There was a clock chiming somewhere, the sound of a horse and carriage, and shouting voices further down the street.

The room we entered was dark, but I could make out several dozen sleeping forms because I could see a faint glow around each. There were no beds, only blankets and piles of rags. We hovered near the ceiling for a few minutes, and I realized we were in a children's orphanage.

Suddenly one of the children stirred and sat up. He rubbed his eyes, then walked the short distance to the window on his knees. The gaslight from the street lit his dirt-streaked face. His eyes were big, round, and brown, and they drew me closer to him.

Manyfeathers hovered behind me as I floated down towards the boy. As soon as I got near enough to look directly into his eyes, I felt an electric connection. There was no doubt: this was Angel.

My entire spirit body trembled with the joy of recognition. Love poured out of me, and I could see waves of pink light flood over the child. Great tears rolled down his face. He clasped his hands and began to pray silently though I could hear him well, "Dear God, I can feel your angels near me. Tell them to bring me food, please. I am so hungry. Amen. Oh—

and God? Have the angels bring enough food for everybody, so we won't fight over it. Thank you. Amen again."

Compassion surged through me. I couldn't help myself. I wrapped my spirit arms around that child. I know he felt me because he sighed and relaxed a little though his tears still flowed. A few moments later, he fell asleep with his head on the window sill.

I was still holding him when Manyfeathers moved closer so that he stood at the boy's back. He clasped his hands and ran his thumbs up the child's spine. I felt the little one quiver in my arms. The Guide did this several more times until a bright glow came from the top of the boy's head. The glow intensified and lengthened, and I saw the child's astral body hovering above his physical form. A slender lighted cord ran between the spirit body and the physical body.

Manyfeathers addressed the Spirit of the child, "Anthony, I am your guardian angel. You are much loved."

I was still holding the boy's physical body. I looked up at the golden spirit body floating just above me. It looked much like the child but was translucent and luminous. I could see a kaleidoscope of patterns and bright colors in the center of this glowing form. The boy was asleep, but his Spirit was awake and looking directly at me.

"I know you," I heard the thought come from the Spirit of the child. "I have two angels come to help me."

A rush of emotions pulsed through me. I could not believe that I was finally talking to my mate though Angel was in the form of a small boy.

"Yes," I gushed, "it is I—and I'll help you however I can. I love you so much, little one."

Manyfeathers turned the child's spirit form towards him and asked, "We angels don't eat food or carry any with us. How would you like to go to a place where there is no hunger?"

"Yes, please," I heard from the boy's Spirit. "Soon, please."

"All is well, Anthony. We love you and will watch out for you," said Manyfeathers.

He then used his hands to gently glide the spirit form back into the physical body of the boy. I wanted to carry the sleeping child to a more comfortable spot but realized that I could not physically accomplish this, and besides there were no comfortable spots. In the dim light of pre-dawn, I could see the squalor, filth, and dust and dirt in the air. I wanted to get that boy and all the children out of that horrible place.

Manyfeathers and I watched from a perch near the ceiling as the children woke up. They were a tattered lot, all boys between ages four and twelve, their faces dark with dirt. There was a pail in the corner for urination. A larger boy pushed a smaller one out of the way so that he could use the pail first. The little boy cried and wet himself.

A great clanging came from below. The eighteen boys scurried down the wooden stairway. Manyfeathers and I floated through the floorboards of the upper room so that we could observe the scene on the level below. A fat man was banging a pot with a spoon, a signal for the boys to come and eat. A hefty woman in a large soiled apron spooned globs of mush into wooden bowls, then spun them onto the table. There were only three spoons, which the older boys grabbed. The other children ate the porridge with their dirty hands.

The fat man hit one of the boys on the back of the head and snarled, "Simon, it's your turn to dump the pee bucket."

"Let me eat first," said the boy as he ducked from another swipe of the big man's hand.

Anthony crouched at one end of the table with the younger boys. They gobbled their mush, keeping their heads low and their eyes on their food.

The woman spoke, waving her cooking spoon, "I want every one of you boys to go down to the public trough and wash your faces. Sister Margaret and Sister Claire are coming today with blankets and clothes for you ruffians. I don't want your dirty faces to scare away the nuns."

The room emptied quickly. Having eaten every bit of mush, the boys headed out into the street—all but Simon who trudged unwillingly up the stairs to do his chore.

The street outside the orphanage was busy. There were horses and carts, horses and carriages, and many pedestrians passing by.

Manyfeathers and I followed the boys. They divided into two groups, the younger lads headed in one direction and the pack of older boys in the other. Anthony tagged along with the older group. There were seven of them headed down the street toward an outdoor market a few blocks away.

The tallest boy instructed the others as they walked, "Remember our plan. You, you, and you—distract the vendor. The rest of us will steal fruit off the other side when he's not looking."

"Then we share!" demanded one of the boys who had been told to distract the fruit merchant.

"Yeah, yeah," the older boy said dismissively with a wave of his hand.

We watched from above as the pack of orphan boys circled the market.

"Let's do it!" I heard one boy say. "I'm still real hungry. Get me a pear! I want a pear!"

"Shhhh!" the leader whispered, hushing them as they drew near the fruit stand.

The merchant saw trouble coming and shouted, "You imps, move along unless you can show me your money."

Three of the boys pretended to be digging in their pockets for coins while the other four, including Anthony, moved to the far side of the stand. Without consulting Manyfeathers, I moved closer to the little boy who had Angel's Soul. I shook my head in disbelief. Astara, Nua, Yulanna Carlotta, Little Elk, Nunzah, Soliya, Gabriel, Shalia—so many names, so many lifetimes all wrapped up in this dirty street urchin.

As the boys crouched behind the fruit stand, I heard Anthony say to another boy, "I dreamed of two angels last night. One told me I won't be hungry anymore. Maybe we'll get some fruit today."

The next series of events happened very fast. The fruit vendor began chasing away the boys who were trying to distract him. The four hiding behind the stand saw their chance and began grabbing apples and pears. The merchant turned in time to see the theft taking place. He whirled around and came charging.

Anthony, who was the youngest of the four thieves, was just reaching for an apple when the vendor began yelling, "You filthy little thieves! I'm going to thrash you and teach you not to come near my stand!"

Empty-handed, Anthony ran around the stand toward the street. The oldest boy who had his arms full of fruit tossed a ripe yellow pear to him.

I could see the sun glinting off the pear as it sailed through the air. I could also see hunger in the face of the boy. Anthony wanted that pear; he wanted to grab that pear and run. He followed the fruit with his eyes and backed up so as to be in just the right position to catch it. Just as the little boy reached for the prize, a horse-drawn milk wagon came upon him. The horse knocked him down with one of its huge hooves, and the heavy wagon, laden with containers of milk, ran right over the poor child.

The street went quiet. The driver pulled up his team and climbed down.

The boys and the fruit merchant forgot about their confrontation. The six orphans carried Anthony to the side of the street. Two of them were crying. The others looked sad.

"I never saw the little fellow," the driver said, scratching his head under his cap while the vendor shook his head and went about picking up his scattered goods.

Manyfeathers and I had zoomed quickly to the boy's side as soon as he was hit and stayed close as the other boys carried him.

"That death was very quick," said Manyfeathers.

"The little one did not feel a thing."

"Are you sure he's dead?" I asked. I didn't need an answer. With my own eyes, I saw the golden Spirit of the child float out of his body just as the other orphans were laying him down.

This time there was no connecting cord; this time, the Spirit was free of the physical body. The newly-detached Spirit hovered a few feet above the scene watching the other boys stand around his lifeless body.

Manyfeathers moved closer to the boy's Spirit, and I followed. My heart was thumping wildly as I took my place on one side of the disoriented Spirit who looked just like Anthony but was translucent and golden.

"That's me!" exclaimed Anthony, pointing to his body on the ground.

Manyfeathers stood behind the Spirit boy, putting one arm around him and another on his head.

He spoke softly to the child, "It's all right, Anthony. You're with us now. We've come to guide you to the place we talked about last night."

"Where are they taking me?" the Spirit boy cried as his orphan buddies carried his crushed body down the street.

"We can follow them and see," said the Guide, "or we can move on. You do not need to be here any longer. We can go together to a better place."

The Spirit child looked at Manyfeathers, then at me. We radiated love to him. I pulsed wave after wave of pink light as my heart pounded with love. Then I wrapped myself around him and hugged Manyfeathers in the process.

"I'll go with you," said the boy. "I never want to go back to that place. I never want to be hungry again! Ever!"

So I took his left hand, Manyfeathers took his right, and the three of us rose up, up, up above the street, above the neighborhood, above the bustling city. Even though it was a sunny day, a bank of fluffy clouds appeared.

Manyfeathers knew the way and led us into the clouds.

I kept my hand clasped tightly on the boy's, and once we entered the cloud bank, I put my arm around the child. This was Angel's precious Soul. I was not going to lose her now.

∞ ∞ ∞

The Spirit child's eyes were wide as we rose higher and higher. Finally, the sounds of the Earth plane faded away, and silence surrounded us. We traveled for a while as the clouds thickened and became a luminous vapor.

The Native Guide led us to a great portal with columns and steps of crystal. The three of us glided up the shining steps and between the columns. We were in the great room where I had arrived when I last passed from life on Earth. Manyfeathers brought the Spirit child into a brightly lit circle, then stepped back, motioning for me to do the same. The little one stood there rubbing his eyes.

As soon as Manyfeathers and I were out of the circle, an extraordinary thing occurred. Dozens of tall luminous Beings manifested around the child. Some shone so brightly I could not look directly at them. These were more than the Angel Initiates who greeted me. These were the Archangels.

"The Angels take special interest when a child passes over," Manyfeathers informed me. "There are an unusually large number of them here today—perhaps because this Soul is their namesake."

The splendid Beings around the Spirit child obscured him from our view for a while. We waited patiently. Eventually, the tall brilliant figures grouped in a semi-circle behind the boy. Manyfeathers stepped forward and entered the circle of light. He knelt before the boy and took his hand.

"I am your Spirit Guide, Syd Manyfeathers."

The child nodded.

"My job was to bring you safely home to a place where there is no hunger. I have done that. You are here."

I moved closer. I didn't want to miss a thing.

"Do you know how lucky you are to have all these Angels around you?" asked Manyfeathers.

The boy looked at the group of Angels standing behind him and nodded again.

"I want to take you to a room where you can rest. The Angels picked it out especially for you."

The native Guide looked at the host of Angels, then scooped the child into his arms and glided quickly to the far side of the room. I followed. We stopped before an ornate oval door, which slid open when Manyfeathers spoke a few words in a tongue I did not understand.

Behind the golden door was a small room with pink floor, walls, and ceiling. There was a comfortable bed and a round window. A very peaceful feeling came over me as I gazed into the little room.

"This is for you," Manyfeathers told the boy.

"I've never seen a room like this!" the child exclaimed.

"This room is designed to make you feel very good," continued the Guide. "You can stay as long as you wish. We will be nearby. You go in and rest now."

The child looked at me, at Manyfeathers, then back at me. He then stepped right into the pink booth. The walls began to glow.

"Are you all right?" the native Guide asked him. "I am going to close the door. You can open it whenever you want. You rest now, little one."

The child nodded at us and sat on the bed as Manyfeathers placed his hand on one of the ornate decorations, and the door closed.

He then beckoned me to follow him. We circled around through a curved hallway near the pink booth, passing through an oval opening to a dimly lit room that had seats and benches. I gasped because this room had a window that allowed us to look into the pink room where the child was. I watched the little boy remove what was left of his tattered clothing and lie down while I sat on the bench closest to this viewing window.

Manyfeathers joined me.

"Very often when Souls depart the Earth plane, they need time in this booth," he told me. "Not enough love in that boy's life. Not enough love on Earth. Maybe you and Angel can change that."

"Change it? How?" I asked, wondering if he was referencing our mission.

The native man turned his eyes to the resting child. There was a soft glow in the Love Power Booth and a ray of pink light beamed right on the boy.

"You two show those on Earth how much love there is in the universe. You will see."

He switched his gaze to me and said, "Stay with the little one. I must go and take care of the formalities. This one was called back early, so there is much to do."

"What sort of formalities?" I asked, wanting to know everything.

"A Spirit Guide officially signs on before a child is born to assist while that Soul walks the Earth in human form. When the Soul returns to the spirit plane, there is a sign-off procedure, there's the death imprint to file, and discussions on what is next for that Soul."

"The discussions . . . ?"

"You will be a part of them, Darci, and so will Angel once she is re-energized and ready. You stay and watch what occurs in this Love Booth. I shall return."

He headed toward the door but vanished before he reached it. I wondered when I would be able to do that.

For a long time I sat in the dimly lit room with my eyes on the changing conditions in the Love Booth. The Spirit child rested quietly.

The energizing rays in the Love Booth went through many phases. There were often strong pulsing pink lights, then there would be a steady pale pink light or a deep rose hue in the little room. Occasionally spirals of gold would circle up from the floor to the ceiling. I found myself mesmerized by this play of light and color, so much so that initially I did not notice that the spirit form of the boy was changing.

I was taken aback when I saw a longer and decidedly more feminine form on the bed where the child lay. My curiosity and passion got me off the bench. I pressed myself against the viewing window. The figure on the bed was turned away from me.

"Let me see you." I sent the thought to Angel. "Turn to me so I can see you," I asked, sending this thought several times, the last time with a heart full of love. The figure turned over to lie facing me. Angel's eyes were closed. Even in sleep she had responded to me.

I looked at her luminous form and saw the curves, the indentations, the little hills and valleys of the one who had been my mate in so many lifetimes. Her spirit body seemed to be liquid, then vapor, then light as the colored rays shifted and danced in the little room.

Suddenly a very bright golden ray lit her face. My heart raced, and I vibrated from head to toe as I watched her features change. There were so many faces that blended smoothly from one to the next. I recognized quite a few as the amazing metamorphosis went on and on. Angel shifted her position again, lying on her back. A beam of white light engulfed her so brightly I couldn't see her, and I was afraid she might be transported away. I sat with my hands clenched on the sill of the viewing window until I could see her form lying there. I sighed. I needn't have worried.

"Certainly you have learned to trust the process by now," murmured Manyfeathers, standing behind me.

"We've just been reunited. I don't want to let her out of my sight. Surely you understand," I replied.

Manyfeathers put his hand on my shoulder and replied, "You two are a team. You know this."

"What is happening to her in there?"

"She is receiving a love bath."

"But she is transforming! I saw her face change again and again!"

"The spirit body is much more malleable than the physical one."

"Is this usual for a Spirit that has just returned from Earth?"

Manyfeathers paused before answering as if he were searching for the best way to explain.

"No. What Angel is going through is not the norm. Most Souls keep spirit forms similar to the physical bodies they inhabited during their most recent lifetimes, as you did. I think perhaps your presence is influencing Angel as she adjusts to being in spirit form."

"Is that all right, Manyfeathers?"

"It shows how strongly you are bonded. She is reaching out to you even in her unconscious state of rest."

We both gazed through the observation window at the sleeping Soul. I wondered if she really knew I was there. I wondered if she knew about our mission.

"She feels you near her," Manyfeathers answered my thoughts. "Beyond that, she is simply adapting to her spirit form and absorbing a great deal of love. She needs much love after her last incarnation as the orphan Anthony."

Sitting, watching, and waiting by the observation window became a meditation for me. Manyfeathers left, returned and left again, but I stayed as close to Angel as I could get, which was that seat by the window.

If measured in Earth time, it would have been days that I sat outside the Love Booth, but the spirit world has no linear time frame. It didn't matter to me. At last I knew where Angel was, so that's where I wanted to be.

As I sat there noticing the deep hue of the rose-colored light in the Love Booth, my dear mentor Sottrol appeared in the doorway. He joined me on the bench near the window.

"She loves you very much," said the elder.

"She knows I'm here and who I am?"

"Oh, she knows. Now that she is getting her energy back, her life-force is restored. She is dreaming, dreaming of you, Darci."

"I wish I could know her dreams."

"Reading dreams is much like reading thoughts. You just have to extend your psychic mind to probe a little wider and a little deeper. You're accessing visuals when you look in on someone's dreams. Take a deep breath and try it."

I breathed a few times very deeply, then visualized a wide connection cable that went from my mind to hers.

Sottrol saw what I was doing and made some suggestions.

"Visualize the connection as being even wider and much more luminescent. See it sparkling and floating gently between the two of you. It is a connection of love, so link your hearts as well and send love to her in the cables you have visualized. Then open your heart and mind and see what you receive from her."

I tried to do what Sottrol instructed, but there was a block of some kind.

"I'm having difficulty," I said, squirming a bit on the bench.

Sottrol placed both his hands on my head, "Relax. Just let it come."

A flood of golden light washed over me. Suddenly I saw myself in a field of yellow flowers. There was bright blue sky overhead, and the flowers went to the horizon in every direction. I felt a presence, turned, and there was a lambent female figure standing at a distance.

This was it! This was Angel's dream, and I was in it with her! I instinctively moved towards the female.

As I approached her, she changed. At first she was glowing white. Then her form became yellow-gold, much like the flowers.

As I got closer, she transformed to light pink, then deeper pink, then rose. I reached out my arms towards her, and she did the same. Sparks flew those few yards between our fingers. I felt the electric energy crackling through me and jumped out of my meditative state.

Sottrol patted me on the back. "There! That wasn't too hard to do, was it?"

I couldn't respond, for I was still catching my breath from the dreamtime experience.

"It won't be long now," the elder assured me. "She's getting her strength and power back. Be patient. You know Angel. She is very thorough. She won't leave the Love Booth until she has all she needs."

"Can I help her?"

"Pray and send her love. She needs our prayers, Darci, for she is at a turning point. As you know, her Soul has been caught in a deep karmic pocket which has kept her trapped in dealing with basic lower wheel lessons."

"Like what?"

"Survival, food and shelter, and love. As you may know, she is a Soul who progressed very far and then took a tremendous dive. She is recovering. However, her next decisions and resulting actions will determine if she truly reverses her downward spiral."

"I thought she did well as the crippled Shalia."

"True. She began balancing the karma from the curse she put on her own leg when she was Gabriel, but she did not develop social skills in the lifetime in India and remained very self-absorbed. Hence, she was propelled into her next incarnation where she was orphaned early in life and had to develop abilities for interacting constantly with the other boys."

"Group living, never being alone. I saw the conditions she was dealing with in her last life," I mused aloud. "They were horrible—squalid and filthy. She may have learned how to interact with the other boys, but there wasn't much affection between them."

My mentor nodded and said, "They were together because of circumstance, not because of conscious choices they made."

"They were just children. Tell me, Sottrol, what did Angel miss by returning home early from that incarnation?"

"She missed working herself out of hardship and poverty. Anthony's right leg would have eventually gone lame, and she could have worked off more of that curse."

"That already lasted through Shalia's lifetime. When can Angel be free of it?"

"That depends, Darci, so pray for her. She will be at your side soon, conscious and burning with questions."

Sottrol and I sat silently. I prayed and he prayed. My heart went out to Angel, for I knew she still had a long road in front of her.

I would travel it with her. I resolved I would do my utmost to help move her up and out of the karmic pocket Sottrol had mentioned.

When I again raised my head, the deep rose light in the Love Booth was flickering very fast. The atmosphere in the little room seemed filled with white and pink sparkles. All of this faded slowly to a blue-white light that was peaceful and still. The figure on the bed stirred, rolled over, and slowly sat up.

I stood up. I was vibrating, brimming over with anticipation.

"I must go to her."

"Sit," Sottrol said, placing his hand on mine.

The door to the Love Booth opened, and Manyfeathers stepped into the small room. When I saw this, I did sit down. It made sense that her most recent Guide would be the first one to greet her. He sat next to her on the bed and talked to her while he checked her eyes and her energy field.

She was glowing with a rich pink light. Although she was turned away from me, I could see her spirit form had changed from a boy to a small woman who appeared to have long hair and graceful arms. Manyfeathers gave her a pink and silver robe to wear, which she drew on over her head. Once clothed, she stood, twirled in the new gown, and ended up facing the observation window and me. She bowed.

"I told you she knows you are here," Sottrol chuckled, poking me with his finger.

As for me, I was lost in emotion. When Angel faced me, I saw her eyes. My insides quivered, and I noticed that suddenly thousands of tiny comets were circling around me in my energy field.

Sottrol moved behind me and whispered, "Breathe, Darci. Breathe!"

Manyfeathers began talking again to Angel, so she turned toward him. I could hear low murmurs but could not distinguish what was being said.

"When can I talk to her, Sottrol? When can I hold her?"

"I've arranged some private time for you two before the next meeting of The Elevated Council. Follow me."

As long as I could see Angel, I did not want to leave that spot.

"She will join us there," Sottrol assured me.

Still, it wasn't until I saw her leave the Love Booth with Manyfeathers that I, too, moved to go. Sottrol led me through curved and lighted hallways. We glided through the crystal meeting room to a wall just outside the entrance.

Sottrol sent beams of light from his hands toward the wall. The patterns there instantly slid around revealing a small oval doorway. My mentor motioned for me to step through though I had to duck to enter.

"Angel will join you shortly," he called as the door closed noiselessly behind me.

I was somewhat startled by where I found myself. The room was circular, no surprise, but it was also padded. The floor and walls were cushioned. There was a wide plush bench that went around the circumference. I looked up to behold a small dome of crystals similar to the one in the great meeting room. The light for this cozy, cushioned room came through the crystals in the dome above. Everything was white.

I sat on the floor and leaned against the bench, energized and a bit crazed with anticipation, so I tried to center and calm myself. I didn't want to frighten Angel with wild vibrations and thought perhaps I was being monitored, for it was not until I had evened out my energy that the door of the white chamber opened.

I tried to maintain a sense of calm as I saw Angel step through that oval entry, but it was impossible. I wanted to take her in my arms and cry and laugh, but I just sat there cross-legged in my purple robe with my heart racing.

She stood just inside the doorway that slid closed. Her eyes fixed upon me. They were violet, nearly the color of my robe. Her hair was a lovely, reddish brown with golden highlights, which reminded me of the color of one of my favorite horses during my last lifetime in England. A decidedly pink glow surrounded her. I could also discern rings of deep rose light circling her.

"Thank you for your prayers," she began, still standing.

I couldn't speak though my heart cried out, "I love you. I love you."

She took a step towards me, and I began to see why we were in a room with so much padding. Visible bolts of electric energy passed between us as soon as she took that step. Losing her balance, she fell onto the cushioned floor.

She laughed, saying, "What a great impression I'm making. I can't even stay on my feet."

Still speechless, compassion poured from me. I could see waves of golden light pulsing from my spirit body. Now I realized why the room was white. We could more easily see the colors in each other's energy patterns.

She crossed her legs and sat facing me. We were about ten feet apart. I placed my arms on my knees with the palms of my hands facing her. She followed my lead, but as soon as she turned her palms toward me, more bolts of electricity passed between us. It was exhilarating! I had never felt anything like it. I turned my palms to the floor, and the electricity abated.

"I am so glad to see you," I finally said. "I'm glad to have this time with you."

She smiled and replied, "I know you are my partner, my mate though the details of our past together are unclear to me right now."

"It took a while for me to remember. I had help from The Great Book of Lifetimes. I read about many of the Earth incarnations we shared. We both have had many names and have walked the Earth in many cultures in many different time periods."

"I recall only the orphanage," she replied, "and even that is a blur."

"No matter. We are finally together. That's what counts. I want to come closer."

"Wait," she said softly. "What do you call yourself here and now?"

"Darcimon. Darci, really. Darci Stillwater."

"Do I have a new name now I am here? It's not Tony, is it?"

It was my turn to laugh. "No, no. You are called Angel."

"Angel? Like those incredibly tall, unbelievably bright Beings who surrounded me when I first got here?"

"You are their namesake."

"I am far from what they are."

"Ah, but you can become a true angel like them if you wish. You have the potential. We have great potential together."

"I wish I understood more," she said, dropping her head slightly.

"There is much I don't know, and I've been training for a while. I still don't understand why Sottrol—he's my mentor here—why he can appear and disappear, why he can go through ceilings and walls, and I cannot. When I was with Manyfeathers on Earth the day we came to get you, I was able to float through the roof of the orphanage, yet I cannot do that here.

It's all a great mystery to me, and I find the more I learn, the more there is to learn."

Sighing, she replied, "I am such a beginner."

"Not true, Angel. I have read The Great Book of Lifetimes! I know that you have amazing talents. You were my teacher long ago in Egypt. You were a great astrologer and healer in that lifetime."

"What has happened to me, Darci? Why was I in that awful orphanage and not here with you?"

I did not answer right away. I was trying to find the words. She looked at me earnestly, and our eyes connected long enough for more sparks and electricity to fly about the room.

"I did something, didn't I?" she said with a quiver in her voice. "I can feel it, but I don't know what it is."

"Your Soul has knowledge of all your past actions."

"Will you tell me? I can see that you know."

"I want to be closer. I want to touch you."

We both gingerly moved a couple of feet closer, and immediately snapping and sparking filled the space all around us. We were encased in a sphere of electric energy that was firing bolts in every direction. Angel's violet eyes were wide as she experienced the same jolts and rushes I was feeling. After a while, the crazy, crackling energy in the room steadied to an even hum. I could see bands of bright golden light encircling us.

"I guess we'd better take this slowly," I offered.

She laughed a little and stared again into my eyes, waiting for an answer.

"Angel, I don't know everything—far from it. I do know that in many, many lifetimes you were courageous, loving, compassionate, nurturing, generous, wise and strong."

"Then what happened?"

"A challenging lifetime, one that tested both of us to the limit."

With much love and compassion in my heart, I told her in detail the story of Gabriel, Marie, and their first-born son Raphael. As I related the account, tears rolled down her cheeks. I sensed deep feelings surging within her. The atmosphere in the white, cushioned room was laden with strong emotions. Bolts of electricity reverberated between the dome ceiling and the floor.

When I finished with the description of Gabriel's death imprint, I saw the emotional pain pouring from Angel. Great waves of red and black pulsed from her. I couldn't stand it. I had to hold her. I pushed myself up and reached towards her but was repelled by a field of static. My hands burned for a moment. I sat back and focused on sending her love and compassion.

When the atmosphere in the white room was once again calmer, and the harsh black and red waves were no longer emanating from Angel, I ventured more words, "The karmic situation from that lifetime is not yet resolved, but you have made some progress."

I continued, quietly recounting our incarnation in India as Hari and Shalia.

She listened and then sat silently for a long time after I finished. I watched the changing colors in her energy. There were now emerald green and magenta rings of light wreathing her spirit body. I was glad the jagged red and black were gone.

"So I was Shalia, crippled by my own curse," she finally said.

I nodded.

"Then I was Anthony, orphaned at a very young age, and now I'm here."

"Yes."

"What is next for me, for us?"

"The Master Guides have given us a mission."

"A mission? You and me? What is it?"

"I don't know the details yet. I believe we will find out together. I do know why they chose us."

"Tell me, please," she said, inching closer to me as the atmosphere around us again crackled and spit sparks.

"We are bonded through time. Our love for each other and our connection are so strong that the Master Guides believe we will be able to communicate through the barrier surrounding the Earth plane. Our ability to do this will help change life on Earth for the better."

"Wow!" she exclaimed, sitting back on her heels. "Well—I guess I'll be the one doing Earth duty."

"I believe so. We will find out much more when we attend the meeting of The Elevated Council. Angel—I want to touch you."

"Dare we try?"

"I'm guessing, but I think we needed to talk first as we have been doing and discharge that which has been pent up within us. I'm going to move closer."

She nodded, and I shifted my position so that I was within a foot of touching her. The electric sparks flew but not as violently. The crackling sound had lost its scary edge. I looked up and saw we were surrounded by a sphere of golden sparkles that hung in the atmosphere around us. She saw it, too.

"I love you, Angel," I spoke aloud, and as I did so, a great wave of pink light emanated from me and washed over her. I heard her let out a breath that was almost a sigh.

"We have raised dozens of children together throughout the many lifetimes we have shared. Sometimes you bore them; sometimes I bore them. We worked as a team for the benefit of our families, an exception was the lifetime I just told you about when you were Gabriel. Most often, we succeeded very well in serving our families and our community. Now we have the opportunity to serve all of humankind."

"I hope I am ready."

"I will do all I can to make sure you are—we are. Let me touch you."

She reached out her hand.

I took it and clasped her other hand as well. Huge vertical bolts of electricity passed through us from the floor to the dome. My spirit body was buzzing so intensely that I thought I would dissolve. Staring straight into Angel's eyes, I felt as if I were vaporizing. She held my hands and my gaze. The lightning produced by our two Souls touching continued to flash and strike. At one point, I nearly let go because it seemed as if I were disintegrating, but Angel squeezed my hands and clutched them tighter. I focused again on her luminous eyes, now lavender in the bright, rarefied light. Soon the electric storm began to subside. The strikes and bolts turned to continuous vertical rays of dazzling white and gold light. We both breathed great sighs of relief.

"I'm so glad to have you back, Angel. How I've missed you and longed for you."

She pressed my hands, then let go to touch my face. Some gentle sparks flew. I spontaneously encircled her waist and drew her to me. At last we were pressed against each other in blissful reunion. A steady stream of electric energy ran from the crystal dome through us into the padded floor. Lights of all colors flashed. A spiral of lustrous gold wound around us as we embraced. We held each other for a long time until the light show mellowed to an even continuous deep pink glow.

All my passion and yearning for Angel came flooding out as I took her face in my hands and kissed it. Hundreds of thin very bright vertical bolts of electricity ran through us and surrounded us as we kissed. Our spirit bodies seemed to melt into one another's. Never had I felt such oneness, such union with another Soul. For the first time, I knew what it meant to be drawn into a cosmic dance, a dance that knew no boundaries. Although our spirit bodies remained in an embrace in the center of the white room, we seemed to twirl and soar.

It's very difficult to describe the multitude of sensations. I can only say I felt as if I were finally home, that the missing parts were snugly and comfortably in place, and all was well.

The joy I experienced was overwhelming. It didn't matter what was ahead of us as long as we could face it together.

We would have liked to have stayed in that room together for a long while; however, we did not have that luxury. As soon as the energy in the cushioned room again settled to a peaceful hum, Sottrol and Manyfeathers appeared. We didn't see them at first, so both Angel and I jumped a little when we heard Sottrol speak.

"Very impressive, you two. I've never witnessed anything quite like it. You probably couldn't see it, but there was a fountain of pink light spewing through the top of the dome."

"A good sign," added Manyfeathers.

"We've come to brief you for the meeting," Sottrol continued, sitting next to us. He was very agile for one who appeared to be old.

Manyfeathers sat cross-legged on the other side of us.

Sottrol continued, "The Elevated Council is made up of the Master Guides and those Guides who are concerned with the development and evolution of the lower wheel. Earth, one cog on the lower wheel, is getting much attention at this time because this particular plane is nearing a great shift that can bring an opportunity for humanity."

Although I was listening to Sottrol, I was looking at Angel. We were still holding hands, and I was still vibrating intensely.

Sottrol put his left hand on the back of my neck and his right hand on the back of Angel's. My head became extremely clear even though the electric buzzing in my spirit body continued.

"You two have been chosen to help lead humanity into a new era on Earth. What I observed when you reunited today confirms that the Council has chosen wisely."

"Time to go," interjected Manyfeathers.

The two Guides helped us to our feet and escorted us slowly out through the small oval door. The meeting room was just around the corner. The other members of The Elevated

Council were not yet present, so the four of us sat on the horseshoe bench. Angel and I were together, of course, with her Guide close to her and Sottrol next to me.

"Are you all right, Darci?" Sottrol began as he examined my eyes. "You'll do little more than listen at this meeting although you will have the chance to ask questions."

Manyfeathers spoke in low tones, "It is important that you both understand exactly what is expected of you."

At that moment, Chilliwon Mac strutted in through the great portal of the meeting room. He hopped up on the bench and bowed, then looked directly at Angel who had an expression of curiosity and interest.

"My Lady," said the Elf Guide as he bowed specifically to her, "at last you join us. I am Chilliwon Mac, at your service."

"Hello, Sir," said Angel with a slight smile.

I squeezed her hand. How good it was to have her beside me to share all this with her.

Chalherine and her assistant Wachena entered next. They came directly over to Angel. Wachena bowed, then hugged her and took her other hand so as to make her stand. Then Chalherine embraced Angel. I knew what this powerful Guide's hugs were like. I saw tiny shimmering stars shoot out of the top of Angel's head, and since I was still holding one of her hands, I felt a surge of intense love pass through her.

Wachena went to the back of the room to fetch a second chair to put beside the one that was already sitting in the opening of the horseshoe bench. Chalherine then indicated that Angel and I should take these seats.

Esther and Arcillis arrived together, the vaporous female Guide floating swiftly and gracefully to the bench. Arcillis, however, beckoned Sottrol to join him near the door, and they talked together for a short time. When these two reverend elders took their places on the horseshoe, everything went silent. Everyone in the room sat quietly with their eyes closed, so Angel and I did the same. I said a prayer for Angel, for our mission, and for the Earth.

Arcillis stood, removing his hood to reveal his crystal-covered head. I saw the look of surprise on Angel's face. This was all new to her. The Master Guide looked directly at Angel.

"Welcome," he said with a deep bell-like timbre to his voice. "We are pleased that you have arrived safely. Please do not be apprehensive about anything that is discussed here, for nothing will be asked of you that you cannot accomplish and accomplish well."

Angel shifted in her seat. We continued to hold hands.

"I am Arcillis, one of a team of Master Guides who has developed a high-minded plan for the lower wheel of experience which, of course, includes Earth. Because of the ebb and flow of the major cycles, which were created long ago by the One, the Great Spirit, a crucial time is approaching for the lower wheel and for Earth in particular."

He stopped and looked from face to face, ending with a long gaze at Angel and me.

"This Soul called Angel has just returned from Earth," the Master Guide went on. "She knows the conditions there: an abundance of violence, carelessness, hard-heartedness, greed, and disrespect for the very essence of that plane of existence, for the Earth Mother. Even now a great war, which may involve most of the Earth, looms menacingly. People are hungry. Children are hungry."

He motioned toward Angel. I saw a tear roll down her cheek.

"Earth has just entered a period of quickening that leads to the change of great cycles. This has happened many times before on this material plane. Each time the population of humans has decreased due to natural occurrences that come automatically with the quickening and the change. I am speaking of great floods, the eruption of volcanoes, Earthquakes, the shifting of land masses and such."

I felt Angel's fingers tighten on my hand as her eyes widened with concern.

"Even though Earth has been through this over and over, the time that approaches differs in one significant way." Again Arcillis paused, looking around the horseshoe and at Angel and me and said, "The difference is a gift from the Creator."

When Arcillis spoke those eight words, there was a silent explosion of tiny shimmering golden flecks of light. I heard Angel gasp, and I, too, was amazed.

"The power and magic of the Creator is far beyond what we can fathom," the Master Guide continued. "I will explain this gift to the lower wheel as I understand it. You can see that it has a life of its own."

He swung his arm, motioning to the sparkling atmosphere and disclosed, "The gift is a ray of energy that transforms this approaching time of quickening into a time of opportunity. Of course, this places added responsibilities on those of us who watch over and assist Souls on these lower planes. We must make them aware of the meaning of the quickening and the opportunity it brings."

Arcillis stopped and looked at Angel and me. The others turned to us as well. Angel's hand trembled, so I tightened my hold to reassure her.

"Souls incarnated on Earth will have the most to gain or to lose from the upcoming changes," said Arcillis. "You two are the messengers to Earth. Darci, you will work from the Spirit Guide realm, and Angel, my dear, you will be incarnating on Earth again. Darci will receive much training as to the specific information that must be made available to those on Earth. He, of course, as a Spirit Guide, will also have access to all the resources of the spirit world. His job is to get the information to you, Angel, which you then will transcribe and disseminate it to the other Souls on Earth. This means that you two will have to establish strong channels of communication between worlds, not just dreams and visions although these are not precluded. You must be able to consciously talk to one another through the boundaries between the Earth plane and the spirit realm."

Arcillis could see that Angel was trembling and that I was concerned about her. The Master Guide's eyes were full of compassion as he continued, "Such conscious communication between Spirit Guides and humans has occurred before. Several books in the Bible were dictated from Spirit, and there are other examples. You two have been chosen because your bonds are already very strong, and this will facilitate your connection between worlds. Once the conscious link is made, your work together will begin. May I add that the potential for what you two can accomplish is very great. At the very least we wish you to transcribe the information about the quickening and the opportunity it brings. This will be your first task once you connect through the veil."

I noticed Chalherine nodding and Sottrol smiling as if Angel and I had already accomplished this.

Arcillis carried on, "From that point, your mission will expand to include helping humans connect with their Spirit Guides so that each Soul born to Earth has access to divine information specific to that individual. Much can be healed and much karma can be balanced when humans work consciously with their Guides. You two may also show how love can flow abundantly between Souls, no matter where they are. You can demonstrate how love lasts through time and moves through the barriers between worlds. Your story and your work can change human perceptions and attitudes and may result in major changes on Earth."

Sottrol spoke up, "What is next for Darci and Angel?"

Arcillis responded, "If they are willing, they will train together for this mission. That's where we shall start. The quickening has already begun on the lower spiral. It is time to proceed with our preparations on the spirit side. Let me conclude by saying that the gift from The Great Spirit, the transformational ray of energy, is one of the most spectacular phenomena I have ever witnessed. This is truly an extraordinary time." He nodded at us and sat down.

Esther then rose from the bench and addressed the group.

Her extremely fluid form made it impossible to focus on any details of her spirit body, save her exceptional eyes.

She began, "Dear members of The Elevated Council, Darci, and Angel—as you may know, my specialty is relationships, so it was I who recommended this couple for the mission. There are a number of other Souls who are linked through time, space, and all dimensions much as these two are. I suggest that we station as many couples as we can in a similar way. Then Angel and Darci will have support."

The others in the Council nodded their approval.

"If all goes well," Esther added, "you two will also tell your story. In fact, Angel, you will write about this very meeting when you and Darci were given your mission."

Chalherine stood up as Esther took her seat beside Arcillis. The chancellor lifted both her arms and said, "Let us offer our prayers for the success of this mission."

We all bowed our heads and silently prayed. I added a prayer for Angel who was overwhelmed by everything she had seen and heard.

Arcillis was the first to speak after the silent prayers. "Does anyone have any comments or questions?"

He looked at Angel and me. "Both of you will have plenty of opportunities to ask detailed questions during your training."

Pausing, he glanced around the room and then stated, "If no one has anything further, then let us move on. This meeting is adjourned."

Mac stood on the bench as the Master Guides rose from their seats. "Angel, Darci," the little man spoke up, "you will have much help from the elves. I guarantee it." He bowed, hopped to the floor and literally skipped away.

Arcillis, Chalherine, and Wachena took turns shaking our hands, then hugging us. They each seemed to impart strength and a sense of focus when they hugged me. Esther surrounded Angel and me with her veils, which wrapped around us like soft fluid arms. I felt an amazing surge of love.

Manyfeathers and Sottrol stayed behind as the others departed. The American Indian Guide moved very close to Angel, looked at me, and said, "We have arranged a special chamber for you while you undergo training."

"Yes," said Sottrol, gliding to my side. "It's called the Infinity Suite. We will take you there now. Follow us."

Once again I was led through unfamiliar corridors. Of course, this place was entirely new to Angel. We skirted around the edge of the wondrous spherical room and passed under a green marbled arch into another set of hallways. The deeper we went into this area, the more peaceful I felt.

Finally, Manyfeathers slowed as he approached a most unusual door. It was shaped like the number eight lying on its side, the symbol for infinity. The shape of the entry reminded me of the symbol on the wall outside the Power Booth except the two loops of this doorway were equal. Sottrol stood on one side, and Manyfeathers stood on the other. They each placed the palm of their left hand on one of the loops at exactly the same time, and the door vanished, opening the way to the chamber.

"You must learn to do this," said Sottrol looking at Angel and me. "This room can only be accessed by two people working in unison. You must always leave and arrive together. One alone cannot open the door to this chamber. Both of you must do it."

"They will have much practice," Manyfeathers added.

The two Guides entered the chamber, Sottrol floating through the left loop and Manyfeathers the right at precisely the same time.

"Now you two try it," instructed Sottrol.

I took Angel's hand, and we glided through the opening as our Guides had done before us.

"Very good," said Manyfeathers. "Welcome to your new home. This suite will serve you well."

"You both need recuperation time," said Sottrol.

"We will leave you to it. Look around. Become familiar with your new chamber. Then rest. All is well."

Chapter Nine:
A Matched Pair

Angel and I were left alone in the Infinity Suite. We had been holding hands since we reunited in the white cushioned room, so we continued to do so as we explored. The entry where we were standing had a warm welcoming glow and was made of two spheres joined together, echoing the shape of the doorway. We stepped together into the next room through a double arch. This area was circular and had a floor that was glowing with gold and white crystals.

Angel hesitated to set her foot upon such a magnificent floor though she followed me once I had done so. A soft, pleasant musical tone sounded each time we took a step. There were seats around the circumference of this room, prompting me to think that we might receive some of our training there. Light radiated from the floor and also through the crystal dome overhead.

There were four doors to this central room. One was the double archway through which we had come, and two were single arched doorways across from each other that each contained a cot and a meditation seat for one. The fourth doorway was another double archway.

Once we stepped through it, we both knew this room was where we wanted to stay. It was the honeymoon suite of the spirit world. A great round bed commanded the center with padded circular walls and a padded floor. There were seats at varying levels around the wall and a giant kaleidoscope on the ceiling. When we first looked into this amazing room, everything was golden, but as soon as we stepped through the doorway, the room changed to a deep emerald green. The exception was the ceiling, which had a myriad of vibrant colors dancing in an ever-changing kaleidoscopic fashion.

Without exchanging words, we lay down on the great round bed and watched the light show above us. Mesmerized, we were lulled slowly to sleep.

I awoke to find Angel's hand still in mine. Our spirit bodies were pressed together in a rather unusual position— almost as if we had been dancing in our sleep. The kaleidoscopic ceiling moved very slowly and was not as bright as before. Letting go of Angel's hand, I put my arms around her and held her close to me as she slept. Joy vibrated through every part of me as I realized that not only were we reunited, we were now a team. We had been given a mission, an important one.

Just as I was wondering what was next for us, Sottrol appeared standing by the bed next to me. Manyfeathers was behind him but turned and disappeared into the central room.

"Don't wake Angel," my mentor whispered. "She needs all the rest she can get. You and I can talk."

I shifted my position slightly so I could easily see and converse with my mentor.

"You hold on tight to that precious one," the elder smiled. "She is the key to the success of the mission."

At that moment, I felt a rush of love for Angel that manifested in waves of rose-colored light that filled the room and even turned the kaleidoscopic ceiling to shades of pink.

"That's it, Darci," Sottrol nodded. "Let the love flow. The more the better. Remember, you two will be on opposite sides of the boundary between Earth and the Spirit Guide plane. You will have to learn how to communicate with her through that barrier."

Sottrol sat on the edge of the bed as near to me as he could so that we could talk quietly.

"There will be times," the elder continued, "times you may not want me popping in like this. Remember to simply ask for privacy, and it will be given to you."

"Like in the Spirit Guide Creed."

"Yes. We teachers and Master Guides must respect that privacy clause, too. Your request will expire when one or both of you fall asleep. Also, keep in mind that our dear Angel is fresh from Earth and still has some acclimating to do. You can help her."

"How?"

"Love her as you have been doing and heal her with your energy. Your vibration has increased significantly since your arrival here. Be aware that a Soul who has just departed from Earth and is bound by karmic law to return does not usually enter this university complex. Angel is an exception."

"Because of me?"

"Because of your mission together. We had to select a couple with extremely strong ties where one is destined to be a Spirit Guide and the other to be human. You two matched our criteria. From what I saw when you were first reunited, you surpass that criteria."

"Will the difference in our basic energy cause problems?"

"I'm here to give you some tips, so it will not. We have not yet taught you to vanish or pass through walls, floors, or ceilings because we knew you would most likely be in training with Angel for this mission. You cannot be appearing and disappearing when you are around her. Your focus must be entirely on her and on your training. All must be calm, supportive, and friendly for her here so that she can prepare without distractions. Keep your floating around to a minimum. Stay on her level while you train with her."

"I can do that. This won't affect me or my energy adversely, will it?"

"No, Darci, you will not lose any of the experience or any of the skills you have gained through your training to become a Spirit Guide. In fact, your work with Angel can only help."

"Can I talk to her about my training?"

"Yes, as long as you don't begin training her. Her work is on Earth, and her path leads her there. She may elect to become a Spirit Guide one day when she has earned the opportunity as you did."

"This is all highly unusual, isn't it?" I asked, staring at the sleeping female in my arms.

"It is. You may find Angel needs more rest than you do. That is why this suite includes single rooms for rest and meditation."

"At this point, Sottrol, I cannot bear to let her out of my arms or my sight."

"Understandably so," the wise one nodded. "Just remember to take your cues from her. Your powers of observation are strong due to your training, so use them to evaluate her level of comfort and understanding. We want Angel to whole-heartedly accept this mission and undertake it with enthusiasm. I shall go now. The little one in your arms will wake soon, and you may wish to express yourselves in ways that call for complete privacy. Remember to ask."

Just as Sottrol joined Manyfeathers in the center room so that they could exit our suite together, Angel stirred in my arms. When my mate opened her eyes, she saw a very peaceful atmosphere—and she saw me. She stretched, smiled, and threw her arms around my neck.

"So this is heaven," she murmured.

"It is the Spirit World," I replied softly. "Let's treasure this time we have together, for I know it will be all too brief."

"I have to go back, don't I?"

"To Earth? Yes."

"You made me a promise. You and Manyfeathers said I would never be hungry again."

"There is no hunger here."

"There is on Earth, and when I go back . . ."

"Sh-h-h." I rocked her gently. "I'll do all I can to keep you from hunger once you return to the Earth plane. Let's enjoy each other now. Sottrol was here, you know."

"When? While I was sleeping?"

"Yes. He said it's highly unusual to have an Earthbound Soul in the Spirit Guide area; however, our mission is important enough for exceptions to be made."

"I'm glad to be with you, Darci, no matter how it happened."

"The facts are that if it weren't for our strong bonds and this mission, we would probably not be together for a long, long time."

"We're together now. That's what counts."

Love and passion intertwined and rose from a place deep within me. I embraced her, holding her tightly. She sighed, kissed my neck, then in a quick and unexpected move, which reminded me of Nunzah, rolled on top of me. She laughed. It was the first time I had heard her laugh since our reunion, so I rolled on top of her. We both laughed and continued to tumble across the big round bed.

"I want to show you how much I love you," I said as I held her under me, our eyes only inches apart.

Then I sat up and said, "First I must do something that Sottrol suggested when he was here."

Angel sat up, too, and eyed me quizzically.

"Beings on this plane can appear out of nowhere. Sottrol and Manyfeathers did. I don't know how to do this myself, but I do know we can keep away sudden ill-timed manifestations of these Guides."

"Put a sign outside the door?"

"No," I replied, laughing, "Sottrol said we need only ask for privacy, and we'll get it—so I respectfully ask for privacy here and now."

"I hope it works, Darci."

"It will. Sottrol has never steered me wrong—or us. He was our friend in Manchuria."

I stroked Angel's hair as I told her about that incarnation, making certain she knew that Sottrol helped us as Raffa in that lifetime. As I recounted the birth of our daughters, Angel's eyes widened.

"Twins? Our first birth was twins? How did I do?"

"You were magnificent. You birthed sixteen children in all. Our offspring now populate much of that part of the world."

She pulled the hood of my robe over my head.

"Oh, Darci, how could you? Sixteen children?"

"That's what was needed at the time," I responded, pulling her on top of me. "Our mission is much different now."

"Darci . . . can we become intimate like Nua and Shu even though we don't have physical bodies?"

"I think so. Sottrol told me that I have been maintaining a certain spirit form so that I can relate to you easily, and we can train together. Would you like to try?"

"Oh yes!"

"Spirit bodies are made up of energy—so surely we can find ways to combine . . . "

I never finished that sentence. Angel was kissing me so expressively that I was vibrating wildly all over. What followed was passionate and profound. Our love for each other showed us the way, just as it had so many times on Earth. We learned how to relax and let the energy of the other come deep inside. The vibration of my energy field was higher and more advanced due to my training, so I was careful at first not to overdo. Yet Angel responded to me so beautifully, so positively, that I dared to increase the vibrations I was pouring inside her spirit body.

When dealing with pure energy and not physicality, it is difficult to describe precisely what took place. We experimented and found areas of our spirit bodies where we could more easily take in the vibration of the other. Altogether we located seven such points of entry and sharing. Each one provided a different sensation.

After a while, we did not need to speak aloud about what was occurring. I could read her feelings and her thoughts; from how she was acting and reacting, I believed she could read mine. We rested, then began again until we had found a way to bring each other to ecstasy at each of the seven entries. I was fascinated by the colors. I could see my energy penetrating and filling her. Then she would reciprocate, and I watched her love fill me. It was entirely wondrous, and I did not want to stop.

Angel did tire and needed rest, so I held her as she slept. I was tingling from the experience. Our spirit bodies glowed with love, and the kaleidoscope above us slowly waltzed with gold and pink light. I was amazed at what Angel and I had discovered. I replayed the love-making over and over in my head, thinking of new approaches to try and new subtleties to add.

When Angel finally woke, I looked into her eyes and said aloud, "I respectfully request more privacy."

She laughed and kissed me. We began again. I realized I had more control of my energy and more power because of my higher vibratory base, so I carefully increased the intensity of the vibration I was pouring into her spirit body. She loved it, but was sometimes so lost in bliss that she was drifting out of consciousness and not responding.

I remembered Sottrol cautioning me not to overdo it. One thing I could not help doing. When Angel was filled with my higher vibration, floating with rapture, I took her in my arms and danced her around the room high above the padded floor. Mini lightning bolts flashed between the walls of the room and the two of us. When I laid her back down on the bed, she was breathing quite heavily.

Once she calmed and caught her breath, she exclaimed, "I didn't know you could fly like that!"

"I didn't scare you, did I?"

"You surprised me—that's for sure. Your training is showing, Darci."

She took a long deep breath and noted, "Everything is so new—so different here."

"Please know that most of what we did and shared was new for me, too."

Love and compassion for this dear Soul poured out of me in a great flood of emotions. Angel could feel it. She relaxed, exhaled, and smiled.

"I wish I could keep up with you, but I'm feeling tired again. Stay close while I sleep, please."

"Always."

∞　∞　∞

Once again I had visitors while Angel slept. This time Chalherine appeared in the doorway of the room. Her radiance brightened the double-arched entrance. I caught a glimpse of Wachena behind her though the tutor did not enter our room.

"My, the atmosphere is sweet in here," the Chancellor began as she stepped into the room. "There is some concentrated, rarefied love energy in this chamber!"

"Hello, Chalherine. Thank you for helping reunite Angel and me. It's marvelous!"

"You're not exhausting her too much, are you, Darci?"

"I don't mean to."

Chalherine glided to a seat on the wall near me. She looked at Angel sleeping soundly with her head in my lap.

"She deserves such peace and happiness," the Chancellor began, "though I come to tell you that the training must begin soon. Events on Earth are picking up speed, and we need to position both of you before the turn of the millennium."

"The year 2000 on Earth? I never thought I'd see it."

"You will, but from the spirit side. It is Angel who will be on Earth celebrating with the rest of humanity."

"Who is going to train us?"

"Sottrol, two other Guides, and me. The circumstances are extraordinary. We've never prepared anyone for such a mission before."

"Can you tell me more about it?"

"Earth has fallen behind in her evolution. Most of the other planes of experience on the lower spiral have progressed much further. Highly evolved teachers who have walked the

302

Earth during the last two millennia have made a difference. For example, there is much more charity and compassion now than there was before Christ. Still, this is not enough. The Earth realm is whirling toward major change, and as Spirit Guides to that plane, we are called to inspire humans to make this a positive transformation."

"What is this gift from the Creator, the ray that Arcillis spoke of?"

"The ray of energy is our ally. It gives spiritual depth to the quickening on Earth."

"I don't understand, Chalherine."

"Events on Earth are speeding up. Technology is taking over and focus on material gain is increasing. This new ray of energy stirs a longing within each human for something more, something spiritual. That's where you and Angel and many others come in. You show humanity how much more there is. The ray provides an opening in the veil between worlds. You and Angel will instruct humans on how to take advantage of this gift."

"Angel should hear this."

"She will. You'll cover all this in detail during the training, which as I mentioned before, must begin soon."

"Do we train here?"

"Yes, mostly in the center room."

"The room with the musical floor."

"Yes. Sottrol will start your lessons since he knows you both so well. When he next arrives, you will know it is time to begin. Rest now. You will need it. Oh, and Darci? Try not to completely exhaust your lovely partner."

With a smile and a nod she was gone.

Angel was still sleeping soundly. I gently pulled her on top of me and cradled her. The new information from Chalherine rolled around in my mind. Eventually I slept also.

Bright flashing lights woke the two of us. The kaleidoscopic ceiling was putting on a spectacular show with vivid colors and quickly changing shapes. We lay there watching it when it occurred to me that this light show was meant to rouse us.

"Are you rested?" I asked my mate. "I think our training is about to begin."

Angel didn't have a chance to respond because Sottrol appeared in the doorway with a large book in his arms.

"Greetings, you two. Are you ready to begin?"

He bowed and swept his arm towards the central room. I helped Angel up, and we accepted the elder's invitation to join him in the training area. Manyfeathers sat along the wall.

On the lighted crystal floor in the center of the circular room were three oval chairs set in a triangle. The floor made tones as we walked across it, and we heard a chord play when we sat on the chair. This amused Angel, so she stood up and sat again just to hear the sound once more.

"Your child-like curiosity will serve you well once you return to Earth," Sottrol told her. "It will help lead you to Darci."

Angel and I immediately looked at each other. The thought of being separated again was unpleasant. I saw a hint of sadness cross her face.

Sottrol continued, "I'm here to get your training started. Let me begin by saying that we have designed this program especially for you and your exceptional circumstances. We'll begin simply with some exercises in telepathy. Darci, clear your mind. Angel, think something to Darci. Don't say it. Think it."

I took a breath and put a blank screen up in my mind. It immediately was filled with the image of Angel and I making love.

I heard her voice in my mind saying, "Darci, I love you so much. Can we try this again?"

I answered her aloud, "Yes, I love you, too—very much!"

"Angel, now you clear your mind, and Darci, send her a thought."

I knew this was all new to Angel, so I chose something we had done often in all the lives we had shared. I visualized taking her face in my hands and kissing her.

"I feel you kissing me," she said almost immediately.

"Good, good," Sottrol noted and then nodded.

"Now, Darci, tell Angel what Chalherine said during her visit."

"Chalherine was here?" Angel asked.

"Yes," I responded aloud. Then I sat quietly for a moment thinking over what Chalherine had told me.

"I'm not getting anything." Angel said, shifting in her seat.

"That's because I haven't sent it yet!" I replied and poked her playfully.

Composing myself, I sent the following thought, "The new ray of energy is making an opening in the veil between worlds."

Angel closed her eyes and screwed up her face a little as she concentrated.

"Just blank your mind and see what comes," offered Sottrol.

"I see a ray of sunshine coming through a bank of clouds, she finally said. "Is that close?"

"Not bad," our teacher replied. "I can see you're better with images than with words. It's a good start. Angel, you must be able to understand words and sentences sent to you telepathically, so let's try single words."

We worked back and forth with Angel sending me words, and then me sending a word at a time to her. She would often get an image or a picture rather than the word itself. Sottrol suggested we try something else.

"Put your heads close together and imagine a great, wide, connecting cord between your minds. See it as bright gold, very luminous and strong."

We did as the elder instructed. We stood, put our hands on each other's shoulders, and touched our heads together. There was some sparking when we visualized the connection.

"Now keep that cord of light between you and step apart. In fact, Darci, go to that side of the circle and Angel, this side."

Once we had separated, Sottrol asked me to send Angel a word. I chose "intellect" because it did not have an image associated with it.

"Intelligence," said Angel.

"Very close. Very good," said Sottrol, who could, of course, read both our minds.

We continued working very hard until Angel could easily receive single words from me telepathically. When Sottrol said that was enough for now, Angel looked weary but pleased.

"It took a while, but I got it," she smiled.

"Yes, you did well, little one," Sottrol said as he hugged her. "Now I want you to practice. Your next lesson will begin once you have rested."

The elder and the American Indian Guide vanished into twinkling mist, leaving Angel with an astonished look.

"You can't do that, can you, Darci?"

"No, not yet. I'd like to point out that we're alone again."

"I get the feeling we're never entirely alone here in the Spirit Guide World."

"That's why I ask for privacy—now."

Angel got a very playful look in her eye and giggled a little when I spoke those words. She ran her hand down my spine, so I lifted her in my arms and floated into the room with the great round bed.

"We're going to practice, right? Just like Sottrol said," she said playfully with laughter in her violet eyes.

"We'll practice," I replied as I placed her on the bed, "more than just words." I got on hands and knees and perched over her so our faces were very close and added, "After all, the more ways we connect, the more successful our training."

She lovingly pulled me down and began kissing me. It wasn't long before we surrendered to the love and passion that flowed between us. Once again, we found new exhilarating ways to share our energy.

At one point after we had been pouring love into each other through the solar plexus, I telepathically asked her if she would like to see the kaleidoscope up close. I was pleased to hear her send "yes" back into my mind, so I lifted her, and we floated gently up, up, up. The great lighted panels on the ceiling responded by flashing so quickly they shimmered. Angel was thrilled.

"I'll learn to fly like this someday," she said aloud, obviously enjoying herself.

"I know you will. Let's try one more thing."

Staying near the ceiling, I circled the room, then descended and placed her on the bed with her head at the center and her feet on the edge. Next I lay in line with her, my head also in the center and feet on the edge. The tops of our heads were aligned and touching. I began to pump love energy out of the crown of my head into hers. I couldn't see what was happening to her, but I did notice that the room and the kaleidoscope above us turned rosy pink. I began to feel her love enter me through the top of my head and was ecstatic. Waves of love flowed from my head to my feet, back up through my head to her head, then to her feet. Sheets of pink light like colored rain passed over us, and we both began floating.

Although I could have gone on and on, I knew Angel tired much sooner than I, so I rose and glided around, taking her in my arms.

"Time to rest, dear one."

"I've never felt anything like this, Darci. Can we do this sort of thing once I'm on Earth?"

"I don't know, but I bet we'll find a way."

We rested. Angel slept, and I lay thinking of new ways to please her. I felt such musings were more than just my desire for new pleasures with my mate. The stronger our bonds, the easier it would be for us to reconnect through the barriers around the Earth plane. I finally slept, too.

∞ ∞ ∞

This time tones and chords from the floor of the adjoining room awakened us. I rose to see Chalherine in the doorway with an unfamiliar Guide. This Being was male and so tall that his shaved head nearly struck the top of the arches. He wore a sleeveless cream-colored robe, which showed his strong arms. He also wore a belt of large crystals and was carrying a tool of some kind.

"I hope you are rested," Chalherine began," because your new teacher is here. Darci, Angel, meet Gotharn Ginall."

My partner and I scrambled off the bed and bowed as a greeting to this large new teacher. Gotharn nodded his head and motioned us to join him in the training area. Chalherine waited until we were seated on the musical floor with the new Guide towering over us before she took her leave.

In a deep voice, Gotharn began our lesson with these words, "Within each of you must live a kernel, a seed. This seed contains the drive needed to propel you forward on your mission. This seed also provides strength, for you both will need to be strong and focused for this mission to be successful."

Angel and I looked at each other. I heard her ask me telepathically, "What is he talking about—a seed?"

I shrugged and looked back at Gotharn, certain we would soon know.

"Strength, drive, and focus—these are the attributes I come to give you. My method is simple. We Guides will infuse a pair of crystals with these traits, and I will implant one in each of you. We will do this as a ceremony. You will receive the stones simultaneously for an optimal shared experience. Do you understand?"

I nodded "yes"; Angel shook her head "no."

"Let me show you," said the giant Guide.

He moved the crystal belt around his waist so that the purple pouch that had been behind him was now in front. Opening it, he removed a lavender cloth. Bending over so we could see, he opened the cloth on the palm of his hand, and there were two perfectly matched crystals. Each was the size and shape of a bean seed.

Angel and I looked at these spirit stones, then at each other, then back at the crystals.

"Hold them," said Gotharn. "Your left hands, please."

We each extended our left hand, and the giant Guide placed the crystals at the same time. I brought the small stone up to eye level and examined it.

It was alive! It had tiny rings of incandescent light that spun inside it along with what seemed like hundreds of minuscule glittering stars. I turned the stone in my fingers and eyed it from every angle. It radiated a very distinctive white light that had just a hint of the entire color spectrum. Angel was also taken with the crystal in her hand.

"It's so beautiful," she exclaimed with much awe in her voice.

"These spirit crystals were especially designed for you and your mission. We have used crystals this way before; however, this is our first twin implanting."

"Will it hurt?" asked Angel. Her innocence moved me.

"There is no pain here in the Spirit World, little one. Nor will you feel this once you are back on Earth. It will affect you though. It will do what I described. Each crystal is programmed to stimulate your strength, your drive, and your focus for this mission. This will happen automatically. For you, Angel, the effects will strengthen as you gain years on the Earth plane. Once you become conscious of your spirit path and of Darci, the crystal will become fully activated. Any further questions?"

I spoke up, "Will the crystals help us communicate?"

"They may—though that is not their primary function. The fact that the stones are a matched pair and will be implanted in you two at exactly the same moment may help you connect."

"What's this about a ceremony?" queried Angel.

"Your Guides and teachers will gather to honor you and the sacred moment of implantation."

Gotharn looked back and forth between Angel and me. He put out his hand that still held the lavender cloth, so we could return our crystals to him. As we did so, he said, "You will need to practice breathing together. The implantation will be synchronized with your breathing."

"We've done some breathing together," I told Gotharn as I shot a sideways glance at Angel, who dropped her head, smiling shyly.

"Good. I want you to practice this . . ." the Guide took a deep breath in, then let it out in short puffs. "One deep breath in, seven short breaths out. Let me see you do it together."

Although Angel and I did this nearly perfectly the first time, Gotharn asked us to repeat it over and over. He watched us carefully as we followed his instructions.

"Practice this and one more exercise."

He placed his large foot on the center panel of the lighted floor, set off a tone, and said, "Breathe in. Then sing this tone as you breathe out. Try it."

We took deep breaths, and as we exhaled, Gotharn stepped again on the crystal panel so that we would sing the tone at exactly the right pitch.

"Again," he instructed. We did this over a dozen times.

"Come back to us, little one." Gotharn placed his hand on Angel's head. "She is drifting into bliss," he explained, looking at me. "You are much more accustomed to the high energy levels here. That is why you must help her stay focused. You both must be in exactly the right state to receive the crystals."

"How can I help?"

Gotharn looked into Angel's eyes, nodded, and then continued, "You are back with us. Good. Darci, as you two practice, monitor her closely. If she begins drifting, pull her back."

"How?"

"Extend your energy field vertically. Then place your hands—both of them—on her head. She will come right back."

We went over both exercises again, and when we began singing the tone, I saw Angel's eyes close and her head tilt back.

Gotharn nodded to me. I did as the Guide had suggested, and Angel opened her eyes and stared right into mine.

"Oh, Darci—did I drift off again? I'm sorry. I guess I'm a bit overwhelmed."

"That's enough for today," our teacher informed us. "Practice what you have learned here. The ceremony will be soon. And, Darci—please let this one get some rest. She will need it."

Gotharn bowed, turned, and took long strides as he crossed the musical floor. Chalherine appeared next to him, and the two exited.

I took my partner's hand and asked, "Do you want to rest?"

"I guess so," she said. "I'd like something else more."

Angel then telepathically sent me an image of the two of us making love. I was surprised because the picture was of something we had not yet tried. I automatically imagined the exchange and felt a warm rush pass through me. I smiled at her.

"I ask for privacy here and now," I stated.

Angel asked, "In the training room?"

I nodded and replied, "Right here on the musical floor."

We began seated where we were. This time at Angel's suggestion we sent our love energy in a vertical circle, which connected us through the heart and the solar plexus. Once we got the current going, we stood facing each other and curled the flow one way through us, then the other.

Angel became momentarily unsteady when we changed the direction. Then we daringly made two streams of love energy, each circling through the same points but in different directions. This was highly stimulating. We embraced. Our spirit bodies shuddered as we came together with the two circles of rotating love energy whirling faster.

I began to sway gently, and we danced, moving slowly around the crystal floor, setting off tone after tone. Angel's laugh was full of joy as we twirled faster. After several rotations, I swept her up and glided into the bedroom where we continued to make love.

I expanded the rotating circles to include our heads and groins. That's when the entire room began glowing with rose-colored light, and I found myself trembling with ecstasy. Angel, too, was quivering, and I heard her sigh my name.

We rested. Angel slept while I went over our lessons in my mind. Then my thoughts drifted to our most recent magical exchange of love and I shook my head.

"When we were coupled on Earth, our mating was always passionate," I thought to myself, "but this—this is extraordinary!"

"And we've just begun," Angel's voice answered in my mind. She had heard my thought and had responded telepathically.

"We are making progress," I thought back to her.

She giggled a little and said aloud, "In more ways than one."

We held each other for a while, then both felt restless and knew it was time to practice what Gotharn had taught us. We began by sitting across from each other on the round bed doing the first breathing exercise. At that point, Angel thought it best to return to the central training room to go over the second exercise.

"I don't want to guess at the tone," she said to me. "I want to get it exactly right."

We stood holding hands, positioned on either side of the center crystal panel. It was just large enough for us both to step onto it when it was time to exhale and sing the tone. We rehearsed this for a while until I could see Angel's fatigue.

"This ceremony will not happen as we wish it to if you are not rested," I told her as I led her back to the bedroom. "I will stay right here and hold you, but I insist that you rest."

She did not resist. As soon as she was deep in sleep, the archway to the bedroom lit up, and Chalherine and Sottrol materialized. They glided over to me and took two of the seats along the wall.

"Her aura is lovely," observed Chalherine. "You have been sharing much of your energy with her."

"Yes, we have been sharing with each other," I replied.

"Which is how it should be!" Sottrol jumped in.

"How did you get on with Gotharn and his lessons?"

"Very well, I think. I do have some questions about the implantation he spoke of."

"That's why we visit," Chalherine responded. "This is an unusual ceremony, one that is rarely performed. In fact, I've witnessed it only twice."

"And I've seen it once," said Sottrol. "It was with the woman who became known as Joan of Arc."

My heart leapt, and I pleaded, "She came to a tragic end on Earth. Please tell me Angel is safe from such a fate."

Both Guides nodded yes.

"Your path is far different. Times have changed on Earth. A new approach is called for," Chalherine assured me.

"Tell me about the implantation ceremony," I requested again, still a bit apprehensive.

Sottrol moved quietly to my side and sat on the bed next to me. Then he said softly, "I will stand with you and help you. Chalherine will stand with Angel. Simply follow the instructions, and you will be fine. We're going to do this soon, are we not?" The elder looked at Chalherine for confirmation.

She nodded and then spoke, "Once Angel has rested, we will gather in the adjoining room. We'll leave you for now."

The two vanished in a glittering mist which hung next to me for an instant before it disappeared.

∞ ∞ ∞

Lying there holding Angel, I felt peaceful, and wished we could stay wrapped in each other's arms just like this, but I knew that couldn't be. I also knew we would become restless and would want to actively help in some way. We were sure to get our chance.

I finally slept too; I'm not sure for how long. I awoke with Sottrol standing by me smiling and holding a cream-colored robe with gold trim.

"For you," he said, handing it to me.

At that moment, Chalherine appeared in the arched doorway and glided to Angel's side. She was holding a similar robe.

"Wake her, Darci," prompted the Chancellor. "Time for you both to change into these garments. We'll wait in the next room."

She laid the robe by Angel, and the two powerful Guides moved to the center room.

Anticipation manifested in my energy field. Prickles of magenta light raced up my torso and neck. I held Angel's head and woke her with kisses.

Once her sleepy eyes opened, I looked directly into them and said, "It's time."

"Time?" She questioned groggily.

"The ceremony is next. We're going to receive our crystals. Look, we have these fine new robes to wear."

She looked at the robe, then at me.

"Can't we ask for privacy and spend the time with each other instead?"

I laughed. "I'd like that. However . . ."

"I know; I know. I'm a little scared though, Darci. Those stones are beautiful, but I'm not sure I want one implanted in me."

"You know it won't hurt—and it can only bring us closer."

Her face brightened considerably when I said that.

She whispered, "And afterwards we can ask for privacy."

"Yes," I laughed again. "Who knows what these crystals may add to our exchanges."

Angel and I dressed in the matching robes and entered the circular training room, consciously trying to move as a unit. The room was filled with Guides. They all hovered about a foot off the floor. When we entered, they all lowered themselves onto the musical floor at slightly different times, which produced a sweeping series of tones. It was very dramatic.

Sottrol and Chalherine were in the center with Gotharn. I recognized Syd Manyfeathers, Hespahba, and Wachena in the group though most of the other faces were unfamiliar. Angel and I made our own tones as we walked across the floor to the center. I stood by Sottrol, and Angel by Chalherine.

Gotharn looked around at the group, looked at us, and then began, "Creator, bless this ceremony. We perform this sacred rite to join Darcimon and Angel and unite their Souls in purpose and direction to strengthen their bonds."

At that moment, Chilliwon Mac jumped out from the group of Guides and landed on a crystal panel next to us, producing a tone. To my surprise, the Beings sang this tone. Then the Elf Guide jumped to another, and the assembly sang that tone as well. This went on and on. After a while, it started to sound like a song or hymn.

Chalherine indicated that we should sing, too, so we did. The light streaming through the dome brightened to a rich gold. By the time we concluded, I was feeling very good.

Next, Gotharn said a blessing over the crystals that were lying on a silver plate he was holding. As he passed his left hand over the stones, sparks flew around the plate. I saw both awe and apprehension in Angel's eyes, so I stroked the back of her hand with my thumb. Chalherine moved close behind Angel and Sottrol behind me.

"Begin now with the first breath I taught you," instructed Gotharn.

As we did so, the giant Guide passed his left hand up and down in front of our spirit bodies. All our practicing had paid off; our breaths were precisely synchronized. I felt Sottrol move in very close behind me and saw Chalherine do the same to Angel.

Then Sottrol positioned his arms securely around my chest and whispered, "Lean on me. Relax."

I saw Angel rest back on Chalherine, who held her tightly.

Angel and I continued the breathing technique we had learned, taking one long breath in and exhaling in seven short puffs. We were only a couple of feet apart at a slight angle so we could see each other, hear each other, and keep our breathing synchronized.

Gotharn then set his large foot on the center panel, and the assembly sang the familiar tone. As voices united, he blew on both stones, and they glowed brighter. He repeated this six more times until the spirit crystals were so brilliant it was difficult to look directly at them. The giant Guide held up the silver plate. The glowing stones sent beams of light around the room.

"As these blessed stones are energized, so shall you be. May these crystals strengthen your resolve and guide you through a successful mission."

He released the silver plate, and it floated above us.

"Now do the second of the breathing exercises," Gotharn said to us quietly.

He watched us carefully and stepped on the panel just when we needed to exhale and sing. The group of Guides joined us in breathing and singing. The suspended silver plate that held the crystals slowly lowered until it hovered between Angel and me. I kept my eyes on her, for I knew she might slip into a semi-conscious state. Gotharn, too, was observing us both closely.

Chanting the tone was very powerful with all the voices joined. An astonishing white light filled the room as Gotharn conducted the breathing and singing. He slowed down the in-breath and the chanting until I thought I might drift into bliss. I looked at Angel. Chalherine had a tight hold on her and was coaching in a whisper.

Sottrol said softly in my ear, "Angel is all right. Stay with us, Darci. Focus on the crystals on that plate."

After a few minutes of group breathing and singing, Gotharn had us all take one deep breath and hold it. He then stepped with both feet onto the panel. As we exhaled singing the tone, he lifted both crystals from the plate, one with his left hand and one with his right. In one swift movement while we were still exhaling, he pushed his left hand into my solar plexus and moved it up towards my heart. Everything stopped for a moment. I seemed suspended in time, space, and dimension. The circular room rotated around me.

I heard Sottrol's voice; it seemed so far away.

"Breathe in, Darci. Breathe in slowly, gently. You can do it. That's it."

I inhaled, blinked, and looked at Angel, whose eyelids were flickering as she looked at me. A beam of white light was radiating from her chest just below her heart. Suddenly I realized there was one coming from me too. I could feel the implanted stone in the center of my spirit body. Sottrol stood me upright as Chalherine did the same for Angel. Gotharn placed his large hands on our heads, his left hand on me and right hand on Angel.

"May these two be blessed. May they walk in light. May they unite in purpose and direction, and may they bring much love and awareness to those they serve. Go in love, Darcimon and Angel. You are blessed."

A great cheer rose up from the group, and Chilliwon Mac jumped right in front of Gotharn. The little Guide looked even smaller next to Gotharn's huge form.

"Good job, my giant friend," he congratulated the Guide. "Such precision, such perfection in timing! I've never seen the like."

Angel and I were still stunned, unused to the change in our spirit bodies. We stood quietly while the Guides who had attended the ceremony came up to us one by one to wish us well. Sottrol and Chalherine stayed very close to make sure we were all right. Finally, the last of the Guides either exited through the archway or vanished, leaving Gotharn with Sottrol, Chalherine, Angel, and me.

"You both did well," Gotharn told us in his deep voice. "This was a very successful implantation. The crystals are fired up and quite alive. They will mellow as they settle into their new homes. For now, take care of each other, and report any discomfort or problems to Sottrol or Chalherine. It has been a pleasure serving you."

He bowed and departed with long giant strides.

Sottrol hugged me, and Chalherine did the same to Angel. Then Chalherine embraced me, and Sottrol enfolded Angel. They stepped back.

Angel and I stood facing each other, our sense of destiny heightened by this experience. As we reached for each other, sparks flew between our hands.

The two teachers took another step back.

I was not afraid; in fact, I was exhilarated, so I stepped forward, placing my hands on Angel's waist. She followed my lead and laid her arms on mine. Electricity ran up and down our arms and zapped into the room behind us. When I looked into the eyes of my mate, I saw love and excitement, so I bravely pulled her to me, and we embraced. The moment our spirit bodies touched, there was a huge crackling sound. A great stream of energy flowed from the floor up and out the dome ceiling with the two of us in the center of it. We were standing in an enormous bolt of lightning! Our bodies quivered. We breathed together, feeling the electricity pulse through us. Even though we were vibrating wildly, we held on. I knew we had to discharge the energy, so I clasped her close to me and kept my breathing synchronized with hers. Slowly the intense energy abated until at last we stood in a sphere of glowing golden light. Chalherine and Sottrol joined us in the sphere of energy. Stage two of our training was complete.

∞ ∞ ∞

Our teachers stayed for a while—probably to make sure that we were stabilized, and there were no immediate problems. I told Sottrol that Angel and I had been successfully conversing telepathically.

"Good," said the elder. "Continue to practice. Chalherine will return after your break to begin a new set of lessons. Please use some of the time to rest."

He winked at us as he motioned for Chalherine to exit with him. The two Guides used the doors this time.

Angel wore a serious expression and uttered, "Darci, I feel different. Do you?"

"Yes, I feel the stone. It seems like it's shifting—turning a little."

"Mine, too."

"Gotharn said the crystals would calm down once they have settled in. Let's take our minds off them while they adjust to their new placement."

"I don't know if I can. It feels funny in there. I hope the crystal finds a position it likes and stops moving!"

"Your mate has an idea," I told her as I guided her towards the bedroom. "Do you want to hear it?"

I heard Angel's voice in my mind saying, "Show me," so I sent her back an image. She gasped and then giggled a little.

Even though I had been told to stay on Angel's level while we were training, I couldn't help occasionally floating or hovering. This had become second nature to me now. Angel didn't seem to mind. In fact, she had really enjoyed it when I carried her up close to the kaleidoscopic ceiling. We had not yet used my hovering techniques in our love exchanges. This was what I suggested to her.

"Please be patient with me, Darci. This is all so new to me."

"You're thriving," I replied as I scooped her up and carried her to the bed, "and you know it."

We tumbled and laughed and kissed.

"Let's lose these robes," I said to her. "My idea will work better without them."

As I slipped out of my ceremonial garb, I spoke the words that now brought a flutter to my heart, "I ask for privacy."

The fidgeting implanted crystals were forgotten as we focused on new ways of sharing our love. After several electric exchanges, I saw that Angel was losing focus either from over stimulation or fatigue. It was time to rest. We had been through a lot that day and needed repose.

I lowered us back down to the bed where we slept still wrapped around each other. The entire room glowed with gold and pink light as we rested.

∞　∞　∞

I awoke with a sense that someone else was there. Chalherine was sitting on one of the higher perches on the wall. I used my elbows to push myself up as Angel continued to sleep with her head on my heart.

"Let her sleep, Darci. We have some matters to discuss. The situation on Earth is deteriorating. There is a world war taking place. Humans have chosen to develop heinous weaponry. Your mission takes on an even greater significance with the unfolding of these events."

"Chalherine, we must not send Angel into the middle of a war! We will not have a chance to fulfill our mission."

"You are right. We will wait until the battles are over although we are not sure how much of Earth will remain."

I lay looking down at my beautiful partner. Part of me did not want to let her go back to the Earth plane, which I knew to be a tricky and dangerous place.

"Much must be done to prepare her," said Chalherine, "and to prepare both of you. It will not be easy. You were on Earth not long ago. You know how toil and trouble can overwhelm a Soul; you saw this happen to Angel. You know your partner still must face Earth lessons. She will be doing double duty once she returns there."

"What do you mean?" There was a flicker of doubt in my mind. Perhaps our mission would not succeed.

"Angel has her own karma to deal with, plus she will be driven to complete this mission."

"Can one work with the other?"

"To some extent. Her choices may be difficult at times. Angel's Soul Contract for this upcoming Earth incarnation will be complex indeed."

At that moment, the subject of our conversation stirred. With her eyes closed, Angel stretched and then curled back in my arms.

"Hello, Angel, my dear. How are you doing?"

Chalherine floated gracefully down from her perch and sat on the edge of the bed. "Her color is good. Look at the rich rose radiance in her aura. Can you see it?"

"The entire room has turned to rose and pink," I replied, "and yes, I see the glow you speak of. It becomes her."

"She is well-loved, and you are responsible, Darci."

"I assure you, it is a shared experience."

"And well it should be. Angel—Angel, my dear," Chalherine spoke gently as she put her hand on Angel's knee, and the sleeper's eyes fluttered open.

She was looking straight at me. Her violet eyes always moved my heart.

"Is it time to ask for privacy?" Angel said sleepily.

Chalherine and I laughed, and Angel jumped a little.

"Oh, Chalherine, hello. I didn't see you there."

"You two have been rather caught up in each other," Chalherine replied with a kind smile. "That's very good. The closer you are connected, the better the chance this mission will succeed."

She continued, "Angel, I've been telling Darci that there is now a sense of urgency. We must move along with the training. Do you feel rested enough?"

"Not really—but let's move on anyway."

"Are you sure?" I asked, concerned.

"Let's at least begin. Angel, please tell me when you wish to break for rest," Chalherine reminded her, then stood, nodded toward the center room, and glided through the double-arched doorway.

We joined her directly. The floor produced gentle tones as we moved across it. This time there were three suspended oval seats in a small circle. Wachena sat quietly along the wall. Chalherine was also already seated, so we took the other chairs. I helped Angel up into hers.

"Listen carefully," the chancellor began. "Your mission may determine the fate of humanity for generations, indeed for thousands of years."

Angel shifted in her seat, looking concerned and replied, "I hope we can do this. I hope I can hold up my end of the mission."

She looked small in the floating chair. I automatically sent compassion to her. A ray of golden light shot out of my chest and penetrated hers. She smiled at me.

Of course, Chalherine saw this and continued, "We selected you two because we feel you have the best chance of succeeding. We have every confidence that you will do well. You will have much help from the spirit side.

"Furthermore, Angel," Chalherine continued, "it will be more challenging for you because you are the one who will walk the Earth. You will be distracted again and again by the illusions that exist on the material plane. You will feel very lost until you consciously connect with the spirit side."

"Explain what you mean by 'consciously connect,' Chalherine," I said.

Our radiant teacher looked at me, then at Angel and explained, "All humans are connected to their spirit paths and their Guides through their subconscious minds. That's why Spirit Guides often work through dreams and intuition. It is time for humans to begin to expand their conscious minds, and you, dear Angel, will lead the way."

"How?" Angel's eyes were wide.

"By consciously communicating with Darci, by using your logical, rational mind to connect with Spirit, and by teaching others how to do what you do."

"And this is truly possible?" Angel asked with a quiver in her voice.

"Oh yes. Like I said, you have much help. Let's begin by talking about the new ray."

"The gift from the Creator," I spoke up.

"Yes, and a miraculous gift it is. You see, up until now there has been a general lockdown or shut down—a barrier around the Earth. When Souls enter human bodies, they are seemingly cut off from their spiritual origins. This is, of course, an illusion. The Earth plane is every bit a part of the entire universe, but to humans, life on Earth is pretty much all there is. I have been told that the Creator designed it this way so that Souls would focus on the lessons right in front of them on the material plane. Through the ages, there has been much speculation on matters of the Spirit, and many religions and belief systems have been formed. Now, however, thanks to the gift of this new ray, which is piercing the barriers around the Earth plane, humans have the opportunity to know."

"To know?" I questioned, not sure I followed the teacher. "To know what?"

"To know what you two know right now—that Earth life, though important at the time it is being lived, is just one phase of learning for the Soul, that the Soul goes on to other experiences after death, and that the Soul sometimes returns to Earth."

"Karma!" I broke in excitedly. "Humans can begin to see the big picture of how karma works."

"Yes," Chalherine replied, smiling at my enthusiasm. "Also, death will be viewed differently. In short, the spirit perspective will be available to humans through their Guides. The time holds much potential, but humans must be alerted to this opportunity. That is your mission."

Angel let out a deep breath and sat back in her chair and murmured, "It's overwhelming."

"The enormity of it is a bit staggering," I told our shining teacher.

"You two will be fine. Work together. Show others that it can be done—and teach them how to do it. If you can get humans to consciously connect with their Spirit Guides, they will do the rest on their own."

"That simplifies it," Angel responded. "Still, it sounds like a lonely path for me to walk on Earth."

"I'll be with you," I said as my heart went out to her.

"And humans will be ready," said Chalherine, "ready to receive this information and ready to hear what you have to say. The new ray, you see, will not only provide an opening in the barrier around the Earth plane, it will also stir a longing deep inside each human. Humans will yearn to know why they are on Earth and what they are meant to do. They will seek far and wide to find such answers—and you will have them."

"I will?" Angel was incredulous.

"We will," I interjected. "Once we connect consciously, I can find any information you may need here on the spirit side and send it to you."

"Oh, I see," she responded, looking relieved.

"You are not alone in this venture, my dear," continued Chalherine. "In fact, all on the Spirit Guide plane will be ready to help you. When you connect with Darci, then the resources of the spirit world will be available to you. You will, in essence, be our ambassador on Earth. You will speak for us, teach for us, and most importantly you will make the needed connections between Earth and the Spirit Guide plane."

Chalherine warmed to her subject. She rose out of her chair and began to glide back and forth as she talked, "Think of it, Angel. You will be able to help many humans meet their Spirit Guides. You will teach them how to work with us, and as a result, their lives will be immensely improved. All this stems from your ability to connect with Darci through the barriers. This will be the first step once you are again incarnated on Earth."

"How will I know what to do?"

I reached towards her. I couldn't quite touch her physically, but a beam of bright peach-colored light radiated from my hand and caressed her shoulders.

"I will help. I'll be your Spirit Guide, remember?"

Chalherine moved to Angel's side and continued, "You two are a team. We'll do all we can to prepare you. My part of the training is to inform you of the details of the mission. Do you understand what I have told you?"

"Yes," I nodded.

"I think so," said Angel, "though I can't imagine how this will all play out."

"You are tired," Chalherine acknowledged with her radiance brightening as she reached towards Angel. "Time for rest and assimilation. Go over all I have told you. If you have any questions, I will be back. That's enough for now."

She floated up towards the domed ceiling, then lowered herself in front of me.

"Love her, but please don't exhaust her," she said softly.

Then joining Wachena, they vanished into twinkling mist.

I looked at Angel who seemed overwhelmed, took a deep breath, then stood up and stepped on the center panel, which was right in front of my suspended chair. Singing the tone as I exhaled, then breathing in again, I motioned for Angel to join me. We exhaled and sang together. She squirmed just as I felt the implanted crystal twist a little inside me.

"Let's go rest," I encouraged as I reached for her hand.

Angel was very restless in her sleep.

"Did our lovemaking soothe her and allow her to sleep more peacefully?" I wondered.

I had purposely not suggested a love exchange because I knew my mate was tired, but perhaps it would have been beneficial. I began sending circles of golden light through our hearts as we lay together.

She smiled with her eyes still closed and murmured, "I feel that."

Without saying a word, I changed the color of the light to bright pink and visualized it washing over her entire form.

"Oh Darci, that feels wonderful. Will you do that for me when I'm human?"

I pulled her to me and promised, "This and more."

The love light I was emanating seemed to calm as well as please her, so I sent wave after wave. It wasn't long before her eyes reopened.

She asked, "We don't know what will happen for sure, do we?"

"Once you are on Earth? No, humans have free will. As a human, you may choose to completely ignore me."

She punched me playfully in the chest and said, "I wouldn't do that, Darci!"

"You never know."

"Then let's strengthen our bonds even more so that when I am on Earth, I won't be able to help myself."

I was hoping Angel would suggest this because I had been thinking about ways to intensify our exchanges of love.

"I request privacy. Let's try this," I suggested, sending her the picture.

She immediately lined up her spirit body with mine so that we were lying facing each other.

"No. Wait." I suddenly flashed on a variation. "Lie on your back."

As she did so, I rose and floated over her, aligning our bodies as best I could. She was smaller than me, so I focused on our hearts. I hovered about a foot above her and sent beams of love energy to every sensitive point on her body. She opened like a tulip on a sunny day and basked in the love I was sending her. She glowed brighter, and her expression became blissful.

Then she telepathically sent me an image that made me laugh though I moved right away to try it. I lowered myself onto her, rolled her on top of me, and then floated up. I was her magic carpet, giving her a ride. She began sending love energy back to me through all the same sensitive points, and I marveled at the sensations.

My partner was becoming very good at these exchanges of love. I floated with her lying on top of me, allowing her to pour her love into me. The field of energy she generated was so much larger than she was. I could see the glow around us increase in size and intensity.

She shifted her position slightly, and just as I realized that she had aligned the two imbedded crystals, a charge of electricity flew through my spirit body. I felt her tremble, too. The crystal spun around inside me. The proximity of Angel's implanted stone must have triggered this whirling motion. I was overcome with passionate sensations, so I wrapped my arms tightly around her and spun us both. She burst into laughter.

With our hearts and crystals parallel, I guided her up to the kaleidoscopic ceiling. Once positioned under the center point of the kaleidoscope, a shaft of brilliant purple light flew from the ceiling through us to the floor. The patterns above us danced wildly in purple and lavender hues. The violet beam was exhilarating and made my mind extremely clear. We hovered in this ray with sparks flying from us.

When I leaned back a little to look into Angel's eyes, I saw a most unusual sight. Electric current was running between our chests linking the two crystals. Angel saw this, too, and watched with fascination as tiny violet bolts of lightning crackled and sparked betwixt us. I could feel the spirit stone vibrating within me.

Then I sent a circle of love energy connecting our heads and groins. As the deep rose light circled through us, we spun, and the crystals within us spun until this cosmic dance produced a rainbow of light around the circumference of the room. I was vibrating so intensely and was so lost in bliss that I didn't notice Angel becoming overwhelmed until I felt her go limp in my arms.

Immediately I lowered us onto the bed. Her body was emitting rings of pink and purple light, and there was a rainbow of colors streaming from the top of her head.

I stroked her cheek. She did not respond, but the expression on her face spoke of true ecstasy. Still, I was concerned. Our teachers had told me many times not to overdo the lovemaking. But it all flowed so naturally, and Angel was so willing.

Finally, she moved her head a little. Without opening her eyes, she said quietly, "I'm all right, Love."

I held her and let her rest in my arms. The room had taken on a lovely golden-pink glow as I had seen in many sunsets on Earth. The crystal inside me had settled down, so I joined my partner in sleep.

∞ ∞ ∞

Two things woke me: first, the fragrance of gardenias and then the purr of a cat. I opened my eyes to see the cat I had befriended earlier in my chamber walking around the rim of the bed. He noticed I was awake and came directly over to me so that I could pet him.

"Hello, old friend," I said stroking his head. "Wait 'til Angel sees you. You look just like a cat we had on Earth."

The aroma of gardenias became even stronger, and I looked up to see Sottrol in the arched doorway with a new Guide. I gasped a little, for I was so awed at the sight. She was nearly as tall as Gotharn and radiated brilliant white light as well as the smell of gardenias. Her robe was layered— almost as if she was wearing petals. A hood covered her head, so I could only see deep emerald eyes and a slight smile.

"Can you awaken Angel?" Sottrol asked as he escorted the new Guide nearer.

The two teachers looked on as I kissed Angel's forehead and her eyes. The cat brushed against her as though he was trying to help. Her eyes still closed, Angel's hand went out to pet the cat. I noticed Sottrol nodding to the new Guide.

"Angel, we have visitors," I gently prodded her.

"Besides the cat?" she asked, eyes blinking open. She raised herself on her elbows, still managing to pet the cat.

"Darci, Angel, meet Izandra, your teacher for the fourth phase of the training."

We nodded our greetings, and the new Guide did a very curious thing. She stood where she was, yet stretched her arms out to both of us. Her elongated arms were a strange sight, but I quickly forgot how odd this looked when she touched me. She lay one hand on my shoulder and the other on Angel's. I instantly felt clear-headed and awake. Izandra then emitted concentric circles of pure white light which, when they reached me, brought a very peaceful feeling.

"Shall we adjourn to the center room?" suggested Sottrol. "Join us when you are ready."

I was very surprised at what I saw when Angel and I entered the central training room. First, I was taken aback because the room was filled with Beings. They were seated around the outer rim, and all appeared as glowing golden forms.

In the center of the room stood two rectangular panels with rounded corners. Each was a little larger than I. They were plain and tipped back at a slight angle with a small platform at the base. Sottrol indicated that Angel was to stand before one of these panels and I should stand in front of the other.

"Who are all these Beings?" I asked Sottrol as I positioned myself.

"Most are Spirit Guides-in-Training like you," the elder informed me. "They are here to observe this phase of the training. After all, your mission will affect them and all the Guides who watch over humans."

"They are all gold . . ."

"Yes, Darci. They appear this way because they are not participating, only observing."

Sottrol then stepped back, and Izandra stood before us. As soon as she removed her hood, rays of white and light green shot from her head. I could see now that her skin was a deep bronze color. Her hair, which was wound into a large bun, was pure white. Her emerald eyes flashed with a jewel-like brilliance.

Once again, she elongated her arms—this time placing a hand on each of our heads. At that moment I realized that I had become a little nervous when I saw the room filled with onlookers, so her touch calmed me and cleared my mind.

This extraordinary Guide then spoke, "Blessed be these two who step forward to serve humanity and the universe."

Her voice had a ringing sound to it, and I wondered if she might be a Master Guide.

Moving close to Angel, she ran her hands around my mate's Spirit body.

Angel looked at me. I heard her ask me telepathically, "What is she doing?"

Izandra answered, "I am clearing your energy field."

I watched with fascination as the light around Angel went from a soft rosy gold to bright white. Izandra did the same to me. She was just a tad taller, so she easily reached all around me. As she did this, I felt myself vibrating faster. My perceptions were sharpened. I began noticing every detail of the room, which kept me occupied until our new teacher spoke again.

"I am here to teach you how to connect and work through barriers. Almost every plane of experience on the lower spiral has some kind of veil or barrier around it. These barriers serve a useful purpose. They allow the residents to focus on the lessons of that particular plane."

Our teacher continued, "There has always been some contact through the veil between worlds. Up to now, this has been sporadic and fleeting. Now with the gift of the new ray of spiritual longing, communication of all kinds can pass much more easily between the planes of experience on the lower spiral and the Spirit Guide plane. Do you understand?"

Angel and I looked at each other, then nodded.

"The ray provides this opportunity, but you must learn how to use it. The two of you can show others on Earth how to do this. Some will find their way to it themselves, but many will sense a yearning for such a connection yet will not know how to achieve it. You can help them.

"Here are your tools. The first is prayer, which is already used on the lower wheel. The second is specialized breathing. You have learned some of this from Gotharn. The third is meditation. Darci, you are more familiar with this than Angel because of your many years in a monastery. The fourth is visualization. Motivation, sincerity, intent and trust round out the list. Do you both understand everything to this point?"

"Yes," I responded.

"I think so," said Angel.

"I am going to have you do some exercises to put these tools into practice."

As soon as Izandra spoke those words, the two panels rotated so that Angel and I were facing away from each other. I could now see only the line of golden Beings along the wall.

"Let's begin with a silent prayer," I heard our teacher say.

Closing my eyes, I prayed for thorough training and a successful mission. I also prayed for Angel and gave thanks that we were reunited.

Next Izandra taught us a simple breathing exercise called the balanced breath. She had us breathe in for a slow count of four, hold for a count of four, breathe out for a count of four, then hold for a count of four. This was very calming.

The teacher then appeared in front of me and asked me to relax into a meditative state.

"Take your time," she told me. "I will work with Angel for a while to show her how to meditate."

I did as she asked but was curious to know how Angel was doing. I realized that this was the first time my partner had been out of my sight since we were reunited. I knew she wasn't far from me, yet I wanted to see her to know how she was getting on with all of this.

A long time went by. I was almost to the point of lapsing from meditation into sleep when Izandra again materialized in front of me.

"Darci, you must help Angel. Be strong, loving, and persistent, please."

I nodded.

"Visualize a wide channel of golden light between you and Angel. I have moved her, so she is not where you last saw her."

"How am I to do this, then?" I asked. A pang hit my heart at the thought that Angel might be gone.

Izandra's green eyes zoomed in close to mine, her body following afterward.

"Darci Stillwater, trust the connection between you and your partner. You know it is powerful."

"I do. I do." I said firmly. My face and neck felt flushed.

"As if your bonds weren't strong enough going into this mission, now you have an added link through the imbedded crystals. Focus, Darci. Send out the wide channel of golden light. Angel is waiting."

I did my best. Although a part of me wanted to see my mate, I tried not to let that distract me. I had more success when I opened my heart and sent love to her. Then the wide golden channel seemed to manifest more easily.

"You've learned your lessons well, Darci," Izandra told me. "Love is all. Love is the basis for all true connections. Now send a message through this channel you have visualized. Go on."

My heart, my mind, my entire being yearned for Angel. This longing flew through the channel I had visualized along with the words, "I want to see you. I want to be with you."

To my surprise, I received Angel's reply right away. It resounded in my mind and heart. I felt a great rush of love as I heard Angel's voice in my mind.

"Darci, where are you? I miss you. Let's get through this exercise!"

I sent back the words, "Where are you?"

Angel's reply again came quickly, "I've been put in one of the single meditation chambers."

Izandra had been watching me closely through all of this and monitoring our telepathic exchange.

"All right, Darci, stand on the center panel, and without moving from that spot, determine which room she is in."

I stepped off the platform onto the panel. The resulting tone seemed very loud. I faced one doorway, then turned and faced the opposite door. They looked exactly the same, so I closed my eyes and tried to sense which room held my beloved Angel. I was confused because I was sensing love behind both doors.

Izandra glided next to me and urged me, "Breathe, Darci, and focus on the crystal."

I did more than that. I prayed and breathed and placed my hand over the spot on my chest beneath which was the implanted spirit stone. I let love energy flow from me to one of the arched doors. Strong steady love came back to me, and I was about to declare that this was the room where Angel was hidden when Sottrol's face appeared in my mind.

I telepathically received his voice saying, "I have many crystals, but I do not have the mate to yours."

Without wasting a moment, I turned and faced the opposite direction and sent love energy to that chamber. A torrent of love flowed back to me along with a few crackles and small bolts of electricity. I had located Angel.

"This door," I told our teacher. "Angel is in this chamber. Sottrol is in the other meditation room."

"Excellent, Darci. You determined that quite quickly. You may go fetch your partner. We will take a rest break."

The golden Beings who had been observing our training began to move around a bit. I took long strides across the musical floor to the single chamber, opened the door to find the room nearly dark, and easily spotted Angel's glowing form. She was lying on the pallet with her knees up, one hand on her heart, and the other just below it over the implanted crystal. Rays of light shone from between her fingers. I knelt by the cot. Her eyes were closed.

"Are you all right?' I asked, stroking her forehead.

She smiled.

"I've learned to meditate," she replied. "What did you learn?"

I sighed with relief.

"I learned how to find you!"

She sat up, and as we hugged, the small chamber blushed with rosy golden light.

"We're on a rest break," I informed her. "Are you tired?"

"Not really. After all, I've been meditating for most of the time we were apart. I would like to talk to Izandra."

"I escorted Angel back into the central room. Dozens of Spirit Guides-in-Training were milling about talking to one another. Izandra stood in the center expecting us. Angel walked a little ahead of me setting off gentle tones on the musical floor.

"Izandra," she began as she neared our new teacher, "I received what I think was a vision. I know I wasn't asleep, so it couldn't have been a dream. I want to ask you what it means."

"Go ahead, child," said the Guide.

My partner waited until I was beside her. She grasped my hand, then spoke, "I saw destruction on Earth—war, death, soldiers in monstrous-looking masks. There were weapons firing and explosions in the air!"

I could feel her trembling, so I put my arm around her.

"What does this vision mean, Izandra?" Angel asked with a quiver in her voice.

"It means you are still strongly connected to the Earth plane. A little over a decade has elapsed since you left. A serious war has begun, a world war. It is truly a dark phase for this plane of experience."

"I find these images very troubling. What can I do?"

"Pray and send love. Love knows no boundaries, no barriers, which is the basis for the lessons I bring in this fourth phase of your training."

"Yes!" I interjected excitedly. "Once I allowed my love to flow out to Angel, the channel of communication was easily established."

"And so it shall be once Angel here is back on Earth."

"Will that be soon?" I asked, concerned that my mate might end up in some crossfire.

"No, it will be a while. After all, Darci, you are still in training to become a Guide. You must finish your studies before you can officially sign on to be Angel's Guide."

"I had nearly forgotten that, Izandra. I've been so caught up in . . ."

". . . your partner. I know. Do not concern yourselves with timing. The Master Guides have it all well in hand. You two will bring much joy and light to the Earth plane following a time of darkness and war. For now, send your prayers to Earth. I have word that the situation will worsen in the decades ahead."

Angel shuddered. I hugged her, and our extraordinary teacher lengthened her arms and hugged us both. With the addition of Izandra's rarefied high vibration, the three of us were surrounded by blinding, bright white light. I felt Angel relax in my arms and was glad she had stopped trembling.

Izandra moved us back to our positions in front of the panels. She circled and examined us from head to toe.

"You must even out your vibrations, so please do the balanced breath that I taught you, and do it together. Ready?"

The teacher counted for us as we slowly breathed in, held, breathed out, and held. I watched Angel as we repeated this exercise over and over. Observing her energy field, which at first was a sphere of glowing greenish white light, I saw it gradually change to an elongated vertical pattern as we did the breathing. After even more balanced breathing, I could discern a shaft of white light running through her as if her spine was illuminated. Finally, I saw white light beaming from the top of her head.

"Very good, you two."

Our teacher held up her hands indicating we could stop the regimented breathing. She walked away from us to address the Spirit Guides-in-Training.

"Here you see the synchronization of energy fields through using this balanced breath technique. Notice how their energy patterns are matched, and they both have strengthened their vertical flow. This is an exercise that you can do with your assigned human to increase clarity in telepathic communication."

As soon as she finished her statement, the panels rotated, and once again Angel was out of my sight. Sottrol appeared next to me and took my arm.

"Come, Darci," he whispered. "Follow me and float! Do not step on this musical floor. We want our exit to be a silent one."

I didn't want to leave, so I hesitated, pulling back. Sottrol winked at me and waved me forward.

I telepathically said to him, "As long as I'll be back with Angel soon."

"Yes, yes, of course," I heard in my mind.

We didn't go far, only into the room with the round bed and the kaleidoscopic ceiling where Angel and I had shared so much passion. Our most recent exchange came to mind, and I uttered a little sigh.

"Good, Darci. Call up those deep feelings. Your job now is to radiate love energy to Angel from this location. Her task now is to locate you. I must go and sit in one of the single chambers as I did for you. Chalherine will be in the other small meditation room, so Angel will have to distinguish which essence in which room is yours."

"That's more difficult than the exercise I did. You and Chalherine always emit such strong love energy. How will she know . . .?"

I didn't even get a chance to finish asking because Sottrol quickly disappeared.

Lying on the bed, I vowed to do all I could to help Angel find me. First I stirred my love energy further by recalling each and every time we had shared passion in that magic room. The room glowed brighter and brighter with rosy pink light as I did this. I must admit to becoming quite aroused by this string of recollections. Then I began telepathically calling her. I did want her with me so very much. She didn't come to me, but not giving up, I next tried the visualization Izandra had taught me.

I started by simply pouring love energy out to Angel and picturing a wide channel connecting us as I said over and over, "Come to me. Come to me, Angel. I am waiting in the bedroom. I am waiting in the bedroom to love you."

My heart did a little flip when I saw her standing in the double-arched doorway. She looked so beautiful in the cream-colored robe with the dancing sparkles of pink light around her. Gleefully running then jumping on the bed like a little child—which I reminded myself, she had very recently been—

she bounced a couple of times before kneeling by me. I pulled her on top of me, and we laughed and rolled around the giant bed until we heard Sottrol's voice.

"All right, you two. It isn't quite play time yet," said my mentor.

We stopped and looked up to find Chalherine, Izandra, and Sottrol watching us from just inside the entry. Crowded into the arched doorway were a number of the golden Guides-in-Training. My partner and I became serious very quickly. We stood up and walked over to the line of teachers.

"No need to look so solemn," said Sottrol. "You have done well."

Izandra reached out and touched our shoulders.

"You will find your way to each other through any barriers. You have the desire; now you have the tools."

"Phase four of your training is nearly complete," added Chalherine. "Take some time together and review what you have learned. If you have any questions or want clarification, we are available. Just ask and we shall return."

"For now, rest, relax, assimilate, and enjoy," said Sottrol smiling widely. "You have earned it."

The three teachers turned and moved through the doorway, herding the golden observers back into the central room.

We were alone. Angel and I looked at each other, clasped hands, and said in unison, "We ask for privacy."

Chapter Ten:
Lessons in Healing

Angel and I enjoyed a lengthy period of rest, rejuvenation, and lovemaking. Our teachers allowed us all the privacy that we requested. Sottrol and Chalherine visited only once during this time, and it was at Angel's request.

She and I were talking about the training we had received from Izandra. Angel expressed the concern that once she was reincarnated on Earth we would be lost to each other. I felt in my heart that we would most certainly reconnect, but then I was the one maintaining a spirit perspective. It would be easy for me to locate her, especially if I became her Spirit Guide. Angel was the one who would be putting on the blinders that came with being human.

Chalherine and Sottrol manifested in the doorway almost as soon as Angel called them. They sat in seats on the wall; we perched near them on the edge of the big bed.

"I'm not sure at all that this will work," Angel began, relaying her fears. "It's one thing to do exercises in a training room here on the Spirit Guide plane. Darci was never that far away when I had to locate him. It's a completely different situation once I'm on Earth. The barrier between this room and that room is . . . just a door. The barrier between this world and Earth is formidable!"

Sottrol listened with kindness in his eyes and asked me, "What say you, Darci?"

"I understand Angel's apprehension. I have the advantage of remaining in spirit form and operating from a place of knowledge. I will know where she is on Earth."

Chalherine rose and glided to Angel's side, saying, "My dear, we know this will not be easy. It is true that your conscious connection with Darci will be cut off as soon as you take a physical body on Earth. Many years may pass before you can once again activate this connection, but you will."

"You will be driven to it," Sottrol jumped in. "The crystal implanted below your heart will stir a yearning and a restlessness that will keep you searching until you find the door that leads to Darci."

"There's a door between Earth and here?" Angel asked, still unconvinced.

"There are many," Chalherine responded. "Spirit Guides use them all the time. Humans don't see them and don't know about them, but that is changing."

"That's what the gift of the new energy ray of spiritual longing is all about," Sottrol said as he, too, came closer. "The new ray will illuminate these doors, so to speak, making humans aware of the Spirit Guide plane and the opportunity to communicate with their Guides. You, Angel, can be one of the first to find your way to those doors and to Darci. You have the tools to do this, and you have much help from the spirit side."

Chalherine picked up the thread, continuing, "You are going to be on Earth at a very exciting time in human evolution. Due to the increased vibrations brought by the new ray, humans can activate more of their brains."

"And begin to use telepathy, for example," Sottrol interjected excitedly. "We Spirit Guides have great hopes for the human race now that the gift of this new ray has been made."

Chalherine looked directly into Angel's eyes and spoke, "You are right. It will not be like the training exercise you did here. You will not be reunited with Darci in a matter of moments. It will take you years to mature to the point where you can communicate with him."

Angel looked sad.

Sottrol took her hand and encouraged her, saying, "He'll be with you even if you don't see or hear him. He'll be your

Life Guide, your protector, and your dear husband. He'll be as close to you as your own breath."

"But I won't know it," Angel said sadly and pouted a little.

Chalherine smiled and reassured her, "Part of you, your subconscious, will know it. You will feel his presence. Perhaps you will even meet him in dreams. Eventually you will be able to talk and share thoughts and feelings as you do now."

"I hope I live long enough to see it happen," sighed Angel.

"It is true that your last two lifetimes were short," Sottrol admitted.

"Why, she was only a child," I blurted emotionally as I remembered watching Anthony's death.

"Yes, Darci," Sottrol said, patting my hand, "and Shalia had not yet reached twenty years on Earth before she departed. This lifetime will be different."

Chalherine looked me straight in the eyes and added, "Mr. Stillwater, it is your job to protect her from harm while she matures during her next lifetime. She will need at least forty years of Earth experience before she is ready to begin the mission."

"Forty years?" Angel's eyes widened.

"We expect you'll live to be a treasured elder," Sottrol responded, smiling.

"Darci and I have to be apart for forty years?"

"I'll be there," I said taking her hand. "You may not consciously know it, but I'll be there."

Angel sighed and looked down.

Chalherine put her arm around my mate, gently saying, "We understand it will be difficult for you to give up the closeness and intimacy you share now with Darci. Know in your heart that you shall reconnect in this way and carry out the mission which will help many on Earth."

"A worthy cause," said Sottrol. "Don't you think Earth is a worthy cause?"

"Oh yes!" Angel verified, looking up. "I love Earth—but I love Darci, too."

"And he shall be with you—and through him you can receive help from all of us."

"How do you mean?" I asked.

"You still have some studying to do, Darci," Sottrol replied, poking me with his finger. "You will learn that the Life Guide ushers other spirit helpers in and out of the life of the human to whom that Guide is assigned."

"You mean I can bring you to visit Angel on Earth if I wish?"

"Once you are her Spirit Guide, yes. Speaking of which—you must return to your studies soon. You need to be fully trained and ready when Angel is called to go back to Earth."

My mentor then patted me on the shoulder, adding, "Don't look so concerned, Darci. You'll graduate in time."

"Unless you have more questions, we will leave you to your repose," said Chalherine as she floated up. "Our next visit will be to tell you that it is time for you to return to your studies, Darci."

"And what about me?" asked Angel sounding like an eight-year-old.

"Oh, we have plans for you, little one," chuckled Sottrol. "Don't you worry. We'll keep you busy while Darci serves his apprenticeship."

The two Guides then vanished leaving behind more questions than they answered.

∞　∞　∞

Angel and I took advantage of our private time. We knew all too well how temporary and fleeting it was. By watching her eyes, I could tell when she was lost in the beauty of our deep connection and when she was cognizant of her return to Earth. It was a strange mix of bliss and melancholy. After one of our vibrant exchanges of love, I noticed a distant look with a touch of sadness on her face.

"You're thinking of Earth, aren't you?" I said as I stroked, then kissed the top of her head.

She didn't answer for a while. Then she stared into my eyes and replied, "My feelings are mixed up. I sense that something horrible is happening on Earth, and it scares me. Then I feel a surge of courage and want to go to Earth and help. Then I become frightened, for I am just one little Soul. Then I'm sad because I don't want to leave you."

Tightening my embrace, I held her close to me and whispered in her ear, "I'm with you now, and I will always be with you."

She sighed and I felt her tremble and wondered if perhaps she was sobbing quietly. When she looked at me again, her gaze was intense.

"You know we will be residing in two different worlds. You know there will be barriers between us. You know I will be in a human body. You know it will not be like it is here now."

"Of course, I do, but let us savor this space and this moment. Let us entertain the possibility that there may be a great advantage to one of us having a human body."

"Well, that would be me, but what do you mean—an advantage to having a human body?"

"You've been in the flesh more recently than I; however, I recall many pleasurable sensations from Earth life."

"Oh, Darci, I don't. I just remember being hungry—cold, dirty, and very hungry."

"You poor thing," I lamented, hugging her again. "My last Earth life was much different than yours. I was a country gentleman in England with a fine estate, woodlands, fields, and a pond. I had horses, two dogs . . ."

"And plenty of food," Angel broke in, "but you and Manyfeathers promised I would no longer go hungry."

"The promise will be kept. You will not be hungry once you return to Earth."

"Earth," she said quietly with a faraway look in her eyes. "What shall my life be like this time?"

"Much improved from your last experience," I said although I wasn't sure of this but was determined to remain positive.

"That would not be too difficult," she retorted. "So tell me of your favorite Earth sensations, Darci."

I thought for a moment, then replied, "The smell of a spring morning as the Earth is bursting into bloom . . . the warmth of the sun upon my face . . . the sound of the dawn chorus of birds . . . the feel of the wind through my hair as I ride my galloping horse . . . the colors of a breathtaking sunset . . . a warm bath . . ."

"Perhaps you should be the one to return," Angel pulled on my ear.

"Ah, no. Don't you see? It is your turn to experience such glorious sensations. Angel, listen . . . we shared some magical moments when we were together on Earth."

"Tell me."

"Long ago we lived in Central America. You were a mountain woman, and I lived on the plains below."

I proceeded to tell her about our lives as Zontyl and Nunzah, describing in detail our favorite grassy meadow where we had conceived our second child. This led to another round of lovemaking—with Angel insisting that we pretend the round bed was the grassy field.

As we lay relaxing in the blissful afterglow of our love exchange, Angel murmured, "We have to find a way to do this once I'm on Earth."

"We will. We'll find a way," I murmured, stroking her hair and kissing her forehead.

We had not rested long when we heard tones coming from the central room. We had visitors, a group of them. Sottrol appeared in the doorway.

"Join us," he motioned with his arm.

Angel and I looked at each other. This was it. Our recreation and relaxation period was over. The mission lay before us.

∞ ∞ ∞

The center room was filled with Beings. Many appeared as luminous golden forms. Chalherine, Wachena, Sottrol, and Arcillis were waiting for us in the center. Angel and I held hands as we walked across the musical floor to join them. Arcillis hugged us first. Then Chalherine, Sottrol, and finally Wachena put their arms around us.

I had come to love these embraces because they always imparted strong energy to me. Wachena held Angel a little longer than the others did. I watched compassion flow from the Spirit Guide to my dear mate.

"We have gathered for two purposes," Arcillis addressed Angel and me. The bell-like timbre of his voice reverberated throughout the room. "First, we celebrate the completion of your training, and second, we bring the news that the time is short, and you must move now to the next step of preparation."

I glanced around. The room was crowded; the golden Beings encircled us. Angel looked so small next to them.

"We are dealing with an Earth situation," Arcillis continued, "so linear time is a factor. The quickening of events on that plane is beginning, which means we here on the Spirit Guide plane must also increase our pace. We still have much to do to get you both ready before you take your positions with you on Earth, Angel, and you as her Life Guide, Darci. Your mission is to help humans connect directly with their Spirit Guides, a joyful task. You will also bring news of the new energy ray of spiritual longing, which will allow humans to shed the blinders they have worn for so long and see what else exists besides Earth. It is an auspicious time!"

The musical floor then played a series of tones. There were so many Beings crowded in that room I could not see which of them were touching the panels.

"Before we begin the celebration," Arcillis continued, "I wish to bring forward Sashma, a fine Spirit Guide with much experience."

A tall gentleman stepped from the crowd into the center circle. As he did so, he turned from gold to bright blue. Everything about him was blue. His closely-cropped beard was deep blue, his eyes and his robe were blue, even his skin had a bluish hue. I wondered if he might be related to my former instructor, Beminer.

"Sashma, meet Darci Stillwater—and Angel. The others you know."

The tall blue Guide bowed, and we did also.

"Darci, you will be Sashma's apprentice. He will help you complete your studies to become a Spirit Guide. Now, Regina—step forward, please."

Once again, a golden form stepped into the circle and magically changed color. She was a smaller Guide with dark hair and dark sparkling eyes. Her gown was a deep blue-violet, her complexion dark. She glided next to Angel.

"Angel, you will study with Regina," Arcillis informed us. "She will teach you special skills that will be useful to you once you return to Earth."

Regina did a combination curtsy and bow. I saw Angel eye her curiously as we bowed to her.

Arcillis raised his arms and announced, "Now that these introductions have been made, let us enjoy the benefits of this wonderful space and celebrate with music and dancing."

The golden Beings moved back just a bit so that Chilliwon Mac who always seemed to appear out of nowhere and another small elf-like Guide had room to leap around on the panels and play music for the group. The golden forms swayed and twirled to the sounds. I was fascinated by the scene and noticed Angel watching it all with delight.

Floating to my side, Sottrol whispered in my ear, "Lift Angel up in your arms and take a few turns around the room. I know you dance well together. After all, this is a celebration."

I noticed Wachena and Sashma dancing. Their luminescent robes contrasted pink against blue and seemed to shimmer as they moved effortlessly around the floor. I took Angel in my arms, floated up off the floor just a little and began gently waltzing. She let me guide her as we twirled faster.

I heard her ask me telepathically with laughter in her eyes, "Can we dance our way into the bedroom?"

"Soon," I responded, holding her close as we spun even faster.

The celebration went on for a while. I didn't interact with any of the golden Beings. However, Angel and I did engage our new instructors in conversation. Regina and Sashma were talking, so we joined them. I was especially curious about what might be in store for Angel.

"I look forward to being your apprentice," I addressed Sashma. "Have you been assigned a human?"

Sashma looked me over. His blue eyes were piercing but kind. He responded, "Mr. Stillwater, glad to have you aboard. Yes, I have my assignment, and it is a challenging one. I expect you will learn much."

I turned to Regina. The deep blue-violet of her robe extended into the radiance around her.

"What do you have planned for Angel?" I asked.

"Many things," she answered, her voice a bird-like chirp. "We will focus on the arts. Self-expression will be a big part of her next Earth incarnation."

"Will I make art?" Angel's face brightened. "Then surely I will have food."

My heart went out to her as I explained to our teachers, "Angel experienced much hunger during her last Earth life."

They nodded.

"We will begin soon," Sashma said as he put his hand on my shoulder, so you two must rest. There is much to do."

I felt a strange surge of anticipation.

Sottrol joined our group at that moment and said, "Yes! Much to do. Best you both retire to the adjoining room now and rest. Darci . . . hear me . . . I mean rest!"

He then escorted us to our room where Angel and I lay down together. She did seem quite tired, so I held her as she drifted into a deep sleep.

My mind was filled with images of the celebration and of our new teachers, but finally, I, too, fell asleep.

∞ ∞ ∞

Upon awakening, I immediately sensed a presence. Turning, I found Chalherine and Wachena perched on two of the higher seats on the wall. When they saw that I was awake, they glided down next to the bed.

I kissed Angel's ear and whispered, "We have visitors."

Once my partner stretched and opened her eyes, Chalherine began talking to us, "You both seem well-rested. That's good. You now begin a new phase—one that will take you to the point where you will officially embark on your mission."

"That's when I go back to Earth and become a human baby," Angel said, rubbing her eyes.

"Yes, Angel," Chalherine continued, "at this point, you two will study separately. It is very important that Darci complete his studies to become a full-fledged Spirit Guide."

My heart tumbled in my chest.

"Study separately?" I questioned, taking Angel's hand. "Will we not see each other anymore?"

Chalherine put her hand on my arm, and I felt calmer as she explained, "Unusual circumstances surround your studies, Darci. The Elevated Council discussed your unique situation. We have arrived at the following plan, which I think will please you. You both will be studying in the wing of the university that I oversee. Although you will go your separate ways when you work with your individual teachers, you can reunite between lessons."

"We can tell each other what we've learned," chimed in Angel.

"Precisely," Chalherine replied, smiling. "Now Wachena and I have come to take you to your new quarters."

"Why can't we stay here?" I asked. I had become very fond of the room with the kaleidoscopic ceiling.

"For several reasons. This suite, as you may recall, can only be entered in twos. There may be times when you are away with Sashma, and Angel might wish to rest. If you stayed here, she would have to wait for your return to enter this suite. Also, there may be another group using the central training room, so it is best if we relocate you."

Angel and I nodded and stood ready to go. We took one last look around the room where we had shared so much.

"Not much to move," Angel remarked as she picked up her ceremonial robe.

I also took my alternate robe, and off we went. We took care to exit as we had entered—at exactly the same time. Wachena and Chalherine did this also.

Keeping my arm around Angel as we glided through hallway after hallway, I remembered how disoriented I had been when I first arrived. I knew all this was unfamiliar to Angel. Plus, she could not hover and float as I could, so I carried her as we moved along behind the two female Guides.

At last we arrived at a lovely oval entry with an ornate interlocking scroll pattern around it. There was a symbol on the door that I hadn't seen before. It looked like a star atop a wavy stick. The Chancellor placed her hands on either side of this symbol, and the door opened.

We entered our new temporary abode, a much cozier chamber than the last suite we were in. Once we stepped through the oval, we were in a comfortable circular sitting room with chairs at different levels. Beyond this was a smaller circular room with two single-seated alcoves located across from each other.

"For meditation and the practice of telepathic communication," Chalherine pointed out as we moved past them.

The third room was dimly lit. Once we entered, I immediately scooped Angel into my arms because the floor dipped away. The room was a perfect sphere. The lower half was padded and had a flat, slightly raised portion that served as a bed. The upper half of the spherical room was covered with crystals through which came a filtered, diffused light. As I gazed around, I felt as though we were inside a crystal. The room was small and intimate, meant for two, so Chalherine and Wachena circled, then stood in the doorway. I set Angel on the raised bed area. There was something missing.

"Yes, Darci," Chalherine had read my mind. "Angel's presence in this wing and, indeed, at this university is unprecedented. Up until now, there has been no need to accommodate Spirits who are Earth-bound. We will install a ramp or some stairs for you, Angel, so that you can easily access the resting area. Wachena will return directly with this alteration. For now, Darci, look after Angel. Settle in. Your teachers will let you know when they wish to begin instruction."

The two Guides disappeared into a twirling, incandescent mist, which then dissipated. Angel and I sat in the center of the spherical room looking around us with wonder. We really didn't know what to expect next, so we held each other silently. I savored every moment with her because I knew I would soon be off somewhere with Sashma.

"Do you think when we're apart that we'll be able to talk telepathically?" Angel asked me.

"You mean now in this interim before you return to Earth?"

"Yes, now—and later, too."

"I'd like to think so."

"Let's practice. Would you carry me over to the center area? We can try using the alcoves."

I lifted her and floated from the bed to the doorway. We then each sat in one of the alcoves facing each other. The egg-shaped alcove made me feel safe. It also amplified my energy and helped me project across to Angel as we spoke to one another telepathically.

"Are you comfortable?" I asked.

"Yes—but I do feel left out. I'm the only one around here who can't float and fly," she answered me.

"You are an honored guest on this plane," I responded. "Please don't feel left out. Feel privileged to be here. I feel fortunate that the Master Guides saw fit to bring us together. Angel—I love you so much."

A flood of love, pouring spontaneously from me, accompanied my last thought. The alcove in which I was sitting lit up with a warm pink glow. I watched my love energy stream across to Angel and illuminate her alcove.

"That feels wonderful," I heard Angel's response. "Here—for you."

She sent back a rolling wave of deep rose light, which stirred me immeasurably as it filled the niche and me.

We kept the love energy flowing back and forth between us until Wachena arrived carrying a ladder-like stairway. The Guide stood in the passageway watching our exchange. Angel stopped when she saw our visitor.

Wachena stepped forward.

"I do not wish to interrupt," she smiled. "You do very well together."

I rose from my seat and helped set the ladder in place, then Angel tried it.

"Good," said my partner. "I can easily reach the bed now. Thank you."

"Do we have more time to rest before our studies begin?" I asked Wachena.

She nodded, bowed, and left.

I joined Angel on the resting pallet, touched her arm, and remarked, "It's not as big as the bed under the kaleidoscope."

"No matter. We're together," she said, smiling. "That's what's important."

"I want to hear you say the same thing to me once you are on Earth."

She rolled her eyes and replied longingly, "You may have to remind me. Oh Darci, neither you nor I really know what's in store for us. Let's . . ."

"Ask for privacy," I finished her sentence.

She laughed, "Yes—say it."

"I ask for privacy for Angel and me, here and now."

I then rolled onto her and began kissing her. Our exchanges of energy when we were sitting in the alcoves had aroused me, and I was glad to have the opportunity to express my passion. Angel was a fiery lover. The more intimate setting seemed to concentrate our energy.

We tried perfecting something we had first done in the Infinity Suite, which was looping our energy in a figure eight pattern. I began by sending love from my heart to hers. Then she radiated it diagonally down to my groin area. Next I moved it across to her groin, then she raised it on the diagonal up to my heart, and then I began the cycle again. We were able to get the love energy flowing through us in a wide channel, then increased the speed until we both began quivering.

Suddenly a ray of bright white light shot down from the center of the crystal-covered, spherical ceiling illuminating us. The white light poured through the tops of our heads and down our spines until we were both vibrating at a very high rate. The crystals above us were glowing with increased brilliance. They seemed to sparkle and dance with tiny rainbows inside each one. Angel and I became completely lost in each other and the blinding white ray of light that engulfed us. It was more than bliss.

∞　∞　∞

We were smart to have taken this opportunity to share our love and to enjoy each other because everything was about to change. The spherical room was still glowing from our passionate exchange when Sottrol and Sashma manifested in the alcove room. They peered in to see us resting on the raised pallet.

"Meet us in the front chamber," said Sottrol.

The two Guides had an orb of white light around them. Even Angel could see it.

"They have halos that go around their entire bodies," she remarked as we got ourselves up and ready.

"You could see their energy fields?" I asked, as I pulled on my purple robe.

"Yes, they were unusually bright," Angel responded.

We hadn't even taken seats in the front room when Sottrol began speaking, "Sashma must return to Earth, and Darci, you are to go with him." The elder looked back and forth between Angel and me and then continued, "This separation will be an excellent time for the two of you to try telepathic communication."

"How long will I be gone?" I asked, reaching to take my partner's hand.

Sashma then spoke, "This first trip will be an orientation and therefore a short excursion."

"You may need to review a few things, Darci," said Sottrol stroking his beard. "We'll see how you do."

I felt Angel tremble. She had a sad look in her eyes.

"And what about Angel?" I asked, looking at Sottrol.

"I will escort her to her first class with Regina. I promise I will take very good care of her."

Angel pointed first at Sottrol, then at Sashma and queried, "Why do you have big white halos around you?"

Sottrol responded, smiling at her, "Sashma and I have just come from a gathering of Guides sometimes referred to as 'The Intensive' where we rededicated ourselves, strengthened our energy, and brightened our auras or our halos as you called them. You have an aura, too, Angel. All Souls do."

"I can't see mine, or Darci's."

"In time, little one. Are you ready to come with me? Regina is waiting, and it will be easier for Darci if you leave first."

Angel and I looked into each other's eyes. There were a few little crackles and sparks of electric energy around us as we embraced. Then Sottrol took dear Angel's hand and led her through the oval entry. One last look, and she was gone.

I heard her voice in my head saying, "Darci, I love you."

Sashma stood in front of me. He was a little taller than me. His intense energy buzzed my energy field as he came closer.

"Do you know what it means to be an apprentice, Mr. Stillwater?"

"I'm not sure—though I did help Manyfeathers when we visited Earth to bring Angel back."

"I am going to provide you with direct experience. You will know exactly what it is like to be a practicing Spirit Guide because you are going to do much of the work—under my tutelage, of course."

"Where are we going?"

"You will see. First take a few moments to increase your energy. Go on now. I will help."

I did the breathing exercises learned when I first began my studies and felt surges of increased vibration, which I guessed were being influenced by Sashma.

"Very good," said my new teacher. "Let us go. A challenging Earth situation awaits us."

We exited the chamber. As we left, I wondered when I would return. Gliding quickly through the maze of hallways with glowing walls, I followed Sashma closely, remarking to myself that I must get a map and begin to find my own way around the massive complex.

"In time," Sashma said, glancing back at me.

We entered the same giant spherical room where I had been with Syd Manyfeathers. I felt like a tiny insect in this gigantic hall. Sashma took my arm to keep me with him as we circled around to a portal that had a small elf-like man standing just inside the entry.

"Hold, Sirs," said the little man. "State your names and your business on the Earth plane."

"I am Sashma Reneir, Spirit Guide to Frederic Marton— and this is my new apprentice Darcimon Stillwater."

"Your destination on Earth?"

"Southern France. I've been away from my charge, and I must return."

"Access granted," said the little man as he stepped aside.

"What was that about?" I asked Sashma as we glided on. "Manyfeathers and I made the journey to Earth with no interrogation beforehand."

"Much has changed on Earth since you and Syd went to fetch Angel. The Earth plane is in a turbulent and dangerous phase. The elves are trying to weed out those Spirits who do not have pressing business as we do. Earth is not for the faint of heart right now—believe me."

"What could be so terrible?"

"War, Darci—a second big war. You will see."

We moved through a passageway with green glowing walls that led to the large corridor with green and blue lights. This meshed with an even larger pathway, which was especially busy. The hum of voices came from below us as we floated along in the gray-blue haze of the corridor. Once in a while I would hear a moan or sob, sounds that tugged at my heart.

Sashma kept me close by him as we rose higher in the crowded passageway.

"Many are passing from Earth now due to this war," Sashma explained.

We moved quickly. The energy in the great passageway was very unsettling, and it agitated me. I was relieved when we reached an opening and exited into a bank of swirling mist. Now I felt much more peaceful as we glided through the clouds.

"Breathe, Darci," I heard Sashma instruct me telepathically. "Don't let your vibration slip to a lower frequency."

We traveled for what seemed like a long time. When the clouds parted, we were over an ocean. The moon was nearly full and illuminated the undulating waters. Soon land came into view. I could see small villages and cultivated patches of farmland. We lowered ourselves over a vineyard with a cottage and two barns. Sashma landed at the edge of the vineyard near a grove of trees. The moon was low in the west.

"Dawn will come soon," Sashma said quietly.

I was caught up in the wondrous fragrances of Earth in springtime and realized we were sitting right under an apple tree in full bloom.

"The human to whom I am assigned has just had his sixteenth birthday. His family owns this vineyard. He has grown up helping with the harvest of the grapes and the production of the wine. He has two older sisters. Both married and moved away. It is just Frederic and his parents now in the cottage."

Although the scene seemed peaceful enough, I sensed an edgy restlessness.

"Times are uncertain here. The Germans are amassing great armies under a new leader," Sashma informed me.

"You said there was a war."

"The Earth experienced a world war less than two decades ago. Many Spirit Guides thought that war would bring an end to all wars. Alas, humans have not yet learned the lesson.

"I selected Frederic because we have a bond. He was my father in a former lifetime in Greece. We were brothers, too— but no matter. I signed on to be his Spirit Guide and assisted him when he wrote his Soul Contract. I escorted him to Earth to take on a human body and a human life. I watched him grow and now help him with his friends, his studies, and his choices."

"Does he know you're helping him?"

Chapter Ten: Lessons in Healing

"Humans rarely understand or acknowledge the assistance they receive from their Spirit Guides."

"How did you help him then?"

"In little subtle ways. You will see. You must learn to do this, too."

At that moment, a light breeze blew. I heard the apple blossoms rustle, and another Guide appeared. It was Jono, the fellow student I had met in the Library.

"Jono!" I exclaimed with surprise.

"Hello. Sashma and . . . Darci, is it?" he responded. "Glad to see you. All has been quiet here."

Sashma did not seem at all surprised that Jono and I had met. The Spirit Guide's focus was not on us but on his assigned human.

"Jono, thank you so much for watching over Frederic while I went to fetch Darci. What became of the cheating incident?"

Jono shrugged.

"The teacher didn't find out—not yet anyway. I brought a wasp into the classroom while the exam was taking place to warn the boy, but he rolled up his test paper and swatted it—then went about cheating as he had planned."

"You are relieved of duty, Jono. You can return to the Spirit Guide plane. I'll have your evaluation shortly. Darci, here, is my new apprentice. I have to make sure he gets off on the right foot."

"All the best to you both," said Jono as he glided on his way.

"My former apprentice," said Sashma, nodding in the direction of the departing Spirit. "Now we are the ones looking after this young man. Let's move a bit closer to the cottage."

As we floated nearer, I heard the first bird herald approaching dawn. A light mist hung on the vineyards, and the moon was setting. There was noise coming from one of the barns, including the crow of a rooster.

"That cock is busy stirring up his hens," Sashma commented. "Frederic will be up soon."

The sky brightened slowly. A hefty white-haired lady opened the door of the cottage, stepped out, surveyed the yard, and shook the small rug she was carrying. We followed her into the cottage. To my astonishment, another Guide was positioned by the hearth. Appearing dark-skinned, she emitted a beautiful golden glow. Sashma nodded at her as we entered.

The front room of the cottage served as the sitting room, dining room, and partial kitchen. There was a stone fireplace and hearth with several chairs in front, a small table with more chairs by the largest window in the room, and shelves along the back wall. I observed that there were a few books, but mostly the shelves held jars filled with beans, grains, herbs, spices, sugar and honey. Off to the side of the hearth was a small cook stove. The woman used a spoon to bang on the metal stove pipe that went into the chimney.

"Breakfast!" she called in French. Opening the stove, she tossed in another stick of wood and stirred the boiling pot on top. "Petit dejeuner!" she called again.

Her husband entered still buttoning his pants. He was silver-haired and slim with a stooped posture and a thin unlit cigarette in his hand. He shuffled to the fireplace, took a stick, poked it into the hearth fire, and then lit his cigarette. His Spirit Guide, a large jolly-looking monk in a burgundy robe, floated into the room behind him. The Guide saw us and bowed. We nodded a greeting.

Finally the young man we had come to help stumbled in and threw himself into a chair at the table. His sandy hair was tousled, and he looked very sleepy.

"School almost over?" asked the father in French as he puffed away on his tiny cigarette.

"One more week," groaned the teen.

"You have more exams, yes?" questioned his mother as she dished porridge into a bowl for him.

"I don't see why I have to be in school at all," said Frederic, slamming his hand on the table. "I'm just going to join the army anyway. I don't need to know how to spell to do that."

"Not so fast," said his father, taking the chair next to him. "We haven't agreed to this. Who will help me with this year's harvest?"

"There will be no harvest. There will be no France if we do not stop the Germans. I must go. It is my duty."

"Duty, bah!" spat his father. "Your first duty is to your family. Besides, the war will not come this far. The Germans will be stopped."

"And I will stop them!" said Frederic, banging down his spoon.

"Hush now," said his mother as she put a loaf of bread on the table. "One day at a time and today you eat and go to school."

Sashma and I followed Frederic as he rode his bicycle down the country lane toward the nearby village. Within eyesight of the school, he diverted to a pathway that led along the riverbank. Two of his friends were there tossing stones into the water.

"Allo, Frederic," one called. "Did you bring tobacco?"

"I have a little," he responded.

I noticed two Spirit Guides sitting together further up the embankment. One was an Asian man with a greenish glow, the other a priest. We acknowledged each other with nods. All four of us were focused on the three young men.

One of the boys began to clumsily roll a smoke as the other watched.

"First class is about to start," said Frederic.

"George and I are going to sign up for the army today. We've made a pact, haven't we?"

The boy attempting to roll the cigarette looked up briefly, saying, "Yes, today."

"We have a mathematics test today," Frederic mumbled, scuffing at the dirt with his shoe.

"We don't need math to fire a rifle!" said the first boy with a gleam in his eye. Then he made the sounds "Pa-pa-pa-pa-pa!" while pretending to shoot across to the far shore. "All Germans, all dead!" he proclaimed.

"Come with us," urged George. "We'll all go together. We'll return as heroes by summertime."

He struck a match to light the crooked cigarette he had rolled; the Asian Guide glided next to him and blew it out.

"Blast! My last match. Oh well, this will have to wait."

He put the cigarette in his pocket and urged Frederic, "So what do you say, buddy? Coming with us?"

Sashma whispered in my ear, "Look at Frederic's aura."

I narrowed my eyes and glanced at the energy field around the boy. Dark blobs were circling his chest and head in a field of pale green light.

"Much weighs on his mind," continued Sashma. "Send him love."

I radiated pink and gold love light to the boy, and the dark blobs faded to a light gray. Frederic seemed to relax.

"Not today," he told his pals. "Tell me what they ask you," he said over his shoulder as he turned his bike around. "See you later."

He rode away. Sashma and I followed.

Frederic left his bike under a tree with others and ran up the steps of the school. He was a few minutes late, but the reprimand from the teacher didn't seem to faze him.

As Sashma and I hovered with a number of other Guides, I noticed that the boy's energy field brightened to a golden-green and extended out towards the young woman he was seated near. She was pretty and had dark eyes and hair. Her peach and yellow print dress showed off her figure. She looked up at Frederic and smiled. Pink light shot out of her upper body and intermingled with his energy. The resulting dance of sparkles, viewed only by the Spirit Guides present, made me think how much humans miss out on and how their lives would be so much richer if they had spirit perspectives.

During the noon break, Frederic sauntered into the school yard. We stayed close by. He stood halfway hidden by a lilac bush, waiting.

"Listen," Sashma instructed. The boy wasn't speaking, but I began to hear his voice in my head.

"Cherie, come over here."

I heard his thought as I saw him peering over at a group of girls. The young woman he had exchanged energy with in the classroom glanced over her shoulder. Frederic gave a little wave that was also a motion for her to join him.

She smiled but turned back to her girlfriends. The look and gesture were not lost on her, though. She lagged behind her friends when they were all returning to class. Frederic took her arm and whispered in her ear. She smiled again and nodded before climbing the steps back into the school building.

It was very interesting for me to watch Spirit Guides at work. There were eighteen students in Frederic's class and twenty-four Guides hovering in and around the classroom. Sashma and I stayed close to Frederic who sat near the back. During the math exam, I saw a number of Guides project soothing blue-green light to their charges. One who appeared as an Asian elder stood right behind a student and periodically placed his spirit hands on her head. Another Guide who was small but very bright actually perched on the shoulder of one of the boys in the class.

Frederic had a lot on his mind, but not much of it was math. He had written a few formulas on a slip of paper that he had slid into the cuff of his shirt, but he didn't seem interested in using the cheat sheet. He gazed for long periods at the young woman he fancied until the teacher, a rather gruff gentleman, scowled at him. Then Frederic looked down at his exam.

"Help him, Darci," Sashma sent me telepathically. "Help him focus."

I thought for a moment, then visualized a golden pyramid of light around him. Next I brought a ray of gold through the apex of the pyramid and through the top of the boy's head. This seemed to help because he set about solving the math problems. Sashma nodded approvingly.

After school let out, Frederic waited for Claire, the girl he had his eye on. She had stayed to talk to the teacher, then a few of her friends, but his patience paid off. Eventually, she joined him as he sat by the bike rack under the huge lilac bush. Her Spirit Guide was a beautiful female in a pink sari. She reminded me a little of Shalia.

We three Spirit Guides followed the two as they held hands and walked along the river. Claire's Guide was protective and stayed very close to her. Sashma and I gave Frederic more room but moved in closer when the two teens sat together in a secluded spot.

Frederic whispered in her ear, then kissed it. He took her hand and kissed it, too.

"Ma Cherie, Claire," he sighed. "You are my inspiration. I go fight the Germans, especially to keep you safe."

"I would not want to see you hurt," she replied softly. "The Germans will never get this far."

"No, because I will stop them," he said boldly, as if he were going to do this all by himself.

He took her chin in his hand and began kissing her on the lips. I was startled to see a red glow appear in his groin area. It grew brighter as he continued kissing her. Claire, on the other hand, had an increased pink hue to her aura; the most intense color circled her heart. Frederic placed his hand on her back and eased her down, still kissing her. The red glow became a brilliant red fire, which flamed up through his head. I saw Claire's Spirit Guide beam white light to her crown, but Frederic was on top of her now, his knee between her legs.

Sashma tugged on my robe, telling me, "Cool him down, Darci. His sexual drive has him heated past the point of reason."

I doused the boy with blue-green light and saw the red flames divide into dozens of tiny red sparks. This surprised me, and I lost my focus. The red sparks reunited in a red ball of fire. The situation was getting out of control as Frederic reached into the intimate area between her legs. Claire's Guide was holding her head, beaming white light right between her eyes.

"Not here, not now, Frederic," Claire managed to say.

The boy was a ball of fiery passion. He had the girl pinned down as he undid his belt with one hand.

Sashma poked me, "Try again to cool him off," he ordered.

Claire's Guide was staring at us with a pleading look.

"Darci, she can influence only the girl. It is up to us to help Frederic bring himself under control."

I didn't see how that was possible. His sex drive was dominating every part of him. He was completely engulfed in bright red flames. At this point, the girl couldn't move much, so she tried to reason with him.

"Please, Frederic—this is not the way. Please let me up. Don't hurt me."

Once the boy flipped her dress up, Sashma did not wait for me to act. He visualized bright green rays streaming vertically down like rain. As the emerald rain hit the red flames, they turned slowly into white sparkles.

Claire's Guide, too, was radiating white light over the girl. At last, the fiery red began to abate. Frederic wiped his brow, allowing Claire to get an arm free to smooth down her dress.

Then I watched Sashma use his hands to manifest a breeze, which caused Frederic, who was covered with sweat, to shiver. Sashma then beamed a powerful ray of gold to the young man's heart. He seemed overcome with emotion, his eyes welling with tears, his entire aura becoming gold.

"Claire, dear Claire," he said softly, lifting himself off her and helping her sit up.

She sat dazed for a moment. Her Guide was sitting behind her, pressed close to her back. The girl was shaking.

"Claire, are you all right?" asked Frederic.

She lowered her head, put her hands to her face, and sobbed. "You scared me!"

"I didn't mean to. I just love you so much. I wanted to show you."

Claire leaned back, slapped him hard, and firmly replied, "That's no way to treat someone you say you love. That's no way to treat a young lady!"

She scrambled to her feet and brushed herself off as she hurried away, glancing back over her shoulder just once. Her Guide trailed close behind.

Frederic was stunned. He held his cheek where she had slapped him and then sat alone by the riverbank and cried. The colors in his energy field fluctuated wildly. Sashma and I stood nearby.

"See, Darci, our young man is confused. Look at the jagged edges on the waves that are pulsing from him; that shows he is agitated. The muddy gray color in his energy field shows confusion. The red circle of light around his groin indicates his sexual arousal. The flecks of gold are the compassionate feelings he experienced when he finally stopped and looked into the girl's eyes."

"There's pink light around his heart," I pointed out.

"Yes, he does love her. He is young. He doesn't know how to show his love properly. I'd say she taught him how not to."

Sashma stepped closer to his distressed charge. I watched him encircle Frederic with layer after layer of light, first pink, then gold, then white. The Guide then repeated this until the sphere of light around the young man was quite large and extended from the embankment well out over the river.

Frederic stopped sobbing. He took a deep breath, wiped his eyes, and blew his nose. I felt much compassion for him.

Sashma pointed to his own ear, then to the boy, so I listened. Telepathically I heard Frederic's jumbled thoughts.

"If she won't see me again, there's no sense me staying here. I'll join the French army, too. Oh, but I couldn't bear to be away from her. But if she hates me now, what's the use?"

"This kind of round and round internal dialogue can really bog down a person," Sashma told me. "Humans can produce a great deal of static with their minds."

I looked closer and saw tiny sparks around his head. They were rather colorless and seemed to race back and forth going nowhere.

"Let's give him a love bath," suggested Sashma. "Stand on the other side of him."

I moved to the opposite side of the boy and observed Sashma who extended his arms out as if he were holding a giant invisible ball. I did the same. The Guide filled the space between his arms with luminescent pink light, so I followed suit. Then Sashma stepped forward and dropped the pink sphere right onto Frederic. The light washed over him. I then moved close to the boy and dropped my sphere of love energy. Pink radiance clung to him as he took a deep breath.

"The angels watch over me," I heard Frederic say as he stood and brushed the dirt and twigs from his pants.

We stayed near him as he walked briskly back to the schoolyard to pick up his bike and floated along behind him on his ride home. Once we arrived at the small cottage, the boy went about doing his chores. He was shoveling out the cow barn as Sashma and I sat under the apple tree and talked.

"You have seen much today," Sashma began. "I'm going to send you back to the Spirit Guide plane to rest and receive some instruction."

"There's so much to learn," I responded, feeling a bit overwhelmed.

"Jono will be here by dusk to show you the way. Besides, I promised I wouldn't keep you too long this first time. Angel will be anxious to see you."

We sat until twilight at the edge of the peaceful vineyard. It seemed inconceivable that war might intrude on this quiet utopian setting.

Jono arrived as Sashma said he would, and I followed him back through the clouds to yet a different entry point. The great corridor seemed even busier as we flew over the slow-moving masses of Souls. As Jono and I entered and began to circle the giant spherical room, I asked him when I would learn the way to Earth on my own.

"A few more visits and you'll know it," he assured me.

We then wound through countless illuminated hallways until I was at the door of my new chamber. I thanked Jono, and he departed.

I was glad to be home. I needed rest and had much to assimilate. Angel was not in our chamber, so I lay down in the cozy spherical bedroom. My mind was filled with images of Earth and of the area I had just visited. Thinking about Frederic, I felt much compassion for him.

I had time to drift into a meditative state for a while.

Then I heard Angel's voice, "Darci, you're home!"

I looked up. She was standing in the circular doorway beaming a wide smile and holding our old friend the orange cat. I could see her aura pulsing with pink and gold as she tossed the cat over to me on the bed and proceeded to climb over using the ladder-like stairs. The cat seemed to recognize me but nimbly stepped aside as Angel threw herself on me and hugged.

"I'm so glad to see you," she murmured excitedly as she kissed my temple, then my cheek, and then my neck.

I felt a warm wave of passion roll through me as I held her and returned her affection. The cat sat right above our heads purring loudly. We laughed.

"Hespahba brought him to me to keep me company while you're away," said Angel as she petted the feline.

"I'm glad," I replied. It felt so good holding her. I was happy.

"Tell me where you've been—please. Who did you see? How is Earth?"

I told her about my visit. I found that relating my experience and describing all I had witnessed in detail helped me assimilate it. She stroked my forehead and then my cheek as she lay in my arms listening intently. The cat pushed his head into her hand demanding some attention.

"Let's name him," Angel suggested as she stroked the length of the fur.

"Do you remember the cats we had in Egypt?" I asked.

"I wish I remembered all our lifetimes together like you do, Darci."

"I don't remember them all, but I do recall having a cat very much like this one when we were husband and wife in Egypt."

"Tell me about that lifetime."

"You're right. Let's name this fellow," I changed the subject. I wasn't ready to tell her about her untimely death and my subsequent grief in that incarnation.

"How about Bilbo?"

She raised one eyebrow and asked, "How did you come up with that?"

"The name just came to me. He looks like a Bilbo, doesn't he?" The cat meowed, and we both laughed.

"Welcome home, Darci," Sottrol's voice came from the doorway. "Your Earth experience hasn't drained you too much, I hope."

"Hello, Sottrol. I'm fine though I could use some rest and some time with Angel."

"No rest for you, Darci. Hello, Angel dear. Are you enjoying your class with Regina?"

She gave an affirmative nod.

The elder continued, "Long have I known you two. I have seen you work together in many situations, in many time periods, and in many cultures. I know what you are capable of creating as a team. I think with training and guidance you can do even more."

Angel looked back and forth between Sottrol and me and asked, "More training for Darci and me together?"

Sottrol addressed her, "Darci is still serving his apprenticeship. He needs more schooling in one area, and you may be able to help."

"What area?" I asked, curious as to where I might be deficient.

"Healing," said the teacher as he glided from the doorway to our pallet. "First, you need to remember what you have already learned and practiced as a healer on Earth."

"In Egypt," I spoke, and immediately I felt a tingling in my chest and at the back of my neck. "How odd," I thought to myself. "Perhaps I have just been remembering that lifetime."

"It isn't odd at all," Sottrol replied, having read my thought. "The cat is a reminder of your life there, and it is time you remember even more."

"I want to know, too," chimed in Angel.

Sottrol smiled answering her, "Yes, little one. You were an important healer then, too. Your presence will help Darci recall more details. To get things rolling, I have brought The Great Book of Lifetimes."

I looked around. I didn't see it.

"I've read about this incarnation already," I informed Sottrol. "I can tell Angel . . ."

"You'll want to read this together, perhaps taking turns reading to each other. There is much more detail in this account that focuses on your work together as healers."

With that, he raised his hands, clapped them above his head, and then snapped his fingers. The huge volume manifested above us and floated down until it laid open on the bed.

"Enjoy," said Sottrol as he rose up and then disappeared into a twinkling ball of lavender mist.

Angel's face was bright with anticipation as she asked, "Can I begin?"

I nodded and lay back to listen.

The book began by describing Angel's birth into a prominent family in Alexandria. At age four, she was found in the courtyard of her home holding a wounded bird. She was sprinkling its damaged wing with water and chanting, "Be healed and fly!"

The bird did, in fact, recover though not at that instant. However, Angel's parents recognized that their daughter might be a candidate for the Academy of Healing. Their little girl also showed a strong interest in the night sky, so she was tutored in astrology as well as in languages, music, color, light, and other subjects generally taught in that culture. She became one of the youngest to attend the Academy of Healing, graduating with honors at age sixteen. She then stayed on as a teaching assistant while practicing both astrology and healing.

Angel looked up at me after reading all this and asked, "Do I still have all those talents? Is all that knowledge still within me somewhere?"

"It's a part of you," I replied. "I guess it's time to awaken these talents."

"Now you," Angel stated, turning the tome around to face me.

I saw immediately why she did this, for the book then mentioned me. It said that I came to the Academy of Healing at age twelve. My first class was in color and toning with Angel, then seventeen, as the co-teacher. A few sentences were devoted to my initial reaction to the new assistant teacher. I was overwhelmed with feelings and experienced my first true arousal while in that beginning class.

Desire to learn coupled with my interest in the young teacher prompted me to be a star student. I always volunteered to try various techniques that we were learning, hoping to get closer to my beautiful teacher. This often worked, and Angel in time became aware of my enthusiasm and talent. As one year passed into another, I did everything I could to make sure I always studied at least one subject with her.

After class one day, Angel asked if she could have my birth information. She explained that she wished to draw up a chart for my potential as a healer. I knew a little about astrology. It was commonly practiced in that time and was used by everyone from street vendors to the Pharaoh, yet I had no idea how much information could be gleaned from the natal chart. I was soon to learn.

The very next day after a class on breath and vocal tones, Angel took me aside. I noticed that her eyes were dancing with excitement, and my heart did a series of leaps and tumbles.

"Hett," she said, taking my hand. As she did so, I felt a thrill rush through me. She continued, "You have the potential to be one of the great healers of our time. In fact, your talents complement mine. I'd like to try healing as a team."

"You a-and m-me? I stuttered. "I'm j-just a student . . ."

"A gifted and enthusiastic student," she replied, smiling as she squeezed my hand.

"First, if we are to work together, please call me Tuura. Second, there is a child coming for a healing this afternoon, and I'd like you to assist me."

I nodded, overwhelmed by the prospect of working with my teacher. She led me to a large room with two windows high along one side. In one corner there were poles with squares of fabric attached to them. A pallet stood waist-high in the center.

"Cover one window with a warm-colored cloth and the other with a cool-colored one," she instructed me, pointing to the poles. "I'll bring in the child and his parents."

I took the pole with the cloth that had rosy orange color. The square fit over the window, changing the sunlight into a beam of rich vibrant gold. Then I placed the pole with the indigo tinted cloth over the other window making a ray of blue light enter the room. I saw that the pallet was on rollers so the patient could be moved from one colored ray to the other.

Tuura returned accompanied by a young couple with worried expressions. The man was carrying a boy of five. With grace and compassion, my teacher escorted the couple to the healing pallet where the father laid the child. I could see that the little one was burning with fever.

Tuura introduced me to the concerned parents, then asked me to stand at the boy's feet and grasp him around the instep. Placing her hands on the child's shoulders, she began singing a tone. She nodded at me, so I joined her. I began to vibrate with the tone and felt prickles in the palms of my hands. I watched my teacher closely, breathing when she breathed and singing the tone in unison with her. At her instruction, we rolled the pallet into the warm golden ray of light.

"We are going to draw the fever up and out the top of the head," she told me quietly. "Send golden light out through the palms of your hands into the arches of the boy's feet. Picture this light cleansing his body. Now go."

We had learned a similar technique in class, but I had never tried it myself. I did as my teacher asked, always observing her for clues as to how I might improve my skills. She placed her hands on top of the boy's head and sang a higher tone. We breathed, sang, and visualized for a while until the angle of the sunlight changed. I was surprised to see perspiration all over the child. It seemed the fever had broken.

We then wheeled him into the blue ray and wiped him with cool cloths. We finished the healing with me again holding the boy's feet and Tuura with her hands on his head.

"We'll now energize the young one for a successful recovery," she told me. "You are the anchor. You know how to do this."

I took a deep breath and planted my feet firmly, visualizing sturdy poles extending from my arches deep into the ground. My heart was racing because I realized that I was going to be receiving my teacher's energy through the child.

As soon as I had that thought, I experienced a strong electric surge, which passed into my hands then throughout my body. I sent the excess out through my feet. Tuura sent wave after wave until again the sunlight moved the ray indicating we were finished. By that time, I was flying, tingling from head to foot. Tuura gently picked up the child, looking into his eyes, and handed him back to his parents.

"He needs to drink plenty of water," she told them. "Keep him from becoming chilled."

The grateful parents thanked us and left.

Next she turned her attention to me. I realized I was perspiring and feeling very light-headed. My beautiful teacher took me in her arms. We were the same height. I was fourteen then and growing. She was a small woman, not more than nineteen. Her embrace calmed me, cleared my head, but also sent an electric charge vertically through me. She pulled back and looked into my eyes. I thought I saw surprise on her face.

"You did well," she said to me, "for your first time."

"How can I improve?" I asked, still tingling inside.

"You must pass the energy through you quickly, thoroughly, and completely. As you know, you were grounding the patient for my work, a potentially dangerous position. You must not take on any of the healing vibrations I send through the patient or any of the illness that we are cleansing. You did well, though. How do you feel?"

She had her arms on my shoulders as she asked me. I suddenly became confused because my body was reacting to her touch, her closeness. My response was a normal one when a male is attracted to a female. I was very glad at that moment that my skin was dark so she wouldn't notice that my face was flushed. I was glad, too, that I wore a loose-fitting tunic, although the faint smile on her lips lead me to believe that she felt my excitement.

Using a damp cloth, she wiped my brow, saying softly, "My star student. You must rest now. We will work together again."

And so we did, over and over. By the time I completed my schooling, we were often requested as a team because our success rate was so high. On the day that I officially graduated from the Academy, Tuura gave me the gift of a white egg-shaped stone that fit neatly into the palm of my hand.

"For your meditations," she told me. "Congratulations. You are now a full-fledged healer."

Then her smile faded and her expression became more serious. She led me to a quieter spot and said, "Hett, I want to continue to work with you."

"I want that, too," I replied.

"Yes, and we will, of course. You ought to know that I have just been asked to join the Council of Astrological Advisors."

"Council to the Pharaoh?" My throat was suddenly constricted and I could barely get the words out.

"Yes," she responded, moving closer and gazing directly into my eyes, "and I have accepted."

The Great Book of Lifetimes went on to describe how Tuura became the Pharaoh's favorite astrologer, not only because she was accurate but also because she was compassionate and colorful in her delivery of information. Her work in the royal court diminished the time she had for other activities.

Although we did several healings together each moon cycle, this wasn't enough for me. I missed being close to her every day, and I contemplated asking her to be my wife. I knew she was fond of me but was concerned that the age difference might be a problem. I was nearly twenty now and had known Tuura for eight years. Now that I saw her less and less as she became more occupied with matters at the royal court, I began to realize how much I missed our talks and our time together, and how very much I loved her. My heart cried out to bring her closer and add intimacy to the strong friendship we already shared.

In those days, there was much travel by barge up and down the Nile. I knew that Tuura would be returning from a meeting of the Council of Astrological Advisors, so I waited by the river for the barge that would bring her home. Fantasies of a possible life with this extraordinary woman galloped through my mind. I sat for hours watching the water and wondering how I could live without her.

At sunset the barge docked, and I saw my beautiful friend disembark. Even though she now moved in the wealthiest and most powerful circles, her dress remained simple and elegant. An older man was walking up the ramp with her as I stepped forward.

"Hett," she exclaimed, with her face brightening considerably, "I'm so glad to see you. This is Rak. The Pharaoh appointed him to be my escort."

"Pleased to meet you, Hett. Our esteemed ruler does not wish his favorite to travel unaccompanied."

I was lost for words. I wanted to be her escort. I wanted to travel with her. I wanted to marry her. The tumult in my heart outweighed my logic, so I found myself unable to respond. Tuura knew me and could see I was engulfed in emotions.

"Thank you, Rak. I am safely ashore. You have done your duty. I wish to spend some time with my friend, Hett."

She said good-bye to the man and took my arm. We walked slowly along the riverbank. She said nothing for a long time. I was so glad to be with her that I didn't need conversation.

She appeared to have much on her mind just as I had much in my heart. We finally both spoke at once, then laughed.

"Please tell me what you are thinking about," I urged her.

"I'm sorry I've been so absorbed in my thoughts. It's good to be with a trusted friend. I have a difficult decision to make, and I've been considering all the ramifications."

"Tell me. You know I will keep your concerns confidential."

"Two events occurred while I was at court. First, the Pharaoh called me in for a private audience and requested that I join the team of healers at the royal residence. This, of course, would mean changing where I live, so I thanked him for the honor and asked him for time to make my decision— which he granted."

She looked quite troubled and sighed. I put my arm around her, glad she could confide in me.

"The very same day, I inadvertently obtained the birth information of one of the Pharaoh's top advisors. His daughter let it slip during a conversation about the man's birthday. All I had to do was ask two innocent-sounding questions, and I had the data I needed. I had a strange feeling in the pit of my stomach as I constructed this man's chart. Hett, he is untrustworthy. I fear he's a deceiver, perhaps even a conspirator. Shall I tell the Pharaoh?"

I pulled her to me, held her, and whispered in her ear, "That would put you in danger."

She pulled back just enough to look into my eyes and reply, "I know. As much as I love being a member of the Council and serving our land in this way, I dislike the political pressures that abound at court."

"And now our ruler wishes you to move there," I noted, clasping my hands around her waist. "You'd be right in the middle of it all."

"My healing work is the most important work I do," she uttered, staring into my eyes. "*We* do," she added. "I must follow my heart on this. I will go only if you will come with me. You are my anchor, Hett. You know this."

I did not hesitate, stating clearly, "Of course, if this is what you wish. Will you be attending only the royal family, or can we continue to offer healings to whoever requests them?"

"I can make that a condition in the agreement with the Pharaoh."

"He must truly like you if you can stipulate conditions."

"I took a pledge to use my healing abilities to help all in need. I must adhere to my own calling. The Pharaoh has other healers. He does not need me all of my waking moments."

My heart yearned to say, "But I do," but I held my tongue. It was enough that she had asked me to go with her. I did not wish to complicate her life further.

"You're a good friend, Hett," she affirmed, taking my arm. Then we began walking again. My heart tugged at me to tell her that I wanted to be so much more. I did give her something that evening by the river—an idea.

"If other members of the Astrological Council were to see this top advisor's chart, would they come to the same conclusions you did?"

"Most definitely."

"Then make the chart available, perhaps without letting on that you're the one who found the information."

"My chart style is distinctive. Still, that's an idea worth considering. Let others interpret the data. No need for it all to be on my shoulders. Thank you, Hett."

She kissed me on my neck below my ear. It was just a friendly kiss of thanks, but it sent me spinning. I vowed at that very moment that when things settled, I would express my love to this woman.

The Pharaoh agreed to Tuura's conditions but insisted she live on the grounds of his palace. I found lodging within walking distance of the court and the healing clinic where Tuura and I had decided to work. She was able to join me only half the time I worked there. It took me a while to get used to the bustle and noise around the Pharaoh's palace. I yearned for quiet times with Tuura, but she was right in the middle of the activity surrounding Egypt's ruling family. I resigned myself to treasuring the time I did have with her when we worked together at the clinic.

Late one afternoon after Tuura and I had performed a healing on two toddlers, a brother and sister with congestion and breathing problems, we walked by the river. I had located a spot made private by the trees and bushes. I had gone there several times to sit, listen to the busy sounds of the city, and watch the river. There was enough of a level area on which to sit, so I spread the wrap that went over my tunic to make a soft place for her.

As much as we were friends, I was in awe of this woman. After all, she had been my teacher for many years, and even though we were now partners in our healing work, she was clearly the leader. The Pharaoh and all of Egypt now knew of her talents, and she was walking with me. My heart galloped wildly as I thought that this might be the opportunity I had been waiting for. I began to perspire.

"I have a great story," she began as we made ourselves comfortable on the riverbank, "one that you will appreciate. In fact, I will relate this to only you. Today I spoke with the head of the Council of Astrological Advisors. You haven't met him, Hett. He's a very wise man, many years my senior. I carefully broached the subject of the Pharaoh's top advisor, hinting that I had some concerns about the man's character.

"He said straight out, 'So, you have come across his birth information and taken a look at his natal chart.'

"I had to be truthful and say that I had. He looked at me with a twinkle in his eyes and said, 'Well done, Tuura. Not many have gleaned that information. I believe I am the only other member of the Council who has drawn up this man's chart.'

"He told me this advisor keeps his birth information top secret, and he knew why. The elder assured me that he keeps a sharp eye on the influential advisor, and he's happy someone else knows this man's potential for deceit. This shall remain between you and me, Hett."

"Of course," I replied as I watched her face. It was glowing. I could see she was relieved to have the situation resolved. This seemed like an appropriate time. I took a deep breath, and just as I was about to express my feelings to her, she asked me to come with her to a celebration at the royal residence.

"It's time you met the Pharaoh and his family. Once they know how powerful and successful we are as a team, I think they will want you to join the circle of royal healers. Besides—" she continued, looking up at me through her dark lashes, "I do much better when you are my anchor. I almost feel incomplete when you are not across from me at the healing table."

Such a compliment gave me hope of deepening our relationship into an intimate one, yet it caught me off guard. I needed to be better prepared and have the right words ready. I wanted them to flow easily. I wanted to show her I would be a worthy husband. However, I needn't have worried. She loved me already, but I was young, inexperienced, and somewhat caught up in my own feelings, so I was unsure.

The celebration was the marking of the tenth birthday of the Pharaoh's eldest daughter. I must admit I was dazzled by the wealth that surrounded me as I walked through the great rooms of the royal residence. The feast was laid out on several large tables, fruit on one, meat and poultry on another, various vegetable dishes on another, and there was a table of gifts. As soon as we entered the room with the guests, Tuura took me to meet the royal family. The Pharaoh and his daughter sat on a raised platform. They were dressed in the most splendid garments I had ever seen. Both wore much jewelry that glittered bright gold in the afternoon light.

"So this is the man you call your anchor," the Pharaoh said in a booming voice. "He looks like a sturdy, strong young man. Let's see what you can do. I have a bothersome carbuncle on my foot. Take it away!"

I instantly became very nervous. I could feel the perspiration forming on my brow and neck. Tuura came to my rescue.

"We would be honored to do this for you, but Sire, do you really wish to lie on the healing pallet now, just as this grand celebration is beginning? Let us work on healing this later."

"Yes, you're right as usual, my little star. Be sure to bring your anchor, and let's do this soon."

We bowed and melted back into the crowd of guests.

"Thank you, Tuura!" I exclaimed as I grabbed her hand.

"He loves putting people on the spot. This is a good opportunity to show him what you can do. It make take a few tries to dissolve that boil, but we can make him feel so good he will not care."

Two days later I returned to the palace to do the healing the Pharaoh had requested. Tuura had prepared a salve, which we were to use at the beginning and end of the session. The Pharaoh was a big man with broad shoulders and considerable girth. I respectfully helped him onto the pallet and took hold of his feet, my usual position in our healing work.

Tuura motioned for me to apply the salve when the Pharaoh barked, "Let her do that!" She obliged the man, giving me a raised eyebrow as she did so.

Soon we started the flow of healing energy between us. Tuura began by laying her hands on the crown of his head while I clasped my hands around the arches of his feet. She and I breathed together. She sent her energy through the man to me, then I let it run through me to ground. I watched her carefully, for although we had done this hundreds of times, this particular healing was important to our future.

We sang tones softly throughout the session. I was able to read the visualizations she was using. For instance, I knew that she began by picturing emerald light flowing from her hands through the Pharaoh to me and sensed exactly when she changed this to blue, then gold. She moved her hands from the top of his head to his brow, his temples, then to his shoulders, and ended by visualizing brilliant pink light flowing not just through the man but all around the three of us. She was smart and powerful. Tuura was right—he wouldn't care about his boil.

The next time I saw her was at the clinic. We were helping a woman with a severe headache when two men brought in their friend who had been severely injured at the docks while loading goods onto a barge. It was difficult to fathom exactly what had happened, as the two men told different stories, but it was obvious that their friend needed immediate help.

Once he was placed on one of the healing tables, we assessed his condition. He was unconscious but breathing. We knew he had suffered a blow to the head because we could see the mark. Also, his back seemed to be damaged. Tuura suggested we begin with the patient face down. She wanted to watch his spine while we worked. I wasn't accustomed to working with the patient in this position.

"Hold him around the ankles. Let's straighten him—gently," Tuura instructed. "Good. Now apply your palms to the bottom of his feet. Let's see if we can send some energy through this poor man."

As soon as she placed her hands on his head, he began to regain consciousness and moaned.

"Be still," said my partner to the injured man. "We will help you."

She began by singing a low tone and sending brilliant violet light from the man's head down through his spine to me at his feet. I joined her in singing but noticed the energy I was receiving was disrupted. Tuura stepped to the side of the table and ran her hands along his back.

"Trouble here and here," she noted, placing one hand on his neck, the other in the center of his back. Then she directed, "Come, Hett. Put your hands on mine."

This was something we had never done before, but that's why Tuura was such a great healer. She approached each situation separately and was not afraid to try new techniques. I watched her carefully as I placed my hands over hers, for this was uncharted territory. Her eyes were closed as if she was journeying within the man's spine to inspect the damage first-hand. At that moment, I was certain that the gods guided her.

To my surprise, the words then disappeared from The Great Book.

"Go on," said Angel who was as captivated by the story as I was.

"I can't," I replied with a bewildered look. "The words have gone."

"That can't be. That was the middle of the story. Let me see."

She moved next to me and saw the blank page. Thumbing through the rest of the tome, she found no words at all. Her face became the picture of astonishment.

"This means we are supposed to do something else," I ventured. "I've worked with this book before. The words will return when it's time for us to read them."

"Oh, Darci! It was just getting good!" Angel pouted. "What kind of place is this where you can't even finish a story?"

"A place of learning," Sottrol's voice echoed in the room even before we saw him. He manifested in the doorway and sat on the ladder.

"Today's lesson is healing. Spirit Guides can offer healing to the humans they watch over. Surely you want to increase your healing abilities, Darci. After all, you will be serving Angel, and once she is back on Earth in a human body, she will need you to help her heal."

Angel and I looked at each other. We had been so caught up in the tale of our life together in Egypt that we had temporarily forgotten the mission.

Sottrol addressed Angel, "You can see that during this time on Earth, you understood energy and used your knowledge to help and heal. You taught Darci and many others. You saved many lives. This is why we teachers want you involved as Darci learns the healing techniques available to Spirit Guides."

"I don't remember any of it," said Angel, looking a little forlorn. "It was so long ago, and so much has happened since then."

"No matter," noted the elder, shaking his head. "Darci needs someone to practice with. Who better than you? Plus this can only further strengthen your bonds."

"What do you wish us to do, Sottrol?" I asked, wanting to know what was next.

"Think of what you have just read—of how Tuura moved energy through the human body in order to heal. You are both still in spirit form, so this will be easier now than when Angel is dealing with the resistance offered by the physical body. It's a good place to start. You two have already shared much love energy. This will come naturally to you both."

Sottrol then glided over and flipped The Great Book of Lifetimes to the back. I heard Angel gasp a little as words appeared on the page, and I began to see how the book manifested whatever text was appropriate at the time.

"Here is a page of exercises in healing. Take your time. Enjoy and learn."

Our mentor then turned and walked out the door.

I read through the exercises and felt a tingle of anticipation. I was to practice healing techniques on my dear Angel. Nothing would please me more. It just so happened that the sleeping pallet was raised above the floor at just the right height so that I could stand by the bed and try the exercises listed in the book. I had Angel read through them, too, for it was her job to give me feedback.

We went through the list one by one. Learning how to send healing energy to each part of her body meant I would start at her head or her feet, depending on what was needed. The initial exercises were easy, first soothing her feet, then her legs, then her knees. For burns, I used a cool blue-green light. For chills, I used gold and orange. When I worked on headaches and neck aches, Angel found white light most helpful. When I visualized adding a touch of blue, she exclaimed that was even better.

For hands, arms, and shoulders, I tried a few things. Sending energy in through Angel's head didn't seem to access the area as powerfully as I wanted, so I tried holding her arm and hand, lighting them from my palm to hers. I could see the golden energy stream to her shoulder. Angel lay there and described what she was feeling. I tried different colors in the visualizations. She often would know exactly what I was doing without my telling her. When she didn't, it was because my healing energy was not reaching the area I wished.

We took a break and talked about what we had tried. The most difficult exercises still faced us. I had to practice accessing the deepest parts of her body. Angel smiled as she scanned the list of exercises we had yet to do.

"Darci, you already know how to bring your energy deep within me. You'll do the same but with different intent."

"Instead of love and pleasure, my energy would be geared to healing," I realized, and as I said this, I suddenly recognized the power of the healer. Intent was everything. Angel saw that I had an epiphany.

"What is it, Darci?" She questioned, moving closer.

I took her hand and shared my insights, "If intent is the basis for healing, then moving energy through the body could be used in a negative as well as a positive way."

"You would never do that . . ."

"I wouldn't—but I realize it's possible, and see how much damage could be done. This knowledge must always be used for the greatest good."

"I agree," she said taking my other hand. "That will be one of our strongest messages when we are teaching and healing on Earth. Please remind me if I am not clear on this. I have no idea how much I'll remember once I'm back in a human body."

"We'll have a conscious link," I replied, tightening my hold on her hands and looking in her eyes. "That means we will be able to talk as we do here and now. I'll be able to tell you anything and everything you need to know."

"Oh Darci, I hope this works. I never knew any humans who could chat with their Spirit Guides."

"Remember that the new ray of spiritual longing is bringing this opportunity not just to you and me but to all Souls incarnated on Earth. There will be an ease about it, I think, because it is time for this to happen."

I pulled her to me, we embraced, and I scooped her off the bed and spun her around, slowly at first, then faster.

She giggled, laughed, and finally said, "You'll have to cure me of dizziness."

I visualized us suspended in a bubble of radiant pink love light. We floated there blissfully, enjoying the closeness of our Souls. The love I felt for her overwhelmed me and flowed abundantly from my heart to hers. It filled the energy field around us, and before long the entire spherical room was glowing with rich pink.

We rested in each other's arms. I thought about the exercises that remained as Angel dozed. I had ideas on how to approach each one on the list, so when Angel stirred, I kissed her ear and whispered, "The Doctor is here."

She laughed a little and stretched. Soon we were back at the exercises. My task now was to practice healing internal organs and systemic problems. From the experimentation we had done while lovemaking, I already knew of a dozen sensitive entry points on her body. Methodically trying each one, I attempted to move my healing energy deep into her. We would focus on one organ at a time, and I would move my energy to that part of her spirit body. I proceeded slowly through the exercises. Near the end of the list was healing trauma to the head. I thought about the story we had just read. The Great Book left off just when Tuura was about to try to heal a head and back injury. I tried to remember what we had done for that injured man.

"You're drifting," Angel said, pulling me back to the present moment. "Come on. I can't wait for the last exercise."

I glanced at the book and smiled. Whoever had compiled the list knew to put the groin area last!

For healing head trauma, I began by pouring white light into the top of her head, then tried beaming gold between her eyes. She responded well to both, but particularly liked it when I brought gold light up her spine to her head. The final exercise lay before us.

"Intent, Darci, remember your intent."

"Yes, healing the lower intestines, the bladder, and the reproductive organs. I know what's on the list."

I did well for a while, starting with a cleansing emerald light, then moving to a pure gold. Before long, I found myself automatically caressing the inside of her spirit body with my energy. Once again, the love simply flowed; there was no stopping it. Brilliant pink and white shimmering light poured from me into her groin area. She trembled. I watched her pull the energy up to her heart and send it back to me. Before we knew it, we were completely engulfed in loving each other. The experience was even more intense than before, for the spherical room seemed to amplify our passion. There were no words spoken, and no need for them. The flow of love energy between us was natural, easy, and tremendously exhilarating.

We slept very peacefully. Waking to find both Sottrol and Chalherine in the doorway, I realized I had neglected to ask for privacy and wondered how much of our lovemaking they had observed.

"We're not voyeurs," Sottrol responded to my thought. "We're your teachers. Still, it was a lovely display."

I felt my neck and face flush. Then I was even more self-conscious because I knew the two Guides could see that, too.

"Relax, Darci," said Chalherine floating to the bedside. "It was wonderful to see such a spontaneous outpouring of love. You know we respect your privacy. However, we were monitoring the way you were handling the healing exercises, and well . . ."

Angel turned in my arms, opened her eyes, and said softly, "Darci did well, didn't he?"

Our teachers laughed.

"Oh, very well," said Sottrol. "I've rarely seen anything like it."

He then became serious and glided over to us, saying, "It's nearly time for you to return to Earth to continue your apprenticeship. Sashma has his hands full. Not only can you help him, Darci, but you can also quickly complete some of the tests you must pass."

"Tests?"

"Yes, you must successfully apply the knowledge you have gained at this university before you can graduate and become a Spirit Guide. Sashma is an excellent instructor. He will help you through it all."

"When do I go?"

"Soon. Take a little time with your mate as you will most likely be away for a long period."

Angel sat up, asking, "Can we finish the story?"

Chalherine and Sottrol looked at each other.

"We were reading about Egypt," I reminded them. "The book did leave us hanging at a critical point."

"Of course," said Sottrol. "Read some more, but I suggest that reliving that entire lifetime is not appropriate right before your separation."

I knew why the elder said this: Angel as Tuura was murdered in that incarnation, and I grieved heavily for years afterward. That was not what I wanted in my heart and my mind as I left to apprentice Sashma on Earth.

Angel's curiosity was aroused and kept asking, "Why? What happened? Tell me."

Chalherine placed her hand on Angel's arm. I could see soothing blue light radiating from the Guide as she explained,

"You were very powerful and had great influence with the Pharaoh. Someone took your life because of that."

"Oh no!" Angel's hands flew to her face. "I was doing so well in that lifetime. How could it be cut short?"

"Humans have free will," said Chalherine as compassion flowed from her to Angel. "The human who ended your life made the choice and incurred the resulting karma."

"Come," said Sottrol to his fellow teacher. "Let them have their time. Darci must go soon."

The two Guides stood side by side. A sphere of light appeared around them, and soon they were lost in its brilliance. The luminous bubble floated up and vanished.

"That was a new way to exit," I remarked to Angel.

It reminded me that I still had so much to learn. Just as I thought this, the pages of The Great Book of Lifetimes flipped over all by themselves. Angel had the astonished look of a child.

"Darci, look! The words are back!"

"You've gotten your wish. Do you want to read or shall I?"

"You read. I want to listen and get lost in the story."

Angel lay back on the pallet, and I turned the tome to face me.

The story resumed just where we had left it. Tuura and I had our hands on the injured man's spine. With me standing behind her and my hands over hers, we radiated white light into the man's body.

"Help me turn him on his back," Tuura requested, "but do so very carefully, very gently."

The man moaned as we did so. He didn't seem capable of turning over on his own. Tuura began sending pure white light into the crown of his head while I stood in the anchor position with my hands around his insteps.

"Ilett, try sending emerald light to me," she said quietly.

I did so, but she shook her head. I knew it wasn't getting through. We switched positions, and Tuura tried the same, but again I received nothing at the head of the man.

Then Tuura did something very unusual and quite brave. She tucked one hand under the man's lower back and placed the other right over his groin. Closing her eyes, she visualized streams of light going up his spine, first emerald green, then gold, then white.

I did receive some of this although it wasn't Tuura's pure energy, for there was some static. We ended this lengthy session with Tuura again at the man's head and me at his feet. She then gave instructions to the attendants at the clinic, prescribing a relaxing potion, a splint on his left leg, and a supportive wrap around his mid-back.

"And much rest," she added. "I'll be back later to check on him. The potion will relax him without making him sleepy. Blows to the head are tricky," she continued, talking to both the attendants and me. "We don't want this man to go to sleep and never wake."

Tuura seemed tired. The healing was a difficult one and had drained both of us. I suggested we go to the secluded spot by the river. She agreed. We walked in silence, her arm in mine.

Although we were both spent, I saw this as an opportunity to express my feelings to her. As soon as we sat on the riverbank, I took her hand, suddenly becoming very nervous. Tuura could tell. She wiped a bead of perspiration from my temple and squeezed my hand.

"Hett, what is troubling you? We did all we could for that poor man."

"It's not that," my voice cracked. I cleared my throat and began again. Just as I was about to speak, our eyes locked, and the adoration and passion I felt for this extraordinary woman welled up inside me. I had to let it out. I had to tell her.

"I care about you so deeply, Tuura."

"I care about you, too, Hett."

"I love you Tuura. I love you like a man is meant to love a woman, only more. I love you like a man loves his wife. Please, please marry me."

"Dear Hett," she replied, pulling me to her. Our embrace was the sweetest, most exhilarating connection I had ever experienced. I kissed her neck. Tears rolled from my eyes. Years and years of feelings poured from me as I realized how long I had loved her and how long I had waited for the right moment to tell her.

"Sweet release," she whispered to me. "Let it flow. I love you, too, Hett. I would be honored to be your wife."

Tears wet my face and her neck and trickled down her back. She began crying, too. We sat by the river, rocking back and forth in each other's arms until nightfall.

Getting married to this woman was no simple matter. The Pharaoh was informed and immediately had me investigated. Rather than have Tuura move in with me after the wedding, he insisted that I relocate onto the palace grounds. He also demanded control of the wedding plans. Although Tuura and I would have preferred a quiet wedding, we went along with the royal decree and were married at the palace.

The experience was a hazy blur for me. Very suddenly and very early on the day of the marriage, four men arrived at my abode. Three of these men were personal servants to the Pharaoh; the fourth was in charge. They took me to the royal residence where I was bathed, perfumed, and dressed. I wondered if the same thing was happening to Tuura.

Indeed, the Pharaoh treated Tuura like one of his daughters. She arrived on his arm at the hall where the ceremony was scheduled. This was highly unusual, and I didn't know if I was more amazed at this or at her appearance.

My bride looked incredible. She was dressed in gold, literally gleaming in the midday sun with golden necklaces, arm bands, and anklets.

After the long ceremony during which the Pharaoh gave a lengthy oration, there was a great feast with music, dancing, and much jubilation. Tuura and I were patient, but after several hours, I asked her when we could be alone. She, in turn, asked the woman who was her attendant, and this woman fetched the Pharaoh. He came to us like a proud father, slapping me on the back and boasting of the greatest wedding present.

"I have ordered a barge outfitted for your pleasure," he beamed. "My man will show you. The crew is reliable, and they have been instructed to give you your privacy. Enjoy! Enjoy!"

We thanked the ruler with all the superlatives we could call to mind and followed our escort. The celebration rolled on almost oblivious of our exit. We walked to the Pharaoh's royal dock with the man, Tuura's attendant, and two other servants carrying food and gifts.

The barge had been luxuriously furnished and decorated to the Pharaoh's specifications. Tuura and I were shown to our compartment, which took up nearly the entire width of the barge. There was an area to wash, a bench, the bed, and a table where the servants placed the food. Two garments made of the softest fabric I had ever touched lay across the pillows. Windows on either side of the room allowed us to gaze out at the river, or we could let down the shades and have complete privacy. The crew was stationed behind our quarters. Our escort introduced us to the navigator, the man in charge of our voyage. He congratulated us, assuring that we would not be disturbed.

The Pharaoh's man, the servants, and finally Tuura's attendant left, and we felt the barge move slowly away from shore. The early evening air was humid and smells of the river wafted through our floating bedroom. Tuura and I looked at each other.

"Shall we change?" I offered.

Not only was I tired of the ceremonial garb, I wanted to feel the soft new tunic on my body. In all the years we had known each other, we had never seen each other completely naked. There was a moment of awkwardness since there was no changing area.

"You face that way to change, and I'll face this way," she suggested with a half-smile.

I nodded, turned my back, and began removing the layers of clothing I had been wearing all day. I must admit I glanced over my shoulder and caught Tuura doing the same. We laughed.

"Come now, Hett. Give your bride a moment."

The bathing area was near me, so I took the time to wash off the sweat of the day. I didn't look back at Tuura, but I knew she was peeking at me. That was all right, for we would soon see and share all.

We sat in the twilight by the window wrapped in each other's arms watching the landscape move slowly by. When it was too dark to see, we began exploring the landscapes of each other's bodies. The soft tunics we had been given were so sensual that touching my new wife through this magical fabric heightened anticipation. I was so excited I was trembling. So many years I had fantasized about running my hand down her back or touching the inside of her leg. Now I was about to caress her in these places and more.

Pulling her gently to a standing position, I knelt at her feet, then moved my hands under her tunic and kissed her feet, her ankles, her legs. Her skin was fragrant, soft, and warm. Then she stepped away, and in one graceful motion, pulled my tunic up over my head and off. My heart raced as I rose to face my new wife. The light was dim, but she could most certainly see my state of excitement.

"You are a very handsome young man," she said softly, moving towards me.

She placed her hands on my chest and kissed my neck as I was quite a bit taller. I couldn't help myself. Lifting her in my arms, I laid her on the bed and kissed her brow, her eyes, her mouth. Although I didn't want to rush, I was as anxious as any young man on his wedding night. I was inexperienced. As far as I knew, we both were, but I allowed my deep love for her to lead me. However, my youthful passion galloped ahead of my intentions, and I moved to consummate the marriage before I had even unclothed her.

"Was that too fast?" I asked as we lay in each other's arms.

"That was only the beginning," she whispered. "Let's start again."

She began kissing me. Now that the nervousness and anxiety of the first time had left, I relaxed and took my time. I learned how rewarding it was to please a woman, and this was the woman I had wanted in my arms since I was twelve. I finally removed her tunic and took exquisite pleasure in acquainting myself with every inch of her beautiful body. Even though this was all new to both of us, our love for each other was our guide.

We were scheduled to cruise for several weeks but ended up enjoying only three days on the water. The boatmen had been poling the barge upriver, docking occasionally. In fact, we had been moored since nightfall in a peaceful area. While Tuura and I were partaking of the first meal of the fourth day, we heard a loud knock on the door of our quarters. It contrasted so sharply with the tranquility we had been relishing that it startled us, and we jumped. The banging came again.

"Orders from the Pharaoh!" shouted a deep male voice outside our door.

I looked at Tuura. I didn't want our time to be cut short.

"It must be important if the Pharaoh is disturbing us," she sighed as we both stood.

I opened the door. It was a royal messenger.

"The Pharaoh's youngest son is very ill. He requests your healing abilities at the royal residence immediately," said the man in a very formal tone.

It was my turn to sigh. Tuura nodded at the messenger, and he shouted to the navigator, "Take this barge down river to the royal docks! Now! Orders of the Pharaoh!"

The trip back took only until late afternoon. There were two guards waiting on the docks to escort us to the palace. On our walk to the royal residence I held my new wife's hand very tightly, experiencing an odd mix of feelings. On one hand, I was anxious because this was the first serious situation I was to address as a healer for the Pharaoh and his family. On the other hand, I was disappointed that this special time with my bride had been interrupted and, indeed, cut short.

"How much control is this ruler going to have over our lives?" I wondered to myself.

Then I said quietly to Tuura, "We must talk as soon as we're done here." After all, I was the number one man in her life now, not the Pharaoh.

The ruler's eight-year-old son was very ill. He lay delirious with fever and had a bad cough. The attending nannies had done their best, but the boy had been steadily growing worse. Tuura questioned the three women who had been caring for the child about his symptoms, his activities leading up to the illness, and his bodily functions. The Pharaoh was not present, but his wife, the mother of the sick boy, was by her son's side.

"I hear you two are the best," she said with a pleading look in her eyes. "Please help my son."

"Of course, Rana."

Tuura put her hand on the woman's shoulder to reassure her, then took her place at the child's head. She and I worked much as we had dozens of times before. The energy that flowed between us was stronger and more powerful than ever. Even without the tools we used in the Academy, we were able to break the fever though this took several hours. Tuura showed one of the nurses how to make a potion that would deal effectively with boy's cough.

The woman who had attended Tuura at our wedding was waiting for us and led us to our new home on the palace grounds. It was a modest sized abode, quite lovely because it opened onto the Pharaoh's gardens. Even though we were tired, Tuura asked what was on my mind. I expressed concerns about the input and control the Pharaoh had over our life together.

Tuura's face wore a very serious expression and said, "We do give up some of our self-determination, Hett, but please remember that my first loyalty is to you, my husband."

"Don't let the Pharaoh hear you say that," I responded. "He acts as if he owns us, but we're not his slaves."

"No, we're not slaves, and I'm sorry if it feels like that to you. I, too, was disappointed that we were called back so soon after our wedding."

"We'll have to take it a day at a time," I uttered with a sigh. "At least we are together now, and no one, not even the Pharaoh, can separate us."

She smiled a tired smile and said lovingly, "I love you so much, Hett. I trust you more than anyone else who walks the Earth. Hold me, please."

So in the creeping twilight, we lay in each other's arms. The evening song of a bird serenaded us as we drifted into sleep in our quiet corner of the palace grounds.

Angel was curled beside me as I read the last words on the page of The Great Book of Lifetimes.

"That's a good place to leave it," she said, stretching. She looked at me with a serious expression, and I saw Tuura's face in hers.

"I wish you didn't have to leave, Darci. I miss you so much when we're not together."

I didn't know what to say. I felt the same, but knew I had to move forward with my apprenticeship. Instead I hugged her close to me and swayed gently thinking of those precious moments by the Nile when we embraced and rocked each other as we were doing at that moment.

"Sottrol may come and take you anytime," she moaned, breathing a muffled sob.

"He won't if I ask for privacy," I whispered.

She leaned back. There was a mischievous look behind the sadness in her eyes.

"Why, Darcimon Stillwater, you constantly amaze me. Those teachers of ours can show up in an instant, so if you're going to ask . . ."

"I ask for privacy here and now," I spoke the words loudly like an orator.

Then I playfully rolled on top of Angel, covering her spirit body with mine. I was going to tell her that I would still be able to do this very thing when she was incarnated in a human body, and I was her Spirit Guide but reconsidered. It was best to enjoy the moment free of future possibilities and concerns.

We took our time and loved each other long, enjoying all our favorite ways of sharing our passionate energy. Images from the Egyptian incarnation flashed into my mind. They did not distract but instead stimulated me. Here in my arms was the Soul who was Tuura. Her essence was the same, and our love for each other was strong if not stronger than when we were Tuura and Hett.

Our teachers allowed us ample time to express ourselves. We even had a good deep rest entwined in each other's arms before Chalherine and Sottrol arrived.

Sottrol gazed at us with compassion and announced, "It is time, Darci. Sashma needs you."

Angel looked back and forth between the two teachers and begged, "Can't we have more lessons here? I know it would benefit our mission."

Chalherine floated to Angel's side, placed her arm around my mate, and said, "I know how you feel, dear one, but circumstances on Earth are quite dire, and Darci must depart now."

I could feel Chalherine attempting to slide her away from me, but my Angel only clung tighter.

"I have had dreams about the wars on Earth," she whispered. "I fear for Darci."

Sottrol moved closer, confirmed this, and added, "No harm can come to him. Please know that this is true. In fact, Darci may help save a human, but he really must go."

"When am I to return?" I asked, hoping an answer might ease the pain of parting.

"There is no telling," Chalherine responded.

"With free will on the Earth plane, many possibilities exist," added Sottrol.

He nodded for me to rise and move away from Angel. It was one of the most difficult actions I ever had to take.

"Angel, go with Chalherine," he instructed gently. "This is best for Darci."

Angel looked so sad that my heart ached. She ran to me and hugged me tightly. I wound my arms around her, holding her close to me. We vibrated with love for each other. The parting embrace was passionate, intense, and heart-breaking, for neither of us knew when we would reunite.

With a sigh Angel turned and allowed Chalherine to lead her up the stairs and through the doorway.

My heart cried out the moment we were parted. So much of my energy was in her and so much of hers in me that I felt ripped in two. Part of me wanted to rush through the door and go after my soul mate, but Sottrol placed one hand on my heart and the other on my head. I felt the powerful elder's energy move through me, calming and centering me. I took a deep breath and told myself that I was becoming a Spirit Guide now. Such a rash action would not further that purpose, nor would it be appropriate.

"You will return to her. You know this," said Sottrol. "The sooner you complete your apprenticeship, the sooner you can come back to Angel."

After inhaling deeply, I exhaled a sigh. My mentor continued to steady and soothe me until I was ready to leave. I knew I must now proceed with my apprenticeship and vowed to do my best for the Earth and for Angel.

Chapter Eleven:
My Apprenticeship

Sottrol and I sat in the front room of the suite, talking while I waited to be escorted back to Earth. I missed Angel terribly but tried to turn my thoughts toward the challenges ahead of me as a Spirit Guide in training and apprentice to the Master Teacher, Sashma.

"Think of this, Darci," said Sottrol responding to my heartache. "Once you are a Spirit Guide and sign on to watch over Angel, you shall not be parted for any reason. Even when she is a baby, you can stay near her. She may not know you are there, yet you can be as close as breath."

"I suppose that is some comfort," I said as I stood and paced. "I am anxious about going back to Earth. I have a very unsettled feeling."

"Well you should. The Earth plane is engulfed in war. Nearly every family is affected. There are some choices being made that are tipping the scales of karma. Many are passing from that plane; many death imprints are being made."

Jono then appeared at the doorway. He greeted us and reached out towards me. I knew I must depart.

This time the journey to Earth seemed longer. We went a different way and were in the giant corridor only briefly. I could see why Jono altered our route. The corridor was densely packed with Souls—most had just come from Earth. They moved slowly below us as we glided in the other direction.

I expected to return to that same quiet vineyard in Southern France where I had last left Sashma, but that was not where we arrived. We moved through clouds into acrid-smelling smoke until we were floating above a convoy. Hundreds of Spirit Guides hovered above the trucks, open vehicles, and columns of men.

The landscape was barren and had a singed look to it. It was not winter; it was war.

Jono took me to Sashma's side. He was gliding along beside a group of men who were tattered and dirty. Their hands were tied in front of them. Soldiers with guns guarded them as they moved along the road. I looked for Frederic but didn't see him at first. I followed Sashma's gaze into the troop of captured French soldiers, and there he was. The teenager who helped his father in the vineyard and who had a crush on his classmate was now a ragged prisoner of war.

I examined the faces of the soldiers who were herding these captured men. They seemed detached, very stern and business-like. Every once in a while, one of the soldiers would yell something in German at a straggling prisoner. My heart went out to the captives. Indeed, compassion flowed from me to all in that bleak scene.

"Good, Darci," said Sashma, "we need all the compassion we can muster."

"It was my natural reaction," I responded.

"You'll make a fine Spirit Guide," Sashma said, patting me on the shoulder. "I'm glad you've come to assist me. We have a great challenge before us."

"Where are we? And where are those German soldiers taking Frederic and the other men?"

"We are in France headed for Germany. Frederic joined the French army, which now no longer officially exists. Paris has fallen into the hands of the German invaders, and many French soldiers have been killed or captured."

"What can we do to help Frederic? He has very little decision-making power now. He is at the mercy of his captors."

"This is when he needs us most. He still chooses what he thinks and says. He chooses his attitude. You will see."

We stayed close to the group of prisoners as the convoy crawled slowly along. I marveled at the number of Spirit Guides around this sad procession. Each human had at least one Guide in attendance. I wished that the beleaguered men could see their Guides. It might give them hope.

Sashma read my thought and said, "Most humans can sense the presence of their Spirit Guides even when they have no idea what the feeling means."

At night the German soldiers halted the convoy and set up camp. The captured men were held in several groups. Sashma and I stayed near Frederic and his fellow prisoners. The French soldier next to Frederic called out to the guards, asking for water. He was ignored for the moment. Eventually one of the German officers strolled up to the group of prisoners and lectured them. He told the captives that France was now a part of Germany and that they must accept that fact. He went on and on about the new order until the same prisoner shouted for a drink of water. The officer made a motion with his hand, and one of the German soldiers struck the thirsty prisoner with the butt of his gun. I saw Frederic flinch.

Eventually water was distributed though the prisoners' hands were never untied. Some loaves of bread were passed along the line of captured men, and each bit or pulled off a hunk. The German soldiers watched, poking a prisoner with the muzzle of a rifle if he ate too much or held the loaf too long. The men were then taken in groups of three to urinate.

We followed Frederic, two other captives, and the two guards as they walked to a long ditch that had been dug.

"Tomorrow it will be your turn to dig," said one of the guards as the men relieved themselves.

I noticed that the Spirit Guides around the prisoners stayed very close to their charges. The Guides belonging to the Germans hovered further away.

"How can we help Frederic?" I asked Sashma again as the three prisoners were marched back to their group.

Sashma sent me the answer telepathically, "You will see."

The captured French soldiers slept on the ground with no blankets, their hands still tied. Once many were asleep, I began to see the Spirit Guides take action. Most worked with the energy fields of the humans, adding soothing green or gold light to counteract the gray and maroon hues that hung over the captured men.

I observed Frederic. His aura was dull with dark, jagged, burgundy-colored lines surrounding his whole body.

"What would you suggest?" Sashma said, turning to me. "You've had training enough to make an evaluation."

Instead of answering, I visualized a golden-green circle of light around Frederic. I tried to make it bright, but the light dimmed as I projected it around the sleeping man.

"He's exhausted and depressed," Sashma explained. "His life force has diminished, and this is dulling your efforts. Do you remember what his energy field looked like last time you saw him?"

"I recall lots of red, then pink."

"Yes, his passion for the girl. Our goal is to revitalize this man. Most Guides do such energy work with their assigned humans during sleep. Sometimes the Soul actually rises out of the physical body to receive the Guide's healing."

Sashma nodded to his left, and I saw a female Guide embracing a translucent whitish-gray form that was rising out of the solar plexus of one of the sleeping prisoners. I watched with interest as she pumped radiant pink light into the colorless form until it glowed.

"Can we get Frederic's spirit to rise out of him like that?" I asked Sashma.

"Some humans allow their Spirits to float out of their bodies more easily than others. Frederic has always kept his Soul tucked securely in his physical form."

"So to help him, we have to radiate our energy into his body."

"Yes. As you can see, the Spirit Guide embracing the Soul that has moved up and out of the physical body has been able to work quickly, thoroughly, and effectively. We will have to proceed more slowly and persevere through most of the night in order to bring Frederic some small measure of relief."

Sashma had me begin. After all, I was training and needed practice. My experience was limited to what I had tried with Angel, but this was an entirely different situation. Angel was open, ready, and eager to receive my energy. This young man lying below us was closed up tight. I could barely find a place to start.

Remembering my healing work as Hett in Egypt, I began at his feet. The poor boy had been marching for days. He had several painful blisters, as his boots did not fit properly and were soaked through. I moved emerald green light into his arches and tried to soothe his aching feet. I could not believe the resistance I was meeting. Only a feeble amount of my light made it into his feet.

It had been so easy with Angel. My light, my love, my energy just flowed into her. With Frederic, I was up against a formidable barrier. I looked at Sashma. He nodded for me to continue to try, so I went to the young man's head and attempted to radiate healing energy through his crown. The gold light I tried streaming into his head turned into static. I asked Sashma for help.

"Try his stomach, his solar plexus," Sashma suggested.

I hovered above the sleeping man. At least he was on his back. Using a ray of brilliant golden green with some success, I watched it slowly fill his abdomen. When I stopped, however, something began pushing the light back out. Sashma could see I was frustrated.

"You need to be much more forceful to make progress with humans," he told me. "Their carbon-based physical bodies automatically offer resistance. Plus these men are under tremendous stress. Most of them realize that they could be executed tomorrow for as small a reason as lack of bread to feed them. Even though they are very difficult to help, they need us more than most humans on Earth right now. So let's get to work. As a team, we may make some progress by dawn."

Sashma hovered over Frederic and motioned for me to join him. We sent powerful rays of energy into his solar plexus. My instructor would telepathically tell me the color he wanted to use. The he'd count "un, deux, trois," and together we'd beam energy into the man. When we changed from blue-green and emerald to bright gold, I saw Frederic twitch in his sleep.

"There—you see?" Sashma remarked, noting the spasm. "The energy is penetrating deeper. Always watch the body of the human you are healing for signs like that one."

We sent some energy to his heart, too, but dawn overtook our efforts.

The next several days were difficult ones. During daylight hours, Sashma and I and all the other Spirit Guides followed the convoy. During the night, we tried to help the suffering humans. I included all who were in the procession because although it was early summer, the weather was cool, damp, and rainy. Everything was wet. Only the officers had tents. The rest of the men were out in the rain day and night.

"The fall of France has caused the skies to cry," I heard one prisoner say to Frederic as they slogged on.

On the fourth day after I had joined Sashma, the convoy arrived at a large encampment inside Germany. The captured men were forced to strip and enter a large shower room, ten or twelve at a time. Frederic and his group were given fresh clothes that marked them as prisoners of war, and their hands were bound again. The captives were loaded into large open trucks. As the vehicles pulled out, we could hear gunfire.

"Executions," snarled one of the guards in Frederic's truck. "You should be glad it is not you—yet!"

The army vehicles bounced and lurched along a dirt road heading north through the German countryside. I marveled at the beauty of well-kept farms, mowed rolling hills, and well-fed livestock in the pastures. Except for the line of army trucks passing through, this area was untouched by war.

The captured French soldiers arrived at a prisoner-of-war camp in the middle of the night. Once behind the many-layered barbed wire fences, the men's hands were cut free. Frederic's wrists were red and raw from the bonds he had worn for days. Compassion flowed from my heart to all the prisoners.

As golden light poured out of me, Sashma patted my shoulder, saying, "Excellent, Darci—let your compassion flow over these men. They need it. Your ability to automatically respond with compassion is one of the reasons you were given the opportunity to become a Spirit Guide. It's a very important attribute for a Guide, and you already had this as part of your character when you passed over into Spirit."

At that moment, a German officer accompanied by several soldiers entered the large room. The officer paced back and forth as he expounded on the benefits Germany was bringing to the world. He motioned to the German soldiers. They grabbed two of the prisoners and sat them in chairs at the front. Two other soldiers proceeded to shave the men's heads, and this went on until all the captives were shaved. Now the prisoners looked similar with the same clothing and nearly bald heads.

As a spirit onlooker, I could still discern marked differences in the energy patterns of the captives. The German soldiers may have been able to homogenize the outer look of these men, but their Spirits were still varied. I bided my time, noting the differences in the auras of the prisoners, the colors, the shapes, and the sizes. Frederic's was rather small and a dark blue-gray with a marbled appearance.

The men were given more than bread for the first time in days, but it wasn't much more. The goop dished out was chunky and brown. Most of the prisoners gobbled it from sheer hunger. Frederic didn't eat all of his, so a fellow prisoner finished it. Shots sounded outside the barracks that caused some of the men to jump.

"We are just livestock, waiting in the pen to be slaughtered," muttered the prisoner who had eaten the rest of Frederic's food.

"They will keep us alive," said another.

"We are bargaining chips."

"Nonsense!" another man whispered loudly. "France has already given in. The Germans have all they want. They do not need us."

"Quiet!" came the order from an officer at the front of the room.

He pointed out three men to four German soldiers, who grabbed these prisoners and took them out. Soon all the captured men would learn why they had been kept alive: the Germans wanted information and hoped to get it from those who had fought to defend Paris.

The men who were removed did not return to the holding barracks, so Sashma and I did not know what was happening until we followed Frederic into the interrogation room. I knew that helping this young man through this ordeal was my next test as an apprentice Spirit Guide.

Frederic looked like a skinny frightened boy as the Germans strapped him into a chair and pointed several bright lights at him. Sashma stood behind him, and I knelt at his feet, wrapping my spirit arms around his legs. I could tell that his heart was racing and he was sweating.

A German officer with the face of a goat entered the room. He carried several long implements: a riding crop, a baton, and some sort of metal rod. He circled Frederic slowly. I could see the officer's Spirit Guide above him near the ceiling and tried to telepathically connect but had no success.

I heard Sashma's voice in my head saying, "That Guide is focused on the officer. Focus on Frederic!"

Realizing that I still had much to learn, I turned my full attention to the boy.

The officer paced, holding the riding crop behind his back. He began by asking which part of France was Frederic's home. Once the boy answered, the goat-faced man fired a line of questions about the organization of resistance in the south of France.

"I know nothing of this," responded the prisoner.

"I was in the army in the north."

The officer cracked the riding crop next to Frederic's head making him jump.

Sashma was filtering blue-green energy into the boy's chest as I moved blue into his solar plexus. We were trying to keep him centered and calm.

"Frederic is a good German name," the officer remarked in a strange high-pitched voice.

"I am French," the boy replied bravely.

Crack went the whip, this time on the back of his neck. Frederic flinched.

"There is no France. What was France is now Germany."

"There will always be France," I heard the boy mutter under his breath.

The interrogator grabbed the baton and struck Frederic across the knees. The boy cried out. I, too, felt the blow as it traveled through my spirit body. The German officer's disdain for the prisoner, his sense of absolute superiority, and his aggressive approach to the interrogation were all apparent to me as I experienced the strike.

I was disoriented for a moment. Then Sashma put his hand on my head, and I focused again on the boy.

The officer kept barking questions. Frederic no longer said a word. This irritated the interrogator. He took hold of the metal rod and threatened the prisoner with it, but the boy remained mute. I could see that the energy field around the officer was becoming dark red.

Frederic's aura was minuscule, reduced to a little blue glow in his mid-section. The boy was shut down.

The officer asked question after question as he paced back and forth. Finally he yelled, "You imbecile! The Third Reich is the future! Accept it! Cooperate!"

Frederic remained still and didn't respond. In one swift motion, the goat-faced interrogator brought the metal rod down hard on Frederic's leg. I heard a crack. This time the boy didn't cry out, just gasped a little.

A tear squeezed from his eye and dropped onto his pant leg.

"Take him away," ordered the officer. "Useless French dung!"

Frederic couldn't walk. Two soldiers had to support him. We stayed as close as we could to the lad. Jagged waves of red and maroon were pulsing from him; he was in pain. The German guards tossed him into a cell with eight other prisoners. All had been questioned and tortured in some way. From the condition of the others, I gathered that Frederic got off easy. Nonetheless, the boy's kneecap was destroyed, and other bones in his right leg might have been broken, too. He slumped into a corner of the bare cell block moaning.

"Relieving pain is not easy," Sashma informed me, "yet it is one of the most common ways a Spirit Guide can help a human. Let's see what we can do for this poor lad. His leg is badly damaged. My heart is very sad to see one human being treat another in such a way."

"Show me how we can help him," I asked my teacher as we floated in the corner above the wounded boy.

"Let's get him to sleep," Sashma said, beaming an engulfing a ray of comforting golden orange.

"At least I am alive," I heard Frederic's thought as he turned on his side and lay on the floor like most of the other prisoners. He closed his eyes, and I saw tears roll across his face.

Sashma indicated that I should position myself at the boy's head while he hovered above his mid-section and the injured knee. We continued using the peach-colored light until Frederic was asleep. Then Sashma did an extraordinary thing, and I began to see why he was one of the best teachers in the field.

"I'm going to examine the damage," he informed me. "Watch carefully. You can use this technique if you pay close attention. Intent and focus are your tools. My intent is to inspect the injury. My focus is on this area only."

With that said, I then observed the Spirit Guide changing form. His spirit body became a sphere of golden light, which floated down so that it surrounded Frederic's injured leg. I was amazed. I had never seen a Guide change quite like that although I had witnessed plenty of appearing and disappearing. As I watched the golden sphere of light rotate and move slightly up and down the leg, I reasoned that, of course, this was possible. After all, we Spirit Guides and our spirit bodies are made up of pure energy. The sphere floated upward, and slowly Sashma's spirit form emerged from it.

"Could you see inside his leg?" I asked, excited by the prospect.

"Yes, and the damage to the knee is severe. This poor lad will always walk with a limp, I'm afraid."

Frederic was restless in his sleep. I could see he was uncomfortable on the hard floor. Sashma and I did all we could to bring him relief. We spent the entire night filling him with soothing blue-green light.

"We can only do so much," admitted Sashma as we heard the dawn chorus. "He needs medical attention, as do many of the men here. Watch over him, please, Darci. I'm going to look around."

"What should I do?" I asked, for I had never been alone in charge of a human.

"Send him as much love and compassion as you can muster. I'll be back soon."

Once Sashma left, I realized how spent I was. During my classes on the Spirit Guide plane, I always had rest and rejuvenation periods. Now that I was out in the field, the demand for my services seemed constant. There had been no time for rest since I joined Sashma.

The prisoners were waking slowly one by one. There hadn't been much interaction among them since Frederic was thrown into the cell. The men were in poor condition, and the cell block was monitored. High in the corner was a speaker and what was probably a microphone. I had never witnessed such oppressive circumstances. Compassion welled up within me and poured out to all the men. Surely there was a way to eliminate such suffering on the Earth plane.

The speaker in the corner crackled, and tinny military music played. Then came announcements in German, then in French. Sashma returned as this was taking place. To my surprise, he had Jono with him and a Guide I had not met before. The four of us gathered in the upper corner of the cell block. The entire cell was filled with Guides. I wished again that the men could see and relate to their spirit helpers.

"Darci, meet Crann, an apprentice like yourself," Sashma made the introduction.

I nodded. The Guide-in-Training was dressed in an emerald robe and had short white hair and a very young face.

"I've heard about your mission, Darci," said Crann, bowing a little. "May it change Earth for the better."

"Thank you," I replied, bowing back.

Sashma turned to me and said, "You need to rest, Darci, so Jono will take you back. Crann will stay and assist me. We are going to try to get these men some medical attention. There is a doctor and a small infirmary on the other side of the camp."

I left with Jono, as the prisoners were getting their morning bread and boiled eggs. As I rose up over the prisoner-of-war camp, I again noted the lush beauty of the surrounding countryside. Then we were in clouds.

∞ ∞ ∞

Jono escorted me all the way back to the entrance of the chamber I shared with Angel. Part of the route to Earth was becoming familiar to me, but each time I traveled there, I was taken a slightly different way. Before he left, I asked Jono if he could show me one route that I could learn; he agreed.

I entered the chamber to find Angel sleeping. I was glad to see her and very relieved to rest myself. Earth was an exhausting place.

I took Angel in my arms and joined her in sleep.

The cat woke me rubbing against my hand. Opening my eyes, I saw Sottrol and Chalherine sitting on the ladder stairs and Angel petting the cat.

"We missed you," she said.

"Feeling rested?" asked Sottrol as he and Chalherine floated closer.

"I guess so," I mumbled, feeling somewhat disoriented.

"Earth can sap your energy," Chalherine responded, placing her hand on my brow. "You must strengthen yourself before you return."

"I'm going back?" I asked, shuddering a little as images of the horror I had witnessed passed through my mind.

"Yes," nodded Sottrol, "but not for a while. You need more instruction on this side."

With a joyful smile, Angel excitedly shared, "You and I will take a class together."

I looked at the two teachers.

"That's right," said Chalherine. "Your training as a team continues . . ."

"In a while," broke in Sottrol. "You must regenerate and regain some of your spirit energy. Once you are a full-fledged Spirit Guide, Darci, you will be on call 100% of the time. You must be ready for that."

"How does Sashma do it?" I wondered aloud.

"You will learn," responded Chalherine, "and you will do just as fine a job. Perhaps you will also train apprentices at some point."

I flopped back on the bed. I couldn't think of that now.

"Darci needs rest," said Sottrol as he tugged on Chalherine's robe. "Angel, come with us. Regina is waiting for you."

The little one didn't move.

"Come child," Chalherine motioned to her. "Let him rest. You'll be back soon enough."

"Never, ever soon enough," said Angel as she reluctantly climbed off the bed and down the ladder stairs.

Sottrol came close to me. He pulled a crystal from his beard and put it in my hand saying, "Rest well."

∞ ∞ ∞

I awoke with Angel lying next to me, stroking my brow and staring at me. I wrapped my arms around her and hugged her close to me.

"Was it awful, Darci?" she asked in a whisper.

"On Earth?" I queried.

"You looked so tired and forlorn when you returned," she said quietly into my ear. "Whatever happened took its toll on you."

Embracing her warmly, I told her all I had seen, emphasizing how difficult it was to help a human who was closed and unreceptive.

"Please don't let them send me back to Earth until that terrible war is over," pleaded Angel. "I won't go unless I know it's safe."

"I wouldn't let you go," I assured her, gently rocking her.

It was so good to be home. I felt much better now after having rested, but the thought that I had to go back to Earth was scratching at the back of my mind.

"I have something to distract you." I heard Sottrol's voice before I saw him appear in the doorway, "Greetings, Darci. You're looking better. You and Angel are going to attend a problem-solving workshop together. We teachers think that this will benefit you—and you'll enjoy it."

I had been hoping for more time alone with my partner.

Sottrol chuckled as he read my mind and said, "You will have your private time, Darci. Let's get this class underway. I've arranged for an excellent tutor for the two of you. Come into the front room and meet her."

"Come meet me, children," we heard from a booming voice from the sitting room.

We followed the sound to a huge female Spirit Guide. She had a voluminous golden robe and orbs of golden light pulsing from her. On her head was a colorful turban with a shining crystal at the crown, a striking contrast to her dark skin. The sight of her was startling, and Angel let out a little "Oh!"

"Come here, child. I shall not bite you."

Angel stepped forward, and the big Guide hugged her. When she stepped back, she literally bounced. I moved toward the matronly Guide and received my welcoming hug. It was like grasping a giant balloon of love. I instantly felt buoyant.

Sottrol made the introductions.

"Angel, Darci, meet Meerah, your new instructor."

The great woman then transformed herself into a giant sphere of pure golden light, bounced between the floor and ceiling a few times, and then manifested as we had first seen her.

Angel gasped, laughed, and exclaimed, "Wow!"

I had seen both Sottrol and Sashma change forms, so I knew it could be done, but Angel had never experienced it before.

"We're going to have some fun," Meerah grinned. "I'll take it from here, Sottrol. Come, children, let's go to the play room."

Sottrol gave me an amused look as Angel and I followed our massive new teacher. We didn't go far this time, only a few entryways along the same hallway. Although the door looked similar, the room within was nothing like our cozy chamber. This playroom was a large oval dome with a circular screen at one end, numerous floating chairs, cubby holes around the edge, and a large oval work table in the center.

"I don't see any toys," remarked Angel. The thought came to me that she probably didn't have many toys during her last lifetime as the orphan Anthony.

"Dear little one," said Meerah, "you shall have toys, but more important, you'll have fun learning with your partner Darci. I'll begin by explaining that this is a class in creative problem-solving. It's mostly for you, Darci, as its completion is a requirement to become a Spirit Guide.

"Angel, this class will benefit you as well, especially since you two will eventually be working together as a team. Darci here has discovered how difficult it is to assist a human. Most Earthlings are totally unaware of the existence of their Guides. Some that have a clue about us shun us. Some even lash out against us because they don't understand that we are there to help them. Only a few on Earth at this time accept and work with their Spirit Guides. We hope you two will change that. Meanwhile, we Guides must devise clever ways of helping."

"Like a sudden splinter or a breeze at just the right moment," I jumped in, remembering the two incidents.

"Yes, we Guides must be inventive, always looking for ways to keep our human charges on the most appropriate path."

"I won't need to use tricks with Angel. She'll know about me once she's back on Earth."

"Yes, Darci, she will at some point. There will be many years during which you must guide her and protect her before she comes to spirit consciousness. You will find that the lessons I bring you in this class will come in very handy, I assure you. Let's make ourselves comfortable."

The big radiant Guide pointed to the floating oval chairs.

Angel and I seated ourselves. Meerah continued to float, touching down every once in a while very lightly and gracefully like a soap bubble ready to land.

"First of all, this is a class in a very specific type of problem-solving. Let me show you a picture."

Our new teacher held her hand out toward us, and a card appeared between her fingers. She then explained, "This is from the major arcana of the Tarot, a deck of cards used on Earth for problem-solving. Look closely; tell me what you see."

I examined the card. Before I had a chance to respond, Angel said, "I see a man, a woman, and an angel."

"What else? Be specific."

"The man is looking at the woman," I said, glancing at Angel, "and the woman is looking up at the angel."

"Yes. Good," said Meerah. "As you can see, this card is called 'The Lovers.' The man represents the conscious mind, the woman represents the subconscious mind, and the angel represents the super conscious—or connection to Spirit. This Tarot card shows the state in which humans have operated since the beginning of their existence. Only the subconscious mind has linked humans with Spirit and with a spirit perspective. The conscious mind has to go through the subconscious, which, of course, includes instincts and intuition in order to receive information and guidance from Spirit. It has almost always worked this way since the beginnings of humanity."

Angel looked a little puzzled, so I tried to clarify by explaining, "In other words, humans receive help from their Spirit Guides through their gut feelings."

"Yes, and sometimes their dreams," added Meerah. "This is the basis of the class. How do you as a Spirit Guide get information and assistance to a human by using this indirect method? Darci, you have been in the field as an apprentice. What did you observe?"

"The human we were trying to help didn't have any idea we were there. Oh, once after he had wept, we sent him much energy, and he mentioned angels. Mostly I found he was closed and difficult to reach."

"Many humans are so caught up in the daily demands of life on Earth that they don't consider how much more may lie beyond the material plane. This course is a requirement because you need to learn how to devise inventive indirect ways to help your assigned human."

Angel piped up, "It would be so much easier if Darci and I could just talk—as we do now." Her directness and innocence were endearing.

413

"Of course," laughed Meerah as she bounced twice in front of us. "Here's the good news. If all goes well, you two will show humans that this can be done. That's right. You, Darci, and you, Angel, will make the link between the human conscious mind and the great super conscious. You will be able to talk directly through the barrier between worlds, and you will show others how to do this. The time is right to manifest the connection that completes the triangle."

She showed us the card again, and I saw what she meant. If I drew a line from the man to the woman, then from the woman up to the angel overhead, the third side of the triangle would be a line between the angel and the man. I reached out and drew on the card with my finger so Angel could see. She nodded to indicate she understood.

Meerah was a jolly teacher. When we grasped this concept, she celebrated by literally bouncing between the floor and the ceiling. Angel laughed at the sight, and I grinned. This class was just what I needed after my grim experience back on Earth. Meerah then landed in front of us.

"You two will have to learn to work without that link in order to activate it later. Darci, during the years that Angel is growing up as well during as many of her adult years, you will have to help her in the same way Spirit Guides have assisted humans for centuries—through her subconscious. Angel will reach a certain point in her life on Earth when you as her Spirit Guide can make the connection to her conscious mind."

"And we'll be able to talk and do stuff like we do now," chimed in Angel.

Meerah laughed heartily and said, "Yes, little one. In order to get to that point, you need this class."

Our teacher finally sat in one of the oval chairs facing us and continued, "Tell me, Darci, as an apprentice, how did you help the human in the situation you were given?"

"I am one of Sashma's apprentices. We mostly used visualizations, sending different colored energy into the young man we were trying to guide."

"Did it help?"

"A little, I think. I did wonder if there was another way to help him."

"That's what this class is about—coming up with as many ways as possible to indirectly assist humans. We're going to have fun with it. After all, this is a playroom." Our teacher then turned her gaze to Angel and asked her, "Would you like a toy, my dear?"

Angel's violet eyes brightened as she responded with her eyes glowing like a child's on Christmas morning, "Oh yes, certainly!"

Meerah reached behind her and produced a box about the size of a large melon. She handed it to Angel who accepted it eagerly. My mate looked at me, then at our teacher, then at the box and asked, "May I?"

Meerah nodded. I watched Angel's face as she lifted the lid. Her expression went from radiant anticipation to surprise to bewilderment.

"What is it?" she asked.

"What does it look like?"

"I don't know—a bunch of slimy strings. Oh! I thought I saw one move!"

"It's a game. Go on and dump it on the floor," said Meerah. "I will show you how to play."

Angel tipped the box and poured out a mass of shiny different colored strings. Meerah rolled forward out of her floating seat and knelt on the floor next to the bright tangled pile.

"Come, Angel. Let me show you."

Angel looked at me, then climbed down and knelt next to the teacher.

"The object of the game is to make a big circle with these pieces. However, some of the colors won't stay next to other colors."

She touched a yellow string, and it jumped, and so did Angel.

"It's alive!" she exclaimed.

"Yes, this game is animated. Now watch. I put the end of the yellow string next to the end of this orange one, and they coexist nicely. But when I put it next to this purple string . . ."

As our teacher tried to put the yellow and the purple strings together end-to-end, the yellow string slithered up her arm like a snake. The purple string stood vertically and looked like a stick. I was fascinated, and Angel was enraptured.

"So I have to figure out which strings to place together to form a circle on the floor?" Angel asked.

"Yes, and there is only one possible combination. As you try to find the correct order, the strings themselves will let you know how you are doing. Darci, your job is to help her without any direct communication. Have fun!"

Meerah then peeled off the yellow string and added it to the pile.

I watched Angel timidly reach out for a blue string and lay it on the floor. She took the yellow piece and tried to lay it end-to-end with the blue, but it leapt away and wound itself around Angel's wrist.

"Oh!" she said with surprise. "It feels slimy and warm."

"The animated strings won't hurt you," Meerah assured her, "but they may frustrate you, and if they tie you up before you figure out the correct order, then the strings win the game."

"And I lose."

"Go on. Give it a try. Darci, help her."

The thought came to me that the logical order of the colored strings would be in rainbow form. I wondered how to get that idea to my mate. Meanwhile, Angel tried to lay an emerald-colored string next to the blue one, and this time the blue string jumped away and wrapped around her ankle. Next, she placed the emerald string with the yellow-green, and they melded into one long piece.

"I think I got one!" Angel laughed.

"Yes, little one. Very good," Meerah confirmed, smiling.

"You'll find that each time two strings combine, you will be able to remove a string that has wrapped itself around you."

Angel tried several other combinations that didn't work, and I became concerned because she had strings wound around both her arms and legs. Another addition might begin to constrict her movement, which would give the strings a distinct advantage. I heard Meerah's voice in my head encouraging me to help Angel. I didn't know what to do. I had to be inventive, and I had to work fast because an orange string just tied Angel's feet together.

"This is odd," Angel said as she scooted on her knees to pick up a turquoise-colored string. She successfully united that piece with the other end of the emerald string, and I knew that my rainbow theory was probably right. I needed to find a way to tell Angel before her hands became tied. I felt in my pocket for one of the crystals Sottrol had given me. I held it out in front of me and visualized a stream of white light moving through it. In an instant, there was a little rainbow pattern on the floor beside Angel. It caught her attention.

"Oh look! How pretty," she said, pointing to it. Then she looked at me. I knew I couldn't say anything, but I couldn't help smiling at her. She glanced back and forth between the rainbow pattern on the floor and me with the crystal. Then she laughed.

"I get it!" she said gleefully.

She then went about connecting the strings in order of their rainbow colors, unwinding them from her arms and legs as she successfully completed the circle. Once she had placed the last piece, the circle lit up and rotated around her.

Overjoyed, she grinned and said, "That was fun!"

"Very good, you two," Meerah said as she moved over to hug me.

She then joined Angel inside the rotating multi-colored hoop and hugged her. I watched in awe as the large golden teacher took Angel in her arms and bounced up and down lightly, buoyantly. Angel giggled, then laughed aloud.

417

I was glad to see her enjoying herself.

Meerah had more to teach us. We settled back into our floating seats.

"Attention," said our teacher. "It's all about attention and inattention. Darci, as you go about watching over Angel once she is back on Earth as a human, you must be able to get her attention and turn it towards what is important. For example, if she is walking in the woods, and there is a big hole in the ground ahead of her, you will want to find a way to turn her aside from the route or call her attention to the hole, so that she will not injure herself. There are all sorts of things you can use to get her attention—or in some cases distract her."

Angel patted my arm and said, "He can say 'Hey, there's a big hole ahead. Watch out!'"

I smiled and our jolly teacher laughed.

"Eventually you will be able to hear Darci speak to you telepathically. However, we have to get you safely through the years before you have direct communication with him. Suppose you are only four years old when you take this potentially dangerous walk. How would Darci keep you from stepping into that deep hole?" She then looked back and forth between the two of us.

"What do I have to work with, Meerah? Can I cause a branch to fall and cover the hole? Can Spirit Guides do that?"

"Good question, Darci. As you know, those of us in spirit form are made up of energy. The Earth plane is also made of energy, but it is crystallized into carbon-based forms. Those in Spirit can affect the physical world, but not easily. It takes focus, and it requires that energy be expended. Your example of the tree branch is a good one. If there was a branch that was already broken and only needed dislodging, then this might be possible. It would be more difficult, however, for a Spirit to break off a fresh green bough. Think of it this way: the denser the object, the harder it will be to move. That's why Spirit Guides often use the breeze or the wind."

"I don't think a breeze would keep Angel from stepping into that hole. What else could I use to distract her?"

"Of course, you will have to take each circumstance separately, but let's say she is only four years old. You could get her attention with a bird, a butterfly, or perhaps a squirrel. She might see one of these and walk towards it, changing her direction."

"Can Darci talk to the butterflies?" Angel asked.

I was wondering how I might get a squirrel to go where I wanted.

"Birds, animals, even insects are aware of those in Spirit. They can see Spirit Guides; they can hear Spirit Guides," said our teacher.

"And humans can't?" Angel was incredulous.

"Most cannot, but you and Darci can change that. In fact, that is part of your mission. Now back to our hypothetical scene in the woods. Darci, you can easily flush out a partridge that would make her jump and perhaps alter her path—or you can shoo a squirrel so she would change direction to follow it. As you can see, you must be ready to improvise because humans change their minds, change direction, and make all sorts of unexpected choices. You have to be instantly inventive, coming up with ways to help your assigned human—in this case Angel."

"This sounds quite challenging," I remarked.

"Oh yes," Meerah grinned. "Being a Spirit Guide is a tremendous challenge. You are up to it. I know you are, Darci. You have much to work with. Not only will the birds and animals cooperate, but also you have the Nature Spirits who will gladly lend you a hand."

"Nature Spirits?" I wasn't sure what she meant.

"You met Chilliwon Mac, did you not? His home is in a glen in Scotland. The elves, gnomes, and fairies are your allies on Earth, Darci, though sometimes you may need to help them, too."

"I'd like to meet a fairy," said Angel who was now very interested in the conversation.

Meerah put her hand on Angel's head and replied, "Yes, little one. You shall. You have already met a few elves."

"At the implantation ceremony," I interjected. "They hopped around on the musical panels and played a song."

"Remember, you cannot move much physically without exhausting yourself. It takes a great expenditure of energy for a Spirit to move something physical, so we teachers do not recommend that approach. Instead, use other tools. You'll get the hang of it, Darci. Let's try another game, shall we?"

"Yes!" came Angel's instant response, and I nodded.

Meerah floated to the wall of cubby holes as the colored strings separated and wriggled back into their box. Our teacher reached into two different cubby holes at once and pulled out two white satchels. She handed one to Angel and one to me. My mate, eager to play, opened hers as soon as she had it in her hands.

"Let's move to the table," suggested Meerah as Angel poked around in her bag. "Empty your satchel here, my dear."

I moved to the table, too, and watched as Angel spread out the contents: a piece of rolled up fabric, some colored sticks, and a bowl.

"Unroll the map and put the bowl in the center," instructed Meerah.

"Now Darci, empty the contents of your bag on this end of the table." In my sack were four cups, a directional compass, and a crystal sphere.

"All right Darci, place your cups on the four corners of the map. Angel, you cannot touch these. Only Darci may touch them or move them. The object of this game is to get the sphere from the cup to the bowl in the center. Go ahead and put the sphere into one of the cups, Darci; it doesn't matter which one. Good.

"Now, Angel, use the colored sticks to make a pathway between the cup in the corner and the bowl in the center.

"You must follow the routes on the map."

"It's a labyrinth," I noted, looking at the complex map. "What is the compass for?"

"On Earth, a compass is used to show direction. The compass in this game will tell you, Darci, when it is time to move the sphere to a different cup. Angel will then have to start over. There are only so many sticks, and only one route that will work. You two must find it with no direct communication. Do you understand?"

"I just lay out these sticks, right?" asked Angel. "And I can pick them up and move them?"

"Oh yes. You'll find you have to. Now begin."

I studied the map as Angel began laying the sticks. They were of different lengths as well as different colors so she could fit them on the twisting turning paths on the map. I checked the compass in my hand, and it was pointing to the cup that held the sphere. The map was complex. Angel ran into a dead end and had to pick up half the sticks. As soon as she got the sticks going on a new path, I felt the compass vibrate in my hand, looked, and saw it pointing to the cup opposite where the sphere was located, so I moved the sphere. Angel had to start over again.

I wondered how I could help her. The routes were so complex that no solution was obvious to me—even from my higher vantage point overlooking the map.

This time, Angel ran out of sticks before she reached the bowl in the center. She had to find a more direct route. I saw a shortcut she could take, but I didn't know how to point it out. Just as she was laying a stick perpendicular to this shorter way, I blew across the map and rolled the stick towards the shorter route. Angel picked up the stick to put it back and spied the short cut; she then laid the sticks in that direction. Before she could complete that route, the compass vibrated, indicating I should move the sphere to another cup.

We played this game for quite a while. Angel was beginning to get frustrated because every time she would get her sticks close to the center, she'd either hit a dead end, or I would change the location of the sphere, and she'd have to start over.

Then I had an idea. Perhaps she should start at the center. Then when I moved the sphere, she would not necessarily have to pick up all her sticks. How could I tell her? I tried illuminating the bowl in the center by visualizing white light pouring into it, but Angel was so caught up in laying the sticks that she didn't notice. Next I tried blowing the sticks toward the center.

At first Angel got upset, but then she stopped for a moment, looked at Meerah and asked, "Can I lay the sticks from the center to the corner?"

Meerah nodded and Angel smiled. "I'll get this yet," she said with a determined look on her face.

It took several more rounds of the game with me moving the sphere from cup to cup. Finally the sphere was in the corner where Angel could put the shortcut I had shown her to use. She quickly completed the path between the bowl in the center and the cup with the sphere. To our surprise, the sticks lit up and the sphere popped out of the cup, rolled along the trail of lighted sticks, jumped into the bowl, and glowed brightly.

"That was hard—but it was fun, too," said Angel, who now looked a little tired.

"I think you two will do fine," said Meerah as she put the cups back into one of the satchels.

"Can you find your way back to your chamber? You've earned a rest period."

We thanked our teacher and returned to our suite. I was so glad to be alone with Angel that I asked for privacy as soon as we stepped through the door. Tired though she was, Angel began kissing me as soon as I said those magic words. Her kisses were playful and light. Soon, however, our interaction deepened into a passionate exchange of vibrant love energy.

Our trust in each other had grown, and so had our knowledge of each other's Souls.

∞   ∞   ∞

As Angel slept, I lay contemplating what it would be like once she was on Earth immersed in human form. Surely she would be easier to reach than Frederic had been. Certainly she would respond to my spirit touch as she did now. I realized that there were no guarantees, and that once Angel reincarnated on Earth, she might choose to ignore me. I trembled with something like a shiver. How could she possibly disregard the deep love I would pour over her daily? No, no, I was sure we would connect. I would be inventive. I would find creative ways to show her my love. I relaxed and joined Angel in sleep.

The next thing I knew, I heard Sottrol saying, "Darci, Darci, it's time to go back."

I felt his hand on my shoulder. My mentor was floating next to me. He looked translucent and glowed brighter than usual.

"Go back?" I questioned, confused. Did he mean the class?"

"To Earth, Darci. Sashma has asked that you return right away."

"He wants me? Now?"

"Oh yes. I'll give you a moment to tell Angel. Soon Jono will be by to escort you."

With those words, he glided backwards and vanished. Sparkles hung in the air where he had been.

I turned to Angel. She looked peaceful, almost joyful in sleep. I truly didn't want to wake her, but I didn't want Jono to come for me before I had a chance to tell her. I kissed her brow, her eyes, her nose. She moved her hand as if she were shooing away an insect.

"Angel," I whispered, "do you want to play a game?" Her eyes blinked open. "Can you guess what happens next?"

"That's the game?" she asked sleepily. "I don't know. We ask for privacy, and then we make love floating around the room?"

"That's your favorite, isn't it?"

"You're my magic carpet of love, Darci."

"I wish we had time for that, but we don't. Sashma has summoned me. The next thing that happens is . . . I hold you and say good bye. I'm going back to Earth."

"But you only just returned to me—to the Spirit Guide plane. Surely you don't have to go so soon. Oh Darci!"

She threw her arms around me and pressed herself against me asking, "Can I come with you?"

"Now Angel, you wouldn't want that. Earth is no place for you now. We decided to wait until the war is over, didn't we?"

She nodded and gave a big sigh. We held each other in silence until we heard a knock at the entry. One last embrace, and I rose to join Jono in the front room. He wore a very serious expression.

"Ready, Darci? We need to get ourselves back as soon as possible."

"Right then. Let's go."

We glided quickly through the maze of hallways to the port I now recognized as leading to the Earth plane. The great corridor was packed with Souls traveling back from Earth. This passageway seemed darker, and there were disquieting sounds, moans, and cries for help. I felt compassion for these Souls in transition and wished I could help them in some way, but we were traveling far too quickly. It took all my focus to keep up with Jono.

Flying through an archway into a bank of clouds, everything was dark. After a while, I caught a glimpse of the night sky, a half-moon just rising. Soon we were lowering ourselves over the prisoner-of-war camp in Northern Germany where I had last left Sashma.

Moonlight filtered through the bars of the cell where Frederic and his fellow prisoners were housed. Jono and I joined Sashma, as he and the other Spirit Guides were hard at work bringing relief to the captured men. The Master Teacher nodded, acknowledging our arrival, and went on with the healing. I hovered in an upper corner of the cell and observed.

Sashma was floating directly over the sleeping Frederic, pouring streams of pink and gold light into his mid-section. I looked around at the other Guides. One prisoner was awake, sitting with his arms around his knees. His Guide, an American Indian female, was hugging him from behind. I watched one very tall guide in a blue robe toss spheres of golden light into the head of a sleeping prisoner.

Jono was still beside me, observing also. He, too, noticed the activity of the tall Guide and whispered to me, "That Guide is sending dreams to his human. Each sphere of light contains a dream image."

Sashma joined us. Crann also appeared.

"I want the four of us to work on Frederic together," said the teacher. "Jono on the left side, Crann on the right. Darci, you are at the feet, and I'll be at his head. Let's take our positions."

Once we did so, Sashma immediately began sending energy through the top of Frederic's head. I could see sparks of white as he poured the light into the sleeping man. I wasn't sure what to do, so followed my instincts. I remembered my time as a healer in Egypt, standing at the feet of many a patient, so I placed my hands around Frederic's arches. I sensed a tiny amount of energy dribbling through. Then Jono began sending golden light through the sleeping man's left hand and arm. I felt a bit more energy coming through. Sashma nodded at Crann, and he began sending emerald green light through Frederic's right hand and arm. I sensed a slight energetic increase.

Sashma said, "Now!"

The three of them breathed deeply and increased the flow through the sleeping human. I *felt* rather than *heard* a pop, and a deluge of smoky gray energy flooded into my hands and arms. I began trembling but did not let go of Frederic's feet. Suddenly I felt dizzy, queasy, and a sharp pain passed through me and down my right leg.

"Breathe, Darci!" I heard Sashma's voice in my head. "Let Frederic's refuse pass through you and out. Don't block it! Let it go!"

I took a deep breath and then another, trying to flush out the murky energy that was flowing in through my hands from the prisoner. It took a while, but at last I began receiving energy from the other three Guides through the body of the captured young man. It was an exhausting experience.

We finished this four-way healing just as dawn broke. Only moments afterward, guards brought two loaves of bread and a tray with a pitcher and two tin cups. One guard used a cup to bang on the bars and rouse the men. The other unlocked the door long enough to shove the food and drink into the cell.

"Ick! Goat's milk again," complained one of the men as he sniffed the contents of the pitcher. "Why don't the Germans feed us any of their famous beer?"

Regardless of this prisoner's tastes, several of the others took turns drinking the milk. All pulled hunks of bread off the two loaves. Frederic was one of the last to take any food. He had lost weight since I had seen him. His complexion was very pale and had a yellow tint to it.

Sashma came to my side and asked, "Are you all right, Darci? Sorry to put you to work like that as soon as you arrived, but we needed to heal Frederic in that four-way formation. He is very ill. He has infection in his blood and inflammation of his liver, which are weakening him day by day. I fear he may not live to see another full moon."

"This is serious," I said to Sashma as I studied the boy. He was sitting, his head hanging down, slowly chewing a piece of bread.

His eyes were sunken, and he had a scraggly, spotty growth of beard.

"The conditions here are poor," Sashma told his apprentices. "Frederic and many of his mates need medical attention."

Having just come from the class on creative problem-solving, I wondered if there was a way to get these men the help they needed.

"Do you want to find a way to end this war, Darci?" asked Sashma jokingly.

"Can we at least get Frederic into the infirmary?"

"You and Crann, go take a look. It's on the other side of this camp," Sashma said, pointing with his chin.

I was glad to leave the overcrowded cell. Crann and I floated through the camp. There were rows of buildings that housed the captured men, then barracks for the German soldiers, and then finally a large house for the officers. The infirmary was a small building next to the cooks' tent on the other side of this house. Crann went right through the door without opening it, so I followed him. This phenomenon amazed me—on Earth I could pass through ceilings, walls, and doors!

Inside the infirmary there were a dozen beds, all full. Most of the men in them were sleeping. Many had their Spirit Guides sitting on the beds with them. A guard and a doctor were talking in a small room that served as an office off the main area. The doctor was remarking that he could fill these cots three times over with prisoners who needed medical attention.

"Maybe we can get the doctor to visit the prisoners," I suggested to Crann.

"Look at him, Darci. He doesn't want to be here at all, let alone traipse into each cell block. There's enough work here for half a dozen doctors."

"There's got to be a way."

I zoomed in closer and saw that his first name was Frederick. I wondered how I could use that to get him to treat our charge Frederic.

At that moment a German commander, an officer, and two German soldiers entered the office. The doctor and the guard both saluted the commander. He had brought the officer in for treatment.

"We need more beds," said the doctor. "We're full right now."

The commander motioned to the two men. They went into the next room, and two shots rang out.

"There," he said. "Now you have room for my officer, and you have another bed free as well."

There were scuffing sounds as the soldiers dragged out the bodies wrapped in blood-spotted sheets. The guard went to remake the cots, and as the commander looked on, the doctor attended to the officer. The man had a fever and a rash.

Of course, the Spirit Guides for all these men were nearby. I was particularly interested in the doctor's Guide. She was a Medicine Woman who appeared as an elder in ceremonial dress. I watched her move near to the doctor as he examined the patient. She stood behind him with her spirit hands on his head. The officer's Guide, a monk, was standing behind him also. The two Spirit Guides formed a golden-green energy field around the two men until a diagnosis was made.

"Bed rest for this man. This ointment may relieve the itching from the rash," said the doctor.

The guard helped the ailing officer into the next room with the commander close behind.

The doctor sat with his head in his hands, mumbling to himself, "I am here to save lives. I will not have my patients shot."

I watched the Medicine Woman put her spirit arms around the doctor as if to comfort him. With Crann right behind me, I approached the elder female Spirit Guide.

"Grandmother," I began respectfully, "I am Darci Stillwater, an apprentice. This is Crann. We observed you helping this human doctor."

"Yes. Greetings," said the medicine woman. She still had one hand on the doctor's bowed head.

"I heard him say he is here to save lives. I know of a life he can save this very day," I said.

"Someone you watch over?"

"Yes. He needs medical treatment. He will not last another week without help. His name is Frederic, too."

"I recognize you now," said the elder Guide. "You were a healer in Egypt. I walked the Earth plane as a human then. In fact, I was one of the children you helped."

"Grandmother, can we work together?" I asked.

She turned to Crann and said, "You are an apprentice, too. I can tell. Come. Put your hand on the doctor's head. Focus here." She pointed to the spot between his eyes. "Radiate soothing blue-green light. He has a headache."

Crann stepped over to do what she asked.

"Now you—Stillwater—show me to your Frederic."

We glided swiftly across the camp to the cell block on the far side where Frederic was being held. It did not take long for the Medicine Woman to see that the young man was extremely ill. Sashma greeted her with a bow.

"You have a very sick boy here," said the elder. "Have you been giving him energy healings?"

"Yes," replied Sashma. "I have three apprentices with me, so we did a four-way healing not long ago. He needs medical help, too."

"That's why your apprentice brought me. The doctor for this camp is my assigned human. He is having a tough day. Helping this young man might improve his mood."

I could see that Sashma was pleased by her words. "There are so many men that need attention," he remarked. "I can understand why your doctor is overwhelmed."

"Nonetheless, let's see if we can get this poor boy some help," said the Medicine Woman as she glided close to Frederic again.

"How do we get the doctor over here to this side of the camp?" I asked.

Then I had an idea and suggested, "Can we plant the thought that a walk in the fresh air might help his headache— and also beam into his mind a picture of this view?" I pointed to the countryside beyond the wire fences.

"Good lad," said the elder. "Smart and inventive. You'll be graduating soon, I can tell. Come with me. We'll try it."

"Once we get him to the outside of this building, we can send him a sign so he knows he should go in," I suggested as we made our way back to the infirmary. "You know this human. What will grab his attention?"

"We'll give him a double flag," she replied. "He won't be able to ignore our signs."

Crann was still attempting to help the doctor who was at his desk eyeing some paperwork. The Medicine Woman wasted no time. She put her spirit hands on the doctor's temples and chanted something in an American Indian tongue. I watched as the doctor took a deep breath, stood, stretched, and walked out the door. He strode slowly at first, then quickened his pace, circling the camp. When he came to the far side, he stopped and looked at the view I had pointed out to the elder. She must have implanted that image in his mind.

I watched carefully as the medicine woman made a motion with her hands and a bird-like sound with her mouth.

She did this several times, then said to me, "The birds, the animals, even the insects can see and hear us. Therefore, they are allies of the Spirit Guides."

A brightly colored bird flew between the doctor and us. It definitely got his attention. He stood watching as it landed in the tree right outside the building where Frederic lay so ill. At just that moment, a fast-moving summer shower passed over.

The doctor moved under the tree for shelter and continued to enjoy observing the colorful bird.

What happened next astounded me and made me realize how powerful the elder Guide was. Rain had wet the side of the stone building making a giant letter F right under the window of Frederic's cell. The bird then flew over and sat on the sill of that window.

"Spectacular!" I complimented.

The doctor saw the signs. His walk had made him more alert, so he saw the double flag, as the elder put it. He went around to the door and entered the cell block. On the inside of the door was a list of the prisoners. Scanning it, he used his finger to keep his place, then stepped over to the bars of the one large cell and said in a very official voice, "Frederic Marton!"

Frederic, who was sitting under the window, looked up, said nothing, and dropped his head.

I saw one of the Spirit Guides blow on the face of a prisoner, and that prisoner pointed to Frederic saying, "Ici."

The doctor motioned for the guard to open the cell door. He glanced around at the other men, then walked directly to Frederic, lifted the boy's chin, looked in his eyes, and ordered that he be escorted to the infirmary. The guard called in another soldier, and the two Germans lifted Frederic up, literally dragging his weak body out the door. As the doctor followed, a few of the other prisoners called out to him.

He turned at the doorway and said in French, "I will return here tomorrow and do what I can for you."

The Medicine Woman Guide, Sashma, two Guides I hadn't met, the other two apprentices and I all floated along behind the Germans and Frederic.

"What made you come in and get the boy?" I heard the guard ask the doctor. "You haven't been over here in weeks."

The doctor smiled a half-smile and replied, "A little bird in a rain shower."

As he examined Frederic, we five Spirits formed a circle around the two humans. We followed Sashma's lead and visualized a sphere of golden-green light around doctor and patient. I was next to the Medicine Woman Spirit Guide, so I asked her how she knew what signs to use to get the doctor's attention.

"I know him well," said the elder. "Not only have I watched over him since he was born, but we shared several Earth lives before I moved on to become a Spirit Guide. That particular bird is his favorite and will always draw his attention. Also, when he was a boy he used to spend summers at a lake. He'd write his initials with water on the dock there. I knew he would notice the F on the wall of the building. The two flags together were powerful signs for this human."

"Not every human notices signs and heeds them," I commented, remembering how difficult Frederic was to reach.

"True. The more connected humans are with their Spirit Guides, the easier it is to get information across. This human and I were close in three lifetimes that were significant to both of us. He senses my presence. He knows he is watched over. I often help him when he is diagnosing patients."

Sashma, who was on the other side of the elder, nodded as she said this. He added, "The key is knowing your assigned humans, then being creative in finding ways to guide them."

I took a deep breath and thought, "If all works out as planned, and I become Angel's Spirit Guide, then I am fortunate. We know each other well."

Once Frederic was resting on a cot in the infirmary, and the doctor and his talented Guide were checking other patients, Sashma, Crann, Jono, and I did another four-way healing on the young soldier. Again I took the anchor position at his feet. I noticed a difference already. Frederic had been given some medication, and it was moving quickly through his system. I made sure to flush out my own energy field after the healing was completed. The four of us hovered over the boy's bed.

"We accomplished much today," said Sashma.

"Indeed, we have saved this young man's life. Darci, you have done especially well. You took the initiative, came up with a plan, and followed through. We can sometimes although not every time involve the Guide of another human as we did here today. You will learn how to evaluate each situation and gauge whether other Guides at the scene can help you."

The Spirit Guide teacher looked at each of us, nodded with a smile of satisfaction, and then said, "I'm sending you three back to take your final exams. I will say 'good luck'; however, I know you will do well."

We thanked Sashma, and Jono led the way back to the Spirit Guide plane. As we three glided above the prisoner-of-war camp, three trucks carrying German soldiers and more prisoners arrived. Rising higher over the Earth, I saw a rainbow in the distance and wondered if it was a sign for us to take heart, for the war would soon be over.

On this return trip, Jono and Crann gave me more detailed instructions on how to find the route between Earth and the Spirit Guide plane. Once we passed through the now familiar portal, Sottrol, Chalherine, and two other Guides greeted us.

"Welcome home, Darci," Sottrol said as he hugged me and patted my back. "So you are ready to take your finals, eh?"

"I guess so. I'd like to rest first," I replied, realizing how fatigued I felt.

Chalherine hugged me and said, smiling, "You're a fine student, Darci. Of course, you may rest and visit with Angel. She has a surprise that she is very excited to show you."

I went directly to my chamber accompanied by my two mentors. As I stepped through the doorway, I was taken aback at what I saw. The sitting room was covered with paintings, and there on the floor sat Angel working on another. When she saw us, she jumped up and threw her arms around me.

"Darci, hooray! You're home!"

"What's all this, Angel?" I asked gesturing to the artwork with a sweeping motion. "Did you paint all these?"

"Oh, Darci, I've never had such fun! Regina is a good instructor. She gave me magic paints."

"Magic paints?"

I began examining the paintings one by one. The colors were vivid, some sparkled, some glowed, and a few actually swirled right on the canvas. Angel had painted many Earth-related pictures, lots of flowers, trees, hillsides, clouds and such. There was a series of the cat and also some very unusual landscapes that were definitely not Earth. I was fascinated.

"These are great!" I exclaimed, hugging her.

"I like them, too," said Sottrol.

"You've done very well, little one," remarked Chalherine as she took Angel's hands. "This talent for painting is something you can take with you when you return to Earth."

"That's wonderful," I said as I hugged Angel from behind.

She was beaming as she said, "When Chalherine told me you were coming home, I wanted to paint a special welcome back picture." Pointing to the painting on the floor, she continued, "It's almost done."

I stepped over to have a look. It was a portrait of the two of us. She had captured my likeness well, especially my eyes. In the picture we were standing side by side, arms linked, but she had not yet finished painting herself.

"Self-portraits are hard," she said. "I guess I'm not sure what I look like now. There are no mirrors around this place."

Sottrol and Chalherine laughed. The Chancellor floated over to the painting on the floor and picked up a bowl of sparkling paint. I moved closer to observe. She dipped four fingers into the paint and flicked them at the unfinished painting on the floor. Angel gasped, and I smiled, captivated, as we watched the shimmering paint literally twirl off her fingers onto the picture forming a very fine portrait of Angel. The most amazing feature of this now completed painting was the radiance around us in the picture; it actually glowed.

"There won't be paints like this on Earth," Angel remarked.

"I bet I spend my whole life trying to find a way to paint light."

"Then Darci will help you," said Sottrol as he moved closer to view the painting. "Very nice. You do good work, Angel. You, too, Chancellor." My mentor then turned to me and said, "Rest is what you need now, Darci. As you recuperate and regain your energy, review all you have learned both here at the university and in your apprenticeship. The final exams are very thorough. Only those who are truly ready will be allowed to move on to become Spirit Guides."

The two teachers departed soon afterward.

Angel took great delight in showing me every painting and telling me the what, how, and why of each one.

I picked up the portrait of the two of us and suggested, "Let's hang this in the bedroom."

As soon as we found a place for it, I asked for privacy. I knew that tired though I was, sharing love energy with my dear mate would help revitalize me and would settle me down after my experiences on Earth. We took our time. We were getting more familiar with what we could do to please each other while in spirit form. Angel loved lying on top of me as I floated gently around the room. She stretched out her arms on my arms, her legs on my legs, and relaxed. Our hearts connected, and waves of love rolled through us. I loved her so much.

Chapter Twelve:
Finally My Finals

Because my early classes at the Spirit Guide University included tests and exams, I was not surprised to be faced with a set of final examinations. After my period of rest and review, I met with Sottrol.

"These are not like any exams you may remember from your days on Earth," my mentor told me. "There will be some written tests, yes—and some oral. The element of surprise plays an important part in these finals. As a Spirit Guide, you will have to constantly deal with surprises because the humans you watch over have free will. Believe me, humans can catch you off guard, so you must be ready and able to handle that. Chalherine and I think you will do quite well. You may even pass the first time. Any questions?"

"How long are these final exams?"

"They are quite extensive. You will take them in stages with rest periods between."

Chalherine manifested near the ceiling of the sitting room and floated down so that she hovered right before me. Her presence was powerful. I had enormous respect for both her and Sottrol.

"You have great compassion and love in your heart, Darci," she began. "Let your instincts assist you as you make your way through the series of tests."

"Focus," Sottrol jumped in with more advice. "Focus and breathe. You will do fine."

My thoughts went to Angel and her activities while I was occupied with these exams. As usual, my two teachers read my thoughts.

"Change is here for Angel, too," Chalherine addressed my unspoken query. "She will begin preparations for her return to Earth."

"What does that entail?" I asked aloud.

"She will undergo a thorough review of her karma," Sottrol responded. "Then she will choose specific areas of learning that she will address once she is reincarnated on Earth. We sincerely hope that by the time she reaches this point, you will be available to help her with her choices. Then she will select her parents. As her Spirit Guide, you can assist her with all of this."

"However, you must first pass the exams," Chalherine interjected. "Is Angel asleep?"

"Yes," I nodded. "She's in the spherical bedroom with the cat."

"Why don't you take Darci to his first round of tests?" Chalherine suggested to Sottrol. "I'll stay here and inform Angel of your whereabouts and of her changing situation."

I had a feeling in my stomach that was similar to what I experienced as a boy standing on a cliff about to jump into a quarry of deep, cold water. It was a strange mix of anticipation and apprehension.

Following Sottrol out of the entry, we climbed up several stories to an area of the university that was entirely unfamiliar to me though my mentor appeared to know it well. We glided through an oval tunnel with glowing walls into a great hall with a very high ceiling and rows of huge columns on one side. Between the columns were doorways of different shapes and sizes. In front of each door was a Spirit Guide at a table with a book. Sottrol moved all the way to the right and approached the Guide at that entrance.

"Exam time again, eh Durcal?"

"Sottrol, greetings! I see you've brought a candidate. Has he completed his apprenticeship?"

"Yes, he has. This is Darcimon Stillwater. I know he is allowed to skip the first two doors because he has served his full term as an apprentice, but I want him to take the entire slate of exams. It will do him good."

"As you say," Durcal responded as he opened the book and turned it towards me. "Place one hand on each page and state your name."

I followed his instructions. When I lifted my hands, I saw they had left imprints that not only glowed; they had moving swirls and waves within them.

"The process of examining your abilities has begun. You may enter."

The Guide stood aside and indicated that I should climb the seven steps and enter the arched door behind him. Sottrol put his arm around me and gave an encouraging squeeze. I took one step forward, heard a tinkling sound, and turned to see that Sottrol had vanished. Two more steps and the doorway itself began to glow. Another two steps and the door opened. I could see nothing but black within. One more step put me directly in front of the entrance.

I took a deep breath and stepped through. The door closed behind me, and I was in darkness. Standing very still, I took a moment to pray to the Creator for help and guidance on my path.

After a few moments, I dared to move forward even though I could see nothing. I remembered the times I had done this and fallen, but that did not happen. Instead, a dim pathway became visible, so I took another step. There was a flash of light illuminating the inside of what appeared to be a cave.

In that brief flash, I also saw two huddled figures on the far side of the cavern. I turned and took a step toward them. To my surprise when I did this, a dim light shone on them. I stepped closer and the light brightened so I could see it was a man and a woman, holding a baby. Once I took another step, I could hear them. The woman who held the child was weeping and the man was trying to comfort her. The baby had just died.

"My little bambino," the woman sobbed. "The light of my life has gone out. I want to die, too."

"Hush, now," said the man. "Hush. You couldn't have known he would react this way to the medicine you gave him."

"We're not sure that's what took his life!" his wife shouted.

"What else could it have been? All he had was a cough and a fever. You gave him that potion you concocted, and two hours later he's dead. Yes, I'd say somehow that medicine contributed to his death," the husband retorted.

"Then it's my fault? Is that what you are saying? Our son would be alive if it weren't for me?" she asked.

"What's done is done," he said.

"How can you be so unfeeling? Our baby is dead! Oh no! I did it! I'm a killer. I just want to die!" the woman cried, clutching the child to her, bent over, and wailing.

The man threw his hands up in the air and walked away.

My test was to help them. I could see this was a good basic exam. Spirit Guides are called on often to help humans deal with death. This death was particularly devastating not only because it was a baby but also because both the man and the woman thought that she had brought it on. Here was a combination of guilt and grief.

I began by radiating love and compassion to the pair. This did seem to quiet the woman's crying a bit. I wasn't sure what to do next, as the two were now separated. The man was closer to me, so I approached him. He couldn't see me, but I could see his energy field, what there was of it. Grief and blame had reduced his aura to an egg-shaped glow in his mid-section.

I thought, therefore, a logical place to start was to try to remind him of the love he had for his wife. Standing behind him, I placed my spirit hand on his heart and breathed deeply, projecting loving images of the woman. His heart opened a little, and he turned back towards his wife. She was still in a crumpled heap. I floated behind her and put my hands on her back. Her energy was very dark. I radiated as much love and compassion as I could muster to the grieving mother.

Then I had an idea. I sent the picture of the little baby as a tiny luminous angel, putting the image first in the mother's mind by placing my hands on her head and projecting. In the image, the baby was alive, happy, and glowing with beautiful little white wings on his shoulders. I heard the woman sigh deeply, and knew the vision brought her some comfort. Then I went back to the man and tried to project the same picture to him, but he was strangely resistant. He was still struggling with the dual images of his wife, one as a loving mother and the other as the agent of the child's death.

He then surprised me by doing an unlikely thing. He rushed to his wife's side and snatched the lifeless baby from her. She began crying again, shaking her head. Now the man had the child, so I tried again to project the angel image to him. He didn't receive it at first, but when he looked into the face of the baby, I saw his expression change. He saw the little one as an angel.

"This child is with the angels," he spoke aloud though he didn't seem to be addressing his wife. "He's all right. He's with the angels."

"I saw that, too!" exclaimed the woman.

She reached out to her husband, and he came close again. I was glad. It was easier for me to help them if they were together. Radiating another round of deep compassion and love to them, I sent another picture. It was time for them to bury the child. The image I projected was of a beautiful ceremony with flowers, candles, and angels singing.

"Let's have a special service for our child," said the man.

"I was seeing just such a ceremony," the wife replied. They hugged, and the scene faded into darkness. My first exam was over.

∞ ∞ ∞

The path back to the entry glowed with a soft golden light. When I walked out and down the steps, Durcal greeted me with a smile.

"You are a natural, Mr. Stillwater. I see why Sottrol has taken such an interest in you.

"How are you feeling? Do you have enough energy to take the second round of finals?"

"I believe I do," I answered, remembering Sottrol's remark that I could have officially skipped the first two tests.

"Very well. Step to the next portal, and good luck to you."

I thanked Durcal and moved to the next table. There stood an elder. She was dressed as a nun, but her habit was rose-colored and so was the glow around her. She greeted me by extending her hands.

I grasped them and introduced myself, "I am Darcimon Stillwater."

"Sottrol spoke to me about you. Pleased to meet you. I am Sister Nina Rose. Please place your hands on the pages of the book."

When I did as she asked, my hands made bright multi-colored prints on the two pages.

"You may enter the portal for exam two," announced the elder.

I climbed the steps to the door between the columns. This entrance was a wide oval that was so low that I had to duck down to enter. Once I stepped through, a panel slid across the entry, and I was again in darkness. This time I smelled incense. I took two careful steps. A pathway glowed dimly beneath my feet, so I continued to move slowly forward. Soon I heard soft music played on a lute. Another step on the path seemed to trigger a beam of light, which illuminated two figures reclining at the back of this cave-like room.

I approached them. The young woman was reclining on her back, the man on his side. He fondled her hair and her ear as they talked. One more step and I was close enough to hear them.

"You love me, don't you?" asked the man.

"Yes," came the response from the young woman. I was near enough to see that her face was flushed.

"Then let me show you my love," said the man, who then kissed her neck and unbuttoned her blouse in one coordinated movement.

"I'm not sure," she replied, grasping his hand.

"It's meant to be," said he swinging himself on top of her and kissing her even more fervently.

I moved closer to assess the situation. The woman seemed to relax as he kissed her. He was gentle and loving. I wasn't sure what this test was about.

The woman sighed a little as he kissed her eyes.

"That's right," said the man. "Enjoy it."

His next moves were so swift and deft that I was sure he had done this many times before. He pulled her blouse open then shoved his hands under her skirt. In that instant, her privacy was doubly invaded.

"No!" she reacted. "Stop!"

Her protests seemed to change him from a loving suitor to an attacker. He was sitting on her legs with his hands still under her skirt.

"Why should I stop when you are so ready for me?" he nearly shouted.

As he removed his belt, I tried to decide what to do. I had witnessed rape scenes before. They were tricky. Emotions always ran high.

The woman's face was now scarlet, and she looked terrified as she called out, "Please, please—no! I've never . . . No one has ever . . ."

Floating to the woman, I put my hands on her head to try to calm her, but when the man used his belt to tie her hands, I changed my focus. I tried to think of what might deter or distract this rapist and immediately sent compassion to both of them. The woman then began weeping, and the man softened for a moment.

"Don't cry," he told her. "It's my love you'll feel. It's a beautiful thing."

"Not this way," she sobbed.

She struggled, but he had her pinned down. Her resistance seemed to excite him.

Since I was in spirit form, I couldn't physically stop him. He seemed so focused, so intent on violating her. Working quickly because he was unbuttoning his pants, I tried to bombard his mind with images that might distract him. He seemed pleased to show the woman how ready he was to enter her.

Her eyes grew wide, and she continued to plead with him, "Please—no!"

I tried sending an image of this woman pregnant by him. He literally salivated.

"If you have my child, you are mine. I will own you!" he crowed, moving over her.

I wasn't doing well at all. That image of pregnancy had the reverse effect. She struggled enough to make it difficult for him to continue. This bought me a few moments.

Searching for something that would reach this man even in his highly excited state, I had an idea and asked to be shown an image of his mother. A picture of a frail kindly woman came to me, and I projected that image as strongly as I could into the mind of the attacker. He paused and looked up. That instant was all I needed. I sent him a steady stream of compassion loaded with images of his mother. Included were scenarios of his childhood interaction with her. He sat back on his heels and blinked, looking disoriented and confused. He had lost the edge of fiery excitement and smoothed down the woman's skirt.

"I'm sorry I got so carried away," he said softly. "My passion and love for you got the best of me for a moment. Are you all right?"

He undid the belt around her wrists and extended his hand to her. She was trembling as she tried to button her blouse. Once he had helped her sit up and refastened his pants, I knew my second exam was over. The light illuminating this couple dimmed, and the path back to the entryway was lighted.

Sister Nina Rose greeted me just on the other side of the oval door.

"Very good, Darci," she nodded at me. "You were able to think fast and change your course of action when what you tried didn't work. This is very important for a Spirit Guide to be able to do. You cannot always predict how a human will react. You must be prepared to change strategies as you did in this exam. Also, you called on the Spirit Guide plane for assistance. It's obvious you have spent time in the field and have a grasp on how we Guides work."

"I was Sashma's apprentice for a while," I replied, glad to know I had done well. "I helped Sashma prevent a rape while I was studying with him. The conditions were similar."

"Congratulations on the successful completion of Final Exam Two. Do you wish to rest? You have this opportunity between each exam."

I took a deep breath.

"I'll go on," I decided. "I have the energy for another test. May I move ahead?"

"Please do. Step to the next table. It was a pleasure meeting you, Mr. Stillwater."

I bowed to the elder and moved to the third table.

∞　∞　∞

I was taken aback because the Being standing there was grotesque-looking. He wore a cloak with a hood, but I could see his gnarled warty hands and face.

"Do not look so startled," said the Being in a deep husky voice. "I appear this way for a reason—well, two reasons actually."

Looking at me closely as if he were choosing his explanation according to my appearance, he continued, "If my countenance is unsettling, that is as it should be. The exams become more difficult with this doorway. We Guides wouldn't want you students to become too complacent. Also, I am royalty among the gnomes where my good looks are appreciated."

I smiled and nodded at the Guide.

"Place your hands, palms down, one on each page of this open book," he instructed.

I jumped a little when there was a sizzling sound and my palms seemed to burn holes in the pages. When I lifted my hands, my prints were illuminated and glowed with a bright magenta light.

"You may step through the entry and begin exam three at any time," he informed me.

I took a moment to breathe deeply and center myself. Each stair lit up as I stepped on it. I had the sense that I was getting to the heart of the exams now. This entry was diamond-shaped with a curtain draped in it. Once I pushed aside the curtain and stepped through, I stood in darkness. There was an overwhelming smell, and it was not pleasant. I recognized the odor from my last Earth life. I had gone to London with my father, and we had become lost. Our carriage happened into a run-down section of the city where residents threw garbage into the streets. It was the foul odor of rot.

Stepping forward as I had done before, I squashed something with my foot. I tried not to be put off by this, for I knew I was being tested. At this point, my path became dimly visible though it appeared bumpy and strewn with garbage. Another step released a particularly rotten odor, but I moved forward. This path seemed longer than the other two. It took a curve to the right. Once around the corner, the tunnel-like hallway opened into a cavern with a trickling waterfall, stalactites, stalagmites, and some crystal formations. At first I saw no signs of life, but as I made my way through the grotto, I heard a whimpering sound.

Gliding quickly around a boulder, I found a woman lying by the underground stream. She was very pregnant. A child sleeping by her looked about eight or nine years old. She was obviously uncomfortable and very close to giving birth. Their situation reminded me of the lifetime in Central America when Nunzah gave birth in a cave while we were on the run. I knew I could help these two through the birth if that's what this test was about. I had done it before; however, this time, I would be assisting from the spirit side.

The woman moaned, and the child shifted his sleeping position.

"That's right. You sleep now, little Jared," she said soothingly. "There won't be much rest for you once the baby decides to come." She clasped her hand to her stomach and groaned louder. "That may happen sooner than we thought."

She pushed herself up into a squatting position, then crawled to the stream for a drink. After washing her face, hands, and arms, she clutched her belly again.

"You are going to make your entrance soon," she spoke to the child in her womb with a grimace on her face. She then shuddered and fell back into a sitting position.

I moved closer and saw that her tunic was soaked from the thighs down. She was ready to give birth.

There was nothing in this cavern except the water. At least when Nunzah gave birth, three of us were present to help her. I felt much compassion for this woman on her own in a rocky, unfriendly environment with only a child and me to assist her. At least the garbage was not strewn around the cavern as it had been on my way in. Still, the sleeping child was streaked with dirt and the woman wasn't much cleaner. I was glad she had washed her face and hands.

I sent her an image of her and the boy bathing in the underground stream. She crawled along the stream until the brook dipped into a pool, swung her legs over and lowered herself in.

"Jared!" she called to the boy. "Come join Mom for a wash. Jared!"

The boy sat up quickly as though he were accustomed to being on alert and saw his mother waving for him to come to her. He rose sleepily and went to the little pool.

"Thank goodness we found this safe spot," she said, extending her hand towards him. "There's room for you. Come, get in and clean off all that dirt and stink."

As he joined her in the pool, she turned away so that he could not see her face contort in pain. I knew she was beginning to have contractions.

After removing the boy's tattered clothes, she washed him. He helped a little. She sat in the pool with her wet tunic plastered on her big belly.

"Can you help me bring this baby into the world?" she asked him softly. "Please, Jared. You're all I have. We are safe here. You needn't worry about the invaders. No one will find us."

"I'll try, Mama," said the boy slicking back his wet hair. "Will the baby come soon?"

Another contraction gave him his answer.

Once it had passed, the woman said, "Find the sharpest cutting stone you can and wash it in the stream."

She pulled herself out of the water. I recognized the look in her eyes. She was in birth mode. I wondered what else I could do to help her.

The boy eventually returned with a palm-sized cutting rock, which he washed thoroughly in the pool. His mother cried out as another contraction rolled through her body.

"Mama!" the boy shouted in concern.

"It's all right. It's just the baby knocking on the door."

"Tell it not to knock so hard," he said with an authoritative tone.

She laughed and then groaned with another contraction. The boy looked frightened.

I floated near them and whispered, "It's natural. It's a natural process. Trust nature." I was hoping that at least their subconscious minds could hear my words.

"Don't worry, Jared," said his mother. "It was like this when you were born, except I was in a proper bed. Can you do as I tell you? You'll have to help. I can't do this on my own."

"I'll try, Mama. I'm scared."

"I know." She groaned again. "Come sit here."

She opened her legs and had the child sit between them and explained, "Your new baby brother or sister will come through this door."

She pointed.

The boy seemed puzzled and frightened as he answered, "That doesn't look like a door."

"You watch. It will open. You'll see the baby's head . . ." Her sentence was interrupted by another moan.

The two of them seemed to be doing fine on their own. What was my test? I positioned myself behind the boy in order to give him guidance and support.

"How long before the door opens, Mama? I'm frightened."

For the first time, she didn't answer. She was focused on contractions and breathing heavily.

"It's natural. It's all natural," I repeated in the boy's ear. "It's how you were born. It's how all Earth babies are born."

The woman gasped, shuddered, took a deep breath and groaned.

The boy was trembling as he cried out, "Mama, Mama! Don't die! Please!"

I held his shoulders and sent compassion to them both. As I beamed a calming blue-green ray of light to the boy's spine and heart, his panic seemed to subside. I wished I could make them both more comfortable. The rocky floor of a cavern was no place to give birth to a child.

The birth was long. I had to steady the boy each time his mother cried out as her contractions came closer. Finally, I saw the head of the baby crown. I took the boy's face in my spirit hands and directed his gaze at the arriving baby. The mother was breathless and unable to instruct him. I sent an image of him taking his clothes, rinsing them, and placing them down for the baby. He did this quickly, as the clothes were nearby and so was the stream.

The woman was perspiring heavily now, struggling with each contraction. I showed young Jared an image of wiping his mother's brow. He used his wet shirt to do that, then returned to receiver position. His eyes popped wide as the head of the baby emerged.

"It's slimy and bloody!" he cried.

I whispered in his ear, "That's good. That's natural. That's how babies come."

He straightened the wet clothing on the ground and told his mother, "Okay. I'm ready. Let the baby come through the door."

Exhausted, his mother was near passing out. Tired before she began labor, the woman was now spent. This was the crucial time when she had to push, but it seemed she had no strength left.

"Come on, Mama. I'm ready!"

But she just lay there weak and weeping. The boy, sensing his mother's situation, became even more frightened.

Abandoning his post, he threw his arms around her neck and sobbed, "Don't die! Don't die!"

I had to act fast. This birth had to happen now or they were all in trouble. Coming closer to the boy, I sent him a vivid picture of stroking his mother's belly. He began doing this immediately.

I said into his ear, "The baby's almost here. Push! Push!"

He repeated these words to his mother who continued to be unresponsive. I moved quickly around to her and poured brilliant golden light through the top of her head. I saw her quiver and then take a deep breath. Next, I rose above her and radiated more deep gold energy into her heart and belly as the boy stroked her stomach and continued to urge her to push.

"It's almost here, Mama. The baby is almost here. Push it out! Push!"

I visualized little flames of orange in the stream of light I was projecting into her. Her eyes seemed to focus and a determined look came onto her face. She took a big breath and bore down. The boy barely had time to step around her leg and prepare to catch the child. It took her only two good strong pushes to move the baby out, then she dropped back, thoroughly exhausted.

"Make sure it can breathe," she said in a weak voice. "Clean its face."

Jared used his wet shirt to wipe the baby's face, but suddenly dropped the cloth when he saw the umbilical cord.

"What's that?" He pointed to it with a grimace on his face. "It looks like a bloody snake—and—and it's coming right out of you!"

The woman was too fatigued to give him much of an explanation. She lifted her head a little and said, "Use the sharp rock and cut the cord." Then she flopped down.

I was very moved as I watched this young boy holding his newborn sister.

He reached for the stone, raised it, and then put it down.

"Where do I cut? There's so much slime and blood. Mama, are you sure you're okay?"

"Yes. Cut it there, near the baby. Is it breathing?"

"Yes, Mama. I have a sister."

He sat down, still holding the babe, and let the cord touch the rocky cavern floor, then used his stone tool to cut it. I put the three in a sphere of brilliant pink love light. The boy brought his baby sister to his mother. She put one arm around him and held the baby with the other.

"Good work, son," she smiled. The baby made a gurgling sound. "Your sister thinks you did a fine job, too. Go wash up."

Jared went to the pool to wash off the birth fluid and blood. I continued to keep the three of them in the sphere of love energy by expanding the orb. The mother looked peaceful and happy as she introduced the child to her breast, and her daughter began to nurse. I wondered if my exam was over now. The crisis here was past and all seemed to be well.

Then we all heard scuffling noises coming from the garbage strewn path. Next the sounds of low gruff voices were audible. Terror contorted the woman's face, and tired though she was, she pulled herself and her newborn behind the bolder. She made a low whistling sound as a signal to Jared. The boy, still dripping from his wash in the pool, hurried to join his mother.

This was all too familiar. I expected to see Meletmuc and his warriors march into the cavern and wondered if all Spirit Guide trainees had to face this scenario. Gliding out of the cavern and retracing my steps, I came upon a gang of men. There were about a dozen, dirty and rough-looking. Most were bearded, though there were a few too young to have full beards. Each was holding a sharpened stick. As they moved along the dim passageway, they poked at the pieces of rotting garbage. One man even tried eating something he had speared, but he spit it out.

I could see they were desperate for food, and I knew my test was to protect the mother and her two children from this hungry gang. My best course of action was to distract them. I couldn't let them get as far as the underground stream, or they would surely discover the three innocents.

Since my suggestions had worked so well with the mother and boy, I moved close to the leader and whispered, "There's nothing here—nothing to eat—no reason to go any further."

Just as I projected this thought to him, another man spoke up, "People have been here. It must lead somewhere."

The leader grunted and continued.

I had to work fast. I had to give them a reason to turn around. I prayed; I asked to be shown a way. Just as I did so, I heard a rustling above me and saw doves nesting on a rocky crag. Remembering the lessons with Meerah, I rose to the nest and showed the birds what I wished them to do simply by picturing it. There were six or seven fat doves, and their wings whistled as they flew over the heads of the men and away from the cavern. The men immediately turned and pursued them.

"I'm not sharing my bird with anyone," I heard one shout, and they were gone.

As I was sending thanks and protective light to the birds, the diamond-shaped doorway appeared before me, and I knew this exam was over. I stepped through, and the Lord of the Gnomes greeted me.

"You found the short cut in that exam," he told me. "Very good. You've learned your lessons well. This exam often takes students three times as long."

"Was the short cut getting the men to follow the birds?"

"Yes, for once the men enter the cavern, the test becomes very difficult. You needn't concern yourself with Final Exam Three any further. Would you like a rest period now?"

"I believe I would like a break. How many exams are there?"

"That depends entirely upon your performance."

∞ ∞ ∞

"There you are, Darci," I heard Sottrol's voice behind me. "I guess I should have known you'd fly through these first three exams. Ready for a rest?"

"Yes, Sottrol."

"Follow me. Your timing is excellent. Your partner could use some support."

"Angel? What has happened?" I asked as we glided out of the hall of columns.

"She's been reviewing her past lives and her tangled web of karma, and is understandably overwhelmed."

"How can I help?"

"Listen to her, comfort her, and love her. She is in a unique situation. She knows you. She is experiencing the high vibrations of the Spirit Guide plane. It is difficult for her to accept that she cannot stay here—that she is a temporary guest—that she must immerse herself in the troubles of the lower spiral of life once again."

"There's no way she can stay here?"

"She must earn the opportunity to become a Spirit Guide just as you did. She still has Earth karma to resolve. Remind her that you are going to be her Spirit Guide and that you will be helping her from this side."

I found Angel in our chamber curled up on the sleeping platform with the cat in her arms. She looked so sad; my heart went out to her. I joined her on the bed and positioned myself so I could look into her eyes.

"Hello, Darci. I'm glad you're back. Sorry I'm so blue. I didn't give you a proper welcome," she said quietly.

"No matter. I'm here now. You can tell me what's troubling you."

"It's me." She spoke louder. "I'm troubling me. Chalherine has been helping me review my past lives—and my choices haven't always been wise. Darci—I fear I don't deserve you."

"That's nonsense, Angel. We're a couple. We're a team. The very fact that you must return to Earth to balance your karma has made us the perfect couple for the mission."

"I nearly forgot about the mission. I've been too caught up in my personal lessons, I guess."

"What did you learn?" I asked.

"I received all the gory details of my life as Gabriel. There were other lifetimes, too—ones without you. It's all so complex."

"You'll work through it all. I'll help you—you know that."

She looked at me with those stunning violet eyes, and compassion automatically welled inside me and flowed to her.

"I got to thinking that I am beyond help," she sighed.

"You know that's not true. Come, Angel. You know every Soul has the opportunity to learn, to grow, to evolve."

"It seems like a long, tough road. How did you rise above it?"

"By doing what you are doing. By paying attention to the lessons that my Soul had to learn and learning them. Angel—

I'll be with you through this next Earth life. I'll be there to guide you. Surely you can take comfort in that."

"If you knew, if you only knew what I've done . . ."

"I love you. None of that matters. I love you, and I know of plenty of good choices you have made. Every time you chose to marry me was a good choice."

Angel laughed a little. I was getting through to her. I held her close to me and rocked her gently, feeling her despair slowly subside. I hummed the hymn that was sung at our implantation ceremony, and she began to look decidedly more peaceful. We fell asleep in each other's arms and rested long. For a while, we were in our own private world.

That was my only respite, for Sottrol returned to fetch me not long after I awoke. Angel and I were talking about using the two meditation alcoves when Sottrol materialized sitting on the ladder.

"Refreshed and ready for more tests?" the elder asked me. "You have momentum now, Darci. Best not to lose it."

Angel and I looked at each other. Our time together was never long enough.

"Angel, my dear," Sottrol said as he floated over to us, "Darci will return soon. Do something for me, will you? As you review your past experiences and your resulting karma, remember where you are now. Not many become honored guests on the Spirit Guide plane as you have—and remember that you are here not by accident but by design."

"I'm here because of Darci," said Angel, pushing me playfully.

"Yes, dear, it's true we need a couple for the mission. A couple means two. You could say Darci is here because of you."

"We're here because of our bond," I interjected. "We're partners. One of us has to go back to Earth as a human, and ..."

"Angel, that's you," Sottrol broke in. "You must have some unfinished Earth karma in order to merit being reincarnated in a human body. Besides, Darci will need something to do as your Spirit Guide. You must have some challenges to address."

Angel rolled her eyes and replied, "Challenges? Oh, Sottrol, you should see the mess I've made of things . . ."

"I know, I know, child," the elder said, lovingly putting his arm around Angel. "It is difficult to look at your mistakes, especially from the spirit level. Just remember, despite the inappropriate choices you have made, you also have much to recommend you for this mission with Darci. Take heart. You can change everything for yourself with this next Earth lifetime."

"I'll do it, too," said Angel with a determined look on her face.

"Come now, Darci. It's time for you to go to the examination area."

I gave a quick goodbye hug to Angel and followed Sottrol out the door.

∞ ∞ ∞

Since the exams were given on an upper level of the complex university, I needed to be led to that unfamiliar area. Once in the great hall, I headed toward the base of columns four and five where my next exam was to be given.

Sottrol grabbed my arm, saying, "Just a moment, oh anxious one. I have something to give you that may help you as the exams increase in difficulty."

The wizard reached up as if he were going to stroke his beard and pulled a white feather out of nowhere, and explained, "This swan feather is small but powerful. Put it in the left pocket of your robe and use it when you need to move energy."

My puzzled look must have prompted him to explain further.

"Sometimes the best way to help is to move out negative energy. For instance, back there with Angel. She had just reviewed her harmful choices.

"This procedure caused her to generate negative energy."

"That's understandable," I spoke up. "Condensing lifetimes of mistakes into one review session can be depressing."

"It took you a while to lift her spirits, and you did it by talking to her, showing your support and your love. Suppose the situations were similar to the way it is with most humans and their Spirit Guides. Suppose she could not hear you or see you. How, then, could you help move away the negativity?"

"With this feather?"

"It is one tool—and a very useful one. Let me show you." Sottrol then made swift sweeping motions with the feather, first around my head, then my torso, then my legs and feet.

"Simple and effective," said my mentor when he was done. "The swan feather may be small, but it is a powerful tool when used as I have just shown you. It is yours to keep."

"Thank you, Sottrol."

"Go now. Step up to the table and sign in for Final Exam Four. Your skills will be truly tested."

The cloaked figure by the table at the fourth portal was very tall, nearly a giant. I noticed several books on this table; the largest lay open. As I stepped up, the giant Guide turned towards me, and I beheld a truly unique Being. His skin was lavender and his nose was the shape of a bird's beak. His eyes were set on the side of his head, also like a bird's. He had no facial hair, nor could I see any hair under the hood of his burgundy-colored robe. I bowed.

"Yes, yes, step forward. If you would be so kind as to sign the register for exam number four."

This time, I took the quill pen that lay on the table and actually signed my name. I noticed that Jono had been the last one to sign before me. The Guide checked my signature. "Darcimon Stillwater, please take the pen and the exam book and enter."

Although the book looked substantial, it was actually quite light when I picked it up. I stood before the arched doorway.

The door simply disappeared, then reappeared after I stepped over the threshold.

I had entered a room that looked like a monk's cell. There was a small table and chair. Light came from two windows high in one wall. I seated myself and opened the book. Words were written in brilliant purple. Page one contained instructions. I was informed that the exam had eight sections; I was to do one at a time. As I finished each, I was told to pull that section out of the book and drop it through the evaluation slot. I looked around. I didn't see such a slot, so I read on. The instructions said that each section would test me differently and that the ink in the inexhaustible pen would change color accordingly.

The first section was filled with a series of questions to which I answered yes or no. The ink in my pen appeared dark blue as I wrote. There were about one hundred questions that tested my knowledge of the differences between the Earth plane and the Spirit Guide plane. When I had made my way through this section, I looked up and noticed that a large gold-trimmed slot had appeared under one of the windows. Following the instructions, I tore out the completed section of the exam and slid it through the slot. There was no going back with these tests.

Next came questions with multiple answers. I was to select the most appropriate response. The ink flowed green as I marked my choices. This section dealt with differences between the human body and the spirit body, and when I had completed it, once again tore it out of the book and fed it through the slot.

Section three was on healing the human body. There were diagrams on which I had to indicate where as a Spirit Guide I would position myself in order to facilitate optimum healing. Then I had to choose a procedure for healing. The scenarios became more complex as I made my way through this part of the exam. The ink flowed with a burnt orange color. I went back over this section several times before I tore it from the book and slid it through the slot.

Section four was on karma, and I was required to write short statements. This time, the ink flowed silver as I wrote my answers. The exam was definitely becoming more difficult. I thought that some of the questions on this karma section could have been answered in several ways, and I did add that observation to my remarks before I deposited this section in the slot.

Part five dealt with interpreting death and birth imprints. The first half showed the imprints, and I had to write essays on what these pictures indicated. The second half gave descriptions of the births and deaths, and I was to describe the resulting imprint. My pen wrote in bright indigo as I tackled this part. I was getting tired now, so when I finally tore that section from the book, I took some time to breathe deeply and stretch.

The sixth section was all about energy, energy fields, and auras. There were numerous illustrations in this part of the exam. The questions concerned everything from analyzing the energy fields pictured on the pages to describing how I might visualize and project energy in order to help a human being. The ink was magenta.

Section seven tested my knowledge of the various planes of existence. I must admit that I guessed at a number of the questions, as I was unfamiliar with some of the levels. I had only vague knowledge of the levels above the Spirit Guide plane. However, I thoroughly answered the questions about Earth and its interconnected levels. One entire section of this part was devoted to nature beings, the elves in particular. The ink was purple as I wrote my answers.

I sighed as I looked at the last part of this extremely lengthy exam. It was the longest section. Twelve scenarios were described, and I had to write an essay on each one. This part tested how I would choose to act given a certain set of circumstances. The scenes ranged from a battlefield to a political banquet, to a birth scene, to a death scene, to a family crisis, to a brutal murder. One was on poverty, another on debauchery. My pen wrote with glowing golden ink as I described in detail how I, as a Spirit Guide, would act to help the humans involved in each scene. It was exhausting work, and by the time I had written my last sentence, I barely had the energy to go back through my essays though I had double-checked every other section of the exam. I slowly read through all my writing and called it finished.

The instant I dropped the final section of this extremely lengthy exam into the gold-trimmed slot, the door to the exam room opened. I stepped through to find both Chalherine and Sottrol talking with the giant Guide. The three of them turned to me as I walked down the steps.

Sottrol spoke first, "There you are, Darci. We were just remarking that you are one of the most thorough students we know. How many times did you go over all the parts of that exam? Never mind, it's done now, and I'll wager you'd like a rest break."

"Yes, please. When will I know if I passed?"

Chalherine approached me, responding, "There is no failing here. You simply retake any sections that you did not do well. Sometimes we offer further instruction before you retest."

She hugged me—her hugs were always wonderful.

Sottrol put his arm around me, assuring me, "I have no doubt you have done quite well. Most students have to redo each step at least once. You flew through exams one, two, and three. You're our star pupil."

"He is driven," said the giant Guide.

"Yes," agreed Chalherine. "Between the mission and Angel, he has much to inspire him."

"May I rest now?" I asked, feeling fatigue set in. I had been focusing on the exam for so long that I felt depleted and a little disoriented.

"I'll take you back," offered Sottrol.

We moved quickly through the complex maze of hallways this time with no conversation. At the doorway of my chamber, I asked my mentor how far I was through the final exams. In my mind, I could see the rows of columns in the examination area extending on and on. If each of those columns was a portal to an exam, I had only begun. Sottrol, of course, saw the image in my mind and knew my thoughts.

"Darci, every student is different. Every series of final exams varies with the student taking them. I will know how you are doing once I get the results of the written exam you just took. Go on and rest now. I'll be back."

∞   ∞   ∞

This time, I found Angel in one of the two meditation alcoves. Rather than disturb her, I sat in the other one across from her. The meditation did help revive me. As I was lifting out of a deep meditative state, I felt a warm, tingling sensation engulfing my spirit body and realized Angel was sending me love. The concave shape of the alcove was amplifying the energy as she sent it to me. I opened myself and drank it in. My entire spirit body began vibrating. My heart burst open, and a flood of love poured out and across to Angel. I heard her exclaim as the wave of love energy filled her alcove. I began looping the stream so that it entered at the base of her spine, spiraled up and out the top of her head, then returned to me at the base of my spine. Angel picked up my lead right away, pulling the stream of energy up my spine, out the top of my head, and back to her. We rode this figure eight pattern for a while until we were both vibrating with intense love energy and the alcoves were glowing with a bright pink light.

"Step out. I want to hold you," I told my mate telepathically.

Watching, I timed my movements to match hers. We met in the middle and embraced. Rings of luminous pink light rotated around us, as we stood there wrapped in each other's arms.

"That was exactly the welcome I needed," I told her as I kissed her between the eyes.

"You were gone so long," she said quietly. "I knew you would be exhausted."

"You are an excellent partner," I replied, hugging her tighter, then sweeping her up in my arms. "Let me fly you to our sleeping platform, my lady."

As I lifted her up and glided into the spherical bedroom, I asked for privacy. We expressed our love for each other with grace and passion.

I rested long. Usually Angel was the one who slept for long periods, but this time I was the one who slumbered. Eventually she stroked my arm and whispered that I should wake because we had a visitor.

I was very surprised to open my eyes and see Hespahba circling the spherical bedroom. The androgynous Guide was amusing Angel by twirling and dancing around the room. Seeing that I was awake, the colorful figure landed gracefully on the sleeping platform. Hespahba then came close to me.

"The news is very good, Darci," said the Guide. "You need further tutoring in only one area. I'm here to begin it."

"The tutoring?" I asked, still sleepy.

"Of course. I am a tutor after all. Here. Put this on and meet me in the front room." He/she handed me a white robe, then flew out the door.

"I've never seen a Guide like that before," remarked Angel. "What will Hespahba teach you?"

"I don't know," I replied, pulling off my purple robe and donning the white one. It was short, ending at my knees. It was sleeveless also, so it looked like a tunic.

I could tell that Angel was about to ask me what was going on so I answered her, "I don't know why I've been asked to wear this or where I'm being taken, but I'll tell you all when I return. And, Angel—I can't wait to come back."

Hespahba was quite talkative as we zipped quickly through the corridors of the university.

"Sottrol is in an important meeting with some Master Guides, so he asked me to fill you in," the Guide began. "First, congratulations are in order. You did very well on all your exams. You will have to retake only one section of exam four. This is very good, Darci. You've done better than most of the students. I'm here to tutor you on the one area where you were found lacking. Then you will retest on this section."

We entered one of the great halls. I wasn't sure if I had been in this grand room before, but Hespahba didn't give me time to ponder. We rose up, up, up, towards the dome ceiling. To my utter amazement, we floated through it and entered an area of blinding white light.

"It will take you a while to adjust," Hespahba told me. "Keep your eyes focused on my blue tunic and stay close."

I could have sworn the Guide was wearing magenta when we began this journey, but I had seen Hespahba change colors before. At one point, I lost the Guide in the blinding brightness. The tutor had to return and grab my arm.

"This way, Darci. You will get used to this level of luminosity. It just takes experiencing it."

After traveling for a while in blinding whiteness, Hespahba sat me in an oversized chair that was white, of course. I was glad to sit still for a few moments. The combination of constant motion and unfamiliar brilliance had made me dizzy.

"Breathe, Darci. Breathe!" prompted Hespahba. "You'll never get through this unless you breathe."

I went back to my very first lesson at Spirit Guide University when I learned to raise my vibration using breath. I took a while using those techniques until I had increased my energy and felt more stable.

"Where are we?" I asked.

"This is the Academy for Angels," came the incredulous response. "You need tutoring on the Hierarchy of Spirit, and this is the best place to receive such information. Are you all right?"

"I think so. What must I learn?"

Magically, a large chart appeared next to me. I blinked. The graphics made no sense.

"The levels of existence above the Spirit Guides plane can only be referenced and referred to generally at the lower levels. We had to journey here in order for me to give you a more detailed picture of the upper levels. This chart gives a brief sketch"

"But—but I don't understand any of it."

"You will. It's important for Spirit Guides to understand the higher levels. You may be called on to work with the Master Guides, the Angels, Archangels, Seraphim, and the like. You must learn their characteristics and their specialties. You must learn how to address them and how to ask them for help. Also, you must learn which to call on for what reason, and if one appears to you, you must know what it means."

Slowly and carefully Hespahba began at the Spirit Guide level and explained how Spirit Guides became Master Guides. He emphasized that the Master Guides were involved in overseeing the lower spirals, including Earth, whereas Spirit Guides did the day-to-day work on these lower levels.

Once my tutor was sure I had grasped this, he went on to explain the different areas at the Academy of Angels and the training each offered. Hespahba talked extensively about refining energy and vibration. I began to get lost when the lecture turned to the higher angelic realms, so my tutor went back over the information. I asked many questions until the strange luminous graph began to make sense to me. This process took quite a while. I wondered if I would really use this information as a Spirit Guide on Earth.

Just at that point in my lesson, I heard a sound. It was a multi-dimensional musical chord unlike any I had ever heard. A glowing presence manifested on the heels of this music. This Being was so large that its head and upper torso were lost in the brilliance above me. I could see hands and a golden cord, which was tied around the waist of this entity.

"Greetings. I've been waiting for you to join us," Hespahba addressed the angel.

My tutor stepped beside me, had me stand, and together we bowed to the great Being.

A voice came from all directions at once. It had such an ethereal timbre and vibration that I could not tell if it was male or female.

"This is the student in question?"

I gulped as Hespahba replied, "Yes, he is being primed for the special mission on Earth. The Master Guide Arcillis, the Chancellor of the University, and his mentor, Sottrol, agreed that this student must acquaint himself with the higher echelons."

"Darcimon Stillwater . . .," The Being spoke, and the atmosphere around us brightened. "Welcome to the third level of Angels. I am your patron on this plane. All is well. I speak for those here on the higher levels. We are pleased that you have agreed to help Earth. There is a turning point coming for this plane of existence. You and your partner will use this opportunity to carry out a mission that has long been planned."

I was in such awe of the splendor of this great entity that I found myself unable to speak.

The resplendent Being continued, "The mission you undertake was conceived at the highest levels and refined by each Angel, each Master Guide as it came through to you. I want you to be aware of the importance of this mission. I want you to have the assurance of the Angels that you and your mate will be aided every step of the way. Pleased to meet you, Mr. Stillwater."

A similar musical chord vibrated around us as the great Being vanished.

"That concludes your lesson," Hespahba said in a manner that seemed a bit too nonchalant.

"Who was that?" I managed to ask though my voice cracked as I did so.

"That great Being is known as Magnia Duria Shellahn Doocan, and that is only one set of names."

My tutor then brought his face very close to mine, and I saw an amused look in his/her eye as he instructed me, "Find your patron on this chart, Darci."

"What? I thought my lesson was over."

"This is a surprise quiz." Hespahba seemed delighted by the prospect.

"You're serious? Well, then . . ."

I examined the complex chart. My tutor did an odd slow-motion cartwheel and then twirled around very quickly, laughing all the while.

"You're teasing me, Hespahba."

"Show me. Show me your patron," the Guide repeated, dancing.

I studied the chart and found the section that represented the third level of Angels. There were no names, only symbols. I ran my hand over these signs, and one of them felt somewhat embossed under my fingers, so I pointed to that symbol and said, "There."

Hespahba broke out into full-blown laughter, slapping me on the back, and replied, "Very good, Darci Stillwater. That is the symbol that this Being, your patron, uses. Well done. Now make a note of the symbol; you may wish to use it in future."

As the colorful Guide did a slow jig suspended a little above me, I felt the symbol again and studied how it looked, trying to commit it to memory. Just when I thought I had done this, the chart disappeared, and my tutor came to my side and linked arms.

"Let's get you back to your chamber. Sottrol is waiting for you with the results of your exams thus far."

I nodded, and we literally flew downward though at times I felt as if I were falling. Hespahba kept a tight hold on me as we traveled.

∞ ∞ ∞

My mentor was waiting in the sitting room. He and Angel were playing a game with floating pinwheels. I suspected the elder was letting Angel win, for she had a ring of these colored pinwheels rotating around her, and Sottrol had only one hovering above his head.

"Ah, Darci, just in time. Angel is about to win this game again," said the elder, greeting me with a smile and a wink.

"Darci, you look brighter!" Angel exclaimed.

"Indeed he does! Darci has absorbed some of the light from the higher echelons. Welcome back."

"Thank you," I responded, not offering more as I was still disoriented from my rapid descent with Hespahba.

Angel hugged me and kissed my chest as that was what was in front of her when she stood before me. I hugged her back.

"Be seated, Darci. We have much to discuss," Sottrol said as he motioned towards one of the seats. "You are a hard worker and a very focused student. You have done extremely well on these exams. You have to retake only the one section of exam four. You just received tutoring on that subject, so you will no doubt fly through that test now." The old wizard chuckled at his pun.

"We in The Elevated Council have reviewed your progress and your exam results," he continued. "We have condensed the rest of your finals into two more exams. Once you complete your retake of that section of exam four, you may move on to one of these mega-finals."

"Is there some reason you have condensed my exams?" I asked, sensing that there was some urgency involved. Sottrol, as always, knew what I was thinking.

"Yes, we want you to finish your finals as soon as possible. The situation on Earth is changing rapidly, and we want you and Angel to be ready to take your positions once the war there is over. Also, Darci, you have done well enough to warrant abbreviating the last of your tests.

Would you like to rest first?"

"May I retake what I need to on exam four right now?"

"Yes, of course. If you're ready, follow me."

"But, Darci . . ." Angel pleaded as she grabbed my hand. "You just got back. Come on and play with me."

Sottrol patted Angel fondly on the head, reassuring her, "He won't be away very long, my dear. If I know Darci, he'll have this test finished quite quickly." The elder turned to me. "Come now, Darci. Let's go."

I followed my mentor back to the exam level of the university and again approached the portal with the giant bird-like Guide. He greeted us with a bow. I signed in as before, and this time was given a much smaller tablet. Even though the entry was the same, the room inside was different. It had a more comfortable floating seat and illuminated walls that gave the exam room a warm glow.

Sottrol was right; I finished the exam quickly. My mentor had waited for me. When I exited from the exam space, he was engaged in a lively conversation with the giant bird-like Guide.

"Oh ho, there we go," said Sottrol when he saw me. "Didn't I say Darci is a fast learner? Done already. Well, leave your tablet here, and let's be off. I want to coach you a bit before you take those last two complex final exams."

I gave my completed test to the giant Guide, we said our good-byes, and then Sottrol took me further down the row of columns.

"Portals seven and eight will hold your last two exams. Much as I'd like to go easy on you, Darci, the Master Guides are insisting on quite a difficult finish. They are looking at the possibility of your working with them on a special project, so they want to make sure you can handle it."

"Another project besides my mission with Angel?"

"An addition to that mission. You will learn all soon enough. I just want to encourage you to be calm and to breathe deeply as you undergo these final tests. The scenarios will be similar to situations you might encounter on Earth. The idea, of course, is so we can see if you are ready to undertake the responsibilities of a Spirit Guide. It can be tough."

"I know. I have a question, Sottrol. When I did the apprenticeship with Sashma, I tired much sooner than he. As you know, I returned to this plane for periods of rest while Sashma kept going and going. How does he do it? How can I maintain that level of activity for such long periods?"

"You are right. Being a Spirit Guide on the Earth plane demands that you be alert and watch over your assigned human often without any rest. Here's the key: once you graduate, your gift is an inexhaustible supply of energy. You will no longer need rest and recuperation. I will caution that you are not there yet and that these next two final exams may tire you so let me take you back to your chamber. Use this break to meditate, center yourself, and gather your strength. You will need it."

∞ ∞ ∞

I was glad to find Angel asleep when we returned. Sottrol hugged me good-bye, and I joined Angel in repose. Later, the cat woke us both by walking on us and purring. Angel opened her eyes. When she saw me, happiness spread over her face. She hugged the cat and me. We rocked back and forth with the cat between us until he wriggled free, and we were left laughing.

Angel's expression changed. She became serious and said, "I have news, Darci. The world war on Earth is over. Chilliwon Mac visited me while you were gone. He said that the aggressors have surrendered but not before much destruction was released because of a new weapon, a bomb. So I must begin the process of choosing the gifts and challenges I will bring to Earth with me. Soon I will pick my parents, too. Mac says lots of couples are marrying and planning to start families now that the war has ended."

"Things are happening quickly. I still have two exams to take," I told her.

"Yes, I know. I want you involved in all my choices on this side, so I will wait until you're done. Chalherine also stopped in briefly to check on me. She told me timing is very important. The Master Guides want me to return to Earth in the first wave of babies born now that the war is over. She said there would be quite a boom of births on Earth in the near future. I'll be among them."

"It's all happening as our teachers said it would," I mused. "We'll begin our mission soon. It's rather exciting."

"And sad. I've grown to like it here on the Spirit Guide plane. I realize it's not my proper place yet, but perhaps someday it will be."

I held her, tucked her head under my chin, and breathed deeply. We both knew that our separation was inevitable, and although I would remain close to her as her Spirit Guide, she would be trapped inside a human body. It would be many, many Earth years before we could converse as we were doing there on the Spirit Guide plane.

Because of this new information, I opted to take the first of my two remaining finals right away. I wanted to be done so I could assist Angel as she prepared to reincarnate on Earth. All I had to do was think that I was ready to proceed, and Sottrol materialized beside me.

"So you think you want to go now to your exam? Let me caution you. It's better for you to take a little extra time to prepare. You don't want to rush into this next test and end up having to take it over."

"All right, Sottrol. But what do you suggest?"

"Meditation, Darci. Spend some time in the meditation alcoves. Have Angel join you—but try not to get carried away," the elder said with a sparkle in his eyes. "You need to conserve your energy; you need rest. I promise you will have some time with Angel before she leaves for Earth. Right, then.

I'll return in a while after you have meditated and centered yourself. I assure you, Darci, you will be glad you did."

Of course I followed Sottrol's advice. As much as I wanted to put the last two finals behind me, I did not want to have to take them again. Angel needed me as soon as I could finish up my schooling.

My mate was more than happy to take her place in the alcove across from mine and meditate with me. We did a series of breathing exercises, too, which I taught her before we began.

The results were excellent. I strengthened my energy, centered myself, and found a place of inner calm. Angel discovered pure bliss.

The two of us were discussing the experience when Sottrol poked his head around the corner. He had been in the sitting room monitoring us.

"I believe you are ready now, Darci," he nodded and turned to Angel, "Angel, thank you for helping him."

"What did I do?"

"You, my dear, were his anchor, his focus, his sounding board, and his amplifier. We Guides chose well when we picked the two of you for this mission. All right, Darci. Let's get on with it. I'll escort you to portal seven."

I gave Angel a long hug, and off I went with Sottrol in the lead. The trip up to the exam level of the university was becoming more familiar to me, but I still couldn't manage to find the way on my own. Two more journeys to this level, and I hoped I wouldn't have to return.

∞ ∞ ∞

A group of half a dozen Guides clustered at Portal Seven. They were many shapes, sizes, and colors, and all were unfamiliar to me. Sottrol knew them, of course, and greeted each with a bow and a smile.

"Is this the star student we have heard about, Sottrol?" queried an elder Being in a burgundy robe.

471

"Yes, meet Darcimon Stillwater," said Sottrol, extending his arm toward me. I bowed.

The Guides offered various salutations, then stepped aside. An old woman sat by the table with the sign-in book. She was dressed in a blue sari and wore much jewelry. I was fascinated and moved to the table.

"Never mind the baubles. Never mind my appearance," said the elder. "You have work to do. Place your palms here," she instructed, pointing to the open register.

I did so. When my hands touched the pages, there was a rumbling sound, and the table and the book vibrated. I looked back at Sottrol who was chatting with the other Guides. He saw my glance and joined me at the table.

"Remember what I told you, Darci, and trust your instincts. Go to it, now."

My mentor gave me a long, warm hug, and I mounted the steps.

The entry to this portal was elaborate, bedecked and bejeweled just like the elder who sat before it. When I stood in front of this ornate door, nothing happened. I saw no obvious latch or knob. I looked back for help, but all the Guides had vanished, including Sottrol and the old woman. I was on my own.

I took a few moments to breathe and raise my vibration and then had an idea. I spoke aloud, "Please allow me to enter this portal."

The door slid up, and I stepped through.

Unlike the other exams, the room I entered was brightly lit and lavishly decorated. If I hadn't known better, I would have thought I was walking into a palace. There was no one around, so I began exploring. I had just begun climbing the regal staircase when I heard sounds coming from the floor above. It was almost as though my step upon the stair triggered the activity.

Voices seemed to be arguing, so I followed the sound. Once on the second floor, I listened and heard the raised voices coming from a room further down a giant hallway. As I walked toward the altercation, I noticed huge paintings—some portraits, some landscapes, all hanging on the walls.

I entered the room with the loud voices. A man and a woman were dressed in sleeping garb standing on either side of an unmade bed and arguing.

"Your duty is to provide an heir! That is the long and the short of it!" shouted the heavyset man with mutton-chop whiskers. He wore a dark blue velvet robe with a gold monogram on it.

"You know nothing about nature or about how a woman's body works!" she replied, wiping tears from her face. Her white nightgown was spotted with blood below the waist. "Leave me be. I cannot conceive now."

"May a thunderbolt strike you if you be lying to me, woman! My advisor says coupling every night for a fortnight will produce an heir, so let's get on with it."

"No! I'm in no condition," she sobbed.

"Blast! I'm the one who does all the work. All you have to do is lie down!"

"Stop! It's not that easy for me."

Stomping around, he grabbed her long hair with one hand, snapping her head back and shouted, "You do as I say, woman, or you will cease to exist! Have I made myself clear?"

She shoved him, shouting back, "Get away from me. You smell terrible!"

"The choice is not yours to make," said the big man as he shoved her, using his superior strength to force her onto the bed. He climbed on top of her as he loosened the tie to his robe.

"This is useless!" the woman cried. "Leave me be. You won't get what you want now."

She resisted, struggling and kicking. One thrash of her knee caught the man in his most vulnerable spot, and he yelled loudly. His face became very red as he kept her pinned down.

Bringing his face very close to hers, he snarled, "I don't trust you. I've heard of women who cut themselves so they don't have to service their husbands. I know your tricks. You must yield to me!"

This last statement was made in such a booming voice that it rattled the crystal glasses on the bed table. The woman went limp, tears streaming silently from her eyes.

I could see that love and compassion were needed in this scenario, so I surrounded the rich man and his wife with an orb of golden light and radiated as much love and compassion as I could into that visualized sphere. They didn't respond. The woman only cried harder as the man pressed his big belly onto hers and fumbled beneath her nightgown. He must have probed a sensitive place, because the woman let out a wail that equaled his roar. He slapped her so hard her tear-stained face showed the print of his hand.

I looked around quickly for some way to distract the big man. The window was slightly open, so I sent a strong breeze into the room hoping to cool down the situation. The man ignored it, but the woman shivered, then yelped, and then let out a long scream. He slapped her again, then he grabbed her ears and began riding her like a pony.

I felt helpless. The encounter was over before I could come up with any other way to help. The man climbed off the bed, tightened the sash on his robe, and headed for the door.

He turned just as he was about to exit saying, "Twice a day until you bear me an heir. Get used to it."

I heard him lock the door behind him.

The woman stayed there, blood on her nightgown and on the bed. She sobbed quietly. I observed her aura changing quite quickly from gray-blue to red. I repositioned myself so I could see her face, which was tear-streaked and contorted. She was angry. She fed the rage and let it stew in her heart and belly. I watched, as her energy field became a ball of fire. I sent compassion and love to her, but my efforts did nothing to calm her. I sat next to her on the bed, blowing a soft breeze over her and humming a peaceful tune, but she was preoccupied.

I could read her thoughts and realized that my test was not so much stopping the man's treatment of his wife as it was preventing his murder. She lay there concocting all sorts of plots and schemes to take her husband's life. This was a serious test because if she succeeded in killing him, then I would fail. She was extremely determined to exact revenge on this man who kept her locked up and visited her twice a day with the intention of impregnating her.

Because of her limited resources, she finally chose two plans. As she washed in a basin, then changed her nightgown and the bedding, she went over and over the details. I tried to break her thought pattern without success. There was a dark almost black ring of energy around her head, and I was unable to disperse it. This was the first time I had witnessed murder being planned and had observed it manifesting in an aura.

I wasn't doing very well on this exam. I had made no difference so far and my greatest test was to come. Looking around the room for tools I could use to dissuade her from taking this dire action, I saw nothing helpful, only the cord she planned to use to strangle her husband and the scissors she had positioned on the night stand as back-up.

She crawled onto the clean bed and fell asleep on her side. I knew this was my chance to make some inroads and waited until she was sleeping deeply. Remembering what I had seen Manyfeathers do in the orphanage, I clasped my hands and ran my thumbs up the woman's spine. A slight shiver ran through her. I did this several more times until a glow came from the top of her head. Because of the state she was in even while asleep, it was difficult to loosen her Spirit as I had seen Manyfeathers do for young Anthony.

I placed one of my hands on her belly, her solar plexus, and the other on the crown of her head, focusing on her Spirit. I sent love to the Soul buried deep in that tormented woman's body. Something clicked, and I felt a connection with her. I tried running my thumbs up her spine once again, and the glow coming from her crown lengthened and grew brighter. Finally I saw the woman's Spirit hovering above her sleeping form, still attached to her physical body by a thin luminous cord. I moved so that I was directly in front of her spirit body.

"Dear Soul," I began, "I have much love and compassion for you."

"You are my guardian angel come to save me," said the Soul of the sleeping woman.

"I am your Spirit Guide, and I am concerned about what you are planning."

"Help me escape, please. Help me get away from this horrible man."

"I will help you. Please trust me."

"How can you help?"

"By showing you how to use your intelligence, love, and compassion."

The Spirit of the woman rotated and looked away. I shifted my position so I could continue to look into her eyes.

"Stronger methods are needed," said the woman's Spirit, which had lost some of its luminosity.

"I know what you are planning, and murder is not the way."

"It is the only way." The Spirit became dimmer still.

"Use your intelligence. He is much stronger than you, so it may be you who gets hurt in such a struggle. If you do manage to kill him, then you will have to pay the price and probably go to prison."

"This is a prison! A prison without that beast would be better than this!"

"So you say. Have you considered other means to free yourself from this situation?"

"What other means? The man is my husband though our families arranged the marriage. He has every right to expect me to bear him an heir."

"But he has no right to brutalize, threaten, and restrain you. If he were kind and loving, would you cooperate and attempt to conceive?"

"Kind? Gentle? Him? He is obnoxious, rude, vulgar, smelly, disgusting . . ."

"I believe he will respond to you if you are loving and kind."

"What? I don't think so."

"Try it."

"Why aren't you talking to him, trying to get him to change? I have no control here. I am at his mercy."

"I am your Guide, not his. I'll be by your side to help you."

"Can you hold him off? Can you keep him from hitting me or from forcing me to . . ."

"I can help you do it."

Once again, her Spirit body turned away from me. During the conversation, some of her radiance had returned, but now it began to dim again.

"I need a gun to protect myself. Can you get me a gun?"

"No. I can show you how to resolve this in a non-violent way."

"Why should I? He is violent to me."

"You show him that you are more evolved, more intelligent, and far more compassionate."

"He won't understand."

"But you will. You'll know."

"All right. What do you suggest?"

"Detach yourself and see the man for who and what he is. In the eyes of the Creator, he is a Soul who needs compassion and love. Here, watch this."

I visualized a sphere of protective light around the woman's sleeping body on the bed below and then suggested, "Put yourself in a bubble of golden light. It will protect you. Then send him love and compassion."

477

The spirit form of the woman again dimmed as she replied, "I know you are asking me to walk the high road, but I still hate him. I want him dead."

"Try these suggestions, please. I will help. I'll be right by your side when he returns. Remember that."

The Soul of the woman then slid back into her physical body, and I kept a vigil. I prayed for her, for her husband, and for me.

As soon as first light crept into the large elegant bedroom, the man returned, a little sleepy and, therefore, not as boisterous. He was wearing a different robe of black silk with the same gold monogram and joined his sleeping wife in bed.

"This is a good start," I thought. "All is calm."

The man lit a candle on the bedside table and peeled back the covers. Lying on his side, he began unbuttoning his wife's nightdress. She stirred. Her nose wrinkled; she could smell him. He began kissing her breasts, and I saw her hand reach behind him for the scissors on the nightstand. She began to tremble.

"Oh you like this, do you?" grunted the big man.

She grimaced and raised the scissors, pointing them at his back. Thinking and acting quickly, I blew the flame of the candle onto her hand. Surprised, she dropped the scissors. The man jerked his head around at the sound. He grabbed the scissors, then held them in front of her face.

"What were you going to do with these? I have a mind to cut off every hair on your head!" he snarled, then stopped. "No—no need to make you any uglier than you already are."

In a few long snips, he cut her nightdress open lengthwise, then threw the scissors out the window.

"No!" she cried, clutching the shreds to her.

"Give it up, woman. You can't hurt me. I'm too strong for you. Now, down to business."

I wondered if she remembered anything of our conversation during the night. She did not resist as much as before.

Her husband was having difficulty though, which made the encounter lengthier. He seemed to need stimulation, so he rolled out of bed, seized his wife's limp body, and slung her over onto her face. Now she protested. The pillow muffled her sobs, as he proclaimed himself a stallion mounting a wild mare. Finally it was over. He gave her a parting slap and left. She lay there, face down, devastated, crying softly.

"My weapon is gone," she murmured, rolling on her side, looking towards the half-open window and bursting into tears. "I'll never bear your child, you horrible, disgusting brute!"

I came very close to her and whispered, "Detach, detach."

She brushed her ear, so I knew some part of her heard. She looked puzzled for a moment, then her eyes grew wide.

"The dream! I had an angel visit me. He said he would help. He gave some advice . . . What was it?"

"Detach. View your husband with love and compassion," I whispered in her ear.

She uttered a heavy sigh.

"Whatever it was, if it doesn't get me out of here, it's useless."

She picked up the cord she planned to use to strangle him and fingered it, picturing the murder in her mind. Her aura became very dark.

Now it was my turn to sigh. I asked myself what I would do on Earth in this situation, and it struck me. I would approach the Spirit Guide of the husband. This had worked well in the prisoner-of-war camp with the kind Guide of the German army doctor who saved Frederic's life. However, every time I had seen the woman's husband, I noticed no Guide present. Sometimes Spirit Guides were not visible to me. I made a mental note to ask Sottrol about that.

While the woman washed again, changed into another nightgown, and brushed her hair, I prayed and asked for help. She then practiced strangling her husband by wrapping the cord around a pillow, her face filled with hatred as she tightened the cord. Something had to change soon.

The man returned later in the day. This time he was fully dressed. He swaggered into the room.

"My blood's a boil. I've been hunting, and now I've come to conquer my wild mare."

The woman hid the cord under the pillow and curled up in fetal position. Her husband ignored his wife's state of fear and hatred and strutted about the room peeling off his jacket, vest, and shirt. As he sat on the bed removing his shoes, she made her move. She whipped the cord around his neck and began to twist it.

The man immediately grabbed at the cord, and a tug of war ensued. She was stronger than I expected. His face began turning red. Where was this man's Spirit Guide? He needed help, and so did I, so I prayed again.

The big man was choking now, and her face was contorted with hate and anger. He lurched back causing her to loosen her grip and quickly snatched the cord. He was now in control. Coughing and sputtering, he rubbed his neck as she backed into the corner of the room with a wild desperate look in her eyes.

"You vixen!" shouted the man in a raspy voice. "I'll show you how to use a rope!"

He lunged at her, and I feared for her life, but he had no intention of killing her. Instead he tied her hands, threw her onto the bed, and lashed the end of the rope to the bedpost.

"Ah ha! I have captured my crazy, wild mare, and now I will tame her! Buck all you want. I'll ride you until you submit to me!"

The woman was consumed with anger. She spat at him, but that only encouraged him. He seemed to delight in her murderous attempts. The challenge of subduing her excited him and only made the situation worse. It was not a pretty picture. The man treated her like a horse. Once again he rolled her over onto her stomach. This time, he twisted her long hair and used it as reins, then slapped her rump as he straddled her.

I was downhearted. I was failing and knew it. I couldn't watch even though I knew I should stay close to the woman and continue to try to help her. The energy field around her was murky brown with flames of red shooting out. I prayed again.

"He is a brute, isn't he?" I heard a voice above me.

I looked up, and in the corner of the room was a small pixie-like Spirit. She lowered herself next to me and said, "Yes, I'm his Guide and will gladly work with you. I've seen you praying. I've heard you ask for my help."

"Why haven't I seen you before now?" I asked, still taken aback by this tiny Spirit's sudden appearance.

"I've been here. I often tuck myself in the big man's pocket. Then it's only a hop, skip, and a jump to his ear. I wanted to see what you are made of Darcimon Stillwater. This is your final exam, after all. You have now asked for my help, and I shall certainly give it to you. I'm Bellar."

"Thank you, Bellar. Let's work together to resolve this."

"You must take the lead as this is your exam, Darci."

The grunts of the husband distracted us for a moment.

I shook my head and said, "From what I can see, they feed each other's negativity. He treats her like an animal, a possession, which fills her with hatred and anger. She lashes out at him, and this prods him to treat her even more like a wild beast. We must break this cycle."

The pixie Guide nodded, "Go on."

"I have already tried reasoning with her Spirit, but the hatred and rage are so strong and so deeply embedded that I made no headway. Why, she asked me to fetch her a gun!"

"What do you propose?"

"Can you get the husband to do one kind thing for his wife? Can you remind him somehow that he wishes her to be the mother of his child? She deserves respect. She deserves to be treated gently, lovingly."

"I can make it possible for you to tell him these things. They will both nap after this, and we will have our chance."

481

Just as Bellar said this, the man was bucking, slapping and yelling, "Ho ho!" Then he rolled off onto his back, exhausted, mumbling, "A fine thoroughbred of a son . . ."

The woman, still tied, was weeping. As her husband began snoring, she rolled over although this twisted the rope tighter and used her feet to kick the covers over her. I could see that her wrists were red from the cord, and she was very uncomfortable with her arms tied over her head. I wanted to cut her free, but as a Spirit, I was not able to do that. I had to convince her husband not only to cut her loose but also to begin treating her as a precious partner.

She kicked him yelling, "Untie me! Wake up, you pig, and untie me!"

The man snorted in his sleep and rolled over. She scooted up towards the head of the bed and curled herself into a ball. This position gave her some relief from the bonds. My compassion flowed to her as I saw her crying quietly. Finally, she, too, fell asleep.

The pixie Guide hovered over the man's face and tickled his nose. He lurched onto his side swatting the air in his sleep, then scratched his nose. I wasted no time. I moved around behind him and used my thumbs, stroking upward on his spine. Bellar was floating above his head helping me draw his Spirit up and out. This process took a while. I do not think this man experienced astral-projection on a regular basis.

Once his Spirit was dislodged from his physical body though still connected by the thin silver cord, I approached him. His Spirit seemed confused. He was staring down at his sleeping body.

"Am I dead?" he asked, looking at his physical form.

"Not at all sir," I replied. "You are sleeping. Your Soul will slide back into your body in a few minutes."

"Who are you?"

"I am serving as your wife's guardian angel, and I have some information that will help both of you."

"Help us? How?"

"You want an heir, am I correct?"

"Yes. I've set up a schedule to insure conception."

"Physical insemination is only part of the process. You and your wife must also attract a willing Soul, a Soul that wants to be your son or daughter. Otherwise, even if she does become pregnant, she will miscarry, or the child will be stillborn."

"I want a strong, healthy son. How do I guarantee that?"

"You must provide an atmosphere of love. This attracts Souls who are ready to incarnate."

"Atmosphere of love? I give my wife everything—fine clothes, a great mansion, servants, the finest food."

"Those are material things. Look at her. You treat her like an animal. You've locked her up and even tied her! Suppose you did conceive a child tonight. The Souls that are ready to come to Earth and would possibly choose to be your child could see this."

I pointed to his wife. She looked pitiful. Her hair was scraggly and wet from tears and his sweat and slobber. Her nightgown was soiled and ripped, and she was curled up like a child lost in the wilderness.

"I did that to her?" he spoke as though he could not believe it.

"She is not only the vehicle through which your baby shall come, she will also nurse and raise the child. She deserves to be treated with gentleness, respect, and deep and abiding love. Then you shall attract a willing Soul."

"My wife needs discipline. Why—she tried to run away. Then she tried to kill me. How can I respect her and treat her with love when she behaves in this way?"

"She is only reacting to your treatment of her. It's a cycle, and I say you must break it in order to achieve your goal of fatherhood. And, sir? What if you have a daughter? Will you treat her this way?"

"Certainly not—my own flesh and blood!"

"Your wife is your family, too."

"So—how do I . . .?"

"Be gentle and kind to her. Treat her as precious, for she is. Love her from your heart before you attempt to love her with your body. Listen to me. I speak the truth. If you treat her this way, she will open like a lovely flower. Her body will respond by conceiving, and the two of you will be like one strong magnet drawing to you the willing Soul of your child to be."

As I said these last words, the pixie Spirit tugged the thin luminous string that connected his Soul to his body.

As the man's Spirit descended, sliding back into his physical form, she whispered in his ear, "Take a bath."

The man woke only a moment or two later. He rubbed his eyes and looked around. He sat up and looked again.

He scratched his head and said, "That was some dream."

Then he turned and saw his wife.

The pixie sat on his shoulder and said, "The mother of your child."

"My dear," he murmured.

On his knees he walked across the bed and quickly untied her. Seeing the raw skin on her wrists, he hung his head. He lifted her face in his hands and stroked her hair.

"I'm so sorry, my sweet woman," he whispered.

She blinked a few times as her eyes opened, then jerked away from him with a scowl.

I glided next to her and whispered, "Love and compassion, love and compassion."

"I don't blame you for cringing at my touch," he blubbered softly. "I'm so sorry for the way I have treated you, truly and honestly. Look into my eyes. You'll see I mean this."

They stared at each other. It was probably the first time they had really looked into each other's eyes in a long time. Something had changed. She was still wary, but her face relaxed a bit.

"You've been crying," he acknowledged, softy touching her cheek. "I've made you weep. Again, I apologize. It's true I want an heir; it's very important to me. What's more important is you, our child's mother."

A look of disbelief crossed her face.

I whispered, "Forgiveness, love, and compassion."

The man stood and began dressing himself, talking all the while. "I had an amazing dream just now. I was floating up there." He pointed towards the ceiling. "I was looking down at myself sleeping. There was an angel—he said he was your guardian angel. He told me physical conception is only the beginning. We need to attract a willing Soul, and to do that we need to create an atmosphere of . . ."

"Love and compassion," the woman interjected. "I dreamed of my guardian angel last night. God is trying to help us."

"I believe it. I know it. And here's something else I know. I care about you. I respect you, and from now on, I will handle you like a precious jewel."

"I'm not a stone. I'm a flesh and blood woman."

"Oh, I know that, believe me." He sat on the bed, took her hand, and kissed it. "I have much to do to make up for how I have treated you. I want you to dress in your finest gown, and I will have cook prepare your favorite meal. We'll dine together in the south room, just as we did when we were first married. Then tomorrow I'll take you anywhere you wish to go."

"I am no longer confined? I can do as I please?"

"I only ask that you give me a chance to show you I have changed."

She looked skeptical, as if this were perhaps another of his games.

I came close to her and put my hand on her heart, radiating as much love as I could.

"Forgiveness, compassion, and love," I said again into her ear.

She took a deep breath, relaxed a little more, and said, "Tell me I am not your wild mare."

"You are my wife. I wish you to be the mother of my children."

I saw Bellar on the man's shoulder. The pixie Guide was projecting an image of the Madonna and child into the man's mind. I did the same to the wife. Her expression changed.

"We'll take it one day at a time," she said slowly.

Bellar turned to me, nodded, and winked. The tiny Guide bowed and extended both arms toward the door. My exam was over.

I walked out of the room expecting to step into the hallway of the mansion. Instead, I found myself on the steps of Portal Seven with an even larger group of Guides by the table. They were talking and laughing. Then they saw me and stopped.

Sottrol, who was in the middle of this group, immediately came towards me. He shook my hand and patted my back, and said, "Good work, Darci. Everyone—for those who haven't met him—this is Darcimon Stillwater."

Some of the Guides bowed, others nodded, and a few said, "Greetings."

"May I rest now?" I asked my mentor.

I heard a couple of chuckles from the group of Guides.

"That was a tough exam, wasn't it?" said Sottrol as he escorted me down the line of columns.

"The hardest test yet," I confessed. "There was so much resistance. I tried . . ."

"It's over now, Darci. Only one more exam to go, and you will be qualified to become a full-fledged Spirit Guide."

"All I want now is rest."

∞　∞　∞

Quickly and quietly, Sottrol lead me back to my chamber. When my mentor and I came through the entry, Angel could see my exhaustion. She threw her arms around me. It felt so good to hold her; I grinned. Sottrol chuckled and smiled, too.

"We were right to bring you here, Angel. Your presence helps Darci a great deal. Darci, I want to have a brief review and discussion with you before you enter Portal Eight for your last exam."

I nodded and hugged Angel tighter. Sottrol left, and we just stood there holding each other. We both knew the time was near for us to become residents of two different worlds.

Once I had rested, and my mate and I had enjoyed some privacy, we lay on the sleeping pallet in the spherical bedroom and began talking. I told her about my most recent exam, but Angel would not speak of her discoveries while I was away.

"I want to tell you," she admitted with a hint of sadness in her eyes, "but I have been instructed to wait until you have officially become my Spirit Guide."

"I wonder if our teachers don't want me distracted or . . ."

"It's procedure. No one but my assigned Spirit Guide can discuss with me the issues and decisions that I must make before I reincarnate."

"Probably both these reasons. I guess we'll know as soon as I get through this next exam. I can't imagine it being more difficult than the last one."

Little did I know what lay ahead for me.

Sottrol took me aside at the entrance to the exam area and reminded me, "All right, Darci, you are doing well, but it's important you are successful with this last test. Angel must return to Earth soon, and if you are not ready to become her Spirit Guide, then the mission will not go forward."

"I understand."

"Two areas of expertise were emphasized in your last exam—working with another Guide and communicating with the Soul. This next exam will be more complex."

"How? Help me, Sottrol."

"I can only say I believe you will continue to do well. Do your breathing exercises before you enter Portal Eight—and, Darci—be ready for anything."

My mentor stood with his hand on my back as I breathed deeply and raised my vibration. His touch helped to calm and center me. Without further words, he escorted me to the giant column that marked the eighth portal. A pang of jitters hit me, and I felt myself tremble. So much was riding on my abilities. I stopped and did more deep breathing. When I opened my eyes, Sottrol was gone.

There stood the table with the open registration book, but no Guide was anywhere in sight. I was entirely on my own. I placed my hands, palms down, on the pages. The book burst into flames! Although I was mightily surprised, I was not burned. When I lifted my hands, I saw deep holes where they had been. The holes went through the book, the table, and seemed bottomless. I had signed in.

With a prayer on my lips, I ascended the steps to the entry. The door was huge, made of iron, and looked very heavy. As before, there was no handle obvious to me. I tried what had previously worked, asking to enter, but nothing happened. Then I noticed two panels just large enough for my hands.

Placing them there, I was taken aback as the door began changing color and became a glowing red. It reminded me of the cast iron stove in my home in Derbyshire when we had it stoked and burning too hot. There was no heat from this great door though or any movement.

"This is terrible," I thought to myself. "I can't even get into the exam."

Then I had the urge to speak aloud. With my hands still placed firmly on the glowing iron door, I said in a very authoritative voice, "I am Darcimon Stillwater here to take this final exam. I am ready. Open and allow me to enter, please."

With a loud creaking and groaning sound, the great iron door opened before me. Once I stepped across the threshold, I was surrounded by darkness and a sense of foreboding.

The door disappeared. I had never felt so absolutely alone. Desolation swept over me, and I realized the environment I had entered was loaded with negativity.

Immediately I put myself in a sphere of protective golden light and paused to take some deep breaths. I also visualized shields around me that would deflect any harmful energy. Thus armed, I carefully took a step forward in the dark murky atmosphere.

I heard singing. The woman's voice was sweet, sad and a little off-key. I followed the sound, and soon a dimly lit passageway became visible. The hall had door after door, all exactly the same. The voice led me to one of the first doors on the left. It was slightly ajar. I peered in to see a young woman in a plain gray dress sitting on the edge of a cot, rocking and singing the same song repeatedly. The room was bare, except for two cots and one window with a cage-like screen over it. I realized this must be an asylum.

Gliding in front of the girl, I tried to look into her eyes, but they were closed. I began to understand the song she sang was a lullaby. There were noises from the hallway and the sound of a key in the lock, which I thought very strange since the door was open when I first got there. Into the bare room came a huge burly man dressed in white, a small man with a mustache carrying some papers, and an old woman in a strait jacket.

"Jeanette, this is your new roommate, Dora. All right, old woman. Treat her better than your last one," said the small man.

He then motioned to the large fellow and said, "Take off the strait jacket."

The big man was a little rough with the old woman but didn't hurt her. Then the two men exited quickly. Sitting on the spare cot, the old woman eyed Jeanette who was still rocking and singing quietly under her breath.

"Hey. Hey! What's yer story, girlie?" Dora raised her voice. "Yer not gonna sing like that all the time. Ya do, I'll hafta strangle ya."

Jeanette stopped singing. I heard her swallow.

"Wanna get outta here?" Dora said in a low voice, leaning towards the girl. "We can do it, ya know. I know how."

Jeanette turned and looked at the old woman for the first time.

"Aha! Got your interest! Stick with me. I know how to get us outta this place."

Dora ran her hand through her short cropped hair, wiped her nose with the back of her hand, and said, "You and me, dearie—we've been through a lot. Time for us to take back our lives. Time to say good-bye to this stinkin' place. You wanna go?"

"My baby," cooed Jeanette softly, then louder. "My baby!" Then louder still. "My baby, my baby, my baby!"

"Easy there," Dora said and held up her hand. "They took yer baby, didn't they?"

"My baby," said Jeanette quietly. She closed her eyes and began to rock.

"I can see you're gonna be a great help. It figures I'd be thrown in with a real loony."

"I'm not crazy," said Jeanette, staring directly at her new roommate. "I just want my baby."

"My plan takes two people. I've been waitin' to be transferred to this floor. It's the only place I can put my escape plan into action."

"Out of here? Really?" Jeanette's expression displayed her doubt.

"That's right, dearie, out and away. We'll be far, far down the road before they come with that slop they feed us for breakfast. You gonna help me? I'm not gonna tell you anything until you swear you'll help and you won't say one word about this. Not one word, hear me?"

"My baby," said Jeanette.

"Yeah, yeah. You can go find your baby. But we hafta break outta here first. Swear to me. Swear on your baby's life. This is our secret now, swear!"

"If I can go find my baby, I swear."

"Good, good. Smart girl. You gotta help, too, ya know. This won't work without you. That all right?"

Jeanette rocked and nodded. The old woman fell silent and stretched out on her cot.

I looked over these two inmates, both in their gray institutional dresses. Dora was stocky with a tough demeanor, her face ruddy and wrinkled with an especially deep furrow across her brow. Jeanette was thin and pale with wrists so delicate they looked as though they could be snapped in two like green beans. Her brown hair had been quite long. I knew this because she still had a few long strands, but the rest had been clumsily chopped off just above her shoulders.

Because Jeanette was alone when I first arrived, I assumed I was to serve as her Guide though I reminded myself to be ready for any eventuality. After a while, two attendants unlocked the door and set down a tray with two bowls, two spoons, and two tin cups of water.

"Hey, you guys. Take a look at her. I don't think she's feelin' so good," Dora told them, pointing at Jeanette who still sat curled up and rocking.

The two men turned their attention to the young woman. I watched as Dora tugged the arm of the shorter man and picked his pocket at the same time.

"I don't wanna catch it—whatever she has. I don't wanna get sick."

"Don't worry, old woman. She's all right. She's been like this since we put her in this room. Relax and eat your stew."

The two attendants left quickly. I could hear the food cart rolling down the hallway as they moved on. Dora ate with gusto.

"Step one accomplished," she crowed between bites of potato. "Hey dearie—Jeanette—eat up. You need your strength. We got a long way to go tonight. Come on. This may be your last meal for a while."

Jeanette stopped her rocking, stared at the old woman with disbelief, then took her spoon and began eating slowly. Dora finished her bowl of stew quickly and talked as the young woman ate.

"I can get us outta this room. The locks on this floor are easy to pick, and now I have this," she announced, flashing a small metal nail file. "I've seen that short guy cleanin' his nails on duty. I knew he kept this in his left back pocket. It's mine now, and so is freedom!"

"What are you going to do?" asked Jeanette, pushing chunks of food around in her bowl.

"It's what *we're* gonna do. I've been in this place for almost five years, and I've been plannin' my escape since day one. Now listen. Two things happen real, real early in the morning. The bread gets delivered and the dirty laundry gets picked up. I know cuz I used to be in the room above the service entrance. We're gonna get into one of those trucks and get outta here."

As soon as it was dark and all was quiet, Dora picked the lock on the door. It didn't take her long.

"Ha! I knew I could do it!" she bragged in a coarse whisper. "Follow me. We hafta use the stairs at the far end of the hall—away from the night guard."

I followed as the two women crept slowly, carefully down the hallway. In the dark I finally caught a glimpse of Dora's Guide who seemed to be keeping his distance. Nonetheless, I nodded at him, acknowledging his presence.

Dora grabbed Jeanette's arm and pulled her closer as they made their way down the stairs. Three flights brought them to the basement utility area where there were shelves of supplies, including stacks of clean linen. Dora pawed through the piles and pulled out two white jackets. She thrust one into Jeanette's arms. Just at that moment, I heard a door open at the other end of the room and saw a silhouette with a flashlight. The women ducked, but the guard caught a bit of movement in his light, so he came into the room to investigate. The two women held their breath and stayed very still as the guard approached. I hovered above Jeanette, who was trembling with fear. I could no longer see Dora's Guide. The beam of the guard's light flashed around the room several times. He took a few steps and pulled the chain on the overhead light bulb.

"Must have been seeing things," he muttered as he extinguished it. Turning to go, he said, "Wouldn't hurt to do an extra bed check." The door closed behind him.

"Drat!" Dora clenched her fists. "They'll know we're gone before we can stow away on one of the service trucks. We've gotta think, dearie. We've gotta come up with a way to distract them so they don't do a bed check. Come on!"

Dora led the girl out the door where the guard had just been. They found themselves in the furnace room. There was a pile of coal and a large boiler that supplied heat for the building, a small table, two chairs where the workmen sat, and a stack of old newspapers in the corner.

"This'll keep 'em busy," Dora whispered as she took a coal shovel, opened the boiler, and scooped out two glowing coals.

"Lord, have mercy!" Jeanette exclaimed louder than she should have. "What are you doing?"

"Sh-h-h-h!" Dora responded as she walked to the corner and slid the coals mid-way into the stack of newspapers.

"Fire!" Jeanette whispered loudly.

"Exactly. None of those night time attendants are gonna think about doin' a bed check when there's a fire to put out. Come on. Let's get outta here."

The women returned to the laundry room, and I followed. Soon the air was thick with smoke. Jeanette coughed, and Dora clapped her hand over the young woman's mouth.

"No noise!" she hushed with urgency in her voice. "And stay close to the floor!"

As the women lay behind the laundry carts, we heard a commotion in the next room. There was yelling and clanging of pails, more yelling, and more smoke. I floated through the dense atmosphere to see what was happening and was alarmed to find the beams and one wall of the furnace room in flames.

Dora had managed to set the building on fire. I knew the two women had to leave their hiding place, or they would soon be overcome by smoke. If Jeanette died, I would have failed the exam.

There was another way out of the linen room through the delivery door, but it was locked as were the two windows. There was certainly no going back the way they had come; the stairwell was filled with smoke. Both women lay with their heads on the floor facing each other. Dora stifled a cough, then grabbed the metal wheel on the laundry basket.

"We gotta get outside. Come on. Help me push this cart through the window. Hey! No time to be scared. Wanna see your baby? Let's go!"

They combined their strength and rammed the metal basket again and again against the window. Finally the cart broke through, throwing Jeanette back onto the floor and Dora forward through the window. The old woman was injured badly. She had impaled herself on a large jagged piece of glass. Jeanette crawled to her side.

"Go! Go!" said Dora. "It's your chance. Take it! Go!"

The young woman climbed out through the broken glass and found herself in the yard of the burning asylum. Screams came from the floors above as smoke filled the building. Jeanette was dazed and traumatized. I came close to her, held her, and put a sphere of protective golden light around the two of us. I could see the flames reflected in her frightened eyes. She drew back into the bushes as the yard filled with people combating the blaze. The scene was pure chaos. A bucket brigade was set up to try to douse the flames, but the fire quickly got out of control.

I wondered if Jeanette might be the only surviving patient, for I could see no one attempting to evacuate the inmates. She retreated further from the pandemonium until she reached the fence that surrounded the asylum grounds. Then she followed it, walking slowly, still trembling. I stayed very close, radiating a calming blue-green light to her. The night sky was glowing, and cries and screams filled the air. She reached the gate eventually. It had been left wide open to allow firefighters to enter. Slipping quietly through, she was free.

Still wearing the white coat that Dora had tossed to her less than an hour before, she wandered up the road, ducking into the bushes whenever a vehicle passed. She continued to tremble from both the shock and the cold. I had to help her find warmth, shelter, and water. As she moved slowly down the road, I scouted the area and located a stream with an old abandoned cabin nearby.

The place was quite run down, but it would get Jeanette out of the cold. When she reached that point in the road where the stream was audible, I asked a large toad to leap into her path. This startled her; she jumped and caught her jacket on some briars. As she was pulling herself free, she heard the stream and realized how thirsty she was. Heading for it, she stumbled and fell once in the darkness but managed to get herself there. She washed her face and hands, then drank off and on for a long time.

I had to show her the old cabin somehow. It was set back from the stream, easily visible in the daylight, but nearly invisible in the darkness. I looked around for tools I could use to guide her to the shelter. There was an owl nearby, but I thought that might scare her. Instead, I sat on the steps of the cabin and radiated love to her. I visualized myself as a great magnet, drawing her to me. I even hummed a hymn I remembered from my last Earth lifetime. She rose and walked right to me. I was pleased and hugged her though she had no idea I was there. Still, my Spirit embrace seemed to calm her further. Her trembling ceased.

The cabin was in disrepair, but the roof was still good and there was an old iron bed with a straw mattress. There were even a few articles of clothing and two blankets. Although it was dark, Jeanette found her way up the creaky steps. She moved slowly, carefully, feeling her way and located the iron bedstead. Before collapsing onto it, she ran her hands over the mattress, then swept it off with her arm. She lay down and curled up into a ball.

As she slept, I wondered how I could best help this lost human. In reality, a Spirit Guide knows his or her assigned human from before birth. I knew only what I had observed since I peered through the doorway and first saw her. She seemed childlike and easily influenced, which might make my job as her protector easier or more difficult, depending upon whom she encountered.

Once dawn broke, I searched the area for resources. There was a small town about eight miles down the road, but I was sure she would be recognized as an inmate of the incinerated asylum. There were several farms dotting the landscape. Perhaps she could find food and assistance at one of those.

Jeanette slept until the sun shone onto her face. Waking, she jerked herself upright with a start because she didn't know where she was. She looked at the sooty white jacket and held her head.

"Fire," she said aloud. "Fire."

Dazed, she sat for quite a while, looking around the old rotting cabin. There wasn't much there, a few tin dishes and cups all covered with cobwebs, an old rusty woodstove, the bed, a pail, and some rags in a broken chair. She sorted through the rags and found a man's blue shirt, which she donned to replace the soiled white jacket. She then took the pail and went to the stream. Once she had rinsed the bucket, fetched some water, and had all she wanted to drink, she sat on the edge of the bed and began rocking back and forth as she had done in the asylum.

"Hungry," she murmured. "Hungry, hungry. No food for me anywhere."

The nearest farm was a little over a mile away. I wanted Jeanette to walk in the direction of the homestead, so I brought the smell of their cook stove to her on the breeze. Whoever was in that farmhouse was frying bacon, an unmistakable aroma. As soon as she sniffed it, Jeanette got up and walked towards it. She lost heart after half a mile, so I encouraged her by wafting the smell of biscuits baking.

"Where are these smells coming from?" I read her thought.

The access road to the farm was soon in view. I employed the help of a rabbit who hopped down the drive attracting her attention. She followed the creature, and before long, the old farm house was in view. She wandered up the drive and stepped onto the porch. A middle-aged man opened the door. He had a ruddy complexion, stocky build, and was clad in overalls.

"Help you, miss?"

"I'm so hungry. Food, please."

He looked her over and noted, "You're a bit of a mess. Where'd you come from anyway?"

"Food, please."

"Don't have any to spare. Go away."

"Please. I've walked so far."

The man's eyes softened a little and he said, "Well— you'll have to earn it. Willing to work?"

"Yes. Food."

"Come in. I was just making breakfast for me and Jim."

Jim sat at the kitchen table. He was about twenty, Jeanette's age, skinny with shaggy brown hair, and wore the same type of overalls as the older man. I followed Jeanette into the kitchen and looked into the eyes of the two men to make sure she would come to no harm. I could tell they were father and son.

"Sit down," barked the father.

She took the only chair. He served up two plates of fried eggs, bacon, and biscuits, slid them onto the table, then went out onto the porch to fetch himself a chair. Jeanette ate with her eyes on the plate. I could tell she was savoring every morsel. Jim ate with his head down but his eyes on her. The son was done with his food by the time the father had cooked more for himself, but he remained at the table, staring all the while at Jeanette.

The older man talked between bites, saying, "Animal doctor comes today. I want you to drive all the cows into the barn, but don't feed 'em."

"Yeah, I know," mumbled the young man.

"Fence repair this afternoon. It's gonna take us the better part of a week to get through that, but now we got ourselves some domestic help. What's your name anyway, girlie?"

Jeanette just stared at her plate and chewed.

"You deaf or somethin'? You gotta name?"

"J-j-jen . . ."

"Jenny? All right Jenny, start by cleaning up this kitchen, then sweep all the floors. That'll keep you busy 'til lunch. Then you can cook us up somethin'."

The girl looked dazed. Jim eyed her suspiciously, asking, "You gonna leave her alone in the house? She might steal somethin'."

"She's on foot. She wouldn't get far. You're not gonna do that, are you Jenny?"

"N-n-no."

"Time to go. The doc'll be here soon."

The two men exited and headed for the barn while Jeanette sat there trembling. I felt so much compassion for her; I surrounded her with love. She took a deep breath and seemed steadier.

It took her a few minutes to figure out how to begin cleaning the kitchen. There was a kettle of hot water on the cook stove, so she poured some into an enamel pan in the sink and washed her face and hands, then the silverware, then the three plates. Just as she was picking up the frying pan, wondering what to do with the grease, Jim came back in. His face was beet red. Jeanette dropped the pan back onto the counter with a clang.

"You come outta nowhere. Where you from anyway?"

Jeanette stood silent.

"That looks like a loony bin dress you got on under that shirt. You escape in that fire last night? They lookin' for you?"

Jeanette didn't think anyone knew of her escape, so no one would be looking for her. She answered his last question by shaking her head no.

"The girl from outta nowhere. I'm gonna keep my eye on you. You sure don't talk much. I thought women were always yappin' all the time."

Jeanette stared at her feet. Jim heard a shout from the barn, turned, and left.

The young woman sighed. She abandoned the dishwashing project and began wandering in the house. The room behind the kitchen was a living room that looked as though it hadn't seen use for years. Dust lay thick on the furniture and cobwebs decorated the corners. The door at the back of the parlor led to a wood shed where an ax was planted firmly in an old stump with slivers of wood scattered around. Jeanette next tried the stairs. The second floor had one bedroom in the front and two smaller ones towards the back. She lay down on one of the single beds, curled up and murmured "my baby" a few times, then fell asleep.

I felt handicapped by my lack of information about her. If I knew what happened to her baby, perhaps I could better assist her. Using my telepathic abilities, I probed her mind as she slept. One picture after another slid by. First she was a little girl with a tall man, perhaps her father, leading her by the hand. Together they looked down a deep well. Next, she was a young woman, probably in her late teens, holding a bouquet of beautiful flowers. A different man was by her side, perhaps her husband. The next image that moved through her mind caused her to moan. She was opening a package that contained her husband's belongings including his wedding ring and his military identification tags. He had been slain in the line of duty, and she shed many tears into that box. There was a tiny baby wailing in the next room; they were both crying.

Jeanette twitched and rolled over as the next image floated past. Loud knocks shook her door; two men entered with legal papers; one man restrained her while the other took the crying baby. I zoomed in on the paper; it was a document declaring her an unfit parent guilty of child neglect.

"My baby," she murmured in her sleep, hugging her pillow tight. "My baby."

I sat by her on the bed and surrounded her with golden light. The poor woman had lost her husband and her child, and was committed to an asylum. Jeanette needed my help to turn her life around, but I wasn't sure how to do it. I prayed for her and for me, asking for help so that I could help her. Right now she was lost and wandering, broken-hearted over the losses in her life. Still, she grasped that her husband was dead and her child was alive somewhere though she did not know where.

I heard a clamor in the kitchen and loud voices. The farmer was calling, "Jenny, Jenny! Where did you go?"

Soon heavy steps sounded on the stairs, and Jim clumped down the hallway looking in doorways as he went. When he saw Jeanette asleep, he called back down to his father.

"Found her! She's sleepin' up here in my room."

Jeanette rolled over and opened her brown eyes to see Jim standing over her.

"Hey, girlie—around here, we work all day. You were 'sposed to get us lunch. Come on! Get up!"

Dazed, the girl raised herself on one elbow.

Jim grabbed her arm, saying, "You're gonna eat our food, you hafta work for it. You didn't even finish cleanin' the kitchen. Let's go. You're gonna make us lunch."

Jeanette got to her feet and was herded downstairs like a stray cow.

The farmer had laid out some meat and cheese on the counter.

"Can we trust you with this?" he asked as he put a slicing knife and a loaf of bread beside the other food. "My son thinks you're from the asylum down the road, but you don't seem dangerous. Make us some plates of food while we wash up."

Slowly Jeanette did as she had been ordered. The two men had to sit and wait for her to finish.

"You'd never make it as a short order cook," remarked the farmer as she set his lunch in front of him. "I'm thinkin' about calling the sheriff to see if any inmates escaped in that fire last night."

Jeanette said, "No" quietly under her breath.

The men didn't hear.

"Well, help yourself. You can eat, too," said the farmer.

She went ahead and cut herself a small piece of cheese and then stood at the window and ate it in tiny measured bites.

Jim never took his eyes off her and asked, "You ever kill a chicken? Wring its neck or chop off its head?"

Jeanette stopped eating.

"Somebody's gotta kill one of those old layers out there for dinner," the young man continued. "You wanna do it?"

Jeanette, still looking out the window, shook her head no.

"We won't make you do that," the farmer laughed as if his son were making a joke. "Besides, I think Jim here enjoys doing it."

The father and son left to spend the afternoon mending fences, and Jeanette was once again assigned to kitchen clean-up. She stared out the window with tears in her eyes as she washed the same dishes again.

I knew that this was not a safe place for her. She needed a home with someone who would treat her gently and show her compassion. Major losses in life had crippled her. Locking her back up in an institution wasn't going to help. I needed to find her a caring, loving situation. As I watched her wash the dishes, unhurried with a faraway look in her eyes, I realized that part of this exam was perseverance. I couldn't rush the scenario. I had to have patience and wait for the opportunity to help her. It came sooner than I thought it would.

As she was half-heartedly scrubbing the counter, an old truck pulled into the door yard with a young man driving. In fact, he looked a little too young to be behind the wheel, maybe fourteen or so. He came around and opened the passenger door. An elderly woman stepped out as he held her hand to steady her. They walked arm in arm to the farmhouse and knocked on the door. Jeanette knew the two men were out in the fields, so she opened it.

"Well lookee here. You a relative of big Jim and little Jim?"

Jeanette shook her head no.

"I'm Izzy from down the road, and this is my grandson, Hank. We stopped by for our eggs and milk. Jim usually leaves our order right in the cold box. Did the Jims mention we might be stopping by?"

Jeanette shook her head no.

"Well, we'll have a look. Hank, dear, check the cold box. We pay Jim once a month when the pension money comes in."

As she explained, the boy lifted the heavy lid on the big box that was in the far corner of the porch and removed two quarts of milk and a basket of eggs from their sawdust nest.

"You do housework for a living, honey?"

Jeanette looked into the kind eyes of the old woman and nodded yes.

"Well then, I have some work for you. Now that Hank is back in school, I could use a hand around the house, especially with the baby."

Jeanette's eyes brightened as she asked, "Baby?"

"Yes, dear, Hank's little brother. My daughter, bless her Soul, passed away last winter in childbirth. Her husband died in the war. Poor girl was broken-hearted."

Jeanette's eyes filled with tears. The old woman patted her arm.

"A terrible thing. So many lives lost, and for what I ask you? Anyway, when you've finished the work Jim has for you, come on over to our cottage. It's eight miles around by the road or just three miles going west over that field there if you're walkin'. Hope to see you soon, my dear. Come, Hank, let's get home now."

"Baby," whispered Jeanette as she watched them go.

I thought a home with this old woman and her two grandchildren might be a good place for the grieving young woman. She could help with child care and would be a good companion for the elder who must miss her daughter. I wondered if Jeanette would have the initiative to go there on her own.

As she watched the old truck lurch and jiggle down the dirt drive, I heard the thud of heavy footsteps. Little Jim had come in through the woodshed. His face was flushed.

"Dad's busy out at the fence line in the north field. I come in to fetch more water," he announced as he moved close to Jeanette.

Feeling trouble brewing, I stood behind her and put my spirit arms around her.

"Water," she repeated.

"I wanna get a better look at you. You and me, we're the same age. Only makes sense we get to know each other. You like havin' fun? I hear the girls in that asylum get put there because they like their fun—maybe a little too much."

He came closer; she could feel his breath on her face. "Well, I like havin' fun, Jenny, and I ain't had much lately. You wouldn't be too bad lookin' if you combed your hair and put on a sexy dress. Come to think of it, I'd rather see you with no dress at all."

He began unbuttoning the gray dress. Jeanette was shaking. I feared a rape or worse. She knew exactly what was happening. She had birthed a child, after all. The boy was clumsy but insistent. Kissing her roughly on the lips, he moved his hand into her unbuttoned bodice.

"No," she said firmly, pushing him away.

He grabbed her hair and yanked her head back, "Hey! You ate my food. You owe me!"

"No!" her voice quivered.

"That's no way to act when we took you in, fed you, let you sleep in my bed. Like that bed? Wanna go upstairs where we won't be interrupted?"

"No," she said weakly as she reached around behind her for the bread knife that lay on the counter and held it behind her back.

"I don't care where we do it. I jest thought you'd be more comfortable in the bed. Your choice, Jenny. I could take you right on this floor."

He had a tight hold on her, but her legs were free, so she struck him in his crotch with her knee. Howling in pain, he released his hold. She bolted for the living room in an attempt to make it out through the back woodshed. He cornered her in the living room, and she pointed the bread knife at him. Tears were streaming down her face.

"You vixen—you're not gonna use that. No, no—you can't even hurt a chicken, little Jenny."

He grabbed her forcefully, saying, "You're gonna pay for kneeing me!"

She tried to wrench free. As I watched them struggle, I looked for a way to end this explosive scene. If either hurt the other, I might fail the exam. Freeing herself, Jeanette backed out the shed door with Jim advancing towards her. She held him at bay with the knife. He jerked the ax from the stump and used it to strike the blade. The situation was escalating.

"My weapon's bigger than yours," said Jim in a sing-song voice.

Jeanette was trembling so much I thought that she might faint. She was gripping the knife so tightly her knuckles were white.

"Come on, baby, put down the knife," cooed Jim as he moved closer with the ax.

"Baby," sobbed Jeanette.

"You want a baby? That can be arranged. I'll give you a baby if that's what you want, loony-bin girl."

He struck out with the ax and hit the knife with a glancing blow, encroaching upon her, "You gotta relax. I won't hurt you. Just lookin' for some fun, Jenny."

Eyes full of fear, she continued to maneuver backwards as he crept forward. She stumbled, and he took advantage of her distraction, grabbing the wrist of the hand that held the knife.

"Drop it! Give up, Jenny. I'll win. I'm stronger than you."

I had to act fast and help her now. Hovering above them in the shed, I looked for anything I could use to stop Jim's aggression and get Jeanette out of there. I saw a cat perched on top of a stack of firewood. Sending the cat an image of what I wished it to do, I made a breeze that ruffled its fur. The feline jumped onto Jim's shoulders and dug in its claws for a solid hold.

Both were startled, but Jim yelled and released his grip. As he flailed his hands to pull off the cat, Jeanette took a few steps backward out of the woodshed.

"Run," I said in her ear. "Run!"

She knew she had to get out of there fast. Whirling around, she looked confused for an instant. I sent her a picture of the kind old woman pointing in the direction of her cottage, and Jeanette took off. She ran west through the field along the tree line. By the time Jim stumbled out of the shed, she had gone far enough so that he did not see her right away. She had been looking back over her shoulder periodically, so when she saw him surveying the area, she ducked into the brush. Once he had walked around to the front of the house to continue his search, she resumed her flight to safety.

My job now was to lead her to the elder's cottage. Though much of the journey was through open fields, it was not a straight and easy path, so she could easily become lost and wander until dark. My goal was to have her arrive by suppertime.

She ran until she was out of sight of the farm. The first field ended with a line of trees; then another began. She rested by a stone wall. Wishing her to continue in the right direction once she had caught her breath, I sent a pair of doves over her head flying directly west. Their wings whistled as they flapped. She looked up, followed them with her eyes, then with the rest of her.

Coming to a creek at the far edge of this field, she drank, then tried to cross by stepping on the stones that were raised out of the stream's flow, but they were slippery and she fell. Examining her aura, I could see flashes of red-orange where she had been hurt. Besides being cold and wet, she suffered pain in her knee and wrist. She got herself up and out of the creek, limping to a spot in the afternoon sun, shivering despite the warmth the sunlight brought her.

I was concerned because she had traveled only halfway. Now that she was injured, the remaining mile or so would be many times more difficult for her to walk. As she sat propped against a tree trunk, I decided to try to do a healing. I visualized bands of golden-green light around her injured wrist and knee, then surrounded her with golden light, then sent her love and strength. I focused very intently on these visualizations until her frown of pain eased.

Because she was still shivering, I placed my spirit hand on her belly and said, "Breathe. Breathe deeply. Take a deep belly breath." I repeated this several times until she did so.

As her trembling lessened and she breathed long and deep again, I worked with her for the better part of an hour until no longer seeing the red-orange flames of pain in her aura. The sun was hanging over the western horizon. She needed to move on if she were to reach the cottage by dark.

"Follow the sun," I said to her, trying to implant the idea in her mind

She got up and began walking directly into the sunlight, limping slightly from her fall but able to keep moving.

The next challenge was a grove of trees at the edge of the third field. Once she entered it, she might lose her way. For a while she did well, continuing west. Then she had to make her way around a large fallen tree and lost her sense of direction. I sent a squirrel scurrying west. It caught her notice, and she turned to follow. Soon she saw the sunlight streaming through the trees and was on track again.

She rested again at the edge of the grove. Poor Jeanette was exhausted. Twenty-four hours before, she was just being introduced to her new roommate. Since then, she had been through several traumas. If I could somehow lead her over the next hill, she would be able to see the cottage.

She groaned a little upon seeing the steep rise before her. The sun went down behind it though, and a chill swept along the edge of the woods. Getting herself up, she began the climb, her sore knee making the hike more arduous. I tried to help her by walking alongside with my spirit arm around her. I sang, and her subconscious must have heard because she walked in time to my song.

At last she crested the hill to see a beautiful valley flooded with the last rays of the sun. The cottage nestled there with wood smoke wafting from its chimney. She hesitated, not knowing if this was the house of the friendly old woman. I used the evening breeze to bring her the sound of the baby crying, and she nearly galloped to the cottage door. The kind elder was holding the baby when she opened it.

"Ah, my dear, come in. You're just in time for biscuits and stew. Here, hold the baby while I dish us out some supper."

The change in Jeanette's energy field was instantaneous. Rays of gold and pink flowed from her heart as the child was placed in her arms. Her face lit up like a lantern, and she smiled.

I was about to follow her into the cottage when I felt a tap on my shoulder. It was my mentor, Sottrol.

"Fine job, Darci. Your charge is safe here—safe, welcome, and useful to this household. Your exam is over."

As he was speaking these words, the scene began whirling. Everything became a blur even as we stood still.

"Look into my eyes, Darci," said my mentor. "Focus on my eyes. Do not concern yourself with what is happening around us."

I did as he asked. It seemed as though we were in the center of a cyclone. There was a deafening roar in my ears, and I felt my robe being blown about in many directions. The tumult lasted for a while, but I was not afraid because Sottrol was there, his eyes kind and gentle, and he was smiling. Finally the tornado around us abated, and we found ourselves standing before the eighth portal in the exam area of the university.

The wizard hugged me and patted me on the back, declaring, "You've done extremely well, Darci. You have officially earned the title of Spirit Guide and all that comes with it. Follow me."

∞ ∞ ∞

We glided together along the row of giant columns, through an ornate archway, and into a labyrinth of passageways.

Sottrol talked as we traveled.

"Ordinarily, you would matriculate with the next group of students who complete the exams. There are several who are nearly finished, but they are retaking some sections now, and it will be a little while before they can graduate. Because of the unusual circumstances, mainly the mission you and Angel have been given, the Master Guides have decided to do a singular graduation ceremony especially for you. Angel needs you as her Guide immediately if the mission is to move ahead as planned. We cannot wait for the next group graduation. We have to prepare you now."

"Prepare? What do you mean?"

"This is not just any graduation ceremony, Darci. This is an initiation during which you receive your gift."

"Initiation? Gift?"

"Remember when you wondered how Sashma could watch over Frederic day and night without rest? You always came back from your stints as an apprentice totally exhausted."

"Yes, I remember. Sashma seemed to never tire. He would send his apprentices back to rest."

"The initiation you are about to undergo imbues you with a new level of energy. You will no longer need to rest or sleep. You will use meditation and deep breath to center yourself and increase your energy. No longer will sleep be necessary for you."

"What about Angel?"

"Angel is destined to become human once again. She will continue to require periods of sleep."

"Will she be there—at my graduation?"

"See for yourself."

We rounded a corner in the maze. The curved narrow passageway opened into a golden lighted dome. I was stunned for a moment by the brilliance of the room. I felt a hand on my arm.

"It took a moment for me to get used to it too," Angel's voice floated into my ears like a sweet song. "Congratulations, Darci. You've done it! You've passed all your tests!"

I took her in my arms. To my surprise, there was a great cheer. Looking up, I saw hundreds of beings filling the golden dome and was taken aback.

Sottrol put an arm around each of us and chuckled, "You see? Many here at the university have been following your progress. A group of Master Guides is here, as well as all the members of The Elevated Council. This is an important step for you, Darci. Not only will you be initiated into the ranks of the Spirit Guides, but also you will also officially begin your mission."

I looked around. Once my eyes adjusted, I began recognizing the faces of the teachers, tutors, and fellow students I had encountered during my long journey through classes and training.

Over a hundred years had passed on Earth while I was studying on the Spirit Guide plane. Now I could return in a changed form, able to help Earth from a fresh perspective.

"There will be plenty of time for visiting and celebrating," remarked Chalherine as she stepped up to hug me. "Right now, your presence is requested in the circle."

At first I didn't know what she meant. Then the luminous figures that filled the dome parted to reveal a circular platform floating a few feet above the floor. This circle was placed in the center of the great dome directly under what appeared to be a giant chandelier. Sottrol escorted me to the circle.

I looked back at Angel who was watching everything with an expression of awe. Chalherine put her arm around my partner and whispered something that made her smile. I smiled, too, and continued to make my way through the crowd of well-wishers.

Arcillis and Esther, the two Master Guides from The Elevated Council, floated into the circle as I arrived. Esther stood on my left and Arcillis on my right. The room became quiet as Arcillis raised his hand.

"We welcome this Spirit, Darcimon Stillwater, into the ranks of the Spirit Guides who watch over humanity and the Earth plane. He has worked diligently and has earned his place. Many of you know about the special mission, a plan of action created by the Master Guides and refined by The Elevated Council. This mission has been in the planning stages for a long, long while. Now, at last, it begins here and now with Darcimon's graduation.

"We considered many couples for this mission. I believe our choice of Darcimon and his partner, Angel, was the right one. He has shown us again and again through his studies, his apprenticeship, and his exams that he is talented, compassionate, intelligent, inventive, and extremely capable. We honor you, Darcimon Stillwater."

Arcillis and Esther each took one of my arms and led me a few steps into the exact center of the circle. There was a glowing spiral design at this spot. They positioned me so I was standing right on top of it.

Esther's incredible eyes flashed before me as I heard her say, "Breathe deeply, Darci Stillwater, and receive your gift."

The two Master Guides vanished. I looked out from this raised platform but could no longer see any of the faces. A veil of light had descended around me. I looked up and observed that the elaborate chandelier-like object had lowered to a point directly over my head. The rays of light that formed the veil took the shape of a four-sided pyramid. I inhaled deeply.

The spiral beneath my feet began spinning, taking me around slowly at first, then faster. At the same time, the chandelier came to life, sending brilliant rays of white light into my spirit body and energy field. The spinning became quite rapid. I took one deep breath after another as a loud tone penetrated my Being.

I felt as if my very essence was being pulverized from every direction, and I panicked for an instant—then realized I had to let go. I surrendered to the initiation process, and as soon as I did this, the tone became higher and the penetrating rays more intense.

Instinctively I uttered a tone that harmonized with the one I heard. Great balls of light began dropping like meteors; they filled the pyramid of light, stacking up around me like bubbles filled with fire. Then the tone changed pitch and became higher. Again, I sang in harmony with every part of me vibrating.

The spiral beneath my feet spun faster still until the globes of fire all burst and flames engulfed me. I felt a giant surge of energy that filled my spirit body from head to foot. The tone turned into the sound of tinkling bells. The rotating spiral slowed, and I stood in a beam of pure white light. I heard singing and realized that all the Beings in the dome had joined their voices in song. The sound was very sweet.

Sottrol and Chalherine glided onto the platform. Each took one of my arms and led me forward to the edge.

Disoriented and a bit shaky, I was glad to have steadying hands on me.

Sottrol spoke loudly, "May I present to you the newest Spirit Guide, the entity who graduated in record time with honors, the leader of the new mission to Earth—Darcimon Stillwater."

A great cheer rose from the crowd. Chalherine whispered that I should bow, so I did. My two teachers helped me off the platform, and I was immediately surrounded by Beings of all kinds wishing to shake my hand, hug me, and congratulate me. At that moment, I wanted Angel. I looked into the crowd, scanning the faces, but did not see her.

Sottrol knew my wish. "I'll find Angel," said my kind mentor. "She should be by your side at such a momentous time."

Beings both familiar and unfamiliar came up to me one by one. Many just shook my hand, then embraced me. Some said, "Congratulations."

Before long, I felt a warm glow on my right, and there was my darling Angel. She looked so small amongst the gathering of great Beings. She was gazing up at me with eyes full of amazement.

"Darci, you're shining like a bright star. You have never looked so radiant!"

"He's now a Spirit Guide," said Gotharn, who was next in line to wish me well. "He has received the blessed gift of energy."

Angel and I looked at each other. We knew this was the beginning of our mission and our separation. I embraced her and held her so long that finally Sottrol tapped me on the shoulder and said, "The celebration will continue for a while, but you two can retire if you wish to."

Chalherine then glided over and added, "Please stay until you've met all who came here to support you today."

I nodded and continued greeting the attendees. Angel stayed at my side, smiling all the while.

At long last, Sottrol escorted us from the dome and accompanied us back to our chamber. Once we were alone, I shared some of my new energy with my beloved mate.

Chapter Thirteen:
Preparing for Earth

Much was different about me once I experienced the initiation. I had been given a great deal more energy and power. As I lay holding my sleeping partner, I scanned my Spirit body. There seemed to be a core of brilliant white light running vertically through me. This core vibrated at a very high rate. Pulses of bright white light shot down my arms and legs like comets. As I held Angel with one arm, I used the other to propel spheres of energy that originated in this core, rolled down my arm, and spun out into the room. I was curious to see how fast I could hurl these balls of light, but they began ricocheting around the spherical bedroom. One zoomed right by Angel's head, nearly hitting her, so I stopped experimenting.

Sottrol materialized in the doorway a moment or two after the light show ceased, asking, "Having fun, Darci?"

"Getting used to my new body. What else am I able to do now, Sottrol?"

"Many things. Your lessons on how to function optimally as a Spirit Guide have only just begun."

"I thought I was done with school."

"We are none of us ever done learning. It is true that you are no longer officially attending the university; however, you are under my tutelage. Your training continues. I will teach you how to use your new powers."

"Let's start now!"

My enthusiasm made my mentor chuckle.

"You will have plenty of time once Angel is born into a human body, especially while she is a babe and sleeps a great deal. Right now, though, preparing Angel for her descent into human form is our priority. We have been waiting for you to assume your place as Angel's Spirit Guide. Now that you have graduated, we can proceed."

"What's next, then? I'm ready."

"I can see you are bursting with enthusiasm and bristling with energy—but Angel needs her rest."

Just as Sottrol spoke these words, Angel stretched, yawned, and a moment later opened her eyes.

As she rubbed them with the backs of her hands, she murmured, "I dreamed there was a fireworks show in here."

Sottrol and I laughed.

"What?" she said, knowing she had missed something.

"Darci was experimenting with his new energy, and it got a little out of hand. All is well, my dear. This is your big day."

"There's no day and night here on this plane, Sottrol," she said, sitting up.

"I'm using Earth terms," the elder responded. "After all, that's what we are going to focus on—all three of us—getting you ready for Earth."

"Just when I was starting to feel at home here," she sighed.

"You remember how beautiful Earth is, don't you?" I posed the question to her.

Angel's eyes lit up and she said, "Yes, although I didn't see much of that beauty during my last Earth life. Can I make some requests for this next lifetime?"

"Yes. Not all Souls have that privilege, but you have earned two requests," Sottrol answered. "Think carefully before you officially place them. They will last the extent of your next incarnation."

"I'm glad I have some say," Angel replied, raising her arms over her head. "I know what I want—and I'm sure of it."

I smiled. Her joy was spilling over me and flooding the spherical room.

"What is it you wish, my child?" said the elder. "I'll make the arrangements if I can."

Angel sat with her legs and arms crossed as if she were sitting at a tribal council and said, "First, I want to be raised in a beautiful place, so as a kid I'll get to appreciate all that's best about Earth. And second, I never want to go hungry ever in my entire life."

I nodded my approval. Both these requests sounded appropriate and reasonable. I glanced at Sottrol who was studying Angel with his wise kind eyes.

"Very well, little one," he responded. "At this point in the evolution of the Earth and humanity, I think both your requests can be honored. We must, however, begin at the beginning. The very first step is for Darci to officially sign on as your Spirit Guide for this upcoming incarnation."

"What do I do?" I asked. "Is there some formal procedure?"

"Oh yes," answered Sottrol. "I will walk you through it since this is your first time. We must leave the university area and go to the Great Hall of Souls. Angel, you come, too. If you're ready, follow me."

Angel looked up at me with a tinge of sadness in her eyes. "This is it, Darci. Our separation begins."

I embraced her and, as I held her close, I whispered, "We are going to be bonded in a new way—a way that ensures we shall never really be separated."

Sottrol came closer and assured her, "He is right, you know. Once Darci has signed on as your Spirit Guide, he is yours. His focus, his responsibilities, his attention, his actions—all revolve around you."

"For the duration of this lifetime," Angel clarified.

"Yes, for this upcoming incarnation," the elder confirmed.

"Then what?" she asked.

Sottrol laughed and replied, "One step at a time, you bundle of curiosity."

Then a more serious look crossed his face as he reminded them, "Know this. You two are bonded through time. The relationship you will experience as human and Spirit Guide will serve to strengthen these bonds."

"So we will continue to work together?" I asked.

"It is likely," Sottrol responded. "Much depends on the outcome of the mission. Now, shall we go?"

The wizard led us on a lengthy journey. At first I recognized some of the areas we passed, but then we entered an unfamiliar zone. We moved slowly because Angel did not possess the higher level of vibration that both Sottrol and I enjoyed. I had to keep reminding myself that it was highly unusual to have her with me on the Spirit Guide plane. We were, however, entering a different area, one where there were other Souls in transition.

At last we arrived in a very formal chamber. It brought to mind the church I had attended during my last lifetime on Earth, but there was no visible ceiling on this room. When I looked up, all I saw was brilliant white light. An altar held a huge book. Curtains in various pastel hues formed a semi-circle around this altar. A golden vase that stood nearly as tall as Angel displayed a dozen or so colorful fragrant lilies.

Angel ran up and smelled them, exclaiming, "Oh Sottrol! They're wonderful!"

"They are for you, little one."

"I love them. I'm going to surround myself with beautiful lilies when I'm on Earth."

The sound of tiny bells tinkled above us.

Sottrol put his hand on my shoulder and directed me, "Step up to the altar, Darci."

As I approached, I realized how high it was. When I stood before it, the book was level with my chest. There were words emblazoned in bronze on the pages. My heart raced as I read the following statement:

> I, Darcimon Stillwater, hereby do solemnly promise to *help, to guide, and to protect the Soul known as Angel. I will stand by her and watch over her no matter what may transpire, no matter what the difficulties, no matter how this Soul may respond or react to my guidance. I promise to adhere to the Spirit Guide Creed in all I do. All my*

actions and reactions will always come from a base of unconditional love, and I will show compassion in all that I do. I make this pledge with the knowledge that this Earth-bound Soul is depending on me for guidance. I sign this with the intention of doing all I can to help this Soul and with the understanding that the consequences of breaking this solemn pledge are very great.

I read these words several times. Neither Sottrol nor any of my other teachers ever described any great consequences. Not that I intended to break the pledge, but I preferred to be aware of all possibilities. No one knew better than I that strange surprises, twists and turns were not only possible but also likely on Earth. Sottrol was standing behind me, following my thoughts. He put his hand on my shoulder and sent me a telepathic message.

"Darci, just as a Soul may rise higher and higher in the great spiral of life, so can that Soul sink lower and lower. As long as you always act for the greater good of the Soul you are protecting, there are no dire consequences for you. Only if you intentionally lead your human charge to make choices that are detrimental, choices that would cause that Soul to slide lower on the spiral, only then would you face such great consequences. You would be demoted and your karma would be seriously in need of balance. It would take you treading a long, hard road to come back to the point where you might be considered to take on the role of a Spirit Guide once again. I'm telling you this because I know you. I know you wish to be aware of all the possible ramifications of putting your signature on this pledge. I also know that you would never ever do anything to harm Angel, so there is no danger of dire consequences. I hope this sets your mind at ease."

I nodded and silently said a prayer for Angel and me. I was ready to sign. I placed my hands on the book at the bottom of the large pages and said, "I agree."

When I lifted my hands, there was my signature in gold followed by a high ringing sound that echoed throughout the elegant formal chamber.

I felt a tug at my heart and turned and looked at Angel. Two things happened simultaneously. A great wave of love for her flooded through me, and a phosphorescent stream of light curled around her then around me, linking us in an oval of luminescence. I floated toward her, and the light surrounding us became more intense. I could see by her face that she, too, was overwhelmed with love. When we embraced, a puff of sparkles lit the chamber.

"This is as it should be," declared Sottrol who was standing off to the side. "The bond is now formed. Angel is now under your guidance and care, Darci—and Angel, every time you take Darci's advice and apply it to your life on Earth, you will be helping him."

Angel still had one arm around me as she turned to the elder. "Would you explain that, Sottrol?"

"There is give and take on both sides of the human-Spirit Guide relationship. Darci is still learning, too. When you accept his guidance and use it, he shines brighter, becomes stronger, and moves forward on his spirit path. Your partnership through the veil between worlds has the potential to propel you both forward in your spiritual evolution, as well as benefiting the Earth and humankind as a whole."

"You mean the mission?" Angel spoke up.

"Yes, but who knows what you two may accomplish? The possibilities are endless, really."

"You want us to focus on the mission, though. Am I right?" I asked.

"Although the mission specifies certain results, you two have input on how these results are achieved. I look forward to seeing how creative you can be. Congratulations, both of you. You are officially bonded as Spirit Guide and human charge. Are you ready for the next step?"

Angel and I answered together in the affirmative, so the elder motioned for us to follow him. We didn't go far this time. The three of us moved along a curved hallway behind the formal chamber. This passageway had many tall oval doorways with circular panels in their centers. Some of these circles had designs in them; others did not.

"What are these patterns?" asked Angel as we passed an elaborate circular design on one of the doors.

"A work in progress," Sottrol replied. "Inside each of the rooms with a design in the circle are a Spirit Guide and a Soul about to set off on a journey to the lower spiral. They are in the midst of a mapping and planning session. The pattern on the door indicates how far they have gotten. Here is your room."

The wizard motioned towards an oval door that had a blank circle and explained, "You will stay here now and work out of this room until Angel is ready to leave for Earth."

"What about our cat?" Angel piped up.

"See for yourself," responded Sottrol, as he touched the circle on the door, and it slid open.

The orange cat was standing there meowing a greeting. Angel immediately picked him up and asked him if he liked the new place.

I looked around. The room just inside the door had floating seats at several levels. It appeared to be a meeting or conference room. I stepped through another oval opening into an area that had two screens on opposite walls and a table in the center, filled with maps, scrolls, and books. Through another smaller oval doorway was a sleeping pallet for Angel with a meditation alcove for me. The head of the bed was also in the shape of an alcove so that the resident could use the pallet for horizontal rest or for seated meditation. It amazed me to think that I would no longer need sleep but would renew my energy through meditation. The triple chamber was warmly lit and appeared very comfortable. This was where

Angel and I would make our final decisions and preparations before our work on Earth began.

Sottrol relaxed in one of the floating chairs as Angel and I looked around.

"This chamber will serve you well," he called to us.

After a while, we joined Sottrol in the front room.

"Where do we begin?" I asked the elder as I helped Angel into one of the floating chairs.

"Angel has already begun by reviewing her past lives. She has yet to see her death imprint from her last Earth life. You will examine it with her and help her understand it. There is also the shuffle of incarnations. Because you have lived so many Earth lives, Angel, my dear, some will not play a part in this upcoming lifetime, and others will. That's what the screens are for. You can review important points in any of your former lives."

"Why is it called a shuffle?" I asked the elder.

"Because the incarnations are shuffled like a deck of cards. The ones that come to the top are the ones that will be more significant in the planning of your next lifetime—along with the death imprint, of course."

"Do we really shuffle cards?" asked Angel, looking as if she were eager to play a game.

"Not exactly," Sottrol said, smiling at her. "The Creator does the shuffling. The incarnations that you have to draw from will be the ones that appear automatically on the viewing screens. Watch and note carefully what is shown to you. I recommend a great deal of prayer around this process. Once you have reviewed these incarnations, you will be ready to begin writing your Soul Contract."

"I just want to be clear," I interjected. "Is this in addition to the mission we have been given?"

"Yes," said the elder as he turned to Angel. "You will have your plate quite full this incarnation, little one."

"Good," Angel spoke with a grin. "I don't want to ever be hungry."

We laughed, and Sottrol remarked, "You will never lack for something to do. You will get busier and more efficient with your time as you grow older and begin to understand what you are on Earth to do. You two have some images to review, so I will leave you to it."

Before we could ask him anything more, he vanished leaving a ring of glittering stars on the seat.

"Do you want to get started, or do you want to rest?" I asked, determined to be considerate of Angel's need for sleep.

"I'm all right. We can start now."

"Tell me when you're tired," I said as I helped her out of the floating chair.

She nodded, and we went into the room with the screens. Two of the floating chairs followed us. We found the cat asleep on the table sprawled across some of the papers.

I took Angel's hands and bowed my head. She followed my lead.

I spoke this simple prayer, "Great Spirit, please bless this process and guide us as we ready Angel for life on Earth."

The room came alive as soon as we finished our prayer. Both screens lit up, and the floating chairs circled us. Angel laughed as the cat jumped up and did a sideways dance off the table.

The image of a man appeared on one of the screens. He was in tatters with a dirty sack over his shoulder. As he walked down a road, he accosted passersby, trying to sell then something from his sack. When one older woman stopped and looked at the scarves and beads he had for sale, he took her coins, gave her the beads, and then used a sleight-of-hand trick to re-pocket them. The old woman never saw it.

"Hey, he just cheated that woman!" cried Angel pointing at the screen.

We watched as the man proceeded to trick and cheat anyone who stopped to buy his wares.

"This is not good," said Angel. "I wouldn't want to be fooled like that. It's stealing."

I sat in one of the floating chairs and wrote down *Integrity and honesty in all dealings and transactions.* As soon as I wrote it, that screen went blank and the other screen came alive. My heart did a little skip when I saw a tall, lean man dressed in dark clothing walk slowly along.

"Uh oh," sighed Angel. "That looks like Gabriel. I knew I would still be paying for the mistakes I made in that lifetime."

She watched tearfully as the image on the screen went through the final phases of that lifetime.

"How could I do that? How could I withdraw and leave you to do all the work, raise the children, and look after me? Darci, how can I make it up to you?"

I took her hand and assured her, "You will."

I wrote down *Self-sufficient, doesn't burden others.*

Angel looked at what I was writing and asked, "Can I add something? After all, it is my life we are designing. Write down *Fiercely independent.* I don't want to have to rely on anybody. No one around me should have to go through what you did as my partner."

I wrote down *Independent.*

Next, Tuura's graceful figure appeared on the other screen. She carried many scrolls in her arms. She unrolled one to show an astrological birth chart. I wrote down *Talent in astrology.*

"I get to be an astrologer?" Angel queried.

"I have a feeling you'll get to be many things this time around."

"I'd better live long enough, then," she pouted. "My last lifetime as Anthony, I barely got out of diapers when I was killed in the streets."

I wrote down *Long life.* Angel nodded.

To our surprise, Angel herself appeared on the screen along with her teacher, Regina. They were painting colorful pictures, so I wrote down *Artistic talent. Love of painting.*

The opposite screen came alive with an image of a sweet little girl sneaking into a fancy room filled with people. She hid under the grand piano as musicians played chamber music.

I wrote down *Love of music.*

Next we heard the rumble of stampeding hooves, and on the opposite screen we saw thousands of buffalo moving across the plains. A young native hunter watched them from a cliff. He made a sketch in the dirt, pulled out one of his hairs, and placed it on the drawing. He then said a prayer, and as he did so, a brightly-colored bird landed on the ground near him. He smiled when he saw it.

I wrote down *Love of birds and animals.*

Angel looked at my notes and said, "Add *healthy respect for nature*, could you, Darci?"

The list was several pages long by the time Angel admitted she was tired and wanted to rest. I accompanied her to the bedroom and used the opportunity to meditate. Once I had centered and refreshed myself, I returned to the center room as Angel slept.

Because I was inexperienced, I was curious about the books stacked on the table. I had never helped a Soul prepare for Earth life and thought perhaps there was information in them. I wondered why I had not taken a class in this since it was my first task as a Spirit Guide.

"That's because every Soul and every situation are different," I heard Sottrol's voice in my head.

My mentor appeared next to me a moment later, clarifying, "We teach students how to think, reason, and act with unconditional love and compassion. Then we give them the opportunity to figure the rest out on their own."

"I don't know where to start, Sottrol."

"Easy. You start with the death imprint from the most recent lifetime. Then you use the incarnations that have been weighted and shuffled to the top—and then you improvise with love."

"I feel I need more guidance. This is my first time and— it's Angel I'm helping. I don't want to let her down."

"Impossible, Darci. You will do fine, but I understand your lack of confidence. That's why I made sure there are many reference books in this chamber. Not only do they give you something to do while Angel is sleeping, but also they will provide you with information and examples. Oh yes—there's a file you might want to have a look at, too. Now, take heart. All is well. I'll leave you to your reading."

Sottrol vanished as he walked away leaving a luminous mist with the aroma of sweetgrass.

The book on top of the pile was a rich crimson color. When I opened it, there were no words at first. Then they appeared. The pages told of another Guide named Hanso who was helping prepare a Soul named Zee for life on the Earth plane. Zee wanted very much to be a woman and bear children during the upcoming incarnation, but the lifetimes that were available as resources were all ones where he had been a man; therefore, the talents included strength, accuracy with a bow and spear, competitive prowess, and so on. Hanso recommended an incarnation as a male, but Zee was determined to have a female body. There was a very amusing section where Hanso pointed out the type of life that might result from such a combination.

The next story was about a first-time Guide like myself who was unsure what to do. This Guide named Matta devised a formula that included all the various ingredients. Just as I began to think that this was a good idea, the Soul to whom Matta had been assigned chose something entirely different. I began to see that there was a great deal of give and take between the Spirit Guide and the Soul.

I moved to a bright purple volume created by one of the Master Guides. In it he wrote many pages about paying attention to detail when preparing a Soul for an incarnation on the lower spiral.

"The Soul in question must have a complete set of tools if there is any hope of this entity taking a step forward on the evolutionary path," I read aloud. "Think of these tools as a resource kit that the Soul opens and uses as she makes her way through her incarnation. The attending Guide would want that Soul to have a complete kit with no tools missing."

I sat back and thought about this. Of course I wanted Angel to be properly equipped and wondered how to make sure this was accomplished. I knew that she had Earth karma, issues and challenges, which she would have to face during her upcoming lifetime. She had already chosen these through her actions during previous lives. I wanted to know what these challenges were.

As I continued through the reference materials, I found the very packet I was seeking. Under the next book was a file, probably the one Sottrol had mentioned. I stared at the cover for a moment because of the unique gold symbol on it. When I opened the file, I gasped because the pages were black with copper-colored writing on them. My heart raced as I took the top page in my hand. It felt warm, almost hot to my touch. At first the symbols made no sense. I automatically said a prayer, and when I looked back at the sheet, the symbols had changed into letters I could understand.

Karmic Pages for the Soul Known as Angel said the title. Each page had a challenge written across the top, followed by a description of how and why Angel had incurred this challenge. The file was thicker than I thought it should be. I wondered how many of these challenges Angel could handle in this next lifetime. After all, we did have the mission to address, but her personal growth was important, too. Reading through these pages, compassion swelled in my heart as I realized all that this Soul had been through. By the time I got to the last few pages, I was trembling, overwhelmed with empathy and love for the Soul who was my partner.

After a short break, I read through the karmic pages again. I knew that Angel had to deal with everything within them eventually, but my question was how much to include in this upcoming incarnation. I said a prayer for help. Then I sent Sottrol a telepathic message requesting his assistance but heard his voice in my head assuring me that I could do this on my own. He said for me to seek balance in my choices.

I took the list of talents and gifts that I had made earlier with Angel and began laying these white pages out on the table. Then I took the stack of black karmic pages and began matching each challenge to a gift, each black page to a white. Sometimes the black page would cling to the white one, and sometimes it would slide away, almost as if the two pages held magnetic charges. Before long, each white page had a black companion, and I had four black pages left in my hand. I returned them to the folder and looked at the table. From this black and white collage, we would make a birth imprint for Angel. I wasn't sure what the next step was, so I took a break and meditated near my sleeping partner, then prayed again. After all, this was my first official assignment as a Spirit Guide, and it concerned my dear Soul mate, so I wanted to do well by her.

When I completed a long and rejuvenating meditation, I checked on Angel who was still asleep and then went back to the work room. The top of the table was glowing, and I was struck by a moment of panic thinking perhaps I hadn't proceeded correctly, but when I looked at what lay there, I was completely surprised. The black and white pages had disappeared. In their place was a large full-color chart, Angel's birth imprint.

I studied it carefully. The circle had about twenty symbols, most of them along the bottom edge of the chart. This graph was similar to astrological charts I had seen when living with Tuura in Egypt, but there were more symbols. I wondered if Angel would recall her expertise as an astrologer and be able to interpret this graph. I didn't have long to wait. I was still studying when Angel made her presence known by throwing her arms around me from behind.

The warmth of her hug sent love and compassion flowing from me.

"I have something for you to see," I told her, grasping her hands. "The Universe has designed your birth imprint, and I want you to see it."

Angel stepped over to the table, eyes wide with anticipation, and said, "It's so colorful—and so many symbols. Why are they mostly along the bottom rim?"

"I was hoping you could tell me. You are the one with the astrological knowledge."

"I need to call on what Tuura knows," she said as she leaned in closer to study the symbols. "I remember this much—when a person is born with most of the planets below the horizon line—or on the bottom of the circle—then the challenges come mostly from within."

"Through meditation and turning within is where you'll find me," I said softly, stroking the back of her head. "It's good that the pattern is set up this way. You may find your way to meditation early in life and develop your telepathic abilities. The sooner you do this, the sooner we can consciously connect."

"I see. Yes, you're right. Well—this is what I have to work with. Since I can access Tuura's skills this lifetime, I will be able to interpret my birth chart myself."

"I saw your karmic pages. Most of them are included in this chart along with the list of gifts and attributes we made."

"Most—not all? Am I coming back to Earth again after this incarnation?" Angel had one eyebrow raised as Tuura used to do.

"I'm not sure. There were four karmic pages left, but I don't know exactly when or how you will resolve the issues described on them."

"I guess I better just focus on what's coming up this time around—lots of inner challenges, that's for sure."

"You won't be alone, my dear. There will be many humans who will be born with patterns below the horizon line.

You are going to be returning to Earth with a great influx of Souls. Now that the big war is over, many couples are starting families."

"I get to choose my parents."

"First, I believe we write your Soul Contract."

"Explain that please, Darci."

"You will sign a contract which states what you intend to accomplish during this upcoming incarnation. We talked about this, remember?"

"When we did, this moment seemed so far away."

I again saw a hint of sadness in her eyes, so I pulled her to me and embraced her. We stayed in each other's arms until I heard her sigh.

"Do you want to begin?" I asked, pulling back so I could see the expression on her face.

"I guess so. Let's not make the contract too hard, okay?"

I laughed a little and assured her, "Come now, you know you'll have everything you need to meet any challenge and accomplish any goal."

"I'll have you on my side, Darci, and that gives me hope."

I looked through the books on the table until I found a ledger that was a rich gold color with white letters that spelled "Soul Contract." The pages inside were blank, the first seven white, and then I came to a section of bright yellow. The word "Notations" was at the top of the first yellow page.

"You tell me what you want to accomplish, and I'll make notes," I said picking up a quill.

Angel began thinking aloud and said, "What I want to accomplish—let's see . . ."

She stared at the birth imprint and words came flowing out, "I want to accomplish building a home in a beautiful location that is safe and protected. I want to accomplish being an artist, an astrologer, and a speaker who helps many people. I want to accomplish good works of high quality. I want to accomplish a balanced partnership, and I want to accomplish much to help the Earth plane.

I guess that's included in our mission."

"Yes. You can do more."

"Like what?"

"You can accomplish communication with all levels of Beings—even the most subtle. You can accomplish communication over long distances that will reach many people. Indeed, you can be a colorful, exciting communicator."

Angel rolled her eyes, then glanced again at the birth imprint. She pointed to two symbols close together near the bottom of the graph and noted, "Mercury, planet of communication, and Pluto, planet of power and deep transformation are near each other—so my words will have power and the ability to transform."

"It will be up to you to use that gift wisely."

"I hope I do everything right, Darci," she sighed.

"You know that's unlikely. Of course, you'll make mistakes—all humans do. My job is to keep you on the right path."

"I'm scared I'll regress like I did when I was Gabriel."

"I won't let you. Trust me. According to your chart, you must include inner work in this contract."

I jotted down "improve self-esteem," "value personal resources," and "heal childhood trauma."

Angel was looking over my shoulder at the ledger as I wrote and questioned me, "What childhood trauma?"

"Think about it, Love. You caused trauma in the lives of all your children when you were Gabriel. You were born with a physical deformity as Shalia, and your parents died leaving you orphaned as Anthony. I'd say you have childhood trauma to face and heal."

She was fidgety and appeared a little upset as she inquired, "It will manifest in this upcoming lifetime, won't it, Darci?"

I could not lie to her; I had seen her karmic pages.

"Yes, it will. Your job is to understand and heal the childhood experience."

She looked once again at the birth imprint. It seemed to calm her.

"Yes. Look here—the moon right at the bottom of the circle. My subconscious patterns will be affected a great deal by my childhood."

"It will be more of an issue for you than for many. Remember, for every challenge, you have plenty of gifts to help you—like your understanding of astrology and the birth chart."

"Understanding the challenges is the first step to dealing with them, but I won't have that as a child. I'll have to endure—whatever."

"I'll be there to protect you."

"But I won't know it."

"You'll sense it; I promise you will."

The two of us worked long and hard on Angel's Soul Contract. I wanted Sottrol or Chalherine to look over what we had done. It was the first time I had drawn up such a covenant, so I wanted to make sure it was done properly. Once Angel went into the bedroom to rest, I prayed, and then asked for help from my teachers. To my surprise, the Master Guide Arcillis manifested in the oval doorway between rooms. His radiance lit the chamber brightly. I bowed to greet him.

"Darci," he responded with a nod. "We Master Guides are monitoring your progress as we are the ones who designed your mission. All is well. I have come to tell you that I will be your supervisor on the mission and will help you all I can. Before I go over Angel's Soul Contract with you, I have an important invitation. The Master Guides wish you to study with them."

"My focus must be Angel."

"Yes, of course, Darci. The studies will not interfere in any way with your duties as a Spirit Guide. In fact, they will enhance your performance and further the mission."

"What are these studies?"

"The Master Guides are preparing information to be disseminated on the Earth plane. We wish you to help us with the final organization of this material. Perhaps Angel can be one of the humans who receives this data. This seems a likely scenario if you help us with this project because you will be very familiar with the information, and you have a strong telepathic link with her."

"What is this information?"

"The Earth plane is nearing a great evolutionary turning point. This naturally occurring cycle is being supplemented and enhanced by a gift from the Creator. In order for humans to make the most of this opportunity, the Master Guides are preparing a manuscript with details on what is happening and simple instructions to help humans."

"I'm very interested, Arcillis, especially since this may provide a focus for me and Angel and our work through the veil."

"Very well. I'm pleased, and I look forward to working with you. Now—let me see this Soul Contract you and Angel have written."

The Master Guide helped me with the wording in several places and added one line that he said was more or less standard of all contracts for humans: the challenge of learning to love unconditionally. We finished going over the contract just as Angel woke from her nap. We greeted her, and she hugged me sleepily, then the Master Guide, too, without reserve or ceremony.

"Your Soul Contract is complete," the Master Guide informed her. "Go over it with Darci. When you are ready, sign it. The next step will be choosing your parents. I must go."

With those words, he turned and took two steps as if he were climbing invisible stairs. Then he vanished, leaving the scent of fresh sage in the air. Angel smelled it and remarked about it.

Although I knew timing was important and there was some urgency, I felt that the process of preparing Angel for her next Earth incarnation was going too fast. She would be gone before long, her Soul implanted in the body of an unborn babe. I knew I would miss her, so I hugged her again and held her until she started squirming in my arms.

"What is it, Darci? What's wrong? Don't you want me to see my Soul Contract?"

"All is well," I replied, holding her head in my hands and looking into her eyes. "I'm just savoring this moment."

She hugged me lovingly, then twisted restlessly in my embrace and asked, "Is my Soul Contract really difficult?"

"There's nothing written in it that you cannot accomplish. It's on the table. Read it for yourself."

I knew in my heart that her Soul was being called to Earth. She seemed driven, and I sensed a new motivation in her. She immediately pulled away from me, focused on the completed contract, scanned it, and then slowly read it aloud.

Soul Contract for Angel Lily Anadonnapolis

I hereby pledge that during this incarnation on the lower spiral plane known as Earth, I will try to learn to love unconditionally; I will dedicate myself to serving the Earth mother, and I will treat the Earth with reverence and respect. I will try to view all on Earth with compassion, to trust the benevolence of the Universe, to be generous, even when I have very little, to give to others with a full heart, to be resourceful using what I have to benefit the Earth, to appreciate all that is given to me, to be thankful for all the blessings bestowed upon me, to love myself as a blessed Soul, a daughter of the Creator, to forgive in love — especially myself, to be open-minded and tolerant, to act with kindness and gentleness in all I do, to be honest and to act with integrity in all my dealings, to honor and respect the elders, and when I walk as an elder myself, to give generously of my wisdom.

She leaned back against me and took a deep breath.

"Are you all right?" I asked her. "We can still alter this. You have not yet signed it."

"There is so much there," she sighed. "I'm no wizard. I don't know if I can do all that. It's too much."

"Oh—I thought you might want to add a few lines," I teased her.

She didn't think it was funny.

"Darci, stop it. Look—I had so very little the last few times I was on Earth that I think it will be very difficult for me to give away any resources I might possess, no matter what they are. I still have fear of starvation and poverty, even here, now, on the Spirit Guide plane."

Compassion for her filled my heart as I responded, "I know, little one. However, you have requested a lifetime without hunger, and it has been promised to you."

"It will take more than that to ease my fears. I'll have to live it, I guess, and perhaps the experience of a belly that is constantly satisfied will neutralize my dread of hunger."

"This contract is only part of the complex process of experiencing a lifetime on the lower spiral. There's your death imprint as Anthony, your birth imprint, your karma—and our mission, of course."

"The mission! I nearly forgot! The mission on top of this? Are you sure you wouldn't like to go to Earth in my place and face all of this?"

Now she was teasing. I enjoyed how we could be so relaxed and informal with each other.

"Sorry, Angel Lily Anadonnapolis. I just signed a contract myself to take care of you and watch over you—and I think I have the bigger job here."

We both laughed.

Sottrol came through the door at just that moment.

"I didn't know preparing for life on the lower spiral was such a barrel of laughs," he joked.

"We are remaining cheerful in the face of difficulty," I responded. "Have you come to see the contract?"

"I'll take a look" said the elder, "though I've come to say time is short, and Angel must choose her parents. Earth now has thousands of pregnant parents, and we must be ready with an equal number of Souls prepared to descend to Earth. There is a great selection of potential parents right now, Angel— although your karma and your birth imprint will narrow the field. Why don't you and Darci go to the selection area and begin the process?"

"Selection area? You mean the place where Angel will choose her parents? You'll have to show us the way, Sottrol. This is my first time as a Spirit Guide, remember?"

"Oh, I remember. You don't need me to lead you. Just go down the passageway to the left. You'll enter the area."

Angel and I followed his directions. We had to travel along the curving hallway for a bit of a distance before it opened into a very unusual circular room. In the middle was a ring-shaped desk with three Guides in the center. Around the circumference of the room were very tall booths. Each booth had at least a dozen small screens stacked vertically. As I glanced around, I noticed that some of the screens were blank and some had images. We walked up to the donut-shaped desk. The Guide who greeted us seemed to know who we were.

"Ah, Darcimon Stillwater and dear Angel Lily. We have been expecting you. Welcome!" said a large jolly Guide with a full white beard and an orange cap. "I'm Pedompa at your service. I'll get you two set up in a booth directly."

He placed his hands on a couple of large lighted panels on the surface of the desk and said our names. The panel rose up and shone brighter than before. Then he removed a glowing disk about the size of a dinner plate.

"Follow me," Pedompa said, motioning with his head.

I was right behind him, but Angel was so caught up in looking around the room that I had to go back and fetch her.

The cheerful Guide led us to a vacant booth. Inside were two floating chairs and the tower of screens. He inserted the glowing disc into a slot at the base of the stack.

"Your information is on that plate," he informed us. "Your most recent death imprint, your birth imprint for this upcoming incarnation, and more are there. Now view your potential parents on the screens provided here. Your personal information has narrowed the field to twenty. I suggest you trim that number down. Each time you decide that the parents you are viewing are not for you—Darci, you put your left hand on this panel and Angel, you put your right hand on the matching one. Let me see you try that. Do it together."

We did as he asked.

"Good, good. The images on the screen will rotate. You can watch them over and over. Take as much time as you want. When you have eliminated all but one couple, we will seal the deal." He chuckled. "Good luck—and remember, the couples you are viewing are only human."

As he left, he slid a door across behind us, giving us some privacy although the screens that rose high above in a stack were visible from the rest of the large room. We heard him click the door into place, and the screens came on. The first image we saw was an Asian woman, cooking fish. She was slender and had long dark hair. Her husband came in, tasted the sauce in the pan, and put a little dab on her nose. She swatted him playfully. The image that had been on the screen right above that one moved down, and the Asian couple moved to the top screen. I realized the pictures of Angel's potential parents were going to rotate. All we had to do was sit there and observe. I urged Angel to take her time and watch carefully.

The first round of images all had couples dealing with food. I suspected this was to reassure Angel that she would not be born into starvation. The second round of pictures showed extended families at play. Swimming was featured in a number of these scenarios, including one in South America and one in North America. I watched Angel as she studied the faces of the pregnant mothers.

Next we observed the expectant parents relating to each other. In two scenes we saw the elaborate wedding ceremonies. In others we viewed husbands waiting on their wives, or hugging, or kissing.

Angel looked up at me and asked, "We don't need to see anything more explicit, do we?"

I smiled and answered, "I don't think so."

Grandparents were featured next. Many had other grandchildren, and we watched them relate, but Angel was especially drawn to the parents of a woman who was expecting their first grandchild.

"I would be the number one grandchild for that whole side of the family," she reasoned. She studied her potential grandmother. "I can see I would learn much kindness and compassion from her."

"Examine this woman's daughter and husband carefully. You will be raised by them, not by the grandparents."

We observed the screens for a long time before eliminating candidates. I could see Angel really wanted to be the first born, so that discounted four of the couples who already had a child or two. Once we took out these, we began to see some of the challenges Angel would face if she chose these couples.

As we went through the remaining candidates, money was an issue in every scene. We watched the couples bicker about it. Most were planning the arrival of their first baby and making purchases. Again, Angel was drawn to the expectant mother with the kind parents. They were very generous with gifts for their daughter and her new baby-to-be.

"I would learn generosity from such grandparents," she pointed out.

Next the screens focused on the pregnant women. Most were happy and very excited to be carrying their first child. The woman with the kind and generous grandparents also had two younger sisters and a younger brother who were almost as excited as she was.

"If I choose these parents, then I will be the first born of the first born, and I'll get a lot of attention," Angel mused.

I agreed that this expectant mother seemed very happy. We watched as she sat with her feet up eating chocolate pudding and singing along to the radio.

"I like her," said Angel.

After more viewing and more elimination, we narrowed the field to two sets of potential parents. One was the couple with the kind grandparents in the United States, and the other couple lived in a villa in Argentina. I preferred the latter set of parents because the setting was very beautiful and the whole extended family lived on the ranch. My reasoning was that Angel would have an entire group of people to raise and influence her, but she thought this would be too confusing and favored the North American couple. We watched one more scene for each pair. The couple in New England was at a family gathering of the husband's relatives who were all Scottish. There was much joking and laughter. The couple from Argentina was at a big outdoor round-up of cattle and were cooking over an open fire.

"I want my mother and father to be these two," Angel said as she pointed to the couple from the United States. "I want to be in on the laughter—and I want to speak English."

"Very well. This is your choice. Are you certain?"

"Yes, Darci. Look how happy they are. Those people know how to laugh. I'd say I'll have a much more cheerful childhood than the last three I experienced."

"Let's do the final step, then."

We placed our hands on the panels to eliminate the Argentinean family. As soon as we did this, the entire column of screens lit up and a long, low tone sounded. The door slid away from behind us, and Pedompa entered the cubicle.

"Very good, very good. I will process this choice for you." He checked some numbers on the console and slid a lighted lever into a slot and said, "You have only a short time before you must descend to the Earth plane and enter the human body being carried by this woman. According to the Earth calendar, she is due to give birth in July, which is not far off."

The screen now showed some numbers.

"Is this the birth date and time?" I asked the Guide.

"Yes, that's it. As I said, not far away. The Soul must be in the fetus for at least three days before the birth, or the melding will not be successful. Please make your final preparations, Angel. Your time is near."

Angel raised her shoulders and wrung her hands in worried anticipation.

She took a deep breath, sighed, and then asked, "What is there left to do?"

"We must finalize your Soul Contract," I reminded her, "and say farewell to the time we have enjoyed together on the Spirit Guide plane."

"You two have been very fortunate," nodded the jolly Guide. "It is very unusual for a Spirit Guide and an Earth-bound Soul to be together for such an extended period. Most have only the exchanges that take place here in this area of preparation for the lower spiral. You have a very special bond."

"We know," I said as I hugged my mate. "Thank you, Pedompa."

"May your mission be successful," he said as he stepped aside.

There stood Sottrol with a lily in his hand, which he promptly gave to Angel.

Her eyes lit up with delight as she exclaimed, "Thank you, Sottrol! It's so beautiful—just like the Earth."

"Come now, you two," urged the elder. "You must finish the Soul Contract and say your good-byes. The summer solstice has arrived in Earth's northern hemisphere, which means your day of birth is a mere two weeks away.

Come, let's return to your preparation chamber."

We followed him as we retraced the steps to our suite. I noticed when we arrived that there was now a nearly completed pattern in the circle on the door.

"I've revised the Soul Contract for you," Sottrol informed us. "You did well with it though I felt it needed a few special additions. Just call if you wish to discuss the changes." He floated up and disappeared.

Angel was tired and asked for a chance to rest before she faced her Soul Contract again. I went with her into the sleep and meditation area and held her as she dozed, wondering what it would be like as a Spirit Guide to hold her when she was in physical form.

I thought back through our many Earth lifetimes together and remembered what it was like when we were both in human bodies. From our small slight forms as Shu and Nua to my towering dark body as Hett holding her golden graceful body when she was Tuura, I perused our many journeys together on the material plane. Angel was very muscular and athletic as Nunzah and very soft, sweet, and elegant as Yulanna Carlotta. The human body had many variations. The same Soul could manifest on Earth in so many different forms.

I even went back in my mind to when I was in a female body as Morning Sky and as Marie, reasoning that this exercise would help me understand Angel once she took the form of a human female. From my perspective as a Spirit Guide, I could see how different it felt to be in a female body as opposed to a male's. There had been no talk about what sex she would be this time though it seemed to me that Angel would have a better chance of fulfilling her particular contract if she were female. I made a note to ask Sottrol about this.

The entire time she slept, I held Angel, for I had no idea how soon she would depart. Whereas she and I had both been incarnated as humans many times, this was my virgin run as a Spirit Guide. I was a bit nervous, so I prayed over and over as I held her.

When she finally woke, she looked up at me with loving eyes and asked, "You've been holding me the whole time. Tell me, Darci—will you still do that when I'm in a human body?"

"I'd like to."

"It must be nearly time for me to go."

"You must sign your Soul Contract."

"It's kind of scary to think I'm going to be immersed in an unborn baby inside a woman. Will birth be painful?"

"I don't think so," I answered, not really knowing. "Sottrol altered your contract. We'd better take a look."

"I remember having children, but I don't remember being born. It was certainly painful giving birth. I never thought it might hurt to be the baby coming through."

"I'll be very close by. I'll help if I can," I reassured her, hugging her. Now was not the time to say that birth was one of the most dangerous transitions for a Soul.

She sighed and drew my arms closer around her.

"I know you'll take good care of me, Darci. What's the worst that could happen? I'll die and be right back in Spirit form with you."

"Now, Angel Lily," I spoke with a stern tone in my voice, "please don't think like that. All our preparations not only for your coming incarnation but also for our mission would then have been for naught. We'd have to start over."

"You're right. I can't disappoint the Master Guides. They've been planning this mission for a long time. I guess I've got to make a go of it. Let's look at the contract."

In the center room, Angel's contract was on the table. It looked quite different because the ledger lay open and the pages were glowing with golden light. My eyes needed a moment to adjust before I could read the words. Much was the same as written before, but Sottrol had added a few lines and had highlighted several already there. These words glowed with a brilliant white light.

The line *dedicate myself to serving the Earth mother* was highlighted, and *trust the benevolence of the universe* was also luminescent white. In addition, Sottrol had added *to walk with joy and appreciation* and *to bravely speak the truth* and *to face with courage and conviction the challenges that Earth life presents to me.*

Angel read it through twice, stepped back, took a deep breath, then glanced at me with a sparkle in her eye.

"I thought maybe Sottrol would edit this down to a couple of sentences."

I smiled at her and loved her all the more for being able to joke at a time when she was faced with serious challenges.

"Sottrol knows that you—that *we* can handle all of what is written there. Remember, we are a team."

"Oh, I do remember, Darci, and I'm counting on you to keep me out of trouble once I have on those human blinders."

She picked up the quill to sign, but hesitated, "I'm afraid I will be swept away once I write my name here."

She put down the pen and moved over to me, saying, "I request one more round of privacy with you before I go. Surely there is time for that."

"I want that too," I replied as my heart did a little flip.

Drawing her to me, I embraced her and said aloud, "I ask for privacy for Angel and me right here right now."

We heard a high ringing sound like thousands of tiny temple bells, and Sottrol's voice came into my mind, "Your request is granted. You have a short time. Enjoy."

Angel hugged me tighter and whispered softly, "I just heard Sottrol say we could . . ."

"I heard him, too," I purred in her ear, and without another word, I began kissing her forehead, her cheeks, her neck, and her lips. She relaxed in my arms and returned my kisses with passion.

There was something different about our lovemaking, probably because we knew this was the last time we would be together like this until after Angel's Earth life. I poured love into every part of her, and with my increased vibration; it was an overwhelming experience for my partner. I might have overdone it. During our exchanges of passion since my graduation, I had been slow and tender when bringing my whirling love energy inside her, but now there was a driving force within me that needed to show her how very much she meant to me. I admit I was not careful, and did not think about being gentle or slow.

I loved her with every part of me and took her on a journey that neither of us will ever forget. Her heart was open and love flowed out to me. The more I received from her, the more I wished to shower it back upon her. We rolled and tumbled, floated and flew until Angel was lost in bliss. Even then I did not want to stop. As she lay with a smile on her lips, relaxed, eyes closed, barely conscious, I still poured love vibrations into her. Sitting at her feet, I held each foot, lit them with my powerful energy, and sent the love up through her until she trembled once again.

Finally, I saw that she lay exhausted with joy, so I lay next to her and held her. Emotions raced through me. Love alternated with compassion and sadness. Part of me did not want to see this beautiful free Spirit, my companion and lover, submerged into the tiny helpless body of a human baby. I kept telling myself that I would be there, guarding her, protecting her, watching over her, but I knew it wouldn't be the same. I realized I might never see such a joyful expression on her face once she was on Earth. We certainly wouldn't make love like that. I asked myself how I could let her go. There was such a sense of loss; my heart yearned for her to stay.

At just that moment, Sottrol appeared at the end of the bed.

"Darci, Darci, please stop. You have never been a Spirit Guide before. You don't know the joys of such a situation. True, Angel will be in a human body, and true, she will not consciously know of your existence for many years, but those years will pass. Think ahead to the time when she does know you. She will be grounded with a corporeal form and can receive and hold the love you send her."

"We can make love . . .?"

"Oh yes—and communicate, and share energy—pretty much everything you do now with one exception."

"What's that?"

"You know as a Spirit Guide, you cannot physically move, change, or alter the dense material world. The Earth plane is carbon-based. Its essence is weight and gravity."

"I know all that, Sottrol. I have returned to Earth several times in spirit form."

"I'm not here to tell you what you cannot do but what you can. Even though the Earth plane is dense, it remains essentially energy. You can still have an influence on the Earth level though it will appear subtle in comparison to gross matter. Remember the spirit crystals you and Angel had implanted. You two are naturally tuned to each other, and the crystals reinforce this. You will be able to share much with Angel, especially once her telepathic abilities are developed enough for you two to have conscious communication."

"When will that be?"

"As a new born and a toddler, she will be able to see you. Once Earth conditioning begins in earnest—around the time she starts putting sentences together—she will no longer see you. This is true of all human babies. What's special about you and Angel is that your unconscious link is very strong. She will feel you even if she has no idea what she is feeling. Eventually, she will know all."

"She'll be a very wise Earth woman then."

"She will. You will help her. You two can write together, teach together, take walks, drives—yes, even make love. Get her to marry you before you try that though, Darci. She will not open up to you without that formality in place."

"Marriage? Between a human and a Spirit Guide? I didn't know that was possible."

"That's why I'm here today—to tell you what is possible once you and Angel are on opposite sides of the veil."

"None of this is certain."

"Correct. It is all potential. Even the mission, which has been prepared and worked on by many, may not fly. It is up to you, Darci, and that little one in your arms. The challenge is great, but you have all you need to meet it and so does Angel. In essence, you two are to set the example for thousands of other pairs of humans and Spirit Guides. You will show how there can be open conscious communication through the veil between worlds. You will demonstrate how Guides and humans can work together to accomplish a great deal. Such joint efforts benefit the humans, of course, the Spirit Guide, and the Earth plane as a whole.

"And know that you will not be alone in this work. Other pairs will be exploring the connection between Guide and human. You will be leaders, helping humanity take a great evolutionary step. The Earth is ready for such a transformation. Together you and Angel will help humans usher in this great change. It is an exciting time to be doing such work on Earth."

I sat for a moment taking all this in. Much of Sottrol's speech I had heard before, but I was still mystified by the prospect of marriage between a human and a Spirit Guide. Sottrol knew what I was pondering.

"Darci, you and Angel are Souls. We all are Souls, just at different stages of development. Love can pass from any level to any other level. No barriers can stop the flow of love. There is no reason you and Angel cannot be husband and wife."

"I'm in spirit form. An Earth husband has certain physical duties . . ."

Sottrol laughed, saying, "You can love her, support her, guide her, communicate, plan, and do many other things. While it's true you won't be bringing home a paycheck, you will support her in every other way."

"I won't have a physical body. Won't she want a human husband?"

"She may. That shouldn't stop you. There will be a time when she is alone. She will choose a period of retreat, and this is when to make your move. Talk to her. She will hear you. She will respond. Remember your incredibly strong bonds and the implanted crystals that link you. Activate these and she will come to you, heart and Soul."

"Your words give me hope, Sottrol."

"Keep in mind that humans have free will, and anything can happen. Also, you two will be connecting when the period of enlightenment is just beginning. You and Angel are among the pioneers. Courage and conviction are needed. You have that. I added them into Angel's contract to be certain."

"You're saying that I can hold her, kiss her, and make love to her as I do now—as I did when we both walked the Earth?"

"Yes. It will not be exactly the same because you are in spirit form and Angel will have a material form—but the exchanges of love between you could be even better. Why don't we leave this right here, Darci? Your priority now is ushering this dear Soul into her new human casing and seeing her through the birth process. Did the selection of parents go well?"

"Yes, I think so. She has chosen a couple with interesting backgrounds. The mother's family has been in North America for over three hundred years, and the father was born in Scotland. She comes from wealthy parents; he comes from a family who immigrated, hoping to improve their lot. Angel will have these two influences during her childhood."

"She will face what she needs and learn what she must. I will go now, but once Angel has signed her contract, I will escort you both to the Earth chute."

Although I wanted to ask him more, Sottrol took his leave. I prayed and then went into deep meditation until Angel awoke. Our cat, who was always nearby, nestled up against us as though he knew we would soon be leaving him.

The meditation helped me to even out my vibration, which was ragged with sadness and anticipation. I wanted to be calm and supportive of Angel as she faced the upcoming transformation. It was my joyful duty to serve her, and I was determined to do it well.

She awoke with a stretch and a yawn, still glowing from our passionate exchange.

"Dear Darci," she said quietly as she put her hand to my face. "My, my, my. Have I transformed into a real angel? I've never felt so light and joyful. You are—why I have no words to describe you as a lover."

"I fear I may have gone a bit overboard. I'm glad to see you are all right."

"I'm tingling everywhere. I feel as though I might float away into eternal bliss."

"That is not on your agenda."

"This is it, am I right? This is the last time we'll be together?"

"Nonsense. I'm your Spirit Guide. I'll be with you for every step you take on Earth."

"You know I mean together here in Spirit, relating one on one. That's over now. I'm about to be fitted with my Earth blinders."

"Sottrol was here while you were sleeping. He informed me that we will be able to do many of the things we have shared here on the Spirit Guide plane—and that includes making love."

"How can that be? I'll be in a human body and you won't."

"It doesn't matter. We'll find a way to express our love. Hold that in your heart, my dear partner, for we must get you to Earth. May I escort you into the next room? I believe you have a contract to sign."

Angel's face was very serious as she climbed off the bed and headed for the central room. I followed closely behind her, for she was a little unsteady. I couldn't tell if she was hesitating or still recovering from all the high vibrations I had pumped into her. Once she reached the table, she asked me to put my arms around her, and as I did, she signed her Soul Contract.

The ledger, which was glowing already, came to life. It levitated, turned, closed itself, and then vanished in a silent explosion of light. Angel and I were both stunned, and as we stood there staring at the place where the golden ledger had been, Sottrol and Chalherine appeared before us. They floated over and hugged us in one great embrace.

"We are your official send-off committee," smiled Chalherine. "Your mission on Earth begins now."

The two esteemed elders began to escort us to the door when Angel ran back to hug our friend the cat.

"You will have many, many feline friends on Earth," assured Sottrol. "Come, my dear. It is time."

We four journeyed through a number of hallways and great rooms. Soon I began recognizing certain markers I had learned when going to Earth as an apprentice Guide. We moved past those to an area that was new to me. There was a great archway covered with elaborate symbols. On each side of the arch stood a Spirit at a podium. Both wore hooded cloaks, so we could see only their radiance shining out.

Sottrol spoke to the Spirit on the left and Chalherine, the Spirit on the right. Both gatekeepers checked something in a log book, then nodded and motioned for us to come across. Angel was trembling a little as we stepped through the archway. I held her hand and squeezed it hoping to comfort her.

Before us was what can only be described as a cosmic carousel. Instead of painted ponies, there were booths that seated two. Everything glowed with a soothing gold light. We watched as the carousel rotated slowly, some doors closed, some open. Just like a ride at a fair or an amusement park, the phosphorescent carousel came to a stop with an open booth before us. This was it—our departure to Earth.

Before we stepped in, we turned to say good-bye to our kind mentors but could see nothing behind us except blinding white light.

"They're gone!" exclaimed Angel. "It's all gone!"

Just then I heard Chalherine's voice in my mind saying, "Many blessings upon you."

Then Sottrol's voice followed saying, "Go in light and love, my dear ones."

"I heard them," said Angel who was still grasping my hand tightly.

"I did as well." I turned to her, saying, "Let's have one more embrace before we go, shall we?"

She melted into my arms, and we swayed, locked in a long heartfelt hug, realizing that this embrace would have to last us for many, many Earth years. It was so hard for me to let her go.

At least we were stepping into the transportation booth together. We were a team, and I told myself that we would not really be separated. Finally I lifted Angel's chin and looked right into her eyes. She was weeping and trembling, so I hugged her close again, but this time led her towards the waiting carousel. We stepped up onto the platform, and with one last long loving look, we entered the cubicle. The door slid closed behind us, and I felt the carousel move, but instead of rotating, it vibrated.

I stayed on the left side as Sottrol had previously instructed, with Angel on the right. We were still holding hands as vibration in the cubicle increased. I was a bit anxious, as I had no idea what was going to happen even though I must have entered the Earth plane with my Guides dozens of times.

The vibration intensified, and I began to see Angel change. I was no longer able to hold her hand. Her spirit form became more translucent at first, then shrank in size and became denser and brighter. Right before my eyes, my dear partner was being distilled into her spirit essence. When the vibrations slowed, Angel was a sphere of bright golden light.

I came close and peered into the glowing ball and clearly saw her beautiful violet eyes. It was she, no doubt about it, now ready to enter the human body she had chosen.

When the door of the booth opened, I saw the starry night sky. My seat became a chute and slid my soul mate and me out into Earth's atmosphere. It felt good to be there, almost like coming home.

Angel was working entirely by instinct and inner direction, so I followed her as we made our way across a channel of water. The crescent shape of a new moon was hanging in the western sky as we followed the shoreline. We passed a major city, and then Angel began descending. She moved slowly over a quiet neighborhood. I stayed close behind as she hovered above a lovely English Tudor style home on the corner of two side streets. The yard was small but full of flowers, and there was a cat crossing the lawn. We floated just above the roof watching cars come up to the crossroads, stop, then accelerate. I followed Angel's lead. She seemed to know intuitively when to enter the home and locate her mother-to-be. The moon set and several walkers passed by below us on the quiet streets. I liked the house. It had a warm glow in the light from the street lamps.

Angel's spherical essence circled around me, and I knew it was time. We glided slowly through the roof of the house directly into a bedroom where a very beautiful pregnant woman lay in bed reading. Her mother came in and sat on the bed. They chatted about a neighbor. Then one of the younger sisters joined them and handed the pregnant woman a poem she had written to welcome the unborn child. We viewed all this from our vantage point near the ceiling.

From the conversation between the mother and the two sisters, we learned that Angel's father-to-be was working in the Mid-West and was planning to come to the East Coast for the Fourth of July holiday and the birth of his first child due July sixth.

"I'm going to be born early," I heard Angel's voice in my mind.

I sent her a telepathic message, "Your new father will be here on your birthday."

Not long afterwards, everyone in the house retired for the night. The pregnant woman, Helen, was the last to turn off her light. She was obviously restless and uncomfortable but eventually fell asleep. As she slept, Angel drew near to her. I stayed close as I watched the sphere of light that was Angel's Soul condense and brighten until it was the size of an apple.

I heard her voice clearly say, "I love you so much, Darci," and was about to answer her when the small luminous ball penetrated the stomach of the sleeping woman. I could see her belly glow with the light of Angel's Soul, and Helen's aura became much brighter overall.

I had been so focused on Angel and her new mother that I hadn't noticed Helen's Spirit Guide. She was in the opposite corner of the room watching the arrival and implantation of Angel's Spirit. Now that this was accomplished, she glided towards me.

"Greetings and welcome to Earth," she said as she extended her arms. "I am Gwenella, Helen's Life Guide."

"Pleased to meet you. I am Darcimon Stillwater."

"Yes, Mr. Stillwater. I was informed of your imminent arrival. It is the dawn of the first of July. I'm very glad you made it in time for the melding to take place."

"The melding? Another Guide mentioned that."

"It takes two, sometimes three days for the Soul to become fully immersed in the human form. The process is starting to occur now for your Angel."

"You know Angel?"

"I know of her and of you. Your mission is widely known among the Guides. I'm pleased to be able to help."

At that moment, Helen awoke, put her hands on her belly and rolled to her side. Gwenella nodded at her change of position.

"She knows something is different. Most mothers can sense when the Soul enters the unborn child. It is one of the few instances where two Souls occupy the same body."

"There are other times when this is so?"

"The potential is there, but I am not the one to school you in that particular ability."

I wanted to find out more, but Helen sat up slowly, stepped into her slippers, and padded off to the bathroom. Gwenella followed, and I stayed at a respectful distance. Once the pregnant woman was back in bed and asleep, I asked Gwenella about the arrangements for Angel's birth.

"They are planning to drive west into the city where there is a very good hospital. I only wish Jim was here."

"Jim?"

"Angel's father-to-be."

Gwenella and I kept our vigil, and when dawn arrived, the household slowly came to life. Since I was the new Guide on the scene, Gwenella introduced me to others who were involved in watching over the family. I was surprised to see the Guide Esther there. When I approached her, I realized it was an entity who looked very much like the Master Guide I had met on the Spirit Guide plane, but it was not she.

"I am named Esther," said the classic beauty, "and I watch over my namesake, Helen's mother and Angel's grandmother-to-be. There are over one hundred Guides trained by the Master Guide Esther who resemble her and bear her name."

I bowed to her and said, "I was first introduced to the Master Guide Esther in a meeting of The Elevated Council."

The household was busy with preparations for the upcoming holiday and the arrival of the baby. I stayed close to Gwenella and her charge. Although I could feel Angel's presence, there was no longer conscious communication between us. Whenever I caught myself becoming sad at the loss of my partner's company, I sent her love, and ended up spending much of my time radiating love into Helen's pregnant belly.

It was a new experience for me to be on the Earth plane operating as a Spirit Guide. When I had come to Earth as an apprentice, I had not yet received my initiation gift of energy. Now that I was a full-fledged Spirit Guide, I possessed more energy and greater perceptions. When Helen was resting with her feet up or sleeping, I would hover directly over her mound of a belly where my dear Angel was making herself comfortable in the unborn human casing. I projected light shows into the womb along with lots of love. I knew Angel couldn't consciously grasp what was happening though I knew her instincts were good, so I was sure she was aware of my presence on some level. I wanted her to know that I was right there only inches from her.

July third, Independence Day eve, many bonfires were lit all across the land. Gwenella informed me of the practice and urged me to take a look. Helen was in bed and seemed as comfortable as she could be, and I knew Angel was not going to be born until the next day, so I floated up and out of the house to view the sight. The smell of wood smoke was in the air as I took myself high over the rooftops. Gliding along, I saw that many people had built bonfires in their yards or nearby fields. When I reached the coastline, bonfires lined the shore. It was a splendid sight and an appropriate way to herald the birth of my dear Angel.

I probably took too much time enjoying the aerial view because when I returned to Helen's side, Gwenella was at the new mother's head sending energy down through her body.

"This baby is anxious to get out. She must have a date with you," joked Gwenella.

I automatically positioned myself at Helen's feet.

"Come to me, dear one," I sent the telepathic message. "Come out and be with me."

As soon as I sent those words, a great gush of liquid came flooding from between Helen's legs. She began calling to her mother, who ran in from the next room. The grandmother-to-be knew what was happening: the baby was coming. She pressed towels against the bedding, dabbing around Helen, then called to her husband to get up and dress. They were about to become grandparents.

"I've got to wait for Jim. I want Jim to be here," cried Helen, who was experiencing labor pains.

"He's on his way, honey," said her mother, "and so is this baby."

The drive into the city was hectic and unusual. All the humans in the car were nervous, even Helen's father who was behind the wheel. Gwenella and I were staying very near Helen, and the prospective grandparents also had their Guides hanging close. This was an important life change for everyone in the car, especially Angel, who was about to transition head-long into Earth life.

Once the hospital attendants wheeled Helen into the delivery room, I heard the news that her doctor was not yet there. It was the middle of the night, so the hospital staff was at a minimum. Helen's father began to pace back and forth in the waiting area, and I became concerned. I saw the nurses administer a drug to relax Helen's contractions and slow down the birth until the doctor could arrive. I wish I could have stopped them. The baby was going to come at the appointed time no matter what they did. The doctor arrived only moments before the baby was due to come out. Helen was so relaxed from the drug that she was barely conscious. I was very anxious, as this was a critical time for Angel. The doctor assessed the situation with me close by his side.

"This baby is ready to be born," he informed the attending nurse. "Can the mother push?"

"No, Doctor."

"She has lost almost all the birth fluid. Forceps please, nurse."

I had seen many births during my numerous Earth lifetimes but had never witnessed one like this. The baby had crowned, the top of the head was visible, and were things happening naturally, this would be when the mother would push and the baby would slide out. I looked at Gwenella who was by Helen's side. The Guide shook her head, indicating that Helen was not conscious enough to push.

The doctor then took a tool that looked like tongs and inserted them around the baby's head. He pulled. He pulled harder. The head moved out a little. He yanked hard. The baby was caught on something, and the poor child was now twisted in the birth canal.

I prayed so hard for Angel. I called to her to come out and join me. Something gave, and at 3:58 AM Angel was delivered into the world.

The doctor quickly and efficiently cut the umbilical cord as the nurse cleaned the baby's face. Then the doctor grabbed the newborn's legs, held her upside down, and spanked her four times until she cried loudly.

I was beside myself with worry. I had never seen such a barbaric practice. No family member was present to welcome the new babe, and Helen was now completely unconscious.

The nurse took the wailing child to a scale to be weighed, and that's when I saw the marks on the baby's head from the forceps. I thought my dear Angel would be scarred for life. How terrible to have this pristine new life both twisted and marred in the birth process.

"Nurse, finish up here," said the doctor. "I have a golf game, and my tee time is 6 AM."

I wondered what kind of world my Angel had been born into. Surely this cold, detached doctor and the harshly lit, antiseptic room were not indications of society as a whole.

I followed the nurse as she took Angel away from her mother, pinned a cloth around her bottom, and put an identification bracelet on her tiny arm. The new baby was then placed in a small crib in a room with about a dozen newborns.

This didn't seem right to me. There was Angel, brand new, her first few minutes on Earth, no father there, her mother drugged, and she was alone in a tiny box. I came very close and examined the marks on her head. I overheard the nurses as they went from crib to crib, checking the babies and changing the cloths.

"Another forceps delivery," said one as she looked at Angel.

"The doctors like that tool. It speeds up delivery."

"It leaves ugly marks though."

"They'll go away in a few weeks."

I was glad to hear that. Angel cried quite a bit during those first few hours. I tried to comfort her, entertain her, love her, but the trauma of the birth was upsetting the little one. I wished so much that I had human arms to hold her and soothe her and show her she was loved. I was standing by her crib, bathing her in love energy when I saw the tired grandparents looking in through a large glass window.

They were pointing at the babies and waving at the one remaining nurse who then walked to the window and heard the proud grandparents call a name. Then she found the right baby and brought her over to the window.

I was puzzled. Why weren't the new grandparents allowed to hold their new family member? I had seen babies born in the hay, on the floor, on the cold ground, and then passed around from father to grandfather to uncle to aunt to grandmother. This society had sterile birth facilities with bright lights and clean floors, but the love and family involvement were missing.

Still, I was happy to see the grandparents smiling and cooing at the new babe. And where was Angel's father?

As I sat through that long morning in the nursery by Angel's crib, I thought about all the challenges this Soul had already faced, and she was only a few hours old. First, the harsh delivery where she was drugged then marked and twisted. Then came the rough handling and the spanking. No father was present, essentially no mother because she was in a drugged stupor, and there were no kind, loving humans to hold her.

Compassion flowed from my heart to my dear mate now trapped in the tiny helpless body of a human baby. There was nothing I could do but love her, so I sent a continuous stream of rose-colored light into her crib. The little one finally fell asleep. I remembered how Angel had requested that she never go hungry in this lifetime and wondered when she would receive some nourishment.

My answer came soon enough. Two attendants entered the nursery with bottles of white liquid and began feeding the babies. Where were the mothers of these children, and why weren't they nursing their babies? What was the liquid that was being sucked through the odd-looking caps on these bottles? When one nurse came to Angel's crib, she had to wake the sleeping newborn in order to stick the bulbous cap in her tiny mouth. Angel sputtered and choked.

In all the many times she had been born onto the Earth plane, her first experience was almost always connection with a mother's breast, receiving nourishment directly. It seemed a tragedy that Angel's new mother was nowhere in sight, and these white-clad women were forcing a strange object in dear Angel's mouth.

She adapted quickly and eventually began sucking on the bottle. She cried a little afterward though, as if to say, "That's not what I really wanted."

Late that morning, a nurse took Angel to see her mother who had finally awakened from her drug-induced slumber. I was glad to see Helen try to nurse the child although the attempt was not altogether successful. The nurse had a bottle ready to hand Helen, so she stopped trying to nurse the baby and stuck the rubber nipple in Angel's little mouth.

The post-war society into which Angel was born was technologically advanced, yet they seemed to have lost touch with much that was natural. I was concerned that her beautiful Soul would not receive what it needed in this situation and was rolling such thoughts over in my mind when Helen had the visitor she had been waiting for—her husband.

Jim was a handsome, wavy-haired man with a winning smile and bright blue eyes. He had just arrived on the train and was greeted by his in-laws with the news of his daughter's birth. He was all smiles as he held the baby and poked at her little hands with his fingers. He asked about the marks on her head.

Helen had many visitors on this Fourth of July, so by dusk she was very tired. As she lay sleeping, and as Angel alternately wailed and dozed in the nursery, I rose to the hospital roof to look around.

I had heard some unfamiliar noises and wanted to see what was going on. A series of loud bangs echoed in the streets below. It reminded me of gunfire, but some boys were merely setting off firecrackers in the parking lot.

"A noisy way to celebrate this holiday," I said to myself.

"You haven't seen the half of it," said a voice behind me.

I turned and saw Esther, the Guide assigned to Angel's grandmother. I greeted her with a bow, and she asked, "This is your first time isn't it, Darci?"

"As a Spirit Guide, yes. Do I seem that green?"

"I could tell by your thoughts and reactions concerning Angel's birth."

"It seemed all wrong to me. The mother was drugged, and a doctor more concerned about making his tee time than delivering a healthy baby yanked poor Angel out of the womb. Why, she came out all twisted and scarred! My poor Angel will have to live with that torque to her physical body all her life . . ."

"Exactly."

"You mean—this was supposed to happen? I thought there was free will on this plane."

Esther came closer. As with the Master Guide for whom she was named, she was covered in veils, but her green eyes were clear and bright as she explained, "The exact circumstances of your Angel's birth were not predetermined, but the results were. In other words, Angel is meant to face physical challenges during this incarnation, and now she has the basics for them set right into her little body."

"So everything that has happened—the absent father, the lack of bonding with the mother—that's all as it should be?"

"All these occurrences set up Angel's life challenges. You know her background, Darci. You know she must face issues with her body and her parents. It is all part of the growth she is here to experience."

"I can't help feeling so much compassion for her—such a harsh entrance into this life."

"And that is also as it should be. You are here to love her, guide her, and care for her. You have the spirit perspective. You can help her understand why she must endure the hardships that life hands to her."

"Thank you for taking the time to explain this, Esther. I have been quite downhearted since the birth this morning."

"I could tell. It is difficult for us to watch the humans we love suffer in any way. The positive side is that we can help them if they let us. As I understand it, you and your charge, Angel, will help humans make great strides in becoming open to help from their Spirit Guides."

"It is our mission," I said just as the sky came alive with an amazing display of fireworks.

With every bright colorful flash, my heart sang out, "Angel is born!"

Chapter Fourteen:
Through the Veil

An entire book can be written about the life of Angel in this incarnation. From my perspective as her Spirit Guide, the important times were the moments we connected. During the first half of her life, Angel had no idea that I existed—at least consciously. My heart would cry out when I saw her suffering, and I used every tool I had to help her. The childhood trauma she endured was heart-breaking.

Indeed, those first forty-three years were very hard for me. I sought counseling from my teachers again and again. Often they would tell me that Angel had to find her own way and that her suffering was part of her karmic path. Even though I understood this, I was still distressed every time I watched her in pain. It was a true test of my ability as a Spirit Guide to persevere through this period of separation. I was with her, but she didn't know me. It was very, very difficult.

There were several instances when we did connect though Angel did not know that it was me, her Spirit Guide, helping her. Unfortunately, most of these times followed tumultuous emotional upsets. Sottrol taught me to stay very near her during these heart-rending upheavals when he showed me how to observe the aura and watch for openings.

My mentor walked me through this technique the first time. We found Angel curled up on her bed, sobbing uncontrollably. Black, gray, and red swirled in her energy field. As she cried, darkness precipitated out of her like rain from a cloud. Slowly, from the inside out, layers of gloom and emotional agitation dropped away. When at last she lay exhausted, her aura was light gray with several holes in it. Sottrol showed me how to send pink and white light into these spaces and surround her with love.

561

Angel was an emotional woman, so I had the opportunity to use this technique many times. Sottrol also taught me how to aid in the cleansing process. Once the gloom began to fall away, I could accelerate the procedure by aligning my energy with hers, then pulling the darkness out of her energy field. Sottrol cautioned against overdoing this course of action because Angel needed to do most of the crying and cleansing herself. I was very glad to have something I could do to help her when she was distraught.

Time and time again, I went to my teachers to ask how to activate a conscious connection between Angel and myself. The elders would inevitably say, "Patience, Darci, patience," or "The time will come," or "The time must be right."

Those forty years as Angel matured and made her way on the Earth plane seemed like an eternity to me. Every once in a while I could see that I made a difference. I would see her relax after I gave her a bath of love light or see her smile when I sent a bird or an animal into her path. I relished these moments.

One bright spot occurred during a time she lived alone while working at her first job as a knitwear designer in a large factory. She had learned yoga and practiced each day at home during her lunch break. This activity aligned her spine and brightened her energy field. My daily routine of sending light into her mind was having effects as well, and I hoped that she would soon be able to hear me speak to her telepathically. I decided to try an experiment.

After doing yoga, she would recline and relax for a few minutes before returning to the mill. I had decided that this was the time to impart a very simple message, but first I wanted her to feel my presence. Bathing her in brilliant golden light, I ran ripples of pink love energy from her feet to the top of her head. I did this over and over. Enjoying the sensation, she stretched and sighed. Encouraged by her reaction, I increased the intensity of the waves until kundalini energy rose up her spine, and she vibrated in ecstasy.

"Who's there?" she whispered after the experience had waned. "Who loves me this way?"

I knew that Angel wondered if she was being loved by Krishna or by some other god. She was not far wrong. I am not a god, but I loved her with my energy just as Krishna had loved the thousand gopis though I focused on her and only her.

Her aura glowed rosy pink with my love. Sending a beam of bright white light into the telepathic center in her brain, I relayed the message, "I love you. Please start a metaphysical library." I thought if she read about Spirit Guides, she might be more open to meeting me, maybe even reach out to me.

She reclined in a blissful state for a few minutes, then rose and penned a few words about the experience in her journal. I was thrilled. She had felt my presence and my love and had received the message.

This was the one and only time during that period that I truly connected with her in a meaningful manner. Sadly, she did not relate to me in such a personal way again until over sixteen years had passed.

Because she came into womanhood during the sexual revolution, Angel had many lovers. My heart was always heavy as I watched her couple with one man after another. I could see that she was searching for a deep soul connection with each one, and after each interaction I knew that she came away unsatisfied. I could not yet tell her about our bond, our many lifetimes together, our shared experiences on the Spirit Guide plane, and our passionate love for one another; this frustrated me. Again and again, she tried to find a deep love connection with a man and failed. Again and again I ached for her.

Perhaps it is not so difficult for other Spirit Guides. My deep love for Angel made the separation and the wait tough for me to tolerate. I often thought of the millions of Spirit Guides who are never acknowledged by the humans they help. It made me sad. I prayed for all of them.

∞ ∞ ∞

Sottrol visited me one evening as I sat near Angel who was asleep alone on her pallet. She had moved to an old pre-Civil War house in Maine. It was the end of summer, and I was watching moonlight play on the leaves of the maple trees outside the old house.

"I know you are concerned about her," said my teacher as he put his arm around me.

"Sottrol!" I was surprised. "This is a rare visit!"

"True," said the elder as the crystals in his beard sparkled in the moonlight. "I don't often pass through the portal to Earth. This is a special occasion."

"Have you come to assist me? Angel is in need of so much help. She has injured her back, lost her job and much of her confidence."

"Ah, you see, this is good," winked Sottrol.

"How can this be good?" I exclaimed. "She suffers so."

"See the bigger picture, Darci," said my teacher softly. "There had to be a breakdown phase in order to slow her pace."

"Angel has been incredibly active," I mused. "She fills every minute of every day—busy all the time. She has lived this way since she became an adult."

"In order for the conscious connection to be made between the two of you, Angel has to let go of much Earth business and slow way down."

I brightened immediately, responding excitedly, "It's time! Sottrol, you're telling me it's time!"

Sottrol chuckled, replying, "A little anxious are we, Darci? Yes, it's time though you must proceed gently. Think of coaxing a seed to sprout, then nurturing the tender young plant as it pushes its way up into the world."

"All right. I understand," I said, perhaps too curtly, "but what's next?"

"For the next few weeks, do the following exercise: as Angel sleeps, activate the vertical energy flow through her body."

"Isn't that easier with two Guides?"

"Very good, Darci. Yes, that's correct. For that very reason, I'm sending you an assistant. She will arrive shortly bringing instructions with her for the next steps."

"Who is she? Where is she?"

"Patience. Caroline will join you soon. There is something you can do on your own. Project an image into her mind."

"An image? Of what?"

"Of you, Darci. Choose carefully. This is how she will picture you for the remainder of her lifetime."

"I didn't learn this in class, Sottrol."

"Each and every relationship between a Spirit Guide and a human is unique. You know that. Many Guides focus on creating auditory connections with their charges because much precise information can be imparted in this way. For you and Angel, both the auditory and visual links can be easily established."

"So I must choose an image to project."

"Yes. Select one she will identify with and embrace. Now flood that little one with love. She has a great journey ahead of her."

My heart swelled with anticipation and love for Angel. I looked at her sleeping, curled up, oblivious to the conference that was taking place by her bedside. When I turned back, my teacher had vanished though he left a hint of sweetgrass in the air.

Pondering what Sottrol had told me, I wondered what Angel would respond to? What would draw her to me? I reviewed the many lifetimes Angel and I had shared. Recalling our time together in Egypt, I speculated that perhaps projecting an image of myself as Hett, tall, dark, and devoted, might stir her, for she was now an astrologer as Tuura had been. When I lived as the Roman statesman, Alger Matticus, I had been handsome and statuesque. Perhaps such a likeness would intrigue her. Then I saw myself as the Mayan corn farmer, Zontyl, muscular and brown. Maybe this picture would entice her, for she grew corn in her garden.

"But no," I stopped myself. "She will not consciously recognize these images. Her subconscious self may know them, but what will speak to her conscious mind?"

Gazing around her room, I found the answer. On the bookshelves were several of Jane Austen's novels. In my last lifetime, I had been acquainted with Miss Austen. Her father was the pastor of the church that my family had attended.

I chuckled when I recalled the day my aunt bustled into our sitting room for a visit. Evidently I was the object of the latest gossip. Word was out that young Miss Austen had written a novel in which one of the main characters was patterned after me. I knew Angel loved this particular story and had read it several times.

Since passing into Spirit, I had continued to use the likeness of myself from my last incarnation; most Souls do. It became clear to me that Angel would easily identify with a spirit friend from that era. It was an image she could see, accept, and embrace.

The next night as I again sat by Angel's bedside, I saw two female Spirit Guides floating across the field from the east. One was slender, wispy, vaporous, and looked very much like the Master Guide Esther. The other Guide radiated just as much luminosity but was plump, rosy, and dressed like a peasant woman.

"Greetings, Darcimon Stillwater," said the slender Guide wrapped in pastel veils. "You know me. I am one of the Esthers."

"Yes, hello. You were Life Guide to Angel's grandmother. I remember you."

"Darci, may I introduce Caroline? She is an expert in health and healing."

The plump female Guide curtsied and smiled widely.

"Caroline, I'm very glad you're here," I said earnestly.

"Angel is suffering tremendously from a very bad back injury. Can you help her?"

"We can help her, Mr. Stillwater," Caroline replied.

"Please, call me Darci, and let's begin right away. Dear Angel needs relief."

Caroline directed me to kneel at Angel's feet while she sat at her head. Esther hovered over us, observing. Caroline worked quickly, first establishing a stream of luminous white and green light between her hands on Angel's head and my hands cupped around her feet. Once the flow of energy was strong, Caroline nodded to Esther who floated to the head of the bed and took over that position.

The plump, rosy Guide then moved to Angel's mid-section and placed one hand above the injured area, the other below. I was surprised to see electricity crackle between Caroline's hands. She continued to pierce the injury with lightning bolts for quite a while. I watched the redness in Angel's aura dissolve into a light peach color.

Caroline looked at me, smiled, and explained, "She'll sleep through the night and awake rested. However, the injury is serious. She'll need more healings and must find help on the physical plane as well."

The two female Guides then led me to a corner of Angel's room. Esther's green eyes glowed as she spoke, "Do you see how this injury is a gift to both of you?"

"A gift?" I uttered, astounded. "How is it a gift? I dislike watching poor Angel suffer so."

Caroline chuckled with understanding and asked, "Have you not been waiting for a chance to connect with your dear Angel?"

I nodded. I must have had a dumbstruck look on my face because Esther smiled, too

"Darci," said the ethereal Guide as she grasped my hand, "this injury to Angel is the key. For one thing it has slowed her down. She will now have time to listen."

"Listen?"

Caroline patted my shoulder, "To you."

Realization flooded through me. It was time for Angel and me to connect consciously through the veil between worlds. I was so elated that I hopped about. The two female Guides laughed but quickly became serious again.

"Darci, please calm yourself. You must prepare her," Esther informed me. "Let me show you." She moved gracefully back to the pallet. I watched as the slender Guide created a sphere of golden energy between her hands and then slowly lowered the brilliant orb into Angel's head.

"Do this daily," said Caroline, as we watched the glow of sparkling golden light emanate from Angel's forehead. "This awakens that part of her brain that receives telepathic communication."

"So she'll finally hear me talking to her!" I blurted excitedly. "How long will it be before . . .?"

"Just keep at it," Caroline replied, putting an arm around me. "How soon Angel responds depends entirely on her."

Promising to return, the two female Guides took their leave. I sat the rest of the night at Angel's head whispering, "I'm here. I love you."

The concept of having a spirit guardian was not foreign to Angel. As I had suggested to her years before, she had collected many books and had read much metaphysical material. I made sure that she had access to a few books about Spirit Guides though not many were available at the time.

The big breakthrough, the moment I had been anticipating for over forty years, came three months later. Throughout those months, I had seen Angel suffer in pain every day. I watched as she searched for help from doctor after doctor. On occasion Esther and Caroline visited, and the healings we did seemed to give her some relief, but the healings did not last.

One bright autumn morning as mist lay in the glen and dew outlined the fallen leaves, I drew very close to my beloved Angel. My heart ached with compassion as I saw her force herself to wash the dishes, a simple task for most but very difficult for her. She primed the old hand pump in the kitchen and laboriously cranked the handle until water spilled into the sink and the kettle. She then lifted the heavy kettle and moved it to the woodstove to heat.

An idea came to me. Perhaps music would cheer her. Angel loved music and had been working in radio until just before the injury. She had a large collection of vinyl records. Projecting the image of a tall, dark-haired, English gentleman, I encircled her with my spirit arms and spoke softly in her ear.

"Might we listen to some classical music today?" I suggested. "You rarely listen to classical."

She stopped. She had heard me.

My heart began pounding wildly. I knew I must continue speaking.

"I'd like to hear some Mozart," I beamed into her telepathic center, "though I believe you have but one Beethoven record."

"Classical?" I heard her say aloud.

She walked into the back room where there was a wall of records. I guided her hand to the one Beethoven album. When she slid it from the rack, her eyes widened in awe, and I heard her gasp, "You really are here!"

She indulged my request, playing the entire record, scratches and all. As we listened, I again sent her the image of myself from my former lifetime, a gentleman of noble birth, handsome and refined, standing tall and proud in an elegant long coat. Her eyes glossed with tears. She not only saw me, she felt our deep connection, nearly swooning as I filled her aura with love. We were together again. This was the sweetest moment I had ever known.

∞　∞　∞

The connection was a solid one. We began conversing like the old friends we were. Angel was so fascinated by the phenomenon of having finally met her Spirit Guide that she spent time every day with me. I was elated. This is what we came to Earth to do! This was our mission, at least in part. Those first days were indeed the most precious because they were filled with the joy, love, and excitement of a new connection. I knew the work would begin soon, so I relished every shared moment.

Angel was still adjusting to her newfound telepathic abilities. Because our connection was so strong, the dialogue between us flowed easily for the first few weeks. During this time, she drove from Maine to Connecticut to visit her mother. I kept her company on the trip.

She planned to continue on to Providence, Rhode Island to see a concert. She was a radio professional and had made many contacts with bands and musicians, including some who were quite famous. Two of her favorite bands, REM and 10,000 Maniacs, were performing on the same show. Before leaving for the concert, she wrote a statement in her journal that was very gratifying to me, and I loved her all the more for it.

"I would rather spend time with my Spirit Guide, Darci, than with my famous rock and roll friends."

One gray autumn afternoon as we walked the country road by Angel's home, she asked me quite pointedly, "Who are you? I know you are my Spirit Guide, but who are you really?"

I suppose I could have answered in a number of ways; however, my heart spoke for me, "Your husband," I said.

As soon as she heard those words, a curtain of static flew up between us and communication was cut off. She mistrusted what she heard, thinking that her imagination had supplied the answer. All had been going so well, but now a wall stood between us.

That evening sitting on the wood pile near the house, I was very discouraged. I had tried several times to reconnect with Angel, but the static surrounding her made any communication between us impossible. I sighed deeply, then perked up as the aroma of sage floated by.

"Ho, Darci," said a familiar voice. "One little setback and you are downcast. That's not like you."

"Sottrol, I am so glad to see you," I said, hugging my mentor with gusto.

The elder settled on the log next to me and continued, "You cannot blame her, Darci. She's lonely. She lives out here on her own away from society. She thinks solitude inspired her imagination."

"She thinks she invented me to ease her loneliness," I added.

"Dear Angel has longed for your connection since her birth. It's difficult for her to accept that it exists and that it is here, now."

"Sottrol, she knows me. Her Soul knows me. Surely she'll come to accept that I exist—that I am real."

"Tell her that and send her love. Love is the one thing that will penetrate that shield of static she has unwittingly erected. Love, Darci—that's your tool. Now use it."

With those words the wizard rose, took two steps toward the house, and disappeared to the sound of tinkling bells.

I wasted no time. Angel was just retiring for the night, so I sat by her bedside and pumped love into that wall of static. I aimed for her heart though I couldn't see much through the crackling and popping. At that moment I wished I'd had a class in penetrating static.

My persistence paid off though it took nearly ten days to clear Angel's energy field enough for us to begin communicating again. She wanted to reconnect. In fact, she sat down with her ukulele and wrote a love song to me, which I treasure to this very day, a beautiful song called "Quarter Turn."

Here you are . . . a vision, clearly in my mind.
Here you are again, a vision . . . vivid in my mind,
But there is something so real about you.
Have you a life of your own? I want to know.

Can the barriers be dissolved
Between your realm and this reality?
Open and warm . . . the greeting, important greeting
I hear your voice coming back to honor me.
Intense and clear . . . recognition, shock of recognition!
Vibrant, alive . . . reveal yourself to me.
Here you are . . . a presence strongly around me.
Here you are again, again, a presence strongly surround
me.

But there is doubt and mistrust inside me.
Can ego-static be stilled? I want to know.
Can communications be clear
Between your realm and this reality?
Now ... take a breath and focus inward.
Now ... meditate and focus inward.
We harmonize and focus inward
Find a rich landscape. Travel free!

The conscious connection between us made all the difference. I was able to suggest ways for Angel to improve her health, and Caroline began working with her on diet. I watched joyfully as Angel moved out of depression and pain. My dear mate loved our connection, too; she said it felt right to her. Indeed, it was the missing piece for both of us.

The week before Christmas Angel visited her Mother. She brought with her fresh-cut boughs of balsam fir, strings of lights, candles, crystals, and decorations for the guest room where she set up a magical environment. In this quiet space she meditated every day and received healings from Esther, Caroline, and me. By the time Christmas arrived, my dear Angel shone bright as a beacon.

On Christmas morning she went to wish her mother Merry Christmas and to have breakfast. The television was on with news of a great revolt in Romania where the people had killed the king and his family. It was horrible news for such a holy day, and Angel was very upset by it. She returned to her room to cry. I could see grief for the plight of humankind pouring from her.

"Darci, when will this end?" she sobbed. "When will humans stop killing and torturing each other?"

I comforted her and watched as the tears cleansed her energy field even further. Once she had cried herself out, she meditated. I was pleased. I could see that her aura was sparkling, and she was vibrating at a very high rate. The daily meditations had truly made a difference.

As I was holding my dear one, Esther floated through the window with the message that Arcillis would be arriving soon and wished to speak directly to Angel. Master Guides do not often make their way to Earth, so I knew this was a significant event. The vibratory rate of a Master Guide is very high, and most humans, even those who connect consciously with their own Spirit Guides, would not be able to communicate with a Master. However, I knew Angel was ready. Just to be sure, I filled her aura with gold and white light.

The weather had been incredibly cold for December, but this Christmas Day the temperature moderated enough for Angel to bundle up and go out for a walk. Arcillis insisted on being the one to introduce her to the next phase of the mission. He began talking to her the minute she stepped into the cold, crisp air. Angel knew immediately that it was not me speaking. She could discern the slight ringing sound that accompanies communications from Master Guides. I stayed very near and listened in on the conversation.

"Greetings. We see your sorrow for the Earth. All will change," began Arcillis.

Angel heard. "I can't wait," she said aloud, walking down the driveway.

"How would you like to be a leader in the new time?"

She stopped in her tracks. "What exactly does that entail?" she asked skeptically.

"First, we'd like you to telepathically transcribe some information and make it available to humanity," Arcillis answered.

"What is this information?"

"Humans are ready to know more about why they are here and how to improve their lives. All the material has been carefully prepared by the Master Guides. We would like you to rise each morning and work with your Spirit Guide, Darci. He will give you the data sentence by sentence."

She agreed to try this and at that moment our mission together began. I was not only ready; I was joyous. At last we would be working together as a team on a daily basis. At last we would be moving forward, pursuing our purpose on Earth.

On December 28, 1989, we began writing what was to become *The Dawn Book*. I taught Angel a condensed version of the grounding and clearing meditation that she could use each morning to get herself in the proper state to receive the information. It worked beautifully. She was a natural at this kind of work.

At first light I would awaken her. We would then sit together in the corner of her bedroom. I would speak and she would write in a notebook. Later each day, she would read that morning's entry. Often it would surprise or astound her. I was proud of my Angel because she was consistent and devoted to the work.

During the year that we were writing this book together, Angel and I became even closer. As data flowed from me to her, our channel of communication strengthened and widened. Even so, I could see a hint of doubt lurking in the back of her mind. I understood this. She had no other friends with conscious connections to their Spirit Guides. She had no one to talk to about this besides me, and she wasn't entirely convinced that I was there. At every turn I tried to reassure her.

Her birthday was usually filled with activities, for she had joined a group of artists and thespians who each year staged a colorful and irreverent parade and play to celebrate the Fourth of July. This year after the festivities she volunteered to take her friend's daughter swimming in a neighbor's pond. During the few quiet moments while she sat by the water's edge watching the child splash and play, I came very close to her, aligned our implanted crystals, and said over and over, "I am real. I am real."

She heard me clearly.

I had secretly made a resolution to court her. Sottrol had told me that a union between us was possible and that although it was not crucial to our mission, it would enhance it. At this time Angel was alone, no man in her life. If she gave me a chance, I could show her that I was the one she had been searching for all those years and that I could love her as well if not better than any Earth man.

That summer we took many walks together. Her favorite path wound through the woods to neighbor's fields. She had several sacred spots along the way, including a grove of trees that formed what she called "the love tunnel." Before she stepped into this grove, she took four deep breaths, then thought and felt love as she walked through. I would join in by flooding her with love. I thought about proposing to her there, but wanted her to be still for a few moments so I could be sure to reach her.

My dear mate also had several old trees along this walk that she liked, especially a giant pine on the path and a huge ash right in the middle of the most remote field. She often sat beneath the great ash and gazed out at the mountains. I decided this was where to ask her.

I waited until she had settled down and her mind had reviewed some recent occurrences in her life. Once again, I sent down a stream of white light into her mind, followed by rays of radiant pink with the message "I love you."

I watched her relax as she received the love bath.

"I love you, too, Darci," she spoke aloud.

I moved so close to her that my spirit body was pressed against her human one, and our implanted crystals were aligned.

"Please do me the honor of becoming my wife," I said, sending the proposal to her while radiating as much love as I could.

She swooned for a moment and then stiffened.

"How can you be my husband, Darci?" I heard her project telepathically. "Can you carry firewood? Can you haul water? Can you fix the brakes on my car? Can you make love to me?"

"I love you so much," I began my answer, "and I can help you with many things. Yes, yes, yes—I can love you better than any Earth husband."

"Darci, I need time. Your proposal is too much for me right now. Let's just focus on completing the book. We can talk about this again after it's done."

I was not disappointed at all, for I had patience and thought her request a sensible one. She would warm up to the idea of becoming my wife because I would continue to love her so dearly that she would not be able to say no.

Doing as she asked, I did not bring up the subject of marriage for many, many months. I did, however, ask her to attend a wedding with me. I wanted to show her that we were not alone, that indeed there were other marriages through the veil.

One warm summer afternoon, I watched her thinning a large spiral-shaped bed of carrots. Her own thoughts rattled around in her head for a while. Then she sensed my presence and said, "Here is some time we can spend together. Do you have a story to tell me, Darci?"

"Yes!" I answered. "I have been waiting for you to ask. The story is about a woman who is similar to you in some ways. She worked in a waterfront bar by the docks in Boston and met with an extremely violent incident there."

"Was she scarred?"

"Yes, she has both physical and emotional scars," I continued. "I'm telling you this because the violent event changed her life and led her to a spiritual path. You have found a gentler way to yours. Soon she will marry through the veil. Her betrothed is a Spirit Guide. I wish to invite you to accompany me to the wedding."

She was amazed at this invitation and asked for particulars, so I came closer and sent the following words into her mind on a ray of pure white light.

"The ceremony is August 9th at 4 PM. Please quiet yourself and enter a meditative state at that date and time. We will proceed from there."

She asked if there were some ways she might prepare, so I requested that she take no alcohol for three days before this date. I also suggested that she tell herself each day until then that she would remember what occurs. She prepared as instructed, and on the designated day, she finished the grounding and clearing process and went into meditation just at 4 PM. I had her do a brief relaxation and then offered her my arm. Her ethereal body joined me while her physical body rested.

The wedding took place on the Spirit Guide plane in a sacred space known as the Chapel of the Angels. There were hundreds of white steps going up to a glowing pointed arch and towering spires at the top. These stairs were filled with Beings of all shapes, sizes, and colors. The crowd was massing on two sides of these wide steps, leaving an open aisle in the center.

I led my mate to the aisle, informing her that those who lined it were human-Spirit couples. As with my dear partner, the humans were represented by their lighted ethereal bodies while their physical bodies rested in meditation. I explained that the human bride was having a small ceremony on Earth at the same time as this grand celebration on the Spirit Guide plane.

Angel stayed close to me, her arm locked in mine as we positioned ourselves on the steps. I spotted Jono, Gotharn, and many other familiar faces. Just as I was about to introduce Angel to my teacher, Beminer, a deep tone heralded the beginning of the ceremony. Another series of higher tones rang out from the great archway, and the processional began.

Angel's eyes were wide with amazement as three angels in blue, wings and all, floated past. They were followed by a figure of brilliant luminescent gold, nearly blinding to look at. Next came two women in white with pink and blue flowers around their waists. As human attendants to the bride, they were radiant. The two who were to be wed walked up the stairs arm in arm. Nancy had shining short blonde hair while Edgar's hair was luminescent white tied back in a short ponytail. They looked incredibly joyful as they made the climb, step-by-step.

The golden Being walked to the center of the arch, which then glowed brighter with radiant white light. A huge angel appeared behind the spires, a Being so tall it was impossible for us to discern his face. His glowing hands were positioned just above the archway and were radiating golden light onto the couple standing before him. We were too far back to hear the vows but were able to congratulate the newlyweds as they descended the stairs after the ceremony. Angel was in awe of the entire spectacle and stood silently by my side as I greeted Guide after Guide, but I knew we couldn't tarry. I had to get my partner back to her physical form.

My dear Angel came out of her deep meditative state with tears of joy in her eyes. She recorded her perceptions of the experience in her spirit journal.

∞ ∞ ∞

It took us nearly one full year to write *The Dawn Book.* By December 1990, she had completed the text and four illustrations. After the holidays, she began typing the handwritten pages on an electric typewriter. War in the

Persian Gulf was occurring at that time, and this upset her greatly. Typing the book brought her comfort.

A few weeks later, Angel had the opportunity to give a talk about our work at a college as part of a community outreach program.

"You are quite a good speaker," I encouraged her. "Please do this."

She hesitated and asked, "Will people understand?"

"You've been a professional radio announcer for years. You've performed on stage with local bands. Your words are colorful and your movements expressive. You can easily do this, and . . ." I increased the beam into her telepathic center as I continued, "Caroline, Esther, and I will take questions from those who attend!"

"Will you really?" She questioned, surprised.

"Yes. We have been waiting for such an opportunity. Some of the people who are there will ask, and we will give you the answers telepathically. Then you, my dear Angel, repeat what we have said, simple as that."

She shook her head and smiled. "I've never done anything like this before—but I trust you. I'll give it a try."

So for the very first time, Angel talked in public about Spirit Guides and used her telepathic abilities to give information directly from us. The talk went well. I was so proud of her and was gratified that our work had moved into the public realm. In fact, one woman who was there asked Angel to do readings for her friends and told her about a hands-on healing group that could help with her back pain.

The Dawn Book was completely typed and ready by the end of April. She made several copies and put them in beautifully decorated boxes for friends to read. I thought it very fortunate that she had people around her who understood our work.

In her search for help for her lower back and hip, Angel first went to see some healers privately, then began attending their monthly meetings. At each gathering, there would usually be a presentation of some kind, then healings, and then refreshments. Angel and I offered information from *The Dawn Book* at one of these meetings, and there was much interest. One of the group leaders even wanted to buy the box of loose unbound pages.

Later that spring, a friend came to Angel with money for her to self-publish a limited edition of *The Dawn Book*. She designed a simple cover. A deep rose color at the bottom that faded to white at the top, it looked like the glow in the eastern sky at first light on a clear morning. In July, 130 soft cover books were ready, and the project, at least in my eyes, was complete. I was pleased and excited, too, because the time had come to once again ask her to marry me.

I had to find a way to show her that I could be a real husband to her. Surely I could touch her as deeply as I had before when we were together on the Spirit Guide plane. Knowing that if I came to her in a dream, it would not be real enough for her, I decided to reach out while she was awake and fully conscious. Besides, utilizing our conscious connection was a part of our mission. I came up with a two-part plan.

I saw the opportunity to implement part one on a beautiful summer day. Angel was in her neighbor's field sitting under the giant ash. The mountains in the distance were misty blue in the hazy summer air.

I moved close so that my energy field nearly engulfed hers, and our implanted crystals were aligned. I sent rays of powerful white light to the crystals and to her entire spine and head, opening all the chakras. Next, I beamed brilliant pink light to her lower chakras and pumped love into her. She was surprised at her arousal.

"Darci, is that you?"

"Yes, dear one. I love you."

"What are you doing?"

"I am showing you that I can love you as a husband loves a wife."

"I wondered when you would bring up marriage again."

"The book is finished, and I would like you to consider my proposal."

"Darci, I'm on Earth. I have to deal with reality. Would marrying you mean I couldn't take an Earth husband?"

"You can still marry a human if you so choose."

"I'll have to think more about this, Darci."

I expected such a response and was glad she was at least considering my offer. I had long ago processed jealousy out of my energy pattern as all Spirit Guides do. If she chose a human partner, I would still love her, whether or not she married me. I would love the man as well, and work with his Guide to keep the two of them on their spirit paths.

Part two of my plan was brilliant—if I do say so myself. Angel was scheduled to lead another healing group meeting. She planned to take the group through a meditation and visualization that would help the members consciously connect with their Spirit Guides. During the days leading up to this meeting, I focused on sending her pure love all day and all night. Never was she out of the stream of radiant pink energy that I was projecting to and around her.

The morning of the meeting, she sat at dawn with Caroline, Esther, and me to prepare. The two female Guides knew of my plan and encouraged me to implement it. We told Angel that after she led the group into meditation, the attending Spirit Guides would bring gifts to their charges. At the end of the meditation, each member would describe what he or she had received.

Angel followed the outline we Guides had designed, including the specific visualizations she was to use. When all were deep in meditation communing with their Guides, I knelt before her with a bouquet of luminous spirit flowers and formally proposed marriage once again.

I poured my feelings out to her, saying, "Dear one, we have been partnered many times. We are bonded through time. I love you so very much and would be honored if you would agree to become my wife."

I followed this with an intense surge of love energy that caused her to vibrate and tingle. Watching her heart chakra open, I saw her love pour out to me. A ray of white light connected our implanted crystals.

I heard her whisper, "Yes."

Overwhelmed with joy, I was filled with such exuberance that I wished to tell my mentors and teachers the good news but had to be patient. Angel was leading a class, and I was there to support her.

Once all the other members of the group had related the experiences they had had in meditation with their Guides, it was Angel's turn. When she told the group that I had proposed and she had agreed to marry me, her Spirit Guide, they were astounded at first, then supportive. Congratulations came from every corner, and Angel invited them all to our wedding. I had done it! We were engaged!

It was some time before we set the wedding date. As an astrologer, my mate wanted to select it carefully. With a little guidance from me, she chose November first. For centuries, humans have held that the veil between worlds is at its thinnest and most transparent on October 31 and November 1. The first of November is a sacred day because it begins the Celtic New Year, an excellent day to begin our married life together.

We were walking together down a country lane near her home. Brilliant autumn colors were splashed across the trees as we talked of our coming marriage. I reminded her of the wedding that we had attended the summer before.

She sent the thought to me, "That was a splendid ceremony, Darci. I'm not sure I'm ready for such a large wedding."

"Let me arrange the event on the spirit side," I offered. "You invite the small circle of spiritually aware friends to your home and handle all the Earth details. As for the size of the wedding—well, my dear, you may keep it small on Earth, but here on the spirit side, there are hundreds who want to attend and wish us well. Someday I will tell you why so many are interested in us. For now, just hold in your heart that every couple who marries through the veil is treated royally on the Spirit Guide plane."

She thought about this, then sighed aloud, "I had no idea such things were possible before you took me to that wedding, Darci. Not many of my friends on Earth would understand."

"Gather a small group of those who support our marriage and have them at your home on November first. Would you like to take our honeymoon by the ocean?"

"We can have a honeymoon?"

"Of course. I want you all to myself with no distractions so I can properly show you my love."

"Will we do what humans do on wedding nights?"

"You can be sure that we will share the highest vibration of love. That's all I will say for now, except to add that once we are married, there will be a difference."

She then asked me about this difference, but I did not say more. For one thing, words could not adequately express the possibilities. They could be understood only through experience, and that could only come after we had sanctified our union on Earth and on the Spirit Guide plane.

Although a formal wedding was not essential to our work and our mission, an official marriage would open many doors between us. I wanted not only the love but also the trust to deepen. We would do our best if we were partners in every sense. Our marriage would mean that we could share everything—that she would open up to me as a wife to a husband.

That autumn was a joyful one for both of us. We prepared for the wedding both separately and together. I studied with Sottrol and others, learning first what is possible between a human and a Spirit Guide, then acquiring certain techniques to facilitate intimacy through the veil. Sottrol made sure that I knew I wouldn't really understand these skills until I had tried them. I was glad Caroline and Esther were taking such good care of Angel, for I wanted to focus on these studies.

Nonetheless, I was present every time Angel needed me. Caroline, Esther, and I functioned as a team during sessions when my partner would introduce a human to his or her Guides. I also took much joy each evening tucking dear Angel in for a night's rest.

Everything was ready for our nuptials by the end of October 1991. All Saints Day dawned cloudy and rainy, but this did not dampen our joy. In fact, the downpour was helpful in making the connection between worlds. Rain cleansed the atmosphere, making it easier for Angel to work with higher vibrations.

The one main room in Angel's little rustic home was clean and filled with white chrysanthemums. The small group of friends brought food, including a wedding cake. Candles were placed around the room and an altar on the table. The elder from the spiritualist healing group stood and gave a blessing.

On the spirit side, there was much activity. Literally hundreds of Guides gathered to witness our marriage. All the Guides I knew from my studies at the university and all my teachers were there, plus many of the Guides we had met through doing readings for humans. The crowd was tremendous. Arcillis, Sottrol and Chalherine stood with me as Angel and I exchanged vows.

An incredible plume of light, a fountain of radiance, rose from that humble little farmhouse. The energy connecting the Spirit Guide plane with Earth was flowing freely back and forth between my partner and me. As the rain poured down, the light got stronger until a beam of brilliant white engulfed Angel on Earth and me on the spirit side. Our marriage not only made this extraordinary bond possible, it made this blessed connection permanent. As long as Angel walked the Earth in a human body, this shaft of white light would connect us. This was our gift from the Universe.

We took our honeymoon by the sea. It was marvelous because Angel had no distractions. I was the only thing on her mind and in her heart. I must admit that I was a little nervous about our first intimate moments together as husband and wife. As Angel drove to the coast, I sang a simple love song to her, one I had written to try to convey the depths of my feelings.

My Love, it is here for you.
My Love, it is here for you.
My Love has withstood every test, every challenge.
My love, it is here for you.

My Love, it is here for you.
My Love, it is here for you.
My Love has withstood every pain, every problem.
My Love, it is here for you.

Through the barrier Love can sail.
Love flows easily through the Veil.

My Love, it is here for you.
My Love, it is here for you.
My Love has withstood even death, even parting.
My Love, it is here for you.

My Love, it is here for you.
My Love, it is here for you.
My Love has withstood the test of time.
My Love, it is here for you.

We arrived at the shore and walked for hours by the sea, talking like the old friends we were. I told her about my last Earth lifetime and that I had died in 1836.

As she found us a cottage to rent by the ocean, I thought about all the other first nights. I remembered how exhausted we were after our extravagant Roman wedding and how we fell asleep waiting until dawn to consummate our union. Those few sweet days we shared as a wedded couple in Mongolia passed through my mind. I recalled when I was Zontyl and took my loving yet reluctant Nunzah in my arms after our wedding. I felt the sting of the fresh burn wounds on my shoulders as Yong Shu and recalled how Nua's gentle touch eventually relieved the pain and allowed my passion to flow. I especially remembered how as Hett, I trembled when I first touched my beloved Tuura, a woman I had loved for well over a decade. Now here we were, paired again, but this time in the most unusual circumstances of all. We were married but on different planes of existence.

Our time together on the Spirit Guide plane had shown me that we didn't need physical bodies to express our love to each other. I wondered for the hundredth time what it would be like for one of us to be in Spirit and the other to be in a physical body. Although I had been instructed by Sottrol and several others on how to use my energy to connect intimately with my new wife, I was not at all sure what would happen. The fact that residents of the Earth plane can exercise free will meant that Angel could react in any number of ways. I told myself that she had come this far. Certainly she would receive me as a wife would a husband.

As dusk fell over the seascape and fog misted the picture window, Angel showered, donned her white nightdress and lit the union candle from our wedding service. She lay on the bed and went into a meditative state. I surrounded her with rose-colored love light and again sang her the love song I had written. As I was singing to her telepathically, I realized that I was in the same predicament of many grooms; I was looking for a place to begin.

I started by asking for privacy. So many Spirit Guides had been at the wedding ceremony, I wished to let them know that this was now our private time and space. Next I visualized a bright connection of blue-white light between my new wife and me. I wanted her to hear and see me clearly for I had spirit gifts to give her. Chalherine had helped me fashion one present. I knew Angel didn't wear much jewelry though she loved earrings, so I gave her a pair: two spheres of pink light with white spirals in them.

"These will help increase your clairaudience," I smiled as I showed them to her. "Let me put them on you."

Her eyes sparkled. I could tell she loved them. She took a deep breath and relaxed as I set the orbs inside her ears. I then surprised her with another present. Sottrol had suggested this one. It was a sphere of white and gold light for her third eye. She willingly let me slowly and gently place the orb of light into the chakra between and just above her eyes.

"This beautiful sphere will help increase your clairvoyance and telepathic abilities," I told her once the orb was in place. I then kissed her forehead and ears, sealing the gifts of light into their new homes.

Angel asked if she might give me a present. I was surprised. My mate had been secretly working on this with Caroline and Esther. I saw her manifest a brilliant gold triangle with a diamond of light in the center. The amulet of energy appeared in her solar plexus. Gently moving it up to her heart where it became brighter, she energized and purified it with her love. She then handed it to me. I was awestruck. Beaming with joy, I placed it around my neck.

We prayed. Although I was tempted to go on as any new husband might, I could see she was exhausted. She sent me a ray of love as she slid into sleep. I gathered her in my spirit arms, surrounding her with love energy. Other grooms might have been disappointed with such a turn of events, but I was relieved. It gave me more time to work with her energy field and search my heart to find the most appropriate way to approach her.

By the time the white and yellow daisies on the wall of our honeymoon room were touched by the light of dawn, I was ready.

"Good morning," I whispered into my bride's ear. "I would like to come to you as a husband comes to a wife."

She stretched and yawned as I had seen her do so many times when we were together on the Spirit Guide plane. She smiled.

"You are my Guide, Darci," she spoke aloud. "Show me the way."

I had decided that the best place to begin was at her feet. I had spent many hours there as the anchor during various healing sessions. Also, this was the most humble place to start and the most modest place to begin touching my new wife. I lovingly held her human feet in my spirit hands. She comprehended what I was doing and relaxed at my touch.

This was it. This was the very first time I was to make love to my new wife through the veil between worlds.

As I sent love energy into the chakras in the arches of her feet, I experienced the wall between the spirit world and the physical Earth plane in an unexpected way, a way that defined that barrier in new terms for me. I already knew that our lovemaking would not be as it had been on the Spirit Guide plane or as it had been when we were both incarnated in the flesh, but I never expected the intense resistance I felt as I tried to move my energy into her body. The flesh, the bone, the muscle, the tendons, the ligaments, the veins and blood were all so dense.

I called on the instruction I had received from Sottrol and others. I had been alerted to the difference in vibration between humans and Spirit Guides, but I was still astounded. My most recent memories were of the free-flowing exchanges of love we had shared on the Spirit Guide plane. I knew our lovemaking would now be different, but I wasn't expecting this wall of tightly-knit molecules. It would take a great deal of patience and perseverance for me to permeate such dense matter. I reminded myself of Sottrol's words that all the schooling and instruction in the Universe would not prepare me for the real test, the actual experience.

I also told myself that I did, indeed, have the patience called for and that this phenomenon of bringing my love energy within my human wife could and would be accomplished. There was no doubt in my mind that this was possible. The questions were how long it would take and would my partner have the patience, too? I could not let myself think about what she might be expecting. I loved her so much that generating love for her was not a problem. Getting this love to penetrate her dense human form in a way she could physically experience it—that was my challenge!

I took a deep breath, said a prayer, and began again at her feet. Using visualizations, I pictured her feet glowing with vibrant pink light as I attempted again to move my love energy in through her arches. The barrier of dense human flesh was great, but after a time I saw that I was able to induce the molecules to vibrate faster. I must have been holding her feet for nearly an hour. She stayed with me—and didn't fall asleep. Finally she told me telepathically that her feet were tingling wildly. I rejoiced!

As I continued, trying to move the energy up into her ankles, I recalled some of our other wedding nights. They were not always successful. As Shu with fresh burns on my shoulders, I was in too much pain for my body to function as a groom would in a wedding bed. It took us several days as Hett and Tuura to find our way to satisfactorily express our passion. Needless to say, I wasn't going to make love to her the way I wanted to at that point. I was sure that eventually we would share passionate lovemaking, but it was going to take a while for me to learn how to bring my energy deep within her human body. She would need to be physically and psychically open to my energy. I was sure she would be, but it would take time— probably years.

This first attempt showed that it could be done, so I was not disappointed. Actually I looked forward to the years of learning, which I hoped would lead us to a complete sharing of our love. I was concerned about Angel though. She hadn't been privy to my instruction. She knew only what other human men had done before me. A great gush of love flooded from my heart and poured over her. She sighed and smiled. We were partners, a matched pair. If any two Souls could connect in such a way, we could and would.

Surrounding her with golden and rose-colored light, I continued to pour out my love. She knew I loved her. She knew I was there, her new husband caring for her, loving her. The sun was beginning to burn through the sea mist, and our first day as husband and wife was beginning. As I scanned her energy pattern, I could see that she was relaxed. Her feet were vibrating with an intense white light while the rest of her lay in pools of varying shades of pink and rose. I had learned a lot from my attempt to make love to her.

One day I would explain all this in detail; one day I would tell her my story. I would relate how I was given the opportunity to become a Spirit Guide and how I then discovered our connection. I would tell her how our bond propelled me through my studies. I'd describe our moments on the Spirit Guide plane as we trained together and shared our love energy. This would come in time.

For now, I bathed her in the highest vibrations of love. I used the glowing mass of white light I had generated within her feet, and instead of trying to move the energy within her, I slowly pulled it up and over her like a soft blanket. I watched as she relaxed further, and her aura changed to a very bright light pink.

"Dear one, can you hear me?" I asked.

"I can, Darci. I can feel your love energy."

"We have only begun our journey as husband and wife. I will get better at lovemaking as we grow closer."

"I look forward to it," she sighed.

"Let us do one thing together before we start this day and our married life. Let us reposition the sphere of light that I gave you last night as a gift."

"Reposition? How? Where?"

"With your help, I wish to slide it deeper so that it sits beneath the crown of your head.

"This will greatly facilitate our telepathic communication and our exchanges of energy."

"I don't know what to do, Darci."

"Just breathe and allow me."

I focused on the sphere and summoned my strength. Once again I faced the formidable denseness of the human body. Her deep breathing released some of the hindrances, and the sphere of light slid deeper into place.

"Now let us join together to energize it," I directed.

I was surprised at how quickly the sphere became bigger and glowed brighter. Now I knew for certain that it was our effort as a team that would make the difference.

And so it would be with our lovemaking. We would learn together through the years how to access true sexual energy. I admitted my inexperience to her, and she did the same. We were both beginners.

This was a marriage unlike any other we had shared for another reason: Angel had to contend with life on Earth. She was often occupied by mundane tasks like feeding herself and driving out to do the laundry or the shopping. Although I always kept an eye on her during those times, I waited for and grew to relish the quiet moments when she would communicate with me.

One evening about a month after our marriage, it was snowing and the house was quiet, so I approached her as she rested. I described our wedding to her as it had occurred on the spirit side.

"My dearest one," I began, "I would like you to know that our entire wedding was staged on another level. I wish to show you. In your home, lovely white mums surrounded you. On the spirit side, we were circled in white roses and white lilies.

"Picture this—a huge, very wide staircase of light-colored stone. Hundreds of Spirits gathered in the cathedral, which was filled with warm golden light. Some stood on the floor, a few lined either side of the twenty-two steps of the staircase, leaving a wide aisle. At the top of the stairs there was an altar surrounded with flowers and covered with a beautiful cloth of white brocade.   On this altar were several holy books, including *The Dawn Book*.   There were also eight white candles, a large golden cross, and a giant crystal. The entire room was ringed with candles.

"The entities gathered were from various planes, yet all were dressed in their finest ceremonial garb. There were many races, many brilliant colors, and much light. Angels attended, too, hovering in the dome above. The music was flute and harp, your favorite. Behind the altar appeared an arc of light. Vertical beams of gold and white light made a curtain effect. The music stopped and a single drum beat began just as it happened in your Earth ceremony, for the ceremonies were connected.

"A Being of brilliant light materialized in the arc and officiated telepathically as all attending could hear this high entity in their minds and hearts. This Archangel raised a hand and all was still. I then walked in, accompanied by Sottrol, Chalherine, and Arcillis.   They were wearing their high ceremonial robes as we stood before the altar.

"Music began again very softly, and at this moment you and your procession began to move down the aisle from the back of the cathedral. First came a flower girl, the lovely spirit child whom we met at Edgar and Nancy's wedding.   She begged me to be in the ceremony, so how could I refuse her? After the child came your friend Greta carrying a basket of flowers, then your beloved grandmother beaming, looking radiant indeed. You looked gorgeous, my dear. I must tell you how my heart jumped when I saw you standing in the arched doorway at the back of this cathedral of lights. Your etheric form was absolutely luminous!   The most beautiful rose-colored light emanated from you as you joined me at the altar. Your eyes melted my heart as our glances met and held.

"We stood during the telepathic welcome and invocation—all this occurred as your ceremony was progressing on the Earth plane. In place of the statement read to the humans in attendance at the Earth site, we knelt and received a blessing from the Archangel. Vows were exchanged, and then all joined us in prayer.

"Once the ceremony was completed, there were embraces all around just as there were at the Earth wedding. You bowed graciously before Arcillis, Chalherine, and Sottrol before hugging them. It's no wonder you have my heart, dear one. Then as you socialized in your home with our Earth guests, we greeted many attendees as husband and wife on the floor of the great cathedral of light. Arm-in-arm, we smiled and often looked at each other as we walked back down the aisle. All in attendance were very, very happy for us.

"These guests on the spirit side were all well aware of the importance of our marriage, as well as other marriages through the veil. The greater the number of strong bonds between the Spirit Guide realm and Earth, the more light and love can flow between them, and more can be accomplished as far as bringing a new way of being to Earth. Now that you have seen how grand and radiant our wedding was on the spirit side, I hope you are happier still. Please know that I, your husband, love you so very, very much."

As I was speaking to her telepathically and relating the details, I watched her heart fill with love and her aura expand with joy.

Tucking her into bed later, I saw that she was taking pleasure in the images I had described earlier. I hovered just above and surrounded her with my love. Once she was asleep, Caroline and Esther arrived to do a healing session.

Caroline nodded at the sleeping woman and said, "Thank you for lulling Angel into a deep sleep. We can do our most effective healing when she is peaceful like this."

I floated to Angel's feet, my usual position, but Esther was already there. The Spirit Guide spoke to me through her luminescent veils, saying, "Caroline and I work alone tonight."

"That's right, Darci," Caroline added. "You have a meeting to attend. We will watch over Angel while you are gone."

"Meeting? Where? With whom?"

Caroline came close to me, her bright jolly eyes staring into mine, as she replied, "You, Darci Stillwater, are to be the honored guest at a meeting of The Elevated Council. You know your way. Now go."

I never liked to leave Angel for any reason, yet I knew that this invitation to meet with The Elevated Council would most certainly pertain to our mission. It was up to me to represent our team on the Spirit Guide plane, just as Angel represented our team on Earth.

The quickest way back was through a small side portal behind clouds that led to the great corridor. I was able to glide along quickly near the top of the broad curved passageway. When I reached the emerald archway with the sentries, I followed procedure and checked in. They had been alerted to my arrival. One of them, a tall thin Spirit with a pale green radiance about him, escorted me directly to the chamber where the meeting was taking place.

The circular room with the dome ceiling seemed even brighter and more elaborate than I remembered. The horseshoe-shaped bench held the Beings I had grown to know and love. Sottrol, my dear mentor, was on his feet first. He literally propelled himself towards me, embracing me for a long time. Chalherine hugged both of us, and the love that flowed was nearly overwhelming. Eventually the two elder Guides moved to either side of me, and the others who were present offered greetings. The two Master Guides, Arcillis and Esther, came forward. Each, in turn, took my hands. I felt their power surge through me. Not to be outdone, Chilliwon Mac hopped up and down on the bench, then sprang very high, landing right in front of me just as the two Master Guides moved aside.

"We are so glad to see you," he bubbled with enthusiasm.

"Congratulations on your marriage. It has helped us all already."

"This room and everything in it seems brighter than when I was last here," I remarked.

"That's because it is," Sottrol confirmed as he took my arm and led me to the single floating chair in the mouth of the horseshoe. "Sit and relax. We have much to tell you."

As he took his seat, Arcillis rose. The hood of his robe slid back and the crystals that covered his head radiated such intensity that I was momentarily blinded.

"Darci, we have called you here to thank you. Your work on the Earth plane with Angel has benefited us all. As you can see, the vitality of our Spirits has increased."

The Master Guide Esther floated towards me, her pastel veils whirling about her as she approached. Her eyes glowed luminous phosphorescent green, and she shared, "You have done very well, Darci." She spoke slowly. Her voice had deep ringing overtones. "Earth's future is changing for the better thanks to you and Angel."

I was stunned. I knew our mission was important, but I had no idea it would affect the Master Guides and the Spirit Guide plane as well as the Earth.

Chilliwon Mac spoke next. He could barely contain himself as he hopped about on the horseshoe bench. I began to see why the others afforded him plenty of space.

"Darci, Darci! My people, the elves, are delighted with the shift in energy on Earth. We want to make you and Angel honorary elves!"

I smiled at the idea and wondered how I would explain this to Angel. All present probably read this thought while Chalherine addressed it, "We wish Angel could be here, too. She has done some very difficult work for all of us."

"Can I not tell her about this meeting and everything you have said to me?"

Sottrol walked to my side. As he put his arm around me, he bowed his head a little as if to honor me.

595

"Angel is a treasure. You know this," he began. "However, you must understand her situation. She has personal karma to burn, a task that is separate from the mission you two were given. She must spend time and energy on Earth lessons. Help her, Darci. She needs you now more than ever as the lessons become tougher."

I looked around at all of them as I replied, "It seems to me that Angel would be heartened to know of your praise. Surely I can relate all you have told me."

My mentor stood in front of me and put his hands on my shoulders. We looked into each other's eyes, and my heart more than my mind spoke, "I love her, Sottrol. I want to share this with her."

The wizard smiled, answering, "Very well. If this is approved by the rest of The Elevated Council, you shall tell her not only of this meeting, but also your entire story, beginning with the transition from your last Earth life."

My heart swelled with joy, and my mind buzzed with excitement as I asked, "Can I tell her everything?"

Chalherine joined us and continued, "Yes, Darci. I believe we all agree that you can tell her about your studies, the lives you have lived together, and the training you shared here on the Spirit Guide plane."

Arcillis conferred with Esther, then stood to address me, confirming, "This is agreeable to the Master Guides with one stipulation. You must wait until Angel has dealt with more of her Earth karma and has raised her personal vibration higher. This may take a number of years."

"How will I know when . . .?"

I didn't even finish the sentence. Chalherine and Sottrol chimed in unison, "You'll know!"

Sottrol hugged me and looked again into my eyes as he continued, "I believe you can convince Angel to write your story as a second book. She has shown that she has the discipline and the abilities, both telepathic and literary. Such a book will help humans understand many things, including karma and death. It will describe Spirit Guides and explain the training you must complete before you are allowed to assist humans. It will be a good story, Darci."

I looked around the splendid room at each of the magnificent Beings I had grown to know and love. I wanted to tell this story, and it would, indeed, be a very good one. After thanking them for their guidance and support, I took my leave.

On the journey back to Earth to rejoin my beloved Angel, I thought about how to begin such a book and decided that, when she was ready, I would start at the very beginning—with my death and my opportunity.

The End

About the Author

Annie Stillwater Gray is a writer, a mystic, an astrologer, a public speaker, a teacher, an audio and visual artist, a healer, a singer-songwriter, and a media veteran. She has been on the air every year since 1974 and currently has her own syndicated radio program, The General Store Variety Show, now in its 15th year. Annie has studied Integrated Energy Therapy, Reiki, and Bach Flower Remedies. She has been helping people consciously connect with their Spirit Guides since 1989. Annie received a BFA from Boston University in graphic arts and writing. She creates songs and designs all the CD covers and publicity for her bands. At the date this book is released, her band is the western quintet Merry-Go-Roundup.

Darcimon Stillwater is a Spirit Guide with a special affinity for language and writing. In a former life on Earth, he served as scribe to the Roman Senate where he developed these skills. He has also accumulated other talents from many Earth lifetimes as well as from experiences on other planes of existence, which he has refined and supplemented on the Spirit Guide Plane. Darci has chosen to assist and serve his human charge, Annie, during this crucial period of change on Earth. Darci has not only completed the lengthy, complicated, and difficult training to become a Spirit Guide, he has also studied with the Master Guides to prepare material to help humans with the great transformation now occurring on Earth.

Annie Stillwater Gray and Darcimon Stillwater have also co-authored The Dawn Book: Information From the Master Guides.

Other Books By Ozark Mountain Publishing, Inc.

Dolores Cannon
Conversations with Nostradamus,
  Volume I, II, III
Jesus and the Essenes
They Walked with Jesus
Between Death and Life
A Soul Remembers Hiroshima
Keepers of the Garden.
The Legend of Starcrash
The Custodians
The Convoluted Universe - Book One,
  Two, Three, Four
Five Lives Remembered
The Three Waves of Volunteers and the
  New Earth
Stuart Wilson & Joanna Prentis
The Essenes - Children of the Light
Power of the Magdalene
Beyond Limitations
Atlantis and the New Consciousness
The Magdalene Version
O.T. Bonnett, M.D./Greg Satre
Reincarnation: The View from Eternity
What I Learned After Medical School
Why Healing Happens
M. Don Schorn
Elder Gods of Antiquity
Legacy of the Elder Gods
Gardens of the Elder Gods
Reincarnation...Stepping Stones of Life
Aron Abrahamsen
Holiday in Heaven
Out of the Archives – Earth Changes
Sherri Cortland
Windows of Opportunity
Raising Our Vibrations for the New Age
The Spiritual Toolbox
Michael Dennis
Morning Coffee with God
God's Many Mansions
Nikki Pattillo
Children of the Stars
A Spiritual Evolution
Rev. Grant H. Pealer
Worlds Beyond Death
A Funny Thing Happened on the Way to
  Heaven
Maiya & Geoff Gray-Cobb
Angels - The Guardians of Your Destiny
Maiya Gray-Cobb
Seeds of the Soul
Sture Lönnerstrand
I Have Lived Before
Arun & Sunanda Gandhi
The Forgotten Woman
Claire Doyle Beland
Luck Doesn't Happen by Chance

James H. Kent
Past Life Memories As A Confederate
  Soldier
Dorothy Leon
Is Jehovah An E.T
Justine Alessi & M. E. McMillan
Rebirth of the Oracle
Donald L. Hicks
The Divinity Factor
Christine Ramos, RN
A Journey Into Being
Mary Letorney
Discover The Universe Within You
Debra Rayburn
Let's Get Natural With Herbs
Jodi Felice
The Enchanted Garden
Susan Mack & Natalia Krawetz
My Teachers Wear Fur Coats
Ronald Chapman
Seeing True
Rev. Keith Bender
The Despiritualized Church
Vara Humphreys
The Science of Knowledge
Karen Peebles
The Other Side of Suicide
Antoinette Lee Howard
Journey Through Fear
Julia Hanson
Awakening To Your Creation
Irene Lucas
Thirty Miracles in Thirty Days
Mandeep Khera
Why?
Robert Winterhalter
The Healing Christ
James Wawro
Ask Your Inner Voice
Tom Arbino
You Were Destined to be Together
Maureen McGill & Nola Davis
Live From the Other Side
Anita Holmes
TWIDDERS
Walter Pullen
Evolution of the Spirit
Cinnamon Crow
Teen Oracle
Chakra Zodiac Healing Oracle
Jack Churchward
Lifting the Veil on the Lost Continent of
  Mu

For more information about any of the above titles, soon to be released titles,
or other items in our catalog, write or visit our website:
PO Box 754, Huntsville, AR 72740
www.ozarkmt.com

Other Books By Ozark Mountain Publishing, Inc.

Guy Needler
The History of God
Beyond the Source – Book 1,2
Dee Wallace/Jarred Hewett
The Big E
Dee Wallace
Conscious Creation
Natalie Sudman
Application of Impossible Things
Henry Michaelson
And Jesus Said – A Conversation
Victoria Pendragon
SleepMagic
Riet Okken
The Liberating Power of Emotions
Janie Wells
Payment for Passage
Dennis Wheatley/ Maria Wheatley
The Essential Dowsing Guide
Dennis Milner
Kosmos
Garnet Schulhauser
Dancing on a Stamp
Julia Cannon
Soul Speak – The Language of Your
    Body
Charmian Redwood
Coming Home to Lemuria
Kathryn Andries
Soul Choices – 6 Paths to Find Your Life
    Purpose

For more information about any of the above titles, soon to be released titles,
or other items in our catalog, write or visit our website:
PO Box 754, Huntsville, AR 72740
www.ozarkmt.com